Leisure & Community Services

KT-549-565

Please return this item by the last date stamped below, to the library from which it was borrowed.

Renewals
Any item may be renewed twice by telephone or post, provided it is not required by another customer. Please quote the barcode number.

Overdue Charges
Please see library notices for the current rate of charges levied on overdue items. Please note that the overdue charges are made on junior books borrowed on adult tickets.

Postage
Postage on overdue notices is payable

	D 13/03/2007	
	CEN · ORP · BEC 26 NOV 2004	
06/05	– 6 MAY 2006	
27-5-06 EMW 17 JUN 2006	15 JUN 2007	
BEC 8 Feb 2010	26/5/09 16 JUL 2011	
27 FEB 2015	BECKENHAM LIBRARY 020 8650 7292	

Marked for
Misfortune

Marked for Misfortune

AN EPIC TALE OF SHIPWRECK, HUMAN ENDEAVOUR
AND SURVIVAL IN THE AGE OF SAIL

JEAN HOOD

Conway Maritime Press

Dedication

To George with love
JH

© Jean Hood, 2003

This edition first published in Great Britain by
Conway Maritime Press,
a division of Chrysalis Books plc
The Chrysalis Building
Bramley Road
London W10 6SP

A member of **Chrysalis** Books plc

www.conwaymaritime.com

ISBN 0 85177 941 7

British Library Cataloguing in Publication Data
A CIP catalogue record for this book is available from the British Library

Editor: Alison Moss
Design and typesetting: Champion Design

Printed and bound in Great Britain

Contents

Acknowledgements

It may be a cliché to say that this book could not have been written without the assistance of many people, but that doesn't make it any the less true, and I owe an inestimable debt of gratitude to individuals and institutions in many countries. I came to the story via a painting of the ship, and to uncover the full story of her ill-fated voyage and to resurrect those who embarked for India in the spring of 1792 could not have been done without the unselfish help, advice and encouragement of so many people. Some of those I contacted knew even less than I did, but their immediate fascination with the story was as valuable a spur as was the help of those who generously put their information at my disposal and those who directed me to where it might be found.

Tony Farrington, Ian Baxter, Tim Thomas, Dr Andrew Cook and their staff at the British Library's OIOC; Nick Pointer and the staff of the Public Record Office; National Army Museum; Royal Geographical Society; National Library of Scotland; Scottish Record Office; Linda Bankier, Berwick upon Tweed Record Office; La Musée de La Marine, Paris; Les Archives de France; Pierre Fardel; the Nationaal Archief, Den Haag and the Nederlandse Scheepvaartsmuseum; P H Sooprayen of the Archives of Mauritius; William T LaMoy, Peabody Museum, Salem; Joseph Judge, Hampton Roads Naval Museum, Norfolk, Virginia; Manchester Central Library; Sandbach Library; my former colleagues Barbara

Jones, Mark Grant and Anne Cowne at Lloyd's Register of Shipping; Guildhall Library, London; Jackie Loos, South African Library; RCS Edinburgh; M S Cavanagh, West Lothian Library Service; Oxford University Press Library, National Maritime Museum.

Lord Jauncey of Tulichettle, The Earl of Dalhousie, David Spens, Jean Spens of Lathallan; Louise Brown; Revd Richard Adams; R H J Griffiths, Richard Larn, Andrea Cordani, Dr Robert Sténuit; Tim Cattley; Jean Sutton, John Barnard, Royal College of Physicians and Surgeons, Glasgow; Erica Hills; Major R Mills, Museum of the Royal Warwickshire Regiment; R Knight, Sir John Hope Bt, Dan Byrnes, David Van Couwelaar; National Portrait Gallery; Bonhams Auctioneers; the late Alan Francis, Naval Historical Library; Wendy Gale; Michelle Desmond; Harry Goodwin; Mr & Mrs A Hay; Miguel Fisher; Stephen Collard; Henri Maurel; National Museum of Wales, Miguel de Avendano, Marco Rameri, Jean Noble and Julie Goucher.

It is always invidious to single out contributors, but I am particularly grateful to John Lee at Conway Maritime Press for sharing my passion for the story; to David Van Couwelaar who translated the report of Pierius Muntz from eighteenth-century Dutch; to Pierre Fardel without whom the eighteenth-century Mauritius papers would have been indecipherable; to Dr Sténuit for everything relating to the discovery of the wreck; to Tim Cattley who helped me crack Dale's private life; to Peter Humphries who transcribed the South Africa material; and to the Reverend Richard Adams who gave me access to material in the family archive. Not forgetting Judy, Peter and Sarah Greenwood who allowed me to share their spare room with various bits of motorbike while I researched in London, my son, Adrian, who explained how to take bearings and my husband George who not only 'financed' the research and covered many miles with me in search of information but who suffered the wreck of the *Winterton* for many more years than those who embarked on her.

But for Colin Denny I might never have heard of the *Winterton* at all. If you read this, Colin, wherever you are, please get in touch!

To err is human. I am more than grateful to Jean Sutton, author of *Lords of the East*, for her suggestions and for correcting factual errors about the operations of the East India Company, and to my eagle-eyed editor, Alison Moss, for spotting inconsistencies and ambiguities in the text, but I take full responsibility for any remaining inaccuracies. If you possess any additional information that would throw further light on the story, I would be more than pleased to hear from you.

Jean Hood
Sandbach

John Dale's Route by Sea

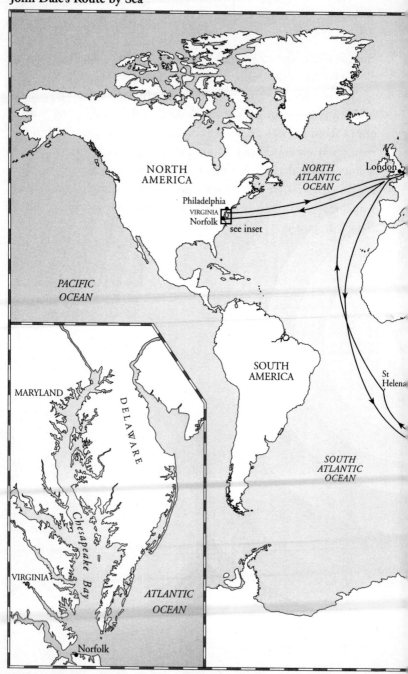

Coastlines of East Africa and India

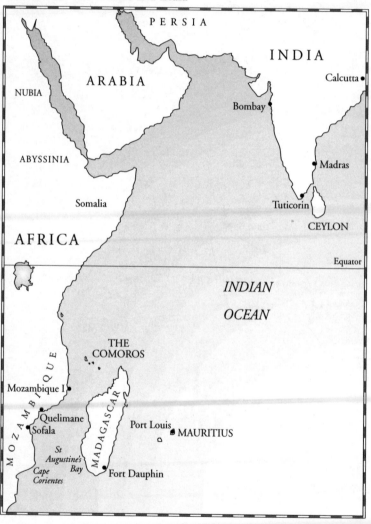

St Augustine's Bay, Madagascar

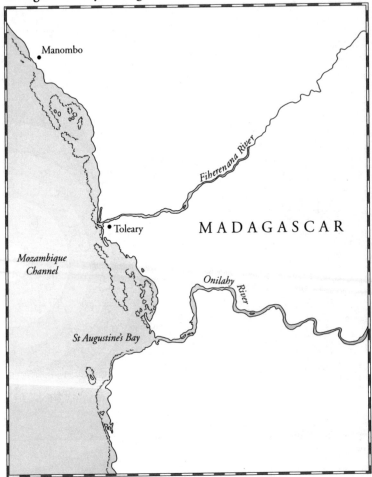

The Mozambique Channel

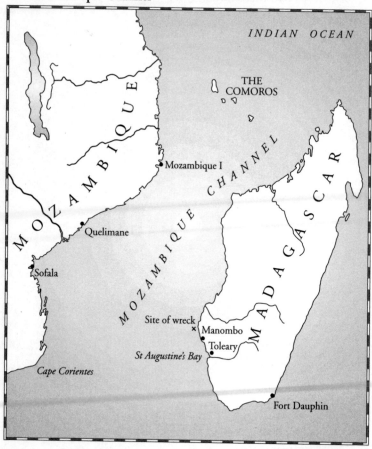

The Mozambique Mainland

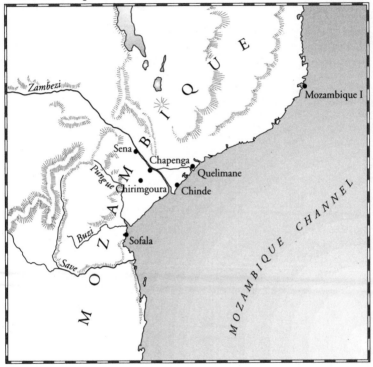

Prologue

'There exists in the human mind a strong and incessant desire to be acquainted with the misfortunes of others. Whether this propensity arises from self-love or from the principles of self-preservation so intimately interwoven in the very nature of our being, I leave it to others more versed in the secret springs of human actions to decide.'

Attributed to John Dale [1]

To the limits of the dark horizon the sea shone satin beneath the brilliance of a starlit tropical sky, reflecting the moon in a rippling strake of gold. From the quarterdeck of the *Winterton*, his night-glass[2] lowered, John Dale glanced at the helmsman to check he still held the ship on her course. The broad, bluff bow rose and fell in its satisfying rhythm, parting the dark water with a deep and heavy plash that no longer disturbed the sleep of the passengers in their stuffy cabins below. Rope and timber groaned and flexed as they restrained the canvas against the south-southeasterly wind, holding the big East Indiaman to a prudent 6 knots. So familiar were the sounds that the absence of footsteps and voices gave an illusion of silence. Dale raised the nightglass to his eye once again and scanned the eastern horizon. Nothing. No breakers to warn of rocks; no fires to indicate coastal settlements. Nineteen days out of False Bay, the *Winterton* was heading ENE up the Mozambique Channel between the coasts of East Africa and the island of Madagascar, bound for Bengal. A perfect night under the new moon: no cause for any more concern than a conscientious Third Officer ought to feel when left in charge of one of the world's finest merchant ships, a cargo worth over £100,000 and the lives of nearly 300 souls. Nevertheless, Dale was anxious. The light wind brought a smell of land to his nose, sapping his confidence in their position.

Captain Dundas might have been one of the first generation of seafarers to benefit from Harrison's chronometers, but he was keen to sight the coast to confirm his calculations. He had admitted as much to one of his passengers that evening. At midnight, when Dale had come on deck for his watch, Dundas changed the ship's course from E to ENE, which would compensate for any inaccuracies in the calculations or the charts by keeping her away from land during the night. He returned to his cabin in the round house, leaving Dale as officer of the watch.

The time slipped by towards 2am. The lookouts on the bowsprit and foreyard were silent and the huge merchantman ploughed on steadily. Unable to sleep, George Dundas came back on deck. The young Third Officer – the Honourable East India Company (HEIC) preferred the naval term 'officer' to the merchant marine's 'mate' – was competent, but Dundas may have thought him inexperienced, though they had sailed together on the *Winterton*'s previous voyage, which was Dundas's first as a Captain, and Dale's first as an Officer. Dale had joined the HEIC as an ordinary seaman rather than as a midshipman even though he was Dundas's second cousin.

Now he was 23, give or take a few days,[3] the sworn-in 'servant' of a company which enjoyed more power than many governments; he had his own cabin where he entertained the less important passengers to dinner, and a uniform similar to that of a naval lieutenant to wear on formal occasions. More importantly, he now enjoyed the perquisites of rank which could turn the modest monthly pay of £3.10.0[4] into a gentleman's living wage. His Captain might have passed the months since the *Winterton*'s return from India at his castle overlooking the Firth of Forth; he, John Dale, had been earning his living as a Second Mate in the less congenial West India trade.

Dundas ordered him to change course to NE by E. The two cousins stood together towards the starboard rail, nightglasses to their eyes. For a further hour Dundas remained on deck; then by the light of the helmsman's lamp he showed Dale the ship's position on the chart, 60 miles from the nearest coast.

'Steer north-east now. On that course we can't make more than 6 miles of easting before daylight. If we are any nearer the land than we should be, you'll see it before any accident can happen.' He went to retire, then looked back and added in his lowland Scots accent: 'But if you do see anything suspicious, act accordingly: don't wait to call me.' He had taken every precaution but one. Believing that they ran no imminent danger of running aground, he had not given orders for soundings to be taken: no leadsman's voice sang out the fathoms.

The ship continued at 6 knots. Although they were far from lumbering tubs, it was common for East Indiamen to shorten sail at night for, with a monopoly of trade to India, there was less commercial pressure to pile on the canvas or take risks with a cargo – the famous tea races of the clipper ship era were more than half a century in the future. To a landsman, the *Winterton* might look like a frigate with her gun ports and gilding, and East Indiamen had deceived more than one hostile naval captain into leaving them alone, but she was broader in the beam, built for trade, and her armament was defensive. Her commander was expected to safeguard his valuable ship and her cargo, not go looking for trouble.

.

The check, when it came, was so slight that, standing by the after hatchway, Dale hardly noticed it. The topmasts shuddered, and he looked up past the bleached and straining mainsail, wondering if some of the spars had broken away. Next moment he was catapulted forward and lurched down the quarterdeck, fighting to keep his footing until he crashed into the helmsman clutching the wheel.

Chapter One

The Company's Orders

Pruned of her yards and topmasts, the *Winterton* sat squat and ugly at her mooring chains on the River Thames. Twenty-one months had passed since her return from India, and the gilding on her handsome square transom was dulled by the smoke from the city; but although she was no longer the largest or the newest in her fleet she still dwarfed the colliers, lighters, coastal traders and West Indiamen navigating the great loop of the river below the Pool of London under the lash of the New Year's sleet. The banks on either side of the ruffled grey water were edged with towering hulls of new ships still on the stocks, ranks of moored vessels narrowed the river to a passage, and northwards lay the renowned Blackwall shipyard from where John Perry could have picked out *Winterton* and thought with satisfaction on the income he would receive from his shareholding.

Not that Perry had built her, though he turned out a steady supply of fine East Indiamen. The *Winterton* had been launched on the south side of the Thames 10 years earlier, in 1782, from one of the two Deptford yards belonging to a company known by any permutation of its partners' names: Barnard, Dudman and Adams.[5] They leased two yards, one at Grove Street, the other at Deptford Green, where during a frenetic decade of building from 1780 they built some 42 vessels, almost all warships or East Indiamen. Why Perry did not build the *Winterton* himself, is hard to say. The order would have come from the ship's managing owner – called a 'husband' in shipping circles – Thomas Newte, who had risen from Captain's Servant[6] to Captain and retired from the sea to follow a less hazardous but equally lucrative career.

With a few exceptions, the Honourable East India Company (HEIC) did not own the ships it dispatched to India and China. Instead, it chartered them even before they were built from consortia of wealthy individuals, headed by husbands, for a certain number of voyages at a specified freight rate. East Indiamen were such specialised vessels, expensive to build and too large for any other trade, that nobody built one on spec. Only a husband could negotiate with the Company and place the construction contract, giving him considerable powers of patronage and influence. The *Winterton*'s shareholders were Donald Cameron, a London banker; John Perry, the shipbuilder; the Rt Honourable Thomas Hanley; John Raymond, a retired Captain; and the young Earl of Winterton whose late father had been one of the original shareholders and after whom the ship had been named.[7]

During the early weeks of 1792, Captain George Dundas remained in Scotland with his young family: East India commanders were far too grand to involve themselves in the early preparations for a voyage, so responsibility for the *Winterton* fell on the Chief Mate, Charles Chambers, one of those archetypal seafarers who:

> '…had been many years at sea and had the appearance of one who had weathered many a gale. He had in his deportment a good deal of what might be called the old school. But though

made of stern stuff he mixed it much with the milk of human kindness.'[8]

He was just one of many chief mates who had failed to make it to the rank of Commander, a step requiring more than competence and experience. His service with the HEIC went back 32 years to the *Plassey*, and he had had his fair share of incident and excitement. In 1774 he survived the wreck of the homeward bound *Huntingdon* off Anjouan; In 1780, he was serving as Second Mate under Nathaniel Dance when his ship, the *Royal George*, and four others of the fleet were captured by the combined French and Spanish fleets.[9] Once repatriated, Chambers was appointed Chief Mate for voyages in the *Montague* and the *Earl of Chesterfield*, but in this position he languished, lacking the patronage or the influence in the right quarter. The HEIC might disapprove of the purchase system, and insist on approving the commander and the first four officers, but the Directors were still some years short of declaring an outright ban.

Theoretically, the captain of an East Indiaman appointed the officers. Provided they had satisfied criteria of age, previous rank and experience they were eligible for promotion, and the captain could present them to the Court of Directors. In practice, the captain's wish to oblige his friends and relations, or simply to provide himself with officers of his own choosing, was limited by the pressure which could be applied by the ship's owners who also had friends, business colleagues and relations seeking favours. Chambers' only chance of becoming a commander now lay in Dundas's dying on the voyage, for it was the convention that a chief mate who completed the voyage successfully would be allowed to purchase the vacant command from the widow or heirs; and there was no shortage of lenders willing to advance the purchase money. His two previous captains having failed to oblige him, Chambers found himself old enough to be the father of all his junior officers and once again recruiting a crew for another man (seven years younger) to command.

Chambers had not served on the *Winterton* before, unlike a number of those who now signed on. Jeremiah Stevens, John Tyler, Daniel Dundas, Henry Dowdall, Thomas Adams, Daniel Percy, Henry Rozier, William Rowland and Daniel Patterson were all on the previous voyage;[10] they must have been content to return to their former ship, for they could have joined the East Indiamen *Thetis* or *King George*, both of which were at their moorings making ready to sail. Not all of them were seamen. East Indiamen carried every kind of tradesman necessary for the 26,000-mile return voyage to Calcutta, from the Caulker who kept the vessel watertight to the all-important Carpenter whose wages were scarcely less than the Second Officer's, and who was, himself, entitled to two mates, a servant, and his own cabin. By the time she sailed the *Winterton* certainly carried a crew of more than 100, including officers.[11]

Before she could set off, there was work to be done. With the ship at her moorings at Deptford, the men set up the top and top-gallant masts, swayed up the yards and topmast rigging, levelled the kintledge (iron ballast) and stowed such heavy essentials as coals, wood, spars and spare anchors. They took on board over 100 water butts and began the strenuous task of filling them. The water that had to sustain some 300 people at least as far as the Cape of Good Hope came straight out of the river into which the sewage of London poured. During the voyage the principal beverages were alcoholic, with weak beer as the staple, so water was used mainly for cooking, washing and hot drinks. Although the organic matter in it fermented out over time, and the better-off passengers brought filtering machines on board, it still made off-tasting tea.

On deck in the teeth of a vicious easterly March wind that whipped up the river bringing the last snow and sleet of the winter, and down in the dark hold that stank of damp wood and bilgewater, the crew laboured. Other officers had joined the ship. Little is known of John Moore, the Fifth Mate, but a young Dublin-born gentleman, Joseph William Wilton,[12] came as Fourth Mate. Even at 21 he was a veteran, having first gone to sea with the HEIC 10 years earlier. Now appointed to the *Winterton* he struck up a friendship with the Third Mate, John Dale, his mess mate and the only officer other than the Captain with previous service on the ship.

There was no seafaring tradition in Dale's family. Originally from Yorkshire, they had been London innkeepers and upholsterers living in the Parish of St Paul's, Covent Garden. By 1720 Dale's great grandfather, William, had become wealthy enough to settle £20,000 on his daughter Dorothea to secure a match with William, Lord Forbes. The commission for Dale's father (also John) in the 6th Regiment of Foot describes the young Ensign as a gentleman. In 1769 that Regiment was quartered at Berwick, and on 29 August Dale, by now a Captain, went with his wife Agnew to have their son baptised with his name at All Saints' church just across from the barracks. Three years later he left England with his Regiment to put down a revolt on the island of St Vincent, and the young John never saw his father again. Fever took a terrible toll on the men and officers. Captain Dale died in 1774 and Agnew remarried that same year.

John acquired a good education, for he was literate, articulate and spoke French. At the age of 14 the apprehensive young man signed on as a seaman on the East Indiaman *Valentine*, owned by Donald Cameron. It was by no means unusual for a young man of good family to take this route into the Company: actual midshipmen's berths were invariably taken up by those with more influence. Before he went to sea his portrait was painted for his mother, showing her blue-eyed, fair-haired son in blue coat and waistcoat with anchors on the buttons at a time when not even Royal Navy ratings wore uniform. The outfit is similar to that of a naval midshipman.

All that is certain is that Dale signed on for a second voyage. Then in 1788 he was appointed as Sixth Mate on the *Winterton* which was owned by Cameron's business partner, Newte, and captained by George Dundas, grandson of the late Dorothea, Lady Forbes, who was also John Dale's great aunt. This formidable woman, who never visited Scotland in her husband's lifetime, had proved a thorn in the side of her in-laws until her death in 1777.[13] She, not Agnew, had been entrusted with the administration following Captain Dale's death, and could well have made sure that the Forbes or Dundas families would do something for his son.

Dale's first voyage on the *Winterton* was not happy. Sickness among the crew and the soldiers on board was common enough on a long voyage, but the officers also had to deal with mutiny, insubordination, and a new rudder which shipped so much water that Dundas feared for his vessel. Rowland, the Carpenter, advised his Captain to put into Santiago for repairs, and with the cargo of lead shifted forward to lighten the ship aft, the officers duly changed course. Once in port trouble broke out among the crew. A sailor had struck the Purser and deserted; another had been put in irons for mutinous behaviour. On 31 May 1788 Dundas's log records:

> 'John Wallis, seaman, refused to go [to weigh the kedge anchor] as did several others, and insisted upon the other man being let out of irons. Upon being threatened to be punished he said that if the other seamen had done as they promised him it would not have been in our power; at the same time he told me he was determined to do no more duty in the ship. Upon which I ordered him to receive 36 lashes, after which he told me I might do as I pleased but that he would find his opportunity to effect his own purpose.'[14]

He was confined in irons for the ship's safety, and two other men were given 12 lashes each. Shortly afterwards one of the earlier troublemakers had a second dose of the cat for striking the Fifth Mate. Flogging was practised in the East India Company ships, as in the Royal Navy, but the merchant seamen were volunteers: they could desert without fear of being hunted down.

Disorder continued when the ship reached Bombay and the officers used pistols to restore discipline. There were problems with cargo that would occupy the HEIC's bureaucracy for months to come; and when the *Winterton* finally arrived back at her moorings on the River Thames on 8 June 1790, Captain Dundas was a relieved man. Dale went off to serve as Second Mate on the West Indiamen *Gloucester* and *Monmouth*, either to improve his experience or because he was not yet wealthy enough to do otherwise. Great grandfather William had been a rich man, but most of the dowry given to Dorothea had been lost in the infamous speculation known as the South Sea Bubble, and much of the money that remained in the Dale family could easily have gone the same way. Once unloaded, the *Winterton* herself returned to Barnard's yard to undergo any necessary repairs and await the Company's orders. All East Indiamen spent this time at the yards of their original builders; only after the order to 'come afloat' had been given were they moved to their mooring chains.

After spending the Christmas of 1791 at home with his mother and step-family, Dale rejoined the *Winterton* for this, her fourth voyage, as Third Mate. Dundas had been successful in presenting his younger relation to the Court of Directors for their approval, and was by implication more than content to have him on board again. The promotion was significant: Dale now had a foot in the Company's door. Given the cost of uniforms, equipment, and supporting himself ashore between voyages, a young man needed capital of anything between £600 and £1000 in order to reach the position of Second Mate, after which he could expect to live on his pay and profit.

On 15 March, at 4pm, with the weather clear and fair, *Thetis* and *King George* left Blackwall. The following day the pilot came on board the *Winterton*, cast her off from her mooring and, under a convenient south-westerly breeze, guided her down the widening grey Thames, slowly leaving behind the wharves, the smoke and the bustle, and the higher land beyond Woolwich to the south. The Kent landscape softened into dull marshland, and the view from the quarterdeck was of a broad monotony, pierced by the occasional creek or church and the rising ground above Erith. From Erith

Reach the *Winterton* made her way into Long Reach, past the hill at Purfleet from where Elizabeth I apocryphally pitied her 'poor fleet' in Armada year, and into St Clements Reach, named after the church at West Thurrock with its landmark tower. In the evening she anchored near the gunports of Tilbury Fort, joining her fellows, *Thetis* and *King George*, and the real business of loading began.

Barges swarmed down the river bringing the stores, and the ships took on their cannon, shot and powder from the nearby Fort (vessels were forbidden to carry guns and powder any further up river). The log of the *King George* records that during the rest of March and into April her crew took on 70 casks of pork, 13 barrels of brandy, 20 pairs of smith's bellows, cordage, military clothing, anchor cables, and shot and shells. While some supplies were for the ship's use, most was destined for the Company's own army and the royal troops serving in India. With winds coming more from the west the weather turned milder but more variable. Two Indiamen passed up, both returning from China; and down from London came the *Busridge, Rose, Belmont, Alfred* and *Earl Talbot*, all due to sail in that season and several of them managed by Thomas Newte. Ships would leave singly or in pairs, taking their own route. Some might call at the Cape of Good Hope, others would go directly to India, meeting their fellows at anchor beyond the Madras surf or laying alongside them in the unhealthy humidity of Diamond Harbour, down river from Calcutta.

Voyages were timed to take advantage of prevailing winds and currents and avoid the storms that could make the coast of India unapproachable. Outward-bound ships battled their way down the English Channel and out into the Altantic, where most commanders shaped a course for Madeira to check their position. A little further south and they could pick up the north-east Trades to take them close to the Equator where the aptly-named Variables could leave them becalmed or fighting for their ships in a storm. Beyond the Variables lay the more predictable south-east Trades which could assist their southerly progress at the expense of pushing them close to the coast of Brazil, and below these lay the powerful Westerlies that could drive a ship to the Cape or on to China. The winds of the Atlantic mattered less than those of the eastern seas. The outward-bound Indiaman needed to reach the Cape after the onset of the south-western monsoon.

Although England was at peace during the spring of 1792, the daily news was unsettling for anyone in business. Between results of the State Lottery, advertisements for concerts, and the salacious detail of sensational court cases, *The Times* provided daily reports from around the world, but particularly from Paris where the French Revolution burned most fiercely and where the will of the new National Assembly was expressed in decrees still issued in the name of Louis XVI. Leading French emigrés, including royal princes now in the German states, campaigned for foreign military support against the new regime, and tension was high around France's borders. William Pitt's government feared both that revolution could spread across the Channel and that Britain would be drawn into a European war.

At home the House of Commons devoted much of its time to bitter and eloquent debates on slavery, with men such as William Wilberforce making passionate abolitionist speeches; others such as Mr Tarleton arguing that the country's prosperity would collapse following any ban on the slave trade; and Lord Dundas winning a compromise vote for a gradual abolition. At Coachmakers Hall the public were regularly invited to debate a motion calling for a boycott of West India goods until the trade was proscribed. News of the death of the German Emperor, the assassination of King Gustavus III of Sweden at a masked ball, reports of the war in India against Tipoo Sultan: all these events combined with the overriding fear of conflict and economic uncertainty to make men nervous.

❧❧❧

George Dundas came down to London some time during the middle of March, stopping off to put his affairs in order before joining his ship. No rough sea dog, he was both a gentleman and Chief of the ancient Scottish family of Dundas of Dundas. Born at Toulouse and educated at Houghton-le-Spring, he had joined the HEIC as a 15-year-old midshipman on the *Speaker* in 1768. For all his lineage and estate, he needed to earn a living. His father had died while he was young, leaving his estate in trust and probably in debt. If he could rise to a Commander's rank he stood a good chance of restoring the family's fortune.

The monthly wages of the mates of an Indiaman were not high, and they were paid only for the duration of the voyage, not during the months of waiting for the next season's trade. If a ship was wrecked, the survivors or their next of kin received payment only up to the time of the loss. Even captains, who had paid anything up to £12,000 for their command, received only £10 per month, payable from the time the ship 'came afloat'. What rendered an HEIC command so desirable was the private trade allowance – the generous amount of space in the hold that the commander could legitimately fill with goods purchased on his own account. Lesser allowances were granted to the other officers. The Company had long taken a pragmatic view of private trade and, knowing full well there was nothing they could do about it, regulated rather than banning it. It saved on wages, threw the element of risk on to those who engaged in it, and gave the officers a stake in the business. Like all perquisites it was invariably and often blatantly abused.

George Dundas was fortunate in his timing, because the name of Dundas had become synonymous with the HEIC. Members of the various branches of the family held high positions in just about every area of the Company's activity, giving them a considerable power of patronage. James Dundas commanded the East Indiaman, *Prime*, and in 1773 George joined her as Third Mate, becoming Second in 1777.

Politics, that other road to wealth and influence, intervened and at the 1784 General Election George stood, unsuccessfully, for the seat of Linlithgow, once held by his late father. On Christmas Eve that same year he married Christian, daughter of Sir William Stirling Bt of Ardoch, and in quick succession became the father of three daughters. In 1788 he bought command of the *Winterton*. With birth, influence and credit on his side, and held to be a good seaman, his path to the quarterdeck had not been unusual. He brought with him his servant, Thomas Marshall; his Steward, James Underhill; and his own cook, James Higgins. Among his personal effects were his charts and his two timepieces.

Although it was well over 20 years since the Board of Longitude had recognised the genius of John Harrison in building a clock of sufficient accuracy to enable mariners to calculate their longitude, few ships carried chronometers. They were far too expensive and production was limited; it was 1825 before the British navy issued them to all its ships. But for East India husbands, or for captains with their heavy investments in private trade, it might be a price worth paying and Dundas had taken one on his previous voyage, making him an early user.[15] For the first few weeks, apart from winding it up, he did nothing with it. Then, suddenly, he tried it out, and recorded the result in his log. Thereafter, like a child with a new toy, he recorded his longitude every day, grasping the value of this new navigational aid. On one occasion, spotting a hill with a fire burning on the top of it, he calculated his position off the coast of Madagascar; on another occasion he worked out the speed of the current. For John Dale on his first voyage as an officer, it had been a fascinating experience to see the new technology adopted, and he was full of admiration for the accuracy with which Dundas made the land.

The Captain still took lunar observations, no easy matter on a rolling, pitching ship with her soaring masts and billowing sails, especially under less than perfect skies, but increasingly they were to confirm the chronometer, not vice versa. By the time he returned in 1790 Dundas was a clear convert to the 'timekeeper', as he called it, and despite a less than successful voyage he or Newte was prepared to invest in a second.[16]

✂

Once the Captain had come on board, the valuable cargo could begin to arrive. The crew hoisted aboard general necessities such as stationery and flints valued at around £2500 and 75 chests containing 300,000 silver dollars weighing 261,600 ounces and worth £68,942.50, all destined for Madras. The Calcutta cargo was less valuable, consisting mainly of broadcloth, spare anchors and steel,[17] but it also included vital medical supplies. The private trade and the captain's stores arrived, together with bedding for the recruits who would shortly embark to join the 75th Regiment.

There is a suggestion that the *Winterton* sailed down the Medway to Chatham to collect the troops,[18] but it is more likely that, as in the case of the *King George*, the soldiers embarked at Gravesend. There were 123 including NCOs, under the command of Lieutenant Henry Quinn Brownrigg, a young officer from an old-established Wicklow dynasty, whose elder brother, Robert, was already serving with some distinction in India. Henry had been one of the founding officers of the 75th, recently raised by General Abercrombie specifically for service in India,[19] and he had been sent back to raise a new draft. These regular troops served under the Company's command, and the Company bore the cost of them just as it paid for its own regiments. Once on board, they were quartered on the gloomy maindeck, with the gratings and portholes to provide light. At night they laid their bedding out on the deck; by day they rolled it up so the crew could get on with their duties. Five soldiers brought with them their wives and children.

✂

Shortly before the *Winterton* was ready to sail, Dundas and his four senior Mates had to return to London to take leave of the Court of Directors at the Company's Leadenhall Street offices, and receive their sailing orders. George Dundas, Charles Chambers, Nathaniel Spens, John Dale and Joseph Wilton changed into their dress uniforms and posted back to the city for this formality, a new experience for the Third and Fourth Mates. Dundas wore buff breeches and waistcoat beneath a blue coat with black velvet lapels, collar and cuffs, and light gold embroidery. The buttons 'of yellow metal' bore the Company's crest. His officers had similar uniforms but, by Company regulations, the embroidery was 'as little expensive as may be'.[20] Since they had to buy their own uniforms, the less well off Mates must have been grateful for this rule. They were all required to have undress uniforms, which differed mainly in the lack of lapels, but officers wore their ordinary clothes while at sea, reserving their undress uniforms for formal occasions on board. They rounded off the day with dinner with some of the ship's owners, drinking to the success of the voyage.

At Gravesend the ship was almost loaded. Dundas had only to wait for his passengers.

Chapter Two

Live Lumber

While its privileges lasted, the Honourable East India Company was the most powerful commercial organisation the world had yet seen. What began as a small trading venture, given its Charter at the end of Elizabeth I's reign, expanded rapidly until by that last decade of the eighteenth century the Company not only traded as far as China but was on the way to the military conquest of India. It had established its own army, a fledgling navy, and a bureaucracy worthy of any government. It minted coins to pay its troops, paid pensions, interfered in Indian politics, and was riddled with patronage, nepotism and a fair measure of corruption. The middle classes avidly sought places in its service, along with the younger sons of the landed gentry and, occasionally, the nobility. The actual pay might be frugal, but there were fortunes, small and large, to be made by those who survived the climate, the diseases and the dangers of the East.

Originally established to bring back spices, by 1792 the trade had expanded. Tea from the whole of the East as far as China was now the most important cargo, but the Company consistently looked for new trading ventures in the region in order to finance its investment in the tea trade, for the success of that investment allowed it to maintain its rule in India. However, the Company had moved beyond commerce alone and in India it also collected taxes. Surplus revenues were sent back to London in the form of commodities such as saltpetre and cloth.

Outward-bound ships carried supplies for the smooth running of the Company's business and settlements, and, most importantly, the men essential to fill the commercial, military, medical, political and administrative operations. Those men might be fine, upstanding and ambitious, regarding their employment as an honour and Indian culture as the equal of anything in Europe; they could also prove to be either unscrupulous fortune-hunters ready to defraud the Company and oppress the local people, or dissolute youths addicted to expensive women, drink and gambling,[21] whose fathers had decided that the cost of shipping them off to a writer's post in India was cheaper than continually paying their debts in England. Whoever they were, and whatever their motives for embarking on an East Indiaman, it would be many years before they saw their families again. Many would never live to do so.

George Buchan awkwardly recalled his emotions when he left his family home, Kelloe, in the Scottish Borders to prepare for a career at the Company's Madras Presidency.

'A voyage to India is now so well understood that in the ordinary course of things it presents little novelty. Though thousands and tens of thousands have pursued…the same track of India adventure, yet the separation that then takes place…[is]…no light thing…I reckon it is indeed impossible…to bid a long farewell to the domestic circle and the native abode without feeling deeply. In truth, on that occasion many an aching heart is hid under a smiling face, for these are feelings that cannot be allowed much to meet the public eye without endangering the character of manliness that most, in making their first step in life, are particularly emulous of asserting. On some of these points I speak a little experimentally, as I remember their being somewhat realised in my own case.'[22]

Earnest, meticulous, and remarkably mature for his 16 years, Buchan was one of the very first passengers to embark on the *Winterton*, arriving on 26 April clutching his letter of introduction. With a Dundas for his mother, and the Lord President Dundas[23] himself present at his baptism, Buchan had an easy route into the Company. His petition for employment, countersigned by John Smith Burges, an influential holder of India Stock, had been accepted. On arrival at Madras he would become a Writer, the lowliest post in the civil administration, and writing would take up most of his time. Letters and documents sent back to the India House in Leadenhall Street were first copied, by hand, in duplicate at least: one or more went by sea, one by the overland route, and one remained on file. Further copies might be sent to other interested parties up country or at another Presidency.

The Company had three Presidencies in India to control its operations, each with its own Governor. They were based at Bombay, Madras and Calcutta, although by 1792 the first two were subordinate to the latter. If communications failed – for ships could sink and overland messengers might be robbed – the correspondence would be copied yet again.

Then there was the bureaucracy within India: correspondence between the Presidencies, between departments and with the various scattered residents. Such labour was boring, but it offered a grounding in the work of the department, and after a year or so of tedium the young Writer could start to expect promotion. Not for nothing were some families prepared to pay a clandestine back-hander of up to £3000 to a Director in order to secure a place for their son, or accept a Writer's position for a relative as a reward for some service rendered.

With Buchan came his baggage for the voyage and beyond, and also his cabin furniture. Passengers needed to buy a wash stand, chest, table and chairs, for although East Indiamen were the nearest things to passenger liners, they offered spartan accommodation. On completion of the voyage, any unwanted furniture could be sold off to passengers about to return to England. When it came to sleeping, it was better to have a cot that could be swung from hooks in the overhead deck than a conventional bed. Cots were difficult to climb into, and many an inexperienced traveller ended up on the deck with his nightshirt round his waist and his cap askew, but when the ship was at sea in anything but the calmest weather they offered a better night's sleep.

The standard of accommodation depended on the number of passengers and their ability to pay. Forward of the Great Cabin on the gun deck were a number of proper standing cabins with shelves and even lockers, while the Great Cabin itself could be used as a dormitory or divided into smaller units by means of wood and canvas partitions. The round house, which opened on to the quarterdeck, was Captain Dundas's domain, but like many commanders he had sold off some of the space to his passengers; and there was nothing to stop his officers from doing likewise. Buchan, however, had secured a wooden cabin on the port side, close to the after hatchway near the Chief Mate's quarters, and a place at his Captain's table where he was sure of better food than that offered to the crew.

In addition to salted meat, all captains carried live stores – chickens, ducks, pigs, even a cow which would provide milk and which could also be killed for fresh beef. To the smell of the estuary, human sweat, bilgewater, and damp wood was added the odour of manure and dank fur. The *Winterton*'s poop deck and boats took on the air of Noah's Ark, and the clucking and snorting of the poor creatures in their coops mingled with the shouts of the crew and the groaning of the ropes.

❈❈❈

Two days later, on 28 April, the majority of the passengers, known irreverently as 'live lumber' by the crew who had to work a ship, arrived at Gravesend and saw the *Winterton* lying at anchor in the Lower Hope. *King George* and *Thetis* had sailed, leaving the other Indiamen in various states of readiness. The passengers were rowed out to the *Winterton* in the boats to find the deck crowded with a jumble of furniture, baggage and trunks, and to realise – most for the first time – that for at least the next four months this cramped and smelly vessel would be their home. Large as she was by the standards of the day, she measured just 143 feet long and 35 feet in beam,[24] and she was to carry a total complement of about 288. With the hold and the lower deck full of cargo and stores, and in any case unpleasantly dark and airless, almost everyone was quartered on the main deck, with its 6 feet of headroom and 26 guns.

Some passengers had already booked their accommodation, others were obliged to bargain with Dundas for the best they could get, which might be no more than a cot or a bed in a cramped cabin-turned-dormitory; but at least no one had reserved for himself the whole of the Great Cabin – something that could easily happen when a very senior officer was travelling. They were shown to their cabins, furniture was lowered through the hatches or manhandled down the stairs; baggage had to be separated from effects destined to spend the voyage in the hold, and reunited with its owners. Cots were swung and furniture arranged so that it was just possible to get in and out of the cabin without having to crawl under the cot. One of the ladies had brought her harpsichord, and watched anxiously as the instrument was carried to her cabin.

The boats were hoisted in and the crew took their ship further down river into the Hope. *Lloyd's List* states that the *Winterton* sailed from Gravesend on the 29th; on the 30th a weary Dundas sat down at his desk, pushed his charts aside and wrote to his lawyer.[25] The letter is peppered with minor errors as though he was too tired to concentrate.

Ship Winterton April 30ᵗʰ 1792
in the Hope

Dear John,
All my passengers are now collected but one or two and I expect
the Purser on board this evening so that if the wind is fair we
will not be detained in the Downs…

You may suppose I am very anxious to be gone, all detentions
now are very tedious and with the crowd of passengers it is only
too pressing.

Before I left London I added Mr. Newte and Mr. Cameron
to the number of my executors in case of any accident to me and I
insured my life for £4,000 as a security to them for that sum
which they advanced me some years ago to pay for the ship and
for which I granted them a bond at that time. I likewise granted
them a bond for three thousand pounds which they have
advanced me just now for my investment so that I owe them
now seven thousand pounds in all. The money they advanced me
formerly being all paid and our Acct. cleared up to the day I left
London.

I mention this to you by way of memorandum in case of acci-
dents.

You will of course let Mrs. Dundas have what money she
may require during my absence and believe me, Dear John
yours very truly

Geo. Dundas

All my policys (sic) of insurance are lodged with Messrs. Newte
and Cameron.
Remember the East India Commanders Fund on the 2nd of
April next £25 –

To John Dundas Esq. WS Edin.

Dundas had already appointed guardians for his children in the event of his death. There was no suggestion he had any premonition of disaster: it was the practical act of any seafarer.

🦋

Buchan arrived knowing no one on board and already homesick, but he struck up a passing friendship with Samuel Hepburn, a young lowland Scot from Midlothian, also embarking as a Writer. Other passengers were more fortunate and came with family connections, but given the level of nepotism and patronage that existed in the HEIC, a subtle web linked many ostensibly independent travellers. Women were by this time going out to India in small but increasing numbers, most with husbands and families already established there, others in the hope of finding marriage. Doyenne of the 10 *Winterton* ladies was 32-year-old Isabella Cullen who was travelling with her two daughters – Miss Cullen and Margaret Cullen – to join her husband. When Captain William Cullen's regiment, the 53rd, had been reduced, he had gone out to Sarnat near Benares as an indigo producer but he remained on half pay.[26] The eldest daughter of Sir Archibald Hope by his first marriage, Isabella was also aunt to Nathaniel Spens, the Second Mate, and moved in the same Edinburgh society as George Dundas.

Because of the cost of bringing out and supporting a European wife, the lack of white women at the Presidencies, and the understandable aversion of many eighteenth-century European women to the idea of living in India, it was common for men to take native mistresses and have children by them. The Bristow girls, Charlotte aged 16, and Mary a year younger, were the illegitimate daughters of John Bristow[27] of Calcutta, one of the HEIC's senior merchants and an extremely wealthy individual. The two girls had been sent to England to be educated, and were now returning to Calcutta. During their absence Bristow had married the beautiful but somewhat notorious Emma Wrangham, an actress from St Helena, who had presented him with legitimate daughters. In 1790 she had left

India to supervise her daughters' education in England, which may have made it easier for Bristow to bring his illegitimate girls back home. In an age of far greater equality between the races, no stigma attached to their parentage: they were referred to as 'young ladies', had their place at Dundas's table, and could expect a good dowry when the right man came along.

Young Isabella Baillie, only 14, was another product of an Anglo–Indian liaison, having been born at Calcutta in 1778 to the native wife of Robert Baillie, while Mrs Bellasis[28] came from a family with strong East India Company links. Of the three remaining ladies, excluding from this number the five soldiers' wives, two were the sisters of young men entering the Company's service. Miss Lyne was travelling with her brother William and Miss McGowan accompanied Suetonius McGowan. Only one, a Miss Robinson, cannot be identified. The ladies had obtained accommodation in the round house beneath the poop, which gave them a degree of privacy and saved them having to go up and down the steps. The disadvantage was that at night they had to put up with the sailors walking about on the poop deck overhead.

About 30 people, including the ladies, dined at Captain Dundas's table. Suetonius McGowan, the Bengal-born son of a former NCO commissioned after the Bhatta mutiny, sat with John Gordon, heir to a baronetcy. Together with the third cadet, William Lyne from Ringwood, they were off to join the Company's Bengal army as Ensigns, and only the 20-year-old Lyne was out of his teenage years. Buchan and Hepburn[29] met fellow Writers, John Hamilton from Strabane, William Frazer and the Honourable Andrew Ramsay, a younger brother of the Earl of Dalhousie. Hamilton's application to the Company was typical:

To the Hon. Court of Directors of the H.E.I.C.

The humble petitioner John Hamilton sheweth that your petitioner has been educated in writing and accounts and

> *humbly hopes to show himself qualified to serve your Honours.*
> *He therefore humbly prays that your Honours would be*
> *pleased to appoint him a writer on the Madras establishment,*
> *and should he be so fortunate as to succeed promises to behave*
> *himself with the greatest diligence and fidelity and is ready to*
> *give such security as your Honours may require.*

Still a week short of his 16th birthday, Andrew Ramsay was fortunate to have the company of one of his brothers. Fourteen-year-old Henry had decided on a career in the Company's marine and was about to embark on his first voyage as a midshipman.

Another of Dundas's company was Thomas de Souza, the nephew of Antonio de Souza, an important Portuguese merchant in Calcutta with wide connections in the mercantile world.[30]

✤

William Dunn, the experienced Purser, joined the ship on time bringing with him the Company's despatches for Madras and Bengal which had been finally closed on the Saturday,[31] 28 April The China despatches had already gone with the Purser of the *Thetis*. Captain Dundas gave the order to weigh anchor, and the *Winterton* sailed proudly down the broadening Thames, past the malarial marshlands of Mucking and Canvey Island on the Essex side and the bleak expanse of low-lying Kent on the other, past the broad entrance to the Medway, and out into the English Channel at Foreland. With the ship in the Downs, there remained the formality of mustering the ship's company, receiving the Company's Inspector on board and sending away the pilot. The wind was fresh, sometimes strong, and passengers and troops were still finding their sea legs by day as their ship tacked within sight of the south coast. The log of the *King George* reported that at noon on 4 May, with the high ground of Portland to the north west, the *Winterton* was in sight. That was the last they saw of her.

The passengers settled down to make the best of the voyage. Together with the changes of watch, meal times punctuated the routine of the day like the religious offices of a monastery. The food served at the Captain's table was the best to be found afloat. Stags' tongues, smoked salmon, red cabbage, mustard, various pickles, preserved damsons, curry powder, coffee, wine, brandy, raspberry jam, oatmeal, mincemeat, and hung beef were among the stores that Dundas had taken on his previous voyage to tempt the palate of his guests, together with everything that might possibly be required for their preparation – hair sieves for punch, wire sieves for flour; a table brush; mills for coffee, chocolate and pepper; ivory mustard spoons, lemon squeezers, larding pins, a long tin pudding pan and assorted knives and steels.[32] In addition, there was the live meat cooped up in the ship's boats and in cages on the poop, and the traditional salted fare. The man in charge of turning such ingredients into a gastronomic *tour de force* on this voyage was James Higgins, who died on 7 July. His was the second death: on 25 May John Hughes, the Poulterer, had been lost overboard while Dale was officer of the watch. Everything was done to save him, recorded Dale, which meant hoisting out a boat and throwing ropes or objects to which a drowning man could cling, but in vain.

On the middle deck John Dale presided over an exclusively male mess for the junior officers and less important passengers, including a number of free mariners. These experienced seafarers were going out to operate the local shipping trade around the coast and between the Company's various possessions in the region. Among them, Mr Collier possessed some education; George Chiene's family was in shipbuilding in India and Robert Gibbs's relatives were already established in Calcutta. The Company exercised a monopoly of the 'country trade' as it was called, and those who wished to engage in it had to apply for permission. This rigid control on potential expatriates was designed to ensure that only men with employment or women with families to support them went to the Presidencies: if there were fortunes to be made, they would be made by the

Company's nominees, and under no circumstances did the Company want its outposts filled with the unemployed. A commander who accepted a passenger without the Company's approval risked immediate dismissal. In practice, hundreds went without the Company's permission. They could sign on as seamen and run – desert – when they had reached India, sometimes with the captain's active collusion.

Among the legitimate passengers was 'a poor man, pretty well advanced in life, who was going out to India, in the mercantile line…he had embarked under much dread of the sea'.[33] His personal effects included a cork jacket, in case of accident.

'I kept no journal regarding the first part of our voyage, and if I had done so it probably would have furnished nothing worth mentioning', wrote George Buchan, overlooking the two untimely deaths in the catering department and a third, seaman Henry White, on 12 July.

'We passed near the Island of Madeira but did not anchor and so far as my recollection goes we saw no other land until we made the Cape of Good Hope on the 18th July', he continued. The voyage was proving to be pleasant. However different the people who found themselves thrown together in an alien and claustrophobic environment, they managed to rub along together, everyone making allowances for the conditions. Not all voyages were so easy-going. Card-sharps fleecing young cadets, sullen or ill-tempered captains wrestling with uncooperative crews, rough weather prolonging seasickness, rain confining passengers to their cabins, even the occasional duel, could all ruin what was at best an uncomfortable passage where privacy was at a premium. The weather was good, there was none of the insubordination and sickness that had marred the previous voyage, and George Dundas won the affection and respect of his passengers. The disagreements that did spring up were minor, and Buchan agreed with Dale that although the ship was crowded 'our voyage was of the most agreeable nature, everyone living in the greatest harmony and the Captain respected by all on board.'[34]

With little entertainment provided, passengers passed the time watching the crew at their work, until the novelty wore off, playing cards, reading, writing as best they could, walking the deck, and just getting to know one another. On Sundays, provided the weather was fine, Dundas officiated at Morning Service, and at other times they could watch the soldiers drilling, or the crew practising gun exercises. Spotting another ship at a distance and speculating on its destination brought unpredicted excitement, and they looked forward to a break in monotony when they reached the Cape of Good Hope. As the *Winterton* sailed further south temperatures rose and skies cleared: the women left their redingotes in their cabins and appeared on deck in dresses of silk and muslin with broad sashes at the waist, white fichus tied across their breasts, and parasols to prevent sunburn. After dinner, there was dancing and music, and here Buchan found his only cause for complaint: there were no musicians among the crew or the soldiers, or at least no players who deserved the name of musicians.

'The chief source of disturbance used to be, perhaps, in a quarter where harmony is reasonably looked for, namely the practitioners in music, particularly on the violin and flute whose notes are somehow uncommonly rebellious in the hands of new performers. "Pass the word for Corporal McCoy" was accordingly a sound of ominous import to all amateurs of musical science.'

There was no Corporal McCoy recorded on the one surviving list of soldiers, only a Private McKey who may well have been the target of Buchan's displeasure; and however bad he was, he went on to enjoy unexpected royal favour.

The view of Table Mountain was always a welcome sight for mariners and travellers. The *King George* had passed without putting in for supplies, but Dundas took his ship into Simmons Bay, and the passengers had the luxury of going ashore in the boats and visiting Cape Town, then in Dutch hands. Buchan was more than glad of the opportunity.

'As a place for the refreshment of ships the advantages it then possessed could hardly be surpassed. We found the climate delightful, and a profusion of fruit and vegetables which constituted a treat which those who have never quitted their own shore cannot rightly appreciate. I had been for some weeks of the voyage much of an invalid and when we reached the Cape was not perfectly recovered, but the change worked with magic charm and a day or two after landing I was enabled to join some of the other passengers on an expedition to Cape Town, a distance of 15 or 20 miles, mounted on the cavalry of the country, without much fatigue. If a long voyage has what some call its miseries it also has its advantages and perhaps I may reckon among the number…the transition of getting on shore and again enjoying the privilege of roaming at large.'

The crew did not enjoy such a holiday, for they were busy stocking up with water and other provisions, as well as carrying out any minor repairs more easily done at anchor. Nonetheless the opportunity to eat fresh fruit and vegetables did much to decrease the incidence of scurvy.

By 1 August the ship was ready to sail, having been detained longer than necessary by contrary winds. Because the season was now so late, Dundas decided to proceed straight for Calcutta and not call at Madras as originally planned.[35]

'Having completed our water and other necessaries in False Bay', wrote Dale in the plain and economical style for which

Buchan patronisingly asked his readers to make allowance, 'we sailed at daylight, with a fresh gale at NW, with which we shaped our course to the SE for two days, when the wind shifted and became variable between the South and East, blowing fresh till the 9th when a SW wind succeeded, of short continuance, for it soon returned to the SE.

'It was Captain Dundas's intention on leaving the Cape of Good Hope to go the outer passage to India, but the winds, as has been stated above, inclining so much from the SE, obliged him to deviate from his original purpose, and on the 10th he accordingly bore away for the Mozambique Channel. Being baffled with light, variable winds and calms for some days our progress was inconsiderable, but on Sunday 19th a SW wind sprang up, which we had reason to believe was the regular monsoon, being then – to the best of my knowledge (for no journals were saved) – in Lat. 25'.

The route up the Mozambique Channel between Africa and Madagascar, known as the Inner Passage, posed several grave dangers to ships, not least the infamous reef known as the Bassas da India which had not yet been accurately marked down on the charts then in use. Before standing to the northward, Dundas wanted to be absolutely sure of keeping his vessel well to the east of this hazard, while at the same time giving a wide berth to the treacherous reef-bound coast of the island, and on 16 August he took lunar observations to confirm the longitude calculations he had made with his timepieces. He aimed to make Madagascar in the vicinity of St Augustine's Bay, a well-known watering place, and then steer north with confidence. In Dale's mind there was no doubt about Dundas's competence as a navigator. 'Captain Dundas had two timepieces, one of which had served him in his former voyage and by it he had consistently made the land with the greatest degree of exactness.'

Sunday, 19 August, was a day of relaxation aboard ship, the nearest thing to a day off that the crew would get; but a constant watch was maintained, and when the lookout spotted what looked like breakers in the distance – an infallible sign of rocks – one of the boats was lowered and sent off to investigate. In his memoirs, William Hickey[36] described sailing up the Mozambique Channel as a passenger on the *Plassey* in 1769 and being invited by one of the officers to look over the side.

> 'I beheld the rocks, as they appeared to me, close to the ship's bottom; but Rogers assured me they were at least 40 fathoms below us. In a few minutes after, however, he exclaimed "damn my eyes if I like this," and instantly ran into the Roundhouse. Captain Waddell…ordered…the lead to be cast; which being done, they found only four fathoms.'

The *Plassey* had a narrow escape, and Dundas had read and heard quite enough accounts of wrecks and near misses to treat the Mozambique Channel with caution.

Then whales were spotted around the ship, and the Captain decided that the distant foam was caused not by the breaking of waves upon submerged rocks but by the far-off spouting of more whales. The signal gun was fired, and the boat returned to the ship.

'The weather throughout the Sunday was clear and fine', reported Buchan.

> 'That is a day when on board of ship, as on shore, people generally appear in a sort of holiday dress, and in a well regulated ship the sailors and soldiers equipped in their best attire present an interesting sight. On the evening of the day I am mentioning this was seen to much advantage. The wind was fair, the sea smooth and everything appeared to prosper, and all was generally cheerful and joyous. I should indeed except Captain Dundas himself who was certainly not without a good deal of anxiety. He had not succeeded in his endeavour to make the land, and though he knew that his distance from

it was not very great he did not know the extent. I well remember standing with him for a considerable time on the Sunday evening at the gangway and his then telling me that he smelt the land distinctly. (The smell of land often extends a long way to sea. In passing Ceylon particularly, hounds on board of ship have been known to open in full cry, probably from the spicy fragrance.) When he retired to his cabin which was I think about 10-o-clock, his last words to me were the expression of an earnest hope that land might be seen by next morning.'

As the passengers went to their beds, Nathaniel Spens, the Second Mate, kept the ship on her easterly course. At midnight his watch ended and he was relieved by Dale. By Dundas's calculations, they were 80 miles off the coast.

'From 12pm till 2am we steered ENE, when the Captain came again upon deck, and observing the lower steering sail to lift, ordered me to keep the ship NE by E. The wind at that time was SSE, a moderate breeze, the ship going 6 knots, the water remarkably smooth and a clear star light night. Every possible attention was paid to the lookout. People were stationed on the bowsprit, foreyard, etc. Captain Dundas and myself with nightglasses carefully looking in the direction of the land; but so perfectly satisfied was he with his time pieces and observations that he never once mentioned Sounding, which was the more surprising as we both were sensible (as well as the other officer in my watch) that we smelt the land: and the Captain in particular compared it to the smell of new hay. But one fatal error was that he depended upon seeing fires on the land before any accident could happen.'[37]

Dundas based his expectation upon past experience. On the previous voyage they had spotted a fire even before they saw land; and he assured Dale that it had been the same whenever he had taken that passage.

Then he went to his cabin with a final warning to his cousin to use his initiative if he saw anything suspicious.

'He had not been off the deck above 7 or 8 minutes when the ship struck…The first shock was scarcely perceptible except to the man at the helm; the water was perfectly smooth, no breakers or surf were heard, and notwithstanding the clearness of the horizon no land was discernible.'[38]

Up on deck, and closer to the centre of the ship than the stern, Dale had hardly felt anything; down below, one of the passengers in the Great Cabin was startled awake by the first thud and instinctively got up. That saved his life, for the second, violent strike drove part of the rudder through the deck, destroying his bed. Buchan woke to the unforgettable sound of Dundas's voice bellowing repeatedly for his First Mate; and passengers and crew, in whatever clothes they could drag on were rushing, aghast, up the stairways to satisfy their worst fears.

Chapter Three

The Ebbing Tide

John Dale had lost his footing but not his wits. Instinctively he ordered the helmsman to put the helm hard a-weather, and shouted to the crew to brail up the driver, haul up the mainsail and shiver the aftersails. By nullifying the effect of the wind he hoped the ship would pay off, but in vain. Time now became their greatest enemy. It was high tide, and a new moon; the waters were at their highest and could only get more shallow. The vessel's keel already beat on the unseen rocks. George Dundas and Charles Chambers were on deck: the latter gave orders for the jolly boat and the yawl to be swung out and lowered. In the darkness, tackles and stays were rigged to the fore and mainmasts and yards, while the bewildered passengers crowded against the rails, staring helplessly out to sea and trying to come to terms with what had happened. Once the boats had been carefully lowered on the leeward side the chosen parties scrambled in and rowed away, the leadsmen shouting out the soundings. Around the ship, the depth was only 3 fathoms (18 feet), and the laden vessel drew 23 feet; but 100 yards astern they found a good 5 fathoms. If they could back her off, disaster might yet be averted.

They braced the yards around, backing the sails so that the wind was affectively pushing the ship backwards. Slowly, in a great grinding and straining, the stricken vessel began to move. Out on the stern gallery in a pool of lantern light, George Buchan listened tensely against the crash of the water and groans from the hull to the crewman beside him heaving the lead and calling out the depths. Hopes grew and excitement mounted as the water deepened and the *Winterton* gained sternway. Cries of 'she's afloat!' went up from all sides, and the passengers began to give thanks for their escape, while the Carpenter was left to assess how much damage had been done. There was no water in the hold: her bottom was sound. All that was needed was to back the *Winterton* from the reef, and steer a course away from danger. They had the craftsmen and the materials to repair her. On the forecastle, Dale was helping to trim the foresails and awaiting the orders to fill them so she could pay off.

> 'The darkness of night had probably occasioned a deception as to the supposed extent that the ship had backed; but before she had gone sufficiently astern to admit of steerage-room, orders were given for again filling the sails, and the ship was once more...precipitated on the reef of surrounding rocks.'

Buchan admitted much later:

> 'It is said that these orders were given by the Chief Mate, but it matters not. Everything was done for the best, and in such trying scenes it would be hard to attach responsibility for every particular measure. If it was that respected officer who gave the orders, he had no doubt, in his own mind, at the time good reasons for what he did.'[39]

The awful, splintering, grinding crash put an end to the euphoria. They had lost the best opportunity of extricating themselves from disaster. With the tide ebbing, there was only one chance left before the next high water: to haul the ship off by main strength. Chambers gave the order to swing out the cutter along with the kedge anchor bent to a 9-inch thick hawser. Dundas objected, wanting the heavier best bower anchor and a thicker cable, but Chambers maintained the kedge would be enough and Dundas deferred to his experience. Once it had reached the deep water astern of the *Winterton*, the anchor was dropped, and aboard the ship the crew began to heave on the capstan, adding their strength to that of the wind to haul the ship off. In other conditions it might have answered; but the *Winterton* was gripped fast by unyielding rocks that tore at her bottom, ripping off the copper sheathing and cutting into the oak.

It seemed a long time before the sky began to brighten. During that time the crew were clearing the upper deck, furling the sails, swinging out the longboat, the one remaining craft left aboard, striking the topgallant masts and yards, and rafting the booms alongside so that they floated rather than added weight. All this would lighten the ship, reducing her draught and easing the strain on her, for as the water receded she thumped more violently. After a night of terror for the passengers and frantic activity for the crew, dawn at last revealed their plight.

They were fatally close to the shore, some 6 miles off and grounded on the western edge of a long reef that ran almost parallel to the low coastline.

'Within the outer reef was deeper water, and half way to the shore was another reef which at high water was covered, dry at half-ebb. That on which the ship struck extended as far to the North as we could see, and quite up to St. Augustine's Bay.'[40]

'Captain Dundas ascertained by an observation which he took on Monday 20th the situation of the wreck to be off Point St. Felix, 63 miles to the north of St. Augustine, which is in about 23°30' south latitude.'[41]

❈

Could Captain Dundas have been wrong in his navigation? Dale refused to believe it was possible:

'I am inclined to the opinion that the whole of the western coast of Madagascar is laid down in our charts too far to the eastward; it has been remarked that ships make the land sooner than they expect. I cannot otherwise reconcile the great error which appeared in our case. Had Captain Dundas been at all doubtful of his timepieces I should not so much wonder; but they had always proved extremely correct: and I cannot imagine (though it is possible) that currents alone should have made a difference of near 90 miles in the space of 15 hours; that is, from noon preceding till the ship struck.'[42]

Back in 1785, beset by unfavourable winds, the previous Captain of the *Winterton*, Raymond Snow, had written in his log book:

'I would recommend to the reader of this journal, should he pass this way, to make the Isle of Madagascar between the Lat. 23.00 and the Tropic as he may depend nothing is to be met with within a mile of the shore and the land is high enough to be seen 10 leagues at sea.'[43]

The wind had then changed and Madagascar was forgotten, but his advice remained in the log, an implicit warning that, as Dale suspected, much of that coast and the Mozambique Channel was imperfectly charted.[44]

To the best of Dale's recollection, the *Winterton* was in Latitude

25°S on the day before the wreck, but either his memory was at fault, or he simply made a mistake when he wrote his account, because it puts the vessel too far south. Sailing at 6–7 knots for the next three hours could never have taken her anywhere near Point St Felix. She certainly approached along that latitude after leaving False Bay, but would have stood to the north by the Sunday, by which time Latitude 23°S is a more likely position.

No longitude was mentioned in any of the surviving accounts, but the accuracy of Dundas's calculations is only one part of the story. Harrison and the clockmakers who came after him had done the seafaring world an inestimable service by making it possible to work out longitude so exactly, but until every sea and ocean was accurately charted navigation remained hazardous. A captain could be certain of his ship's position on the chart, but if that chart proved wrong he could be lulled into a false sense of security, particularly at night or in poor visibility.

There is no way of knowing which charts Dundas carried. It was the business of the captain or his purser to buy the charts, not that of the Company, which only chartered the vessel. They had to approve the charts, but there were few sets to choose from, all quite old and none of them accurate. Madagascar and the Mozambique Channel were a particular problem. In 1791 the hydrographer, Alexander Dalrymple, published a whole set of charts based on those of predecessors and contemporaries. They ranged from the late seventeenth-century Dutchman Keulen, through Thomson and Bellin to D'Apres de Mannevillete, the hydrographer to the French East India Company who shared his plans with Dalrymple. The latter handed out this set of maps to East India captains and asked them to report back on their accuracy.[45] Dundas, with his keen interest in chronometers, may well have had a set in addition to his complete book of charts for the East Indies. Not all Dalrymple's charts showed longitude and those that did give different positions for Point St Felix or its equivalent. The French hydrographers naturally based their longitude on Paris, 2°23' east of Greenwich, so, allowing for the difference, it is possible to compare their positions with that shown on the modern Admiralty Chart and conclude that a chart such as D'Apres 1775 would set the reef well to the east of where it was.

Although Dale was pardonably sceptical that currents alone could have pulled the *Winterton* so far to the east, there is every likelihood that the treacherous and poorly-understood currents of the Channel were the major factor in a set of circumstances that combined with catastrophic results. For most of the year, the reef was marked by white breakers, an infallible sign; but this was high tide and a new moon, one of the few times when the lethal outcrop was covered to a depth that allowed the waves to ride harmlessly over. A few hours either way, and the telltale signs of danger would have been visible, soundings could have been taken, and tragedy averted. However, given all his misgivings about their closeness to land, Dundas's failure to order soundings and his over-reliance on seeing fires amount to negligence.

❦

Not even English oak could take the battering that the *Winterton*'s hull had endured for the past five hours. She was leaking badly, and the soldiers earnestly manning the pumps could do little to stem the ingress of water. By 8am the rudder was beat off, the copper sheathing had come up alongside, and there was only 8 feet of water under the bows. But with the coming of low tide the ship ceased to tear herself apart.

Dundas had still not abandoned hope of getting her off, despite her precarious condition. Breakfast was served; after the long night the crew were tired and ravenous, and for the passengers it preserved a strange semblance of order, albeit a bitter contrast to the cheerful, almost festive meal they had eaten the night before. Everything now depended on the next high tide, due that afternoon, and to have any prospect of success they had to lighten her even more by jettisoning as many of the heavy articles of stores and cargo as possible. Dale was assigned the difficult task of getting the guns[46] overboard. It was not enough simply to hoist them up and drop them over the side: they had to be lowered carefully into the boats and carried well away from the ship, so that, if the crew succeeded in floating her off, she would not strike on them.

While Dale was engaged on that duty other members of the crew were bringing up additional heavy items such as the iron ballast, powder kegs and cannon balls, perhaps also some of the water butts. A party of men was detailed to heave up the rudder and secure that alongside, while the ship herself lay heeled over to larboard.

In the midst of their anxiety and helplessness, the passengers found a strange entertainment:

'Among the things thrown overboard was a pretty general sweep of whatever lumbered on the deck, hen coops and such articles; and it was an object of momentary interest even in our situation to see how delighted the geese were in their new element. But successive surfs soon made them feel they were not now in the peaceful ponds to which they had probably been once accustomed. I do not believe any of them reached the shore alive.'[47]

The surf was caused by a sea breeze setting in, and it soon became so high and fierce that the ship's boats dared no longer come too close, effectively ending Dale's hopes of disposing of all the guns. The surf also tore away the booms that had been fastened alongside, something which was soon to cause serious problems. Dinner was served as usual, which helped to pass the time and keep some semblance of normality, although it could not stop anyone thinking about the next few hours. The passengers had realised, even if they had not been told, that this was the decisive moment. High tide came between 3 and 4pm, and once more, the crew gave their whole strength to the operation of hauling on the kedge anchor to heave the ship off.

With hindsight, their failure, however frustrating it seemed at the time, saved lives. Even with the soldiers taking turns to man the pumps for all they were worth, the water rose relentlessly inside the hull, and had the *Winterton* won free of the reef, she would soon have foundered in deep water.

Dundas summoned his officers to his cabin. The ship was lost: all they could do now was work to keep her together long enough to organise an orderly evacuation, and maintain a sense of calm and optimism among the crew and passengers. The soldiers would stand down from their valiant work at the pumps: there would be no further attempts at refloating.

The crew hacked through the lanyards of the weather shrouds, sending the masts overboard; any useful spars were secured on the deck as raft-building materials, and quantities of food and stores were put into the longboat. From that point on Buchan referred to the *Winterton* as 'the wreck'. Her identity was gone; for him she was no longer a ship.

There was no immediate crisis: the *Winterton* carried four boats which could be used to take people off and land them on shore, but the first task was to establish the best landing place. Dundas gave orders to Nathaniel Spens, the Second Mate, and William Dunn, the Purser, to take the yawl and reconnoitre the shoreline. The boats of an Indiaman, like that of naval vessels, would have included at least one with sails. The crew stepped the mast, bent the sails and loaded the little vessel with firearms, powder, compass and a lantern. At around sunset the two scouts left, with orders not to approach the ship that night unless it was safe to do so.

The *Winterton* crew was not a bad one for a crisis, but Dundas took no chances with them and decided to remove temptation from the seamen by smashing most of the casks of spirits. Before it could seep away, however, a few of the seamen forgot all notion of discipline, threw themselves on the deck, and 'like hogs' guzzled enough alcohol to render themselves senseless for a long time. Some even died as a result.

In the evening, Dundas called everyone together and explained his plan. It was straightforward enough: he had taken the latitude so they knew where they were, and once they had followed instructions and reached the shore they were to make their way south to St Augustine's Bay. He was counting on their finding at least one European ship in the bay, for it was a safe harbour, well known to mariners in the Indian Ocean. Above all, he stressed the need to accept the authority of his officers, promising that he would not leave the ship himself until he was as sure as he could be that everyone was safe. It did the trick: they gave him three cheers and the assurance he required, but his position was now tenuous, as Buchan realised:

'It may not perhaps be generally understood that the author-ity held on board of an Indiaman after such a disaster as ours is held by a much more slender and difficult tenure than in a man of war; the above occurrence is accordingly very cred-itable to the crew of our ill fated ship, and must have been in a high degree flattering to the feelings of our respected com-mander who was much esteemed and beloved…The situa-tion of a commander placed in such circumstances is one of no ordinary trial. The public and valuable property entrusted to him, gone: the lives of those under his command and com-mitted to his charge, to say the least placed in the most imminent hazard; and his personal fortune and prospects greatly impaired, or perhaps ruined.'

A Court of Inquiry awaited George Dundas in London, and there was every prospect that it would find his navigation and conduct at fault. He was already in debt; he had a position in society to main-tain, and a wife and three young daughters to support. Did he but know it, a fourth child was on the way. Not all East India com-manders retired as wealthy as nabobs: the HEIC's pension records show that quite a few, or their widows, were so poor as to merit a pension.

The soldiers stood down from their gruelling work. They had laboured in shifts at the pumps almost since the ship had hit the reef. Now, the water level was the same inside as out.

❀

The idea of landing on an island as little known as Madagascar seems to have held few fears for anyone. Buchan admits to having a confused idea of their being European settlements, which would render them all the assistance they needed, and the seafarers, even if they had never stopped there, knew that the local people were happy to trade supplies. But in 1777 a French East Indiaman, *St Jean Baptiste,* went aground on the Star Bank south of St Augustine's Bay, and of the 39 people who reached the shore only 19 survived seven months of slavery before being ransomed by a Dutch vessel.[48]

❀

The ship's boats that had been lowered earlier were now moored astern: in any event, without the masts there would have been no way of hoisting or lowering them again. Ten men who had been on gun disposal duty remained in the longboat, while the passengers, taking comfort from the fires now burning in the darkness along the distant coastline, and reassured that disembarkation would be an orderly affair, were as cheerful as the conditions allowed. With the sea breaching the Great Cabin, they took shelter in the round house on the upper deck among the trunks and furniture. It was divided by canvas partitions into smaller units, and the ladies shared one of the principal rooms, their bedding laid directly on the deck.

Buchan found temporary refuge in a cabin with Chambers and one or two other passengers. The noise of the ferocious surf crashing against the stern made sleep impossible.

'I do not now recollect at what time we retired to our short rest but we had little sleep. I well remember that Mr. Chambers particularly, notwithstanding the fatigue he had been going through, seemed more inclined to converse than to repose, and that his conversation was that of one who had more anxiety than he wished to express.'

Like his Captain, Chambers was in an invidious position. If it was he who had given the fatal order, then any Court of Inquiry could place the gravest blame on him. Dismissal or demotion would end his career, and he had not made much money out of his position. He was as anxious for his wife and daughters as for those more immediately in his care, and his indulgent boys-will-be-boys attitude had endeared him to the younger passengers and officers.

All this time the wind had strengthened and the surf became increasingly rough around the reef. The three boats moored astern were feeling the full force of the violent sea. Had the Quartermaster[49] in the 30-foot longboat hauled further out, away from the ship and into less turbulent water, all might have been well. He did not, and around midnight those who had managed a fitful sleep or dozed as best they could were roused by a cry that the boats were capsizing. Once again a crisis drove them on deck in the darkness, and above the roar of the surf they heard the ghastly screams of drowning men begging for aid. All they could do from the deck was to throw ropes, desperately hoping that by luck they might fall to hand and that the poor wretch clinging to the other end might not be torn away by the fury of the sea.

'With mingled sentiments of anguish and horror, we beheld the poor fellows in the boats struggling to reach the ship, while the height of the surf seemed to preclude all possibility of it. By the greatest exertions of those on board only three out of ten could be saved; some in the instant of grasping a rope were drove far out of sight and met inevitable death.'[50]

'This last event produced a fearful aggravation of our difficulties and dangers. The boats were our main prop and that now was gone, while the increasing violence of the wind and surf made it a very doubtful thing if the wreck would hold together till morning. I have no distinct recollection of how we passed the remainder of this night; but in such a night of horrors there could have been but little rest. God was pleased, however, to spare us to see the light of next morning, which ushered in the day that was to terminate this part of our calamities...If the wreck had gone to pieces this night, with the numbers then on board, and the circumstance of no preparation having been made then in the way of rafts, to all human appearance inevitable death awaited us.'[51]

The officers had a duty to remain calm and retain control of the situation, but they were not immune to fear.

'The trepidation under which we passed the few hours of darkness can better be conceived than described; the horrors of the night were increased by the ignorance of our situation, and we afterwards found out that we did not even know the real extent of our danger.'[52]

Chapter Four

Miserable Hours

With the sinking of the longboat, jolly boat, and even the cutter which had been moored furthest from the ship, the earlier loss of masts and spars proved critical. At first light, the making of rafts began, but the best timbers were gone, and descents to bring up spare wood from the orlop deck became highly dangerous. Three rafts were under construction when William Rowland, the Carpenter, went to the Captain with an inspired plan to use the poop deck as a floating platform. Dundas seized upon it, and gave Dale responsibility for directing the work.

Unlike naval vessels with their waist between forecastle and quarterdeck, the East Indiamen of the day were already flush decked. Only the poop was raised up, and it could easily, if laboriously, be sawn away and the deck shored up. Cutting scuttles in the floor would allow the crew to lash six empty water kegs around it for improved buoyancy, and ropes around the sides could act as hand holds. Without the ship's plans, the exact dimensions are unknown, but the width must have been less than 35 feet (the extreme breadth of the ship) and probably no more in length. Although a large number could be accommodated on it, there would not be room for everyone. Dale got together a group of men, but with many preparing to leave the ship, and others busy with smaller rafts, he was not well placed to hurry a job on which so many lives depended.

At between 9 and 11am on the Tuesday they spotted the yawl riding the surf, and Dundas hoisted signals, ordering it to stand off rather than risk being overset. Nathaniel Spens managed to make himself heard and reported that the shore, in every direction, was covered by a rough surf. There was no calm landing place. He then turned back and the little craft was soon lost from sight, apparently in pursuit of some native canoes – fragile affairs with outriggers – which had come out in the direction of the wreck. Now it became a case of everyone doing what he could for himself with what little was available. The unidentifiable passenger who had embarked in such fear of the sea, at last found every justification for his cork jacket, and duly appeared on deck wearing it.

❊

Those staring eastwards noticed that articles thrown overboard were steadily drifting inshore. Clearly the wind and current were favourable. The wind had freshened quite markedly, and the surf grew much rougher, breaking over the wreck; now the deck was beginning to rise, a dire warning that the unseen damage below was increasing. The kedge anchor and hawser with which the crew had vainly attempted to heave off the ship remained in place, still keeping the wreck stern-on to the surf and sparing it a broadside pounding. Yet Dundas, fearing it would not save the ship for much longer, was now in a quandary whether to go or stay. The women were in a wretched state, standing on deck in what little shelter they could find under the lee of the starboard side, with the high breakers regularly soaking them, while the few men Dale could muster worked on the poop. Some of the crew were putting the finishing touches to rafts of their own making and were ready to take their chances, but as soon as Dundas broached the idea of taking off the women, several men offered their places. Dundas had actually got on to one of these rafts along with 4 or 5 of the 10 ladies when Chambers went up to him and gripped his arm telling him in no uncertain terms that if they went now they would be drowned.

A heated argument between the two most senior men broke out in front of a large audience. Dundas begged Chambers to get on another raft and take care of the rest of the women. His principal argument was simple: the ship is inevitably lost, we have no means of saving the cargo or treasure: let us endeavour to save our lives while we can! However wild the sea, for Dundas the raft represented the lesser of two great evils. Chambers disagreed vehemently. He had been in the same position once already in his life – when the *Huntingdon* was wrecked off Anjouan – and did not share Dundas's fear that the *Winterton* was likely to go to pieces in the immediate future. Eventually he managed to induce his Captain to remain on board with the women. Inwardly relieved, the men repossessed their rafts and some 60 people said farewell to the surf-battered wreck.

With anxiety knotting their stomachs, those left on board had little appetite for food, and lunched on bread and cheese, waiting for Dale and his men to finish the poop. Their hopes were fixed on the afternoon tide, but either the work could not be completed in time or the sea conditions failed them.[53] The next high tide was not due until the early hours of Wednesday morning, and the perils of a night launch were too great even to consider. Other men, crew or soldiers, scouted around for empty wine chests, hen coops, and anything else that was likely to keep them afloat, and launched themselves into the sea. Nobody, not even the sailors, expressed any concern about sharks, although the Mozambique Channel, like the rest of the Indian Ocean, was home to some of the most feared species. During the afternoon's high tide the evacuees found themselves grounded on the inner reef. Anxious eyes watched through the telescopes until, as the tide flowed, they were once more carried towards the shore.

'In the midst of all this, occurrences that produced something of an occasional smile, flashed across the surrounding gloom. I yet recollect the masquerade, fantastic appearance of some of the crew, dressed out in as many shirts as they could put on their back, with ribbons and all sorts of finery. I remember one or two of them, so attired, quietly amusing themselves in one of the cabins with a tune, so to misapply the name, on a harpsichord. This propensity of sailors for jackdaw plumage at the time of a wreck was not particular to the Winterton.'[54]

The high tide at about 4pm eased the surf, and the bedraggled ladies went down to take shelter in Chambers's cabin. He called for a chair to be brought down; Buchan heard him pronounce it as 'cheer', and one of the ladies answered with a smile: 'I wish *that* could be had.' Soon enough the water drove them back up to the deck and into the dripping round house, which offered little comfort but was at least higher. Buchan joined Dundas in his cabin. Wet, cold and exhausted both mentally and physically, the Captain sat with a length of sail cloth wrapped round him. Quietly he explained that the surf, which was still rising and thundering on the dying hulk, would go on for a while yet. Buchan remembered nothing else of the conversation. Dundas had reached the state when there was nothing left worth saying.

Outside on the quarterdeck, Chambers sat in his chair, as if he were safe at home, oblivious to the fear and confusion around him and the seas washing over the deck. Dale had done all he could with the poop; now he had his own life to think of, and together with the Fourth and Fifth Mates, Joseph Wilton and John Moore[55] he was cutting the driver boom into three lengths. It was not enough to support four or five men: they needed something wider, and the only place to find the timber was down on the dark orlop deck. It was a dangerous expedition with the ship gradually heeling over to larboard, and the water washing loose stores and cargo about with deadly force, but they brought up a spar and were able to make themselves a kind of catamaran before the light failed. A few staves were tied to it, which would serve as makeshift paddles once they were in the water. Chambers watched them from his seat, praising their handiwork, but refusing to join them. 'He remained inactive, declaring he was sensible all his efforts would be in vain; and with the most perfect resignation to his fate, requested everyone to watch over his own safety.'[56] Dale's repeated pleas to him were ineffective: he appeared to have lost the will to live.

As dusk fell between 6 and 7pm the wreck heeled further over until the upper deck lay at a steep angle, the starboard uppermost. Only then did George Buchan suddenly remember his letters of introduction. Without any thought for the appalling risk he was taking, he clambered below to the main deck, and entered his old cabin, now lurched towards the water. The letters were there, safely packed in his trunk, but how to protect them from the water when the time to leave finally arrived? He found a bathing cap, wrapped it carefully round them and stuffed the package inside his waistcoat.

The deck was by now almost perpendicular. Without warning a chest of drawers from some other cabin came tumbling and sliding down the slope, and crashed against the door of Buchan's cabin, trapping the young man. There was no way he could push the door open with so much weight against it, not with the deck at such an angle and no purchase for his feet. All he could to was to knock frantically on the wood and yell for help. By a miracle he was not the only one to have ventured below. Someone heard him and came to the rescue, heaving the chest aside.

A few more minutes and he would have died, for at that moment the hawser attached to the kedge anchor snapped. The *Winterton* was driven broadside on to the rocks and took the full fury of the pounding water. Anyone below had only moments to get out – and there *were* people below. Early on, the treasure had been shifted aft into the lazarette to help trim the ship; men now risked their lives for the plunder. Buchan heard that several seamen drowned because they were still drunk from the day before. As he scrambled out, almost the last person to leave the interior, and pulled himself onto the starboard side of the ship, the shout went up to get on to the poop. One of the quartermasters had found a store of spirits and was violently and dangerously drunk.[57] Although Chambers had abandoned any interest in his own life, he exerted all his authority to restrain the petty officer.

Wilton had been to see Dundas and ask him if he wished to join the three young officers on their raft, but his Captain was holding by his earliest pledge to see everyone safe. Recognising his determination, Wilton then asked diffidently whether they themselves should go or was there anything they could do by staying? Dundas told them to leave. '...there was no reason why anyone with the means of saving himself should have stayed so long'.[58]

With a fearful crash the ship broke apart near the fore-hatch; wind and tide grabbed the forepart to which a number of men were clinging and carried it farther out to sea. Dundas began to help the ladies on to the poop, which was attached only by ropes. Charlotte and Mary Bristow, Miss Lyne, Mrs Bellasis and Isabella Baillie climbed on, along with the five soldiers' wives and their two children. With them went the Cullens, Miss Robinson, Miss McGowan and the servants. Two of the army wives were in a state of sheer panic, but one of the ladies 'gently but firmly admonished them as to the inutility of such complaints'.[59] Various of the men also took up their places. Others remained on what was left of the *Winterton*. Rank did not come into it: Thomas de Souza, Samuel Hepburn and George Buchan all stayed on the condemned hulk, and if the young Buchan had the weak constitution he claimed, he ought to have been a prime candidate for a place on the poop. In his journal Buchan commented:

'Still Chambers made no move to help himself, preferring to

watch with interest the progress of the wreck, putting questions on the subject to a person sitting also by him who had been bred to the sea and who was going out a passenger to India in that line. Mr. Chambers seemed to entertain a faint and momentary idea that, the wreck having divided, the part on which we were might drift towards the shore. At such times even trifles afford matters of future interest to the busy memory. His shoe buckle having loosened, I remember his asking me, in a half joking but significant way, if it appeared worthwhile to replace it. To my friend, Mr. Hepburn…he expressed a request that he would remember him to Mrs Chambers, and tell her that he thought of her in his last moments. On Mr. Hepburn remarking that their chances of safety were equal he said he knew that he would not be saved.'

As the ship's final moments came, there were up to 200 people still on her upper deck. Dale described it vividly:

'The decks were falling in; large pieces of the wreck were dashed with such violence by the surf among us as to endanger our lives; and waiting for a favourable interval, we threw our raft overboard and jumped after it.

'I would attempt just to give a faint idea of the melancholy scene as we went under the stern of the ship. Most of the bottom was gone, so that the upper works lay on their beam-ends nearly. To avoid as much as they could the violence of the sea the people had got close aft on the poop, and the moon which was about three days old, and just setting, shone a faint gleam on their faces that made them just discernible. One solitary light burned in the cabin, which only added to the woefullness of the picture, while the shrieks, amongst which those of the poor females were easily distinguished, at every sea that broke over them, altogether made such an impression as can never be effaced. In a very few minutes the light disappeared.'[80]

The three officers had left the horrors of the disintegrating ship for the savagery of the foaming sea. Experienced mariners as they were, nothing had prepared them for what followed. They got hold of their raft, and pulled themselves on to it, but the surf threw them off, wrenching away most of the staves they needed in order to fight their way to shore. Fortunately they were strong swimmers, and somehow, by luck and by keeping their nerve, they managed to regroup, as Dale describes:

> '...the first that could get on the raft calling to the rest, and before we could well breathe, the same thing would happen again. I lost my hat and shoes this way, and was near to drowning often. I had got on a jacket lined with flannel, which incumbered me so much in swimming that I attempted frequently to disengage myself of it, but it stuck too close; and sometimes when I had got it half off, a sea would go over us...so that I was compelled to keep it on. About midnight, as the sea breeze had abated, the water became smooth. We imagined we saw lights, and thinking it might be the yawl, hailed with all our strength for some time, but had no answer.'

What they must have seen, unless imagination played tricks on them, were fires along the coast; it was highly improbable that Spens and Dunn, together with the crew members who had gone with them, would have put to sea at night when the risks to themselves and their small boat were so great. They could have had no idea that their comrades or anyone else from the ship had been forced into the water. By now, Dale, Wilton and Moore were exhausted. They had been working since dawn, and the life and death struggle in the ferocious sea about the reef had sapped their energy. Despite the danger, cold and discomfort, they found it impossible to stay awake, and every time one of them dropped into sleep the lurch capsized the raft. They lost all but one paddle, but with the dawn they felt sure they had covered the worst of the distance.

They were in for a shock: there was no land to be seen. The wind and current had been too strong for them in their weakened state and had carried them out to sea.

With their lives at stake they could not give up, and at least they knew in what direction the land lay. They started to paddle again. The sun rose, burning hot, which further drained their energy; they had neither food nor water. Each of the trio gave a hundred strokes with the makeshift paddle, then handed it on, and painfully they managed to recover the lost distance.

The elements at last came to their rescue, pushing them on towards the land until they reckoned themselves just a mile from safety. The water had been growing steadily less deep; too tired to work the raft any longer they slipped into the sea, wading towards the beach. The coastal waters of the Mozambique Channel have some of the world's finest coral, but, shoeless, Dale and his friends were in no state to appreciate it as they

'...dragged the raft towards the shore, over a bed of beautiful red and white coral, amusing enough to the eye, but which cut our feet to pieces. Finally, about 3pm we reached terra firma, almost dead with the heat and fatigue; but thankful, after being about 19 hours in the water, for our great escape.'

Their first thoughts were of finding other survivors. All around them the beach was strewn with wreckage and the various effects that had been thrown overboard or washed out of the dying ship. Among the jetsam were the corpses of the wretched ducks and geese who had entertained the passengers by their brief flirtation with freedom. The officers collected as many as they could, hoping there might be a chance to cook them. As they walked along the scorching sand a man in the semblance of a soldier's uniform came towards them and began asking how much they wanted for the poultry. For a moment they looked at him in utter perplexity, astonished by the idea of selling anything to one of their own; then it dawned on them that they were the first people he had encountered since landing and he had taken them for natives. 'We must have been strangely altered to cause such a mistake' thought Dale at the time, but he must have realised afterwards that few people on the ship would have had any real idea of what the native people looked like. Until a few days ago, Madagascar had been no more than an island on a chart. The shipwreck had transformed it into the most desirable place on earth, and only now would they learn the reality.

Chapter Five

Perfectly Hopeless

The ship had gone to pieces that Tuesday evening (21 August) with between 80 and 100 passengers, soldiers and crew on the poop. The night escape that no one had even considered a few hours earlier was now a necessity, and the dangers had multiplied. As the poop began to separate from the ship, at least five of the women panicked and climbed down, seeking what they must have believed to be the greater safety of the mizzen chains. Dundas went after them, trying to get them to return. It was too late. With water breaking over the shrieking terrified people, the poop launched itself into the furious sea. By luck or by providence it remained upright, floating free.[61]

Above them in the failing light towered the menacing black remains of the starboard side, supported only on the yielding beam ends and threatening at any moment to crash down and smash them to pieces. Those on the edges paddled frantically, and the surf carried them clear, but only just in time. At length they drifted into calmer waters, to spend a cold and wretched night in their sodden clothes. They had none of the mates with them, but the petty officers, midshipmen and seamen could read the sky and check the course. They had no provisions; nor could they hope for any rest. The raft rode too low for anyone to be able lie down, even if there had been room to do so; and by morning those on it were anything up to waist deep in water. Men and women held one another up when the strain of exhaustion and hunger grew unendurable.

During those miserable hours they managed to cover one third of the distance to the shore, paddling as best they could. They soon discovered, just as Dale, Wilton and Moore before them, that the morning wind and tide were in their favour. With the poop sinking ever deeper there was no time to look for the best landing place; they simply worked as hard as they could towards the shore, reaching safety an hour before the three officers, and some 3 miles south. Only one person died, and that unnecessarily: a soldier who had supposedly filled his clothes with silver saw how close to the shore they were, decided to swim the rest of the way, and was dragged to his death by the weight of his booty. The rest prudently waited until the poop drove ashore.

They had had ample time to study the coast that confronted them. The rocks extended a way out to sea, and as far as the eye could see the low land above the beach was lined with trees. Among the warm rocks they spotted a cave, and the shattered women retired there to get out of the sun and dry their clothes as best they could while the men recovered from their exhaustion and sent search parties to look for water. Not long before sunset they spotted figures approaching, and apprehension gave way to relief on recognising Dale and his companions. That relief was exceeded only by their appreciation of the supplies that the officers and the soldier had with them. They had seen nothing of the first groups to reach the shore and this was their first tangible proof that others beside themselves had survived the final moments on the reef. If these four had made it, then there was hope for the rest.

Dale's first question was: where was Captain Dundas? To this he could obtain no satisfactory answer. All the party from the poop deck knew was that he had not embarked with them; neither had Chambers. Nothing had been seen of Spens or Dunn with the yawl, so, as a result, Dale became the senior officer present, and his priority, too, was to find fresh water before irreversible dehydration set in. More groups went off on a fruitless search for a stream or spring, while the rest, without the means of kindling a fire to cook their poultry, scraped oysters off the rocks. But even as he was organising his debilitated flock Dale was thinking of the yawl, praying that she had survived. A great deal might be riding on her.

🦋

Barely two minutes after the poop separated, a massive wave reared up and broke on the side of the ship, smashing what was left and washing off many of the 100 or so remaining on it. Some 40 people lost their lives in that single instant, unable to fight their way through the frenzied surf or grab anything to keep them afloat. A great piece of the starboard side, cabins and bulkheads still firmly attached below, became a raft, floating broadside up in a sea of tossing debris and frantic humanity.

Buchan found himself hurled into the water and dragged away from the wreck, his close-fitting coat and breeches hampering his attempts to swim and stay afloat. A plank came to his rescue and he clung on until a powerful wave tore him from it; he found a second plank, and the same thing happened, but he managed to hold on to a third.

'I was in the midst of a wide mass of planks, casks and other such things…and though the sea spared me, how I escaped again and again being dashed to atoms, is truly marvellous. My leg once got entangled in a rope attached to one of the planks, and fracture at least appeared inevitable; but from this too I was extricated.'

His great ally was his youthful optimism and naiveté, and it served him well in those moments, for, never doubting he would survive, he kept his head and neither panicked nor despaired. With disarming honesty he observed:

> 'In fact, our situation on the wreck had been so perfectly hopeless, this probably appeared an improvement, in affording something of a tangible means of preservation. I saw nothing in the darkness but the objects that immediately encompassed me, and I thought I was the only person saved – if such a perilous situation as mine could be called safety'.

He even felt something like buoyant gratification 'in the idea of seeing new countries and new things. In excuse of my ignorance I may say that I had not then numbered many years of life.'

Without knowing where he was, or what had become of the rest, Buchan drifted helplessly where the sea took him, realising only that he was more or less out of the surf. How much longer he could have lasted on his piece of wood he had no idea; suddenly, rising high above him was a mass. He heard voices, and he understood that, by nothing short of a miracle, he had been carried alongside that huge portion of the starboard from which he had been washed, probably over an hour earlier. As he struggled to board it: 'a fine fellow of a sergeant, of whom I still think with gratitude,[62] took hold of me and hauled me up; to my utter amazement and joy, I again found myself in the midst of many of my shipmates.'

Among the 50–60 people who had either kept or, like Buchan, regained their places, were the Carpenter, William Rowland, and passengers Samuel Hepburn, Thomas de Souza, Henry and Andrew Ramsay, and Isabella Cullen. Isabella should not even have been there: she had been one of those on the poop. During the panic that occurred when the poop broke free from the ship, some of the ladies had scrambled back on to the wreck, clinging to the mizzen chains and allied themselves to Buchan's group. In doing so they had made a fatal mistake. After the ship broke up Isabella had seen her daughters washed off the starboard raft by the heavy seas, and distraught, she tried to throw herself after them, preferring suicide to bereavement. Those who were clinging on for their own lives physically held her back, while they showed her 10-year-old Margaret who, by the courage and quick thinking of one of their number had been rescued. Thereafter, Isabella showed a calm resolution, stoically enduring her misery rather than adding to that of the rest.

Of Chambers there was, unsurprisingly, no news. Rowland had seen Dundas with them on the starboard side after the poop had separated; he had spoken with those nearest him, but, 'quite exhausted and unable any longer to keep his hold [he] was washed through the quarter gallery by a heavy surf and rose no more'.[63] His death and that of Chambers had its effect on the survivors:

> 'Much did everyone regret the loss of captain Dundas and of our first mate. The former was one whose equal as a man and gentleman is seldom to be met with. The latter was a good man and much liked.'[64]

There was no sign of Misses Robinson and McGowan, both of whom must have left the poop along with the Cullens, and one man had broken his leg; but the starboard raft had acquired a most unexpected passenger – a frightened pig, which was running about and irritating already frayed nerves. At the time Buchan arrived, they were on the verge of throwing it overboard, but perhaps because he had just been plucked from a watery grave, he intervened on its behalf and it was allowed to remain on board.

If he had felt a relief akin to euphoria at reaching the raft, reality soon hit home. They had neither food nor shelter, and, despite the latitude, the wind felt bitterly cold through their soaked, torn clothing. Many were in shock, and the darkness only increased the sense of helplessness. Although the size of the raft and the woodwork beneath it gave stability, it drew about 8 feet of water, and towards midnight at low tide it grounded for several dismal hours. Daylight showed them that either they had made little ground or that they had been driven back by the wind. Afraid of returning to the breakers they held up every bit of fabric they could find that might act as a sail, no matter how small, hoping the wind would carry them eastwards. At once it seemed their prayers were answered, for they picked up speed, and felt they were rapidly approaching land. Spirits shot up, only to be dashed when they realised that land was much further way than it looked or they hoped. At the next low tide they grounded again, this time on the inner reef, still with a long way to go.

The tide ebbed until 3 feet of water lay on the reef, and some of the men decided to jump off and have a look under their strange lifeboat. Despite the battering it had taken, some of the starboard cabins were intact, and there they found clothes, mostly ladies', and something rather more edible – a hamper of claret and cheese. The impromptu cheese and wine party did a lot to restore morale; they shared equally and kept some back in reserve.

The forepart of the ship that had broken away before the ship disintegrated had also drifted eastwards, and it, too, grounded on the same reef as the starboard. During the morning, Buchan's group were amazed to see three people wading through the sea towards them. Tired and debilitated as they were, and in water still at least waist high, they were all but spent by the time they made it.

Natives in their outrigger canoes came to look at them, crying out 'salamanca dollar', meaning 'give', a term familiar to some of the sailors; but distress signals from the raft were ignored, and the canoes returned to land. Later, another canoe arrived. Its owner had picked up someone from the *Winterton* found clinging to a piece of wreckage, and when the survivors on the starboard signalled to it, the fisherman obligingly came over.

It was their first close view of a native Madagascan, and if they had expected him to conform to their ideas or experience of an African they were to be surprised. He was lighter skinned, a 'bright copper hue not easily described on paper'[65] with long black hair that had been finely plaited and greased, and his features appeared more European to them than African.'[66] Since he had had the humanity to rescue one of the survivors, those on the raft had a second favour to beg.

There was unanimous, almost unspoken, agreement among Buchan's party that something had to be done for Isabella and Margaret Cullen. They were the only women aboard, and they had suffered the most appalling loss. No one knew how long it would take to get ashore on the raft, but by canoe it would be swift. The fisherman was willing to take them, and it only remained to decide which of the five gentlemen should accompany them. All, with the possible exception of de Souza, were young enough to have been Isabella's sons. The selection fell on Hepburn who was most closely connected to Isabella. Buchan was also given the chance to leave, but virtuously declined it. The three of them were helped into the canoe, a sharp craft with outriggers, capable of carrying six people but likely to capsize in inexpert hands, and they set off for the shore, arriving at a small fishing village 10 miles further south along the coast from where the others had landed.

Buchan's group remained grounded on the reef under the baking sun until late in the afternoon when the tide rose but once afloat they made no progress.

❦

The search for water was still in progress when Dale was told that a group of four natives were asking for the Captain. The men were friendly, slightly built, athletic, and naked but for a single cloth twisted round their waist, and in their limited English they informed him that the King of Baba wanted to see him and would provide water and everything else. All he had to do was go with them.

It seemed too good to be true, but, leaving the Fourth Mate, Wilton, in charge, Dale and a couple of others went off with the natives, following the coast south for about 10 miles, part of this distance over the sharp, crippling coral. All they had seen of the island had been the low, rocky coastline bordered by scrubby, dry trees and bushes, and by sunset they were glad to come upon a small village, no more than a few rectangular huts with pitched roofs, all made of rush-covered branches. There was no king there, but as well as the local people they found other survivors who had just come ashore, and they discovered Isabella and Margaret Cullen among them. Dale managed to persuade the villagers to rent out a hut for the two women to give them some privacy in their grief, and exchanged a knife for a mixture of honey and water for himself, the first drinkable liquid he had tasted since leaving the wreck. The fishermen were trading brackish water for a dollar a quart, but it was better than nothing. They spent the night at the village, and the following day, John Slater, the Boatswain, handed over his whistle in exchange for a bullock which they roasted. It was the nearest thing to a feast since Sunday, particularly when washed down with the claret that had come ashore that morning together with a box of lady's shoes (which were of less use!). More items were being washed up, and when Dale had ensured his party had all they needed, he hired a canoe and got one of his men to take the surplus meat and drink back to Wilton.

Having heard by then from the Cullens that there was a large group adrift on a raft, various people begged the natives to go out in their canoes and rescue them, but the appeals were not heeded. It was not a question of deliberate inhumanity: the natives were clearly willing to save individuals, and happy to trade, but they were evidently afraid of large groups, and may have had grounds for their fears if they knew of slaving raids along other parts of the coast.

🔀

After Dale had left them, Wilton's group had continued in vain to hunt for water until, in the evening, a sailor came up with some that had been given to him by a native. Shared out, it amounted to only a mouthful each. The following day, Friday, their luck changed. The sea had torn the wreck apart, clawing out its innards and leaving them to the whim of the tide and wind. A cask of cider arrived on shore, and not far off they found some cheese and a butt of water. By the time Dale's man arrived by canoe with the provisions, they were far more comfortable; and more baggage, food and liquid were being washed up. Wilton organised expeditions to collect up everything from shoes, stockings and bales of cloth for uniforms to casks of pork, cider and porter. Particularly fortuitous was the discovery of a small quantity of black powder, which enabled them at last to light a fire. Surveying his haul on the Friday, Wilton dispatched Dale's man back to him with the news that they had everything they needed and that Dale ought to rejoin them.

❈

Difficult negotiations with the natives concluded with Dale getting a canoe to take Isabella by sea 'for she never could have walked in the state she was in'. Then, with Slater and the rest, Dale retraced his painful route back along the beach. 'Returning over the coral rocks I thought I should have died for without shoes my feet were cut to pieces.'

He returned to a place that looked like some kind of fair or market, with everything laid out and more being brought up. The officers set a guard on it that night, knowing that it represented not just vital supplies but the means of commerce. Among his group, Dale was having little problem with discipline. Used to giving orders on ship, command came naturally to him, and even the soldiers and sailors who were no longer under any obligation to obey accepted his leadership. Maybe he understood instinctively how to exert authority; or perhaps the ordeal they had suffered made the survivors only too ready to defer to the orders of anyone willing to take responsibility.

That night he decided it was time to put Dundas's plan into operation and make ready to walk to St Augustine's Bay. If there were other survivors elsewhere along the coast, that was what they should be doing: the sooner they all reached their destination, the sooner they would know how many had been saved. He had over 80 people with him, including seven ladies and most of the passengers. The groups who had set off on the earliest rafts must be somewhere and also the men whom Isabella and Margaret had left on the starboard side, plus any who had made it ashore as individuals. He had waited as long as he had in the hope that Dundas would reach the shore alive. Now he knew his cousin was dead.

'He was universally respected not only for his professional abilities, which were conspicuous, but for his many other amiable qualities…my only aim is to pay that respectful tribute to his memory, from whom I had received so many obligations and whose loss I do, and ever shall, feel severely. We never found his body….'[67]

Dale called a meeting on the morning of Saturday, 25 August and told them of his decision to set off on the Sunday, giving them the rest of the day to get themselves ready.

'I recommended also to them to behave with order and propriety especially in their conduct towards the natives upon whom we were now dependent and must rely for our subsistence, and pointed out as well as I was able, the bad consequences that would most probably ensue were they to act otherwise.'

His 'harangue', as he called it, was cheered, proof, if any were needed, that he had their trust and confidence. It was also timely: there had been trouble between one man and a group of natives determined to steal the very clothes he had on.

Dale's recollection was that they left on the Sunday; Alexander Thompson, the Free Mariner who kept a journal, stated that they departed on the Saturday evening, a few hours before dark but after the worst heat of the day.

Chapter Six

Under a Relentless Sun

It was fortunate that Isabella and Margaret Cullen were taken off the starboard side by canoe that Wednesday because those left behind made no progress under the relentless sun, even with the afternoon tide, and by the following morning had once again lost ground. They were still endeavouring to work their way east, using their makeshift paddles and holding up cloths to catch the wind, when they spotted half a dozen canoes quite unmistakably heading for them. Rescue had arrived, at last, and everyone stopped what he was doing to watch the natives work up to them. As they came alongside, there was a mad scramble for the canoes.

With more warning and better preparation, they might have behaved rather differently; as Buchan says, they could have drawn lots to decide who should go off in the first flotilla. The remainder could wait, at least secure in the belief that they would, in turn, be saved. As it was, the panic-stricken rush came close to capsizing the unstable boats, frightening the fishermen who immediately paddled clear. Buchan, de Souza and the Ramsay brothers tried to stop the disorder, desperate not to lose the chance of rescue, but nobody heeded them, and they were left to watch their hopes disappearing back towards the shore.

Worse, that short break in their efforts had a further price: yet again they had been driven back out to sea. Any thoughts that the natives would return were soon abandoned; nor did any canoes reappear on the Friday. At the same time as Joseph Wilton was inviting Dale back to share his cornucopia, Buchan's group was surviving on a barrel of salted butter and relieving their parched mouths by sucking pieces of lead. De Souza had the idea that bathing in the sea would somehow compensate for the lack of drinkable liquid. 'Whatever effect it produced', explained Buchan sagely, 'is of course derived from absorption.' Nonetheless, he declined to join his Portuguese companion in the sea, and like the rest was forced to resort to drinking urine: 'salt water in its most loathsome shape'. When the low tide came and the raft grounded they got off and searched in vain for further edible supplies. Buchan found some medical supplies and risked drinking a phial of unknown liquid, with no ill effects. One of the men spotted a cask at a distance and, underestimating his weakness, swam after it. In full view of his fellows he drowned before he reached it.

A few of them tried their hands at raft making, but with no tools and hardly any materials almost all were unsuccessful. De Souza cobbled together some pieces of an old box and launched himself off, but his raft soon capsized, and he swam back, using it as a float. One of the sailors lashed a few sticks together into an open raft, got the young Ramsay brothers, Henry and Andrew, on to it, and left the main party, swimming with one arm and pushing the raft along with his free hand. They disappeared into the distance, leaving Buchan and de Souza as the only passengers among the seamen and soldiers.

That evening a favourable wind sprang up, but despite their

efforts they found themselves carried further out to sea by the current. Since abandoning the *Winterton* on the Tuesday night they had spent more than 72 hours with scarcely anything to eat and drink, and by the time Saturday dawned they had realised there was no possibility of reaching land on the raft. It was too ponderous to paddle against the current; it drew too much water ever to get over the inner reef. However, the shallowness of the water offered the possibility of wading to the shore during the low tide that morning. There was a long way to go, and just a couple hours in which to do it, but as the only alternative was to starve they took their chance – all save the pig for whose life Buchan had so earnestly argued and a man with a broken leg.

> 'We threw off most of our clothes and went two together, those in advance keeping the distance so as to be heard by those who followed. I don't believe we had gone half a mile when we found the water so fast deepening that it was impossible to proceed without swimming – and flying in our state would have been to the full as easy. The tide was by this time just about flowing which left no alternative to preserve the little life that was now remaining to us than a speedy retreat to our raft, and that aggravated the fatigue that this effort had produced. On returning we found a poor fellow whose leg had been fractured, and who was of course unable to accompany us, on the brink of the raft where he had crawled with the intention of throwing himself into the sea.'

For the first time Buchan realised he, too, was staring at death. He had drunk nothing for two days save urine, and the alternate heat of day and the chill of night had taken a toll of everyone. There was only one source of food.

> '...with death advancing in the most terrible shape it was agreed now to avail ourselves of the final resource by killing

the hog. The poor animal having been many days without meat or drink must have been much emaciated but the supply that it afforded was in all likelihood the means of saving the lives of many of us. The part of the meat, I think, which we chiefly ate was the liver, but fearful of the meat increasing our desire of drink we ate little of it. The blood, however, was measured with scrupulous exactness and gave perhaps what was equal to half a small teacupful to each person. I think Mr. de Souza was the only one whose stomach revolted against the blood in such a way that he could not take it, and he gave me his share, a kindness which, if he ever happens to see this, I beg he will be assured I yet gratefully think of. [He also confessed to a twinge of conscience for drinking what was in effect a double portion.]

'So admirable was the conduct of the people to whom my memory yet returns with feelings of attachment that, though we had then before us every prospect of starving to death, no violence was used, and, so far as my recollection goes, the allowance was distributed with as much regularity as the stated rations on shipboard would have been.'

Sunburned by day with the sun reflecting off the sea, and shivering by night, they quietly began to fade. Although it was August, one of the coolest months, the temperature still ranged from 10°C to 26°C in the course of 24 hours, and they were exposed to the extremes without any form of shelter. A weak shower of rain – the Trade winds had lost their humidity as they crossed the high central plateau and the west of the island lay in the rain shadow – brought no relief; during the night someone died.

❦

During the same time period, despite having been spared the terror of the ship's disintegration and the hardships of those on the rafts, Nathaniel Spens was having what Dale, without undue sympathy, considered 'a very disagreeable job of it'. After hailing the *Winterton* to report that the whole coast was surf-bound he had told his crew to make for St Augustine's Bay sailing inside the reef. His hope echoed that of them all: to find a ship at anchor, but the Bay was deserted, and unable to find anyone to whom he dared entrust the precious craft, he had been forced to keep her at sea. During the course of the day he came across the first rafts to be launched from the ship, and the men on them requested help. Spens refused to go to their aid. As Dale later commented in his *Journal*:

'Many of the people confidently affirmed that he had refused to assist them while on the rafts, towards the shore; when they were drifting out. The fact itself cannot be denied, but I should be very sorry to impute it to the same motive as them. Mr Spens saw that the yawl was our only resource in case we should come to execute any plan afterwards for our relief; and as such was apprehensive of trusting her too near them; in case they should have crowded into her, and most likely have sunk the boat. Besides they were in no danger; however they always bore him ill will on that account.'

It would prove not be the only action that earned him the contempt of a particular faction of the survivors.

Disappointed at St Augustine's Bay, Spens sailed northwards to Toleary, changed two of his crew and returned to the *Winterton* at the very least a day after the ship broke up, for he found only the remains of the wreck. His intention to join the survivors somewhere along the coast was thwarted by his crew who insisted on looting as much of the Company's silver as they could rather than leave it all to the natives. As Dale recorded:

'It was to no purpose that Mr Spens presented the danger that would attend it; and seeing they were obstinately bent upon it, he landed, with the Purser; and took out the compass and the firearms: and let them go. They paid dearly for this folly for the boat was upset and two of the men were drowned and lost a couple of oars etc., and it was wonderful that she was not dashed to pieces.'

Spens' companion, the Purser William Dunn, quite literally held the purse strings as the ship's on-board treasurer, a position that was never likely to endear him to his shipmates. Pursers in the navy had a reputation for taking full advantage of their many opportunities to feather their nests. Dunn's station, like that of Mate, Surgeon and Captain's Clerk was considered gentlemanly, but all HEIC ranks, even that of Commander, were considered by many outside the service to be somewhat tarnished by trade.

❧❈❧

John Dale's flock gathered as much as they could carry and shared it out among the most able-bodied, ready for their departure for St Augustine's Bay.

'Our party consisted at first of seventy or eighty people amongst whom were seven of the ladies, most of the passengers and the officers of the ship. Distressed as we were it was impossible to refrain from laughing to see the appearance we made which would have formed a good subject for a sketch book, delicate ladies in great, wide men's shoes, their dress something nondescript, neither perfect man's nor woman's; and each with a small piece of cloth rolled up at the back like a trooper's cloak which served them to lie on; the gentlemen all cropped, both hair and coats, loaded with provisions and bottles.'

Dale himself carried a 5-gallon water keg slung on a pole, as well as his own rations, no light load in such heat for any man. Whether to regain his strength or merely out of amusement he dropped behind on occasions to observe his motley companions. There was no question of hurrying. Although this group had not suffered the same ordeal as Buchan and his comrades, they, too, were short of liquid, and the women were neither equipped nor strong enough for a route march. Ill-fitting footwear, soaked by the sea, baked dry by the sun, and never designed for such walking; hair and clothes full of dried salt; skin tanned by a fiercer sun than they were used to, they were particularly disadvantaged.

Although he makes no mention of it, Dale and his party must have retraced their steps to the huts where he had met Isabella, for the poop had grounded north of it. Here, one of the former passengers, identified simply as Mr C, chose to remain behind, perhaps to wait for the starboard raft to run ashore and tell Buchan and de Souza what was happening.[68] Somewhere along the beach they saw a depressing sight: the timbers that not so long ago had framed a large Portuguese merchant ship – proof, if they needed it, of the treachery of that reef-lined coast. Out to sea, and parallel to the coast as far as the eye could see, the breakers crashed frothing on the rocks. Somewhere out there, beyond the inner reef, were Buchan, de Souza and the rest, but neither silver nor entreaties would induce the natives to go to their aid.

At some stage early on in the journey, Dale sent John Moore on ahead to see what help might be forthcoming. He may well have hoped that Moore, the youngest and most junior of the recorded mates, would make contact with Spens and Dunn of whom nothing had been seen since they had hailed the *Winterton* before she broke up. Dale was keen for news of the yawl. If there were no vessels at St Augustine's Bay, she would be the only means of taking news of their plight to any settlement that might provide help. Anything Dundas had said about the likelihood of meeting a European ship was more to raise the morale of his passengers than with any real expectation; Dale was far from sanguine.

They kept to the beach, knowing that, while it was undoubtedly a longer distance, they ran no risk of becoming lost among the mangroves[69] of the Mikea forest, and had the advantage of the sea breeze. Even so, to walk during the midday heat was impossible; therefore they set out before dawn, rested during the middle of the day, and continued for as long as the light held. While the tide was out they could walk on sand, which, though blisteringly hot, was preferable to the rock. Water remained the most pressing need. Five gallons and some bottles of wine and beer do not go very far among 70 people, particularly in the heat, and were soon drunk. As they trudged along, the men did what they could to keep up the spirits of the women, assuring them that a ship would be waiting for them at St Augustine's Bay, 'and when they were tired, we carried them', Dale added, touchingly.

On the Sunday, frustrated by the slow pace dictated by the women, some of the men decided to push on ahead and fend for themselves. That evening this vanguard found fresh water and a place to stop for the night. One of them wrote a note with directions to the well, and, before they moved on, they stuck it on a pole on the beach, along the route the rest would follow.

It was the measure of their much slower pace that Dale's party had been walking for some hours on Monday before they spotted the instruction to turn left and enter the forest above the dunes. The well lay in

> '…the middle of a nice shady spot of grass. Here we stopped for that day and we almost drunk the well dry. It was one of the pleasantest spots I saw on the island. There were plenty of trees which afforded a fine retreat from the sun, and such a haunt of birds that if the well was left for a minute they would surround it in great numbers.'

Dale is at variance with Alexander Thompson, the Free Mariner, over the dates and the order of events, although he agrees with the details. At the time, he did not keep any written notes and for the next few days Thompson may be the more reliable chronicler.

According to him, they rested by the spring during the day and just as they were about to set out again they were unexpectedly rejoined by John Moore. The Fifth Mate was accompanied by natives in two canoes, and he brought the welcome news that the natives were willing to take the ladies by sea for the sum of 40 dollars.

The relief was double. The women would be spared a hard journey, and the men could travel more quickly. The bargain was struck. It was about this time that a fisherman approached them with news that appeared almost too good to be true. From his limited English they made out that he had come from St Augustine's Bay where the Company's ship *King George* was lying.

Dale's first impulse to discount proof of the very fiction he had invented was quickly suppressed. The women had leapt at it, hardship and exhaustion forgotten while they thought their troubles might be over in a few days at most. If it were true that the ship which had sailed with them back in May and from which they had parted in the Channel was really at the Bay, then boats and parties would have been out looking for them, natives paid generously to bring them by canoe. The *King George* had called at the Cape; it was unlikely she would have any reason to anchor off Madagascar. But he kept his thoughts to himself. Better to get everyone together as agreed before dashing hopes that had already taken a battering.

Neither the walkers nor the canoes went very far for the rest of the day. A crowd of the natives came down on to the beach, which, perhaps for the first time, made the survivors uneasy, and, in any case, the canoes refused to go on. There was nothing for it but to make camp, light fires, and double the watch. The fisherman who had brought the news of the *King George* also sold them a large conger eel, which they were able to cook and eat with relish. While they took turns in sleeping, the natives dwindled away, and the night passed without incident. On both sides there were mixed feelings. Individually friendly and happy to trade, both blacks and whites were understandably apprehensive about large groups.

They awoke around 3am on the Tuesday, ready to begin the day's march, only to face a new disappointment, particularly hard on the women: the canoes had disappeared in the night. The money had been spent to no purpose, and everyone would have to match their speed to the slowest members of the party. They had got up early with the intention of making a long day of it, and now they set off in a body, taking the risk of following the coast around a point while it was still dark.

Without any warning a hail of rocks and stones, some heavy enough to cause serious injury or even death, crashed among them, striking indiscriminately or thudding into the sand. Helplessly they looked round for their attackers, but in the grim pre-dawn could make out only a couple of figures. Some of the men went to negotiate with them as best they could, using their one defence: bribery. While they made a collection of dollars, knives and clothing, the natives held off; then, satisfied with the tribute, they allowed the travellers to move on.

There was now real fear within the party. Reduced in numbers and unarmed, they were helpless in the event of a concerted attack. And, although they did not know it, there was further cause for fear. Fifteen years earlier the French Indiaman, *St Jean Baptiste*, had been wrecked on the Star Bank that cradles the southern end of the island with the loss of 80 lives. Thirty-nine survivors reached St Augustine's Bay in the ship's boat, only to be taken as slaves by the local people. Seven months later, when a Dutch ship put in for supplies, the 19 who remained alive were ransomed by the captain and taken off.[70]

The rest of that Tuesday passed anxiously but at least uneventfully. Short of water, they dug in the ground, finding a meagre and brackish supply; and worn out by anxiety and the early start they stopped for the night at 9pm. By their own estimation, they were walking at $2\frac{1}{2}$ miles an hour; and with frequent halts and a long rest while the sun was at its worst, they managed about 15 miles a day. As the crow flies, the journey should have been around 50 miles, but the need to follow the coast round heads and bays made it considerably longer.

They did not risk another pre-dawn departure. Instead they waited for daylight, only to find that now the local people showed far more friendly intentions. They were given not just water but sweet potatoes, and were able to buy themselves a bullock to joint and roast during the long daytime siesta. The bullocks were fine animals, reared along the rivers and highly regarded by the natives, for although the Madagascans were not nomadic, they did move about; property that could be driven along with them was more valuable than cultivated land.

Later in the afternoon Dale led them off on the second stage of the day, and they walked until the wood came down to the coast. It is possible that by now they had reached Manombo, north of the Baie de Ranobe, where the river of the same name entered the sea, but there is no way of telling from any of the surviving accounts. During their long march they had seen a fleet of canoes, as many as 100, on their way out to the wreck, and they also watched the incredible spectacle of whales coming too close to the surf out on the reef.

'We were often amused with the battle between the whale and the thrasher [breaker]: the former, getting too near the shore becomes entangled, when the thrasher takes advantage of him and beats him with such force, that the noise it occasions we at first mistook for the report of guns; till in some parts of the reef which approached nearer to the shore…we could be spectators.'

They would have plunged into the hot gloom of the trees but for the appearance of a handful of natives who begged them to stay put for the night as the wood was impassable. The appeal left them in a quandary: the natives might be honest and genuinely concerned or they might be gathering for an attack and keen to have their victims where they could easily see them. Communication was not easy, none of the survivors having a word of Malagasy and the natives only a smattering of imperfect English. In the end they yielded to necessity and made camp for the night with a strong guard. There had been no more information about any East Indiaman at the Bay, but in one respect their luck was about to change. At sunrise the following morning a man presented himself and gave them to understand that his king had sent him to be their guide.

The warning that the wood was impassable without a guide turned out to be true; but the passage proved to be only a temporary respite for blistered and cut feet. Soon enough they found themselves back on the beach with its razor sharp rocks. Only the fear of being left behind and the hope of meeting with unspecified assistance kept some of them going. The guide, however, proved reliable, even killing an ox for them on the following day when they once again struck inland. Ten days had passed since the *Winterton* had been wrecked, and now they were desperately trying to follow their agile, athletic guide with the last of their strength, unsure how far they must travel until, on Saturday, 2 September, they met with some of the crew whose news was nothing but good. There might be no *King George* waiting for them, but they were just a few miles from the King's residence at Toleary and the King himself had shown only kindness and generosity.

Toleary lay some 3 miles inland on the southern bank of the Fiherenana, and it was evening before they waded the shallow, muddy river keeping a wary eye out for the crocodiles which proved to be the only dangerous creature they encountered on the island. They entered the village of the same simple rush huts they had seen along the coast, and waiting to receive them surrounded by men armed with spears and muskets, sat a young man, hardly older than Dale who, as the leader of the survivors, stepped forward to be received.

Chapter Seven

The King of Baba

Buchan's group had given up. Their raft drifted with the current and they had neither the will nor the strength to attempt to move it. Everything in their limited power had been tried; now, if rescue did not come to them, they were finished. They had no idea what had become of their fellow travellers, nor that their fate could have any bearing on their own, but on the Sunday when Dale's party had left the little fishing village on the first stage of their walk to Toleary, the fishermen launched their canoes. Buchan notes:

'On Sunday 26th about 8 o clock in the morning while anxiously looking round as usual we saw with difficulty on the
horizon several canoes to the number of 4 or 5 that seemed
to be coming from the shore. We had been so often deceived
in our expectation that a feeling of hope had much ceased to
influence us and we durst not at first allow ourselves to think

that the canoes were approaching towards us. Our fearful anxiety increased as it drew nearer but in vain would I seek words to describe the emotions of joy which we experienced when we saw from the course they were steering that we were the object in their view and that they were the messengers sent to effect our deliverance from the jaws of the terrible death that threatened us.'

For the 30 to 40 who remained on the starboard raft there was enough room in the canoes for everyone. This time there was no scramble for places. Men had learned their lesson, or were too weak to push. In minutes they reached the beach they had for several days striven to gain; it is amazing that they were able to walk. But walk they did, and encountered a group of Madagascans bringing water. This was no charity: they wanted a dollar for as much as a man might drink, and those with money paid for those without, and would willingly have paid more than was demanded.

The fishermen showed them to the tiny settlement of huts where Isabella Cullen and her daughter had spent a night, and there they met up with some of the sailors who had remained behind after Dale's group had moved off. They had found a cask of wine on the beach and were keen to share it with the distressed newcomers. It certainly had the effect of reviving body and soul, but some of those, who, in their weakened and dehydrated state over-indulged, soon became alarmingly drunk. Buchan and de Souza, meanwhile, had met up with Mr C (who had remained behind from Dale's party), and the three of them sat under a nearby tree sharing their stories. It became clear that only fear of too large a group of survivors gathering in their small village had deterred the fishermen from their errand of mercy, and Buchan was left to thank providence that Dale had set off when he did, otherwise rescue would have come too late. Throughout an ordeal that was very far from over he maintained a stoical faith that God would see him through; and rather than lament each new disaster he preferred to consider, at least in retrospect, how fortunate he was to have survived it.

They spent their first night ashore in a makeshift tent of sail cloth erected for them by the elderly man who, without a word of English, first invited them to his hut for a meal of mainly milk and honey – easier on the digestion than any meat or corn. The tent gave them some relief from the night breeze, and protected them from the heavy dew that made sleeping in the open a miserable experience. The following morning Buchan, de Souza and Mr C walked the 8 or 10 miles north to where Dale and Wilton had amassed their stock of supplies. Now abandoned, the place made a depressing sight, the beach strewn with the rotting carcasses of the ship's animals and bits of wreckage, although there were still provisions that they could use. They lit themselves a fire and slept the night in the shelter of some bushes; in the morning the trio took up bottles of wine and spirits, and a quantity of salted meat and cheese, before setting off south in Dale's footsteps. At high tide the sand was covered, forcing them to negotiate the same rocks that had played havoc with Dale's feet. Although Buchan had found a pair of men's shoes to replace the pair sucked off during his struggle in the water, they fitted badly and before too long they were crippling him. Mr C might have been relatively fresh and unscathed, but the other two had suffered appallingly, and Buchan, at least by his own admission, had never been the most robust of youths. The heat of the sun and the weight of their supplies tired them long before they staggered back into the village to sleep.

They had hoped for a friendly reception from the elderly man who had entertained them on their first night ashore, but they were to be disappointed. When they presented themselves on Wednesday morning he made it very clear by his manner that they were not welcome. He may have changed his mind, afraid they would stay around to scrounge off him; or he may have been trying to point out that they would be better off following their friends. Buchan, usually ready to think well of people and put a favourable gloss on their actions, found it hard to understand the hostile attitude, but he took the hint.

They knew from their own experiences that there had been casualties when the ship broke up. The sight of bodies washed up along the beach as they made their way south was a sobering sight for men already grateful for their own survival. Without tools and strength there was no means of burying them decently. With sadness they trudged past, until they came upon a group of fisherman sitting around a fire. Among them was a relative of the old man back at the huts, one of the first men they had met when they landed. Finding him friendly, they accepted his potatoes and the chance to sleep by the fire.

In the morning, Thursday, they tried, unsuccessfully, to negotiate with their hosts for a canoe to take them on. The best they could do was to hire two men to show them the way, and feeling rather more reassured, they set off over the jagged rocks, pausing only for an unlikely breakfast of cheese and rum. Despite Buchan's weakness, they were making better time than Dale's party, and even outstripping their guides. Glancing behind and seeing that the two men had halted, the trio sat down to rest and wait for them to catch up.

To their dismay, they found their guides had been hanging back for a group of seven others to join them, and now all nine began to advance and surround their erstwhile guests.

'Three, weak and unarmed, had no chance against such odds and besides nearly all our provisions they took from Mr. Souza nearly a hundred guineas which he had managed to rescue from the wreck and which we looked to as a mine of wealth…Our situation now was forlorn enough. We only had left a small morsel of cheese in a barren country, strangers to the language and customs of the natives, not sure of our road and far from any place where we could hope for the least supply of water or any other necessary of life. Such proofs, too, of unkindness and outrageous dishonesty at the outset did not lead us to augur very favourably of the future.'

All they could do was to make the best speed possible, and leave the rest to chance. Not far ahead they met a group of eight or nine sailors resting in the shade, and halted for a few moments, but the sailors had barely enough provisions for themselves. Although they would have shared, de Souza, Mr C and Buchan pushed on again and came across the first local women they had yet encountered. They wore the ubiquitous sarong-like garment tied round their waists, and the cloth mantle, but they also covered their upper torsos with a simple tunic. Their hair was dressed in the same fine, greased plaits hanging to just above their shoulders, and they looked sufficiently friendly for the men to approach and beg for food. Two unripe plantains were forthcoming, and these, added to the morsel of cheese that one of the men had managed to retain, provided a mouthful of food apiece when they stopped to eat mid-afternoon.

It looked as if this would be their only sustenance for the remainder of the day, and, robbed of their wine and spirits, they had no liquid. Then, towards sunset they were hailed by three men in a canoe who pulled up on the shore, made a fire and invited the strangers to share it.

'They gave us plenty of beef and broth which revived us greatly as we had scarcely tasted meat and drink that day. We were not however allowed to enjoy our meal quietly. They first began to ask our neck handkerchiefs and then proceeded to demand money. They took from me some money that I had in one of the pockets of my breeches, and were going to lighten me of my watch and seals which I had in the other when I put my hand hastily into my pocket and pulled out at hazard one of the seals which I gave, and they did not search farther. The sea water had made the watch useless but I prized it as the gift of one now no more from whom I received early kindness. The seal was the parting gift of a school companion.'

The leader of this group spoke enough English to make them understand that he had come from St Augustine's Bay where he had seen the *Winterton*'s yawl. This piece of information could explain the false hopes raised in Dale's party. Confusion between the British reigning Monarch King George III and the Indiaman of the same name, and an understandable semantic failure on the part of the Madagascans to distinguish between 'ship' and 'boat' could easily have been misinterpreted by those desperate for rescue. The yawl had apparently gone out to the wreck, and that was where the canoe was also headed next day.

Pressed to remain the night, the three men equivocated, afraid of being robbed of what little remained to them, including their clothes, and hoping that the group of sailors whom they had passed that morning might be close behind them. Much to their relief they turned up within the hour, and the whole party went on together, apprehensive when they realised they were being followed by two armed men, one sporting a musket, the other carrying a lance. It was no time for heroics: they just went on quietly, and soon enough the pursuers left them alone but still fearful of being waylaid. Determined to put as much distance as they could between them and the camp, they took advantage of the clear moonlight and the smooth ground to keep going until midnight. On another occasion it might have been idyllic: the water lapping up the beach and the cool evening breeze catching the trees above the rocks. They halted for the night, unable to make a fire but expecting to sleep well after their long day, only to be woken by 'a heavy dew which wet our clothes as if we had been drenched in water'.

Disappointed in the quest for sleep, they set off as soon as it was light, reaching a village where coat buttons served as currency to buy water, fish and sweet potatoes. The sun was unrelenting, scalding the sand until the walkers could feel it through what remained of their footwear. In the distance, a little way out to sea, they spied canoes approaching them and were more than relieved to find that among the natives was one of their own people, a sailor or petty officer, who told them he was going out to the wreck and to look for stranded or injured survivors. He was quite probably one of Dale's original party, for he knew of the women, although he had not seen them arrive at the King's residence, and he knew the route that the others should follow in order to reach a friendly village for the night. After eating their scanty meal, the walkers carried on, taking to the rocks for a couple of miles as the tide came in, then leaving the coast for quite a way. To their amazement they came upon a few huts by a spring of fresh water.

'There having been either an entire want of water where we had hitherto been or it being so brackish that it was impossible to use it, this was a new and reviving sight and the novelty of such a thing – for there can be no luxury equal to fresh water to those who have been suffering from the want of it – probably made us drink more than was right for us.'

They were on the fringes of the wood which the natives had warned Dale's party not to attempt by night without a guide and through which the King's emissary had subsequently taken them. Buchan's group now procured the services of a guide and went on.

'He led us through wild mountainous places and deep ravines which after what had happened the previous day and added to the darkness of the night raised strong suspicions as to his intentions. They were, however, as suspicions frequently are, without foundation and we reached the end of our journey in safety, but to speak from what I myself felt, wet and tired to the greatest degree.'

The 'Head Man' at the village where they spent the Friday night gave them a warm reception; Buchan was finding out, as Dale had done, that the nearer they got to the King, the friendlier they found the people. Orders to look after them had been issued at a high level, and after drying themselves round a fire and roasting a goat they slept, perhaps for the first time, secure.

Saturday found them eating the remains of their supper before setting off in good spirits with two guides. During the morning they were overtaken by two strangers going their way, and decided to carry on with them rather than their escorts – an unwise decision since the two travellers, 'fresh and naturally possessing the activity of the antelope' easily outstripped them and had no commission to slow their pace. By now they were back on the scorching beach again, which lessened the dangers of getting lost. Buchan began to show signs of a fever, and but for the strong arm of Mr C he could not have continued. 'My feet were so cut from the want of proper shoes that, even if I had been quite in vigour, walking must have been a painful effort; but exhausted as I was it was now a matter of wonder how I got through the rapid long marches we performed.'

Any fears they had on being approached by three natives died away when they realised that the men were looking for them specifically to offer their assistance. Somehow Buchan kept going, and they struck off into a wood where they halted for the night.

All they had to eat were some sweet potatoes, and some Indian corn, more usually ground into flour but pleasant, if indigestible, when roasted. They were only a day's travel from Toleary.

❧❀❧

John Dale and the King of Baba[71] surveyed one another with interest. Dale saw a slight man, around 24 years old, with that typical copper skin, slightly paler than some of his subjects, and a prepossessing, lively face beneath a scarlet cowl and chaplet of leaves. A long robe of striped yellow cloth completed the royal attire as he sat in the shade of a group of large tamarind trees. For his part the King would have seen a long-nosed, slim young officer, with steady blue eyes, his shirt and waistcoat torn, breeches stained by the sand, barelegged in ill-fitting shoes. The sun had burned his fair skin and bleached his tousled fair hair. It was the moment in which to make a good impression for the sake of those who stood exhausted and trusting behind him, and Dale knew it; but it was the King who took the initiative,

'...for he rose from his rush mats and embraced me with much affection. I offered him a present – it was all we had, some trinket or other, which he declined accepting, and directed his interpreter to tell me how sorry he was for our misfortunes and also that he could not think of taking anything from us, but that he would be happy to give us anything he had; that the King of Baba and King George were one brother, and that, as such, he should afford us every protection in his power.'

It was an auspicious and, despite the favourable report of the sailors, an un-looked for beginning. The King spoke a little longer and then told Dale he had ordered a bullock for them and that he would have huts erected as soon as possible. In a haze of relief and gratitude the young officer and his companions joined the *Winterton* survivors who had already arrived at Toleary to enjoy the meal which they had been busy preparing for the new arrivals.

Their reception was totally different from that experienced by the unfortunate survivors of the *St Jean Baptiste*. That had been in the time of the present King's father, or even his grandfather. This young King might simply have been a more humane man, unwilling to add slavery to the other evils of shipwreck, although the Madagascans did practice slavery among themselves. Alternatively, it was enlightened self-interest: a recognition that trade with foreign vessels required confidence on both sides, and that the East India Company was as likely to reward fair-dealing as it was to punish severely any ill treatment of its servants. It was a view his people did not necessarily share.

Chapter Eight

A Precious Craft

The scrubby brushwood stood high enough to exclude any breeze, leaving them gasping for air under the blazing sun. Beneath their painful feet the deep sand was scorching. For Buchan and company it was the final day of their travel, but the terrain and the oppressive heat sapped their strength well before noon. All that had kept them going since sunrise on that Sunday, 3 September, was the nearness of Toleary. It sustained them when, just 2 miles from their destination, they stopped at a village and found that buttons and trinkets were no longer acceptable currency for milk or water. As they came into the royal village at 3pm, Buchan dragged all his physical resources together as he met up once more with his fellow passengers and saw the welcome arrangements made for them.

'Woeful as the difference was I felt as if I had got back to our own country. We had not now before us the immediate fear of being starved, we had a hut to cover us, a comfortable bed of dry rushes to lie on, and we were again among our former shipmates. The most part of them had only reached the end of their journey the day before, so that we had gone over the same distance in about half the time they took…I do not now recollect if any of our party beside Mr. De Souza and myself had been on the last raft but I think not, so that we started with fearful odds against us…This shows what the human constitution is at times capable of. I have never much relished a long walk, and if anyone had told me what I was to go through in this and other ways for about a fortnight the thing would have appeared to myself impossible.'

❦

With almost all the survivors gathered in Toleary and the natives busy erecting huts, it was possible at last to discover who had died and who had survived. Any faint hopes that Chambers, Dundas and Miss Cullen had somehow been plucked to safety or washed ashore alive evaporated. A black servant girl called Frances, Miss Robinson, the wife of Sgt Rose and the sister of Suetonius McGowan were the other female casualties. The Ramsay brothers, Andrew and Henry, had reached the shore, and even the man with the broken leg was alive. Most of the deaths had been among the recruits and the ordinary seamen and had occurred when the ship broke up. In all, about 52 lives had been lost, but at least 230 people were safe.

Toleary was now their home for the foreseeable future, an arid, sandy, unprepossessing settlement on the low coastal strip some 20 miles north of St Augustine's Bay, and they had to make the best of it. The rush huts promised by the King were duly built a short way from the royal village. They were neat rectangular structures, a little over 4 yards long with pitched roofs and a central hole for the smoke, furnished with the same rush beds as the natives used and visited by the same rats. Like the daily bullock that the King began by providing, the accommodation was intended as a gift, but the overseers charged 2 dollars each: 'sad grasping fellows', Dale called them. The King himself remained full of concern, visiting them regularly, sometimes well attended by men carrying spears and muskets and with his interpreter, known as Tom Bush; at other times he was accompanied by no one other than the little boy, Luna, who carried his smoking equipment. He enjoyed listening to the fife, even when played as badly as McKey could manage. They made the acquaintance of the King's wife, a kind, plump woman whom he introduced as Queen Charlotte, but they saw rather more of his mistress, a half-German beauty whose hut lay close to theirs.

Right from the outset Dale had warned everyone that their survival depended on their treating the natives well; but among so many people trouble inevitably broke out. Buchan described the incident as 'one of our sailors having behaved ill...to one of the natives'. Although the natives had frequently made life difficult for them on their journey, there could be no retaliation now. Violence could not be tolerated, and the officers decided to make an example of the unnamed sailor that would deter others and reassure their hosts. The miscreant was duly tied up to receive his flogging when the King arrived and ordered them to release the offender. As they stared in surprise he told them, with a commendable if misplaced confidence in the English legal system, that if one of *his* people had been shipwrecked in England and arrested for a crime, King George would not let him be punished. Therefore, as the situation was reversed, he would not allow King George's people to be punished in his domain. With that he departed, taking the man with him to ensure that his pronouncement was obeyed once his back was turned.

The incident provided food for thought. While rating modern European civilization above all others, young Buchan looked objectively at Madagascan society and found much to admire in their social relationships. However much they might thieve from their new neighbours they were utterly honest among themselves, and if they did enjoy getting drunk, that was a pretty universal failing. The local tipple, *tokay*, fermented from sugar cane, honey and tamarind, was potent and, to Buchan's palate, more than an acquired taste, but though he found it disgusting, other whites soon came to regard it as a preferable alternative to remaining sober. Buchan had no condemnation for the Madagascans who kept slaves and treated them with every kindness, yet as his later records show, he was fiercely hostile to the European slave trade:

> '...one of the severest scourges that Madagascar has experienced from European alliance, and one which Britain has had a large share in inflicting. I cannot recall without painful sensations the sight of the poor wretches whom I have seen landed from the slave ships at Mozambique and the Island of France,[72] many sickly and wasted to shadows, driven along as the lowest description of animals. These poor creatures had been dragged from their homes...huddled on board of vessels insufferably cramped and overheated and brought under the lash of unfeeling taskmasters, the most degrading and degraded part of our species...It would be well if the potentates and ministers of those countries that yet so stoutly in effect oppose themselves to the abolition of this hellish traffic could be made to see such scenes as I have alluded to...They would surely join the cry which the voice of humanity after the slumber of ages has so powerfully and impressively raise, and give their aid in proscribing from the face of the earth the commerce of human blood and misery which has so long disgraced the portion of the world which calls itself civilized.'

With still no sight of the yawl, Dale remained in charge, acting as purser for the group of officers, ladies and cabin passengers who came together to form a mess, buying their food in common and leaving the crew and soldiers to make their own arrangements. The young Third Mate whose shipboard table had been for the junior officers, midshipmen and less wealthy passengers, became a leading member of the limited white society of Toleary, in which a new equality was born. As he states:

> 'We took it in turn to be caterer and cook for the day. The king for a time allowed about a bullock each day, that is while I was there, but said he could not supply us with the other smaller articles such as rice, milk, sweet potatoes etc. These we bought ourselves. The ladies had generally for breakfast boiled milk and rice or sweet potatoes, a mess of beef and other things for dinner, and the cook of the day always served them first and had the honour to dine with them.'

In those early days, they confronted their situation with an element of light-hearted pretence, even naming their dinner 'Baba'.[73] The soldiers and sailors, either because they travelled in larger groups which were harder to rob or intimidate or because they had helped themselves to something of the Winterton's treasure were significantly more affluent than the passengers and officers, enabling them to support a higher standard of living than their erstwhile social superiors.

A few days after Dale's arrival at Toleary, Nathaniel Spens and William Dunn at last arrived, having been out to the wreck with some of the natives. For 17 days the Second Mate and the Purser had been going back and forth in the yawl, afraid to let the boat out of their possession. The sight of it sent a rush of hope though more hearts than Dale's, although he had been speculating on its possibilities ever since he reached the shore. His determination to be the one to go and fetch help never wavered, and the only question was where to aim for.

Although St Augustine's Bay was comparatively well known as a watering hole among seamen in the eastern trade, Madagascar was a closed book to most Europeans, and, to those who knew anything, its recent history was one of ill-fated attempts at colonisation, first by the Portuguese and then by the French who tried repeatedly to establish themselves at Fort Dauphin on the south eastern coast. The Madagascans were willing to trade, but only at Tamatave was there a significant French stronghold. The island had become infamous for two centuries as a haunt for pirates including Captain Kidd; it had been the setting for Defoe's novel *Captain Singleton*. No help appeared likely to be found along its shores, and whatever the King thought he knew of French trading posts he kept to himself in the belief that the French and the British despised each other too much to aid even shipwrecked civilians. Rescue had to come from further afield.

Mauritius, then in French hands under the name of Ile de France, and on major shipping routes, was a strong candidate, but required a long voyage with no charts and few instruments, and Dale had serious doubts whether he would even be able to take sufficient provisions. The same caveat applied to the Cape of Good Hope where Company ships regularly called.

It was Thomas de Souza who suggested Mozambique, the Portuguese colony across the Channel from Madagascar. There were settlements along the coast and ships that traded between them, if not larger vessels out of Portugal. Everything he said convinced Dale that this would be the quickest and most certain means of getting assistance; and, significantly, de Souza was willing to go with him, both as interpreter and, if necessary, to use his family's influence.

❀

The priority was to get the yawl up near the town and guard it day and night. With the water so shallow in many places they had to drag her much of the 3 miles up-river, and they left her to dry under a tamarind tree. The officers held a meeting. With the return of Spens and Dunn – older men with longer experience – Dale slipped to second or even third-in-command. Whether they included Lieutenant Henry Brownrigg, who was in charge of the soldiers, in their councils is not clear; certainly the surviving mates felt that they had as much responsibility for the safety of the ship's complement as if they had been at sea, and they may have limited Brownrigg's role to that of a passenger with responsibility for the recruits. Dale's offer to be the one to get help had been accepted in principle, but they took no decision on where he should go. For the moment they had their work cut out to turn the yawl into a seaworthy, ocean-going sailing vessel, which meant making her ride higher and adding more masts and sails – with few raw materials and less tools for the Carpenter, William Rowland, and his mates to use. Yawls were never intended to be ocean-going: they were designed to take passengers and crew ashore, to water and victual a ship, or to visit other ships. The *Winterton*'s one remaining boat was no match for the unpredictable Mozambique Channel.

To raise her and keep her stable required a false keel, which could only be cut from a single trunk; and good timber was at a premium on that arid coast. There was no question of chopping down the large tamarind tree in the village which was metaphorically, if not literally, sacred, and under which the King was accustomed to hold court; but they did spot some wood which would be ideal for both the keel and the foremast. This, however, belonged to the King who had ordered a new hut. They pleaded with him, and ultimately he yielded to their entreaties and handed over a length for the keel, but he had no confidence in their plan and repeatedly urged them to remain at Toleary under his protection until a ship arrived. He watched their efforts, shaking his head despondently and telling them they would all be drowned. Yet despite all his misgivings he gave up another valuable piece of timber to make the foremast, and the carpenters were able to step a mizzenmast against the after-thwart.

If the King had doubts, some of the crew were highly suspicious of the activity, probably wondering if Spens, who had refused to help them while they were on their rafts, was now hatching a scheme to escape and abandon them. Eventually Dale put an end to speculation by going to their huts to explain the plan, rallying support and asking for volunteers to crew the little vessel. A dozen stepped forward, and from them Dale chose four. Thomas Adams, a seaman, and Thomas Longster, the quartermaster's mate, are the only two whose names are recorded and Adams, like Dale, had served on the *Winterton*'s previous voyage. If nothing else, he knew the calibre of the man in charge of the expedition. Of the other pair, one was Portuguese, and the only foreign-named crewman was Lewis Manuel (but other evidence suggests he remained behind).

Having prevailed with the King to yield up his timber, Dale also needed to persuade the sailors to part with some of the canvas they had managed to bring with them from the wreck, canvas they had intended to make into trousers for themselves. After some skilful negotiation he succeeded in obtaining enough for the foresail. He then went round asking for cash donations with which to purchase enough locally woven cloth for the mizzensail. Around 60 dollars were collected, and at length the vessel was rendered as seaworthy as their limited resources could ever hope to make her.

❧⊁✕⊰❧

Throughout those early days, the local fishermen had been busy going out to the wreck in their canoes and salvaging what they could, in particular gunpowder and silver. John Slater, the Boatswain got a party together and went off to recover what they saw as their own property without thought of the consequences. The following day, while Dale was enjoying a swim in the river, they came back to Toleary in triumph with a quantity of gunpowder taken from a hut while the owner was absent. It was exactly the kind of incident the officers had feared, and they were just admonishing Slater when a wild yelling broke out.

A thousand natives, lances up and muskets prepared, sprang out of the bushes and came screaming down on them. Singling out Spens as the leader, they trained a dozen weapons on him.

Word reached the King just in time to prevent a massacre. The young man peremptorily demanded silence from his outraged subjects and asked them to explain their grievances. Having heard their account he delivered a judgement that would have stood scrutiny in an English court. The powder was to be restored to those who had salvaged it and the British must promise him there would be no repetition of the incident. At the same time, he warned his own people that anyone who showed violence towards his guests would face summary execution. It would not be the only occasion on which he showed a delicate grasp of justice and the international laws of salvage. The people dispersed with dancing and war cries, and Dale strolled back from his swim, completely oblivious to the crisis that had erupted in his absence, to find his comrades in a state of shock. For a few nights afterwards they slept within the hedged compound that surrounded the King's tent.

❧❧❧

With the boat fitting out, two serious problems remained to be solved: provisions and navigation. By cruel irony, the only book of charts to be saved from the wreck was missing the crucial map of the Mozambique Channel and the only instruments were a sextant washed up on the beach and the compass which Dundas had put into the yawl but which now had a broken glass thanks to the men who had capsized the boat. One of the soldiers had managed to preserve a small and very basic geography book with which he was extremely unwilling to part but which, critically, covered south east Africa. Dale negotiated and pleaded until the man reluctantly relinquished it upon promise of payment. However, unless and until the compass could be repaired, discussions about the best destination were academic.

Someone came up with the ingenious idea of boiling goats bladders in the hope of clarifying them, but not one of the attempts produced a transparent membrane. Then one of the ladies came to the rescue with a hand mirror from her pocket book. It was much smaller than the original glass, but with the backing scraped off, and mounted in a wooden frame of the same diameter as the compass,

Dale thought it would serve the purpose pretty well, although it did not show anything like all the compass rose. They fixed it to the top and sealed it with wax to prevent any air and water getting in.

None of the *Winterton*'s supply of salt beef had been saved; in its place they boiled slices of beef in salt and chillies, packed it into clay pots, poured the beef-fat up to the brim and covered the containers with hide and bladders in the hope of slowing decomposition. A few live fowls, some sugar cane, sweet potatoes and cakes made with maize flour completed the stock of food. More vital than food was water. Three wooden kegs had been saved from the wreck and brought to Toleary, but alone they were not enough. The natives used the thick skins of native gourds – calabashes – to store their water, which, when added to the kegs, gave some 25 gallons.

With the time for departure imminent, the officers had still not made their final decision between Mozambique and Mauritius. Dunn and Spens still strongly favoured the latter; Dale and Wilton held out for Mozambique on practical grounds. That was not the only disagreement. Spens and Dale clashed over the composition of the rescue party. The former felt they could spare only one officer; Dale was insistent on sending two.

Spens fought his corner. Only the officers could maintain some semblance of discipline and good behaviour among the sailors and soldiery, and the likely consequences of another failure had already been shown. If he had any inkling of the resentment borne against him by the crew, he may have felt he needed the back-up.

Dale refused to concede. With everything depending on this voyage two heads were better than one. Perhaps more importantly, if he were to die, who would take over? He had few illusions about the crew. He had enlisted four men to go with him, but if they found themselves leaderless they were more likely to look to their own safety than try to complete the mission. More than individual lives were at stake: someone would have to negotiate for a ship on behalf of the HEIC in a foreign port with little more than their word of honour to trade on. In the end, it was Wilton who settled the argument. Asked by Spens if he would lead the expedition on his own, the young man flatly refused, adding that he would not go with anyone but Dale.

Dale also won the next round, but not for any of the reasons he had been urging. Mauritius was abandoned in favour of Mozambique so that Dale could charter a ship to take the survivors from Madagascar to the Cape from where they could embark on the next available East Indiaman or, if 'sufficiently sick of their voyage', return to England. This had the advantage of reducing the cost to the Company, a consideration which, incredibly, weighed heavily on some of the officers.

The boat was ready; the list of the lost and saved had been put together; the officers had written a brief account of what had occurred. More than 250 people were pinning their hopes on seven men and an open boat.

Chapter Nine

A Makeshift Compass and a Missing Chart

The ragged crowd, gathered on the shore of Toleary Bay to wave the rescue party off, had receded to little more than a smudge, individual figures and faces seen through the eyes of memory. The seven men in the boat knew how much hope had been invested in them and how many lives might depend on their success, but that raised rather than depressed their spirits. Whatever the risks, action was infinitely preferable to passively waiting for a chance merchantman to drop anchor; and however odd their ship looked with her chequered mizzen and jib sails, they were once again mariners with a purpose and a use for their skills.

Mozambique Island, from where the Portuguese governed their slice of East Africa, lay north north west of Toleary, a journey of some 600 miles as the crow flies, and with good weather and a friendly westerly wind, Dale's men made good progress northwards. The makeshift glass in the compass might only show four points, but it was enough, and the instrument itself responded beyond all expectations. Dale records:

> 'Though the violent motion of the boat…caused it to vibrate extremely, yet in an instant it returned to its place. Sometimes the card was thrown entirely off the balance.'

They were fortunate in having a McCulloch compass, which, as Dale freely acknowledged, was vastly superior to anything else on the market at the time.

Their good luck lasted a mere two days. On 14 September the wind shifted to north north east, and that same day, having finished off the fresh provisions, they opened the first of their preserved rations, a jar of potted beef. It was rotten. So was the bread.

Officers and men stared at one another in an incredulous dismay that might have been comic had not the implications been so serious. Every jar was the same. One of the seamen, either Thomas Longster or Thomas Adams, refused to accept the evidence of his eyes and nose. Frantically he groped among the pots, hoping to find something fit to eat, even chewing a few mouthfuls, only to spit them over the side swearing in disgust that he could not stand it.[74] Their 12 days' supplies had dwindled in an instant to a few raw sweet potatoes and some sugar cane.

Worse was to come. The constant motion of the little vessel soon cracked the calabashes containing the greater quantity of their water. With just the kegs to rely on, they had to limit themselves to a mere half pint of water each per day.

If the wind, now constant from the north east was contrary, the currents were no better, pulling them west rather than north, so that on the morning of 20 September they caught their first sight of the African coast. They were in Latitude 18° South by Dale's calculations,[75] and if he had only possessed that missing chart of the Mozambique Channel he would have seen at once that they were just 20 miles from the Portuguese port of Quelimane north of the

River Zambezi from where ships regularly traded to the capital. But all he had was the soldier's geographical grammar, which made no mention of Quelimane, and provided only the depressing news that they were still 500 miles from Mozambique Island.

To compound their problems, he had begun to feel feverish and ill, and the physical strain of helping to row the boat out to sea to get an offing before the sea breeze set in sapped much of his remaining strength. For three days, with the wind and tide relentlessly uncooperative and Dale now lying helpless, the other six vainly tried to work northwards. Their water supplies were critically low, and they were sacrificing their own rations for the sake of their sick comrade. They were never going to reach Mozambique Island, nor did they dare to touch land to revictual the ship unless their very lives depended on it. They all believed, genuinely but erroneously, that they would be murdered without compunction by the native population, not because the African tribes were naturally hostile but because their Portuguese conquerors, anxious to dissuade rival colonists, had spread a report among them that all other Europeans were cannibals and their enemies. The only safe places were, therefore, Portuguese controlled ports, and the precious book indicated that 150 miles or so to the south lay Sofala.

One hazard on which they had not counted was the large number of whales. It was mating season, and Dale described them as 'perfectly mad, jumping clean up, straight out of the water and often so near as to alarm us'.

Sick as he was, and he had not eaten for three days, Dale was still in command, but ready to hand over to Wilton. His personal view was that even under the most favourable conditions they were at least five days from Mozambique Island without sufficient water to see them through, while, under the prevailing winds, Sofala could be reached in just two. Confronting his possible death with apparent equanimity, he told them that the decision was theirs, and they were not to let his condition influence it. Unsurprisingly, they decided to bear up for Sofala. There was a good deal of democracy within the group, and the courage and dogged perseverance of the four seamen soon caused Dale to admit that he had pre-judged their quality.

The north easterly wind which had so stubbornly barred their progress north, now chose to freshen strongly, and they found themselves having to run before a high-following sea with all the dangers of being pooped and foundering. Lying-to was no option.

'It was really frightful to see our poor little boat sometimes down in the hollow of the sea, and then again mounted aloft on the top of a wave. We owed our safety to the dexterity of one of the seamen[76] who had been brought up as a fisherman on the north coast of England; by his excellent steerage no accident happened.'

Frightening as the episode was, it speeded up their progress and, two days after the decision to change course, they came to the mouth of a large river which they hoped would take them to Sofala.

As evening closed in, darkness showed up large fires along the banks and trusting that they were now close to the town, they sailed up-river towards them, but without meeting a soul. The tide began to ebb; the boat grounded, and just after midnight it was left high and dry.

They had brought muskets and spears from Madagascar, and now took it in turns to watch through an anxious night, uncertain if they were on the shore of the river or on a shoal somewhere in the middle. Either way, unable to see in the darkness or to risk leaving Dale, who was growing delirious, they stayed with the boat until the welcome light of dawn, relieved to find the water flowing again. With no sign of a town, they decided that they had gone far enough upriver, and were about to return to the coast when the sound of voices and the sight of a couple of canoes caught their attention. The voices sounded pleasant and musical, as if the canoeists were singing, but Wilton took no chances: the guns were loaded and presented. Undaunted, the natives came closer, still singing, and with those in the front holding up plantains as peace offerings. Wilton relaxed, and the canoes came alongside. The natives, very different in appearance to the men of Madagascar, apparently spoke no Portuguese, but they took one look at Dale and immediately offered water and coconuts. Then they gestured to the men to follow a little way up the river and into a creek on the north side. Here they landed, though there were no signs of habitation. Dale was carried out of the boat and put down with his back against a tree while one of the natives went off alone, returning with more water and some fowls. This man did have a grasp of Portuguese, so while the men kindled a fire and set the meat to stew he explained that they were only about 20 miles north of Sofala and that, if they could wait a day, he would act as their pilot. If the reckoning is correct they may well have been at the estuary of the Pungue, the site of present-day Beira.

A broth of white meat went a long way to bringing Dale round, and when they had eaten they built more and larger fires to discourage that scourge of the low and swampy mangrove coast: the mosquito. That night they experienced the first rain since the *Winterton* was wrecked, a sharp squall that shook the trees and soaked them through, but the dawn promised a fine day with a fair wind and they waited impatiently for their guide to return. When he failed to come, they sailed down-river, then followed the coast southwards until yet another estuary raised their hopes, the more so as the sight of huts and smoke promised a settlement.

They found no town, but a group of some 20 local people who were friendly and who spoke enough Portuguese for conversation. They confirmed the proximity of Sofala, but warned that the waters were treacherous on account of the shoals, even for a boat with such a shallow draught. One of them, seeing that their visitors possessed pencil and paper suggested that if they wrote to the Governor, he would take the message. Thomas de Souza promptly scribbled a few lines. The man showed them to an empty hut, provided food for them, and left them while he went on his errand.

The disappointment of the previous day left them anxious when they woke, and they walked along the bank of the River Buzi, waiting for the pre-arranged musket signal that would announce the return of their emissary, and entertained by the courtship gymnastics of the whales out at sea. In the river itself hippopotamuses surfaced, breathing noisily, and quite close to their fascinated audience. The natives warned Dale that they were dangerous and responsible for many canoe accidents and that great care had to be taken when hunting them with spears for their ivory teeth. Dale's party, however, had their muskets, and having decided that here, close to their destination, they were among friends, they started taking pot shots at the nearest creature. Not one of the dozen rounds, fired from a distance of less than 30 yards, had the least effect on the hippo's hide. The natives looked on laughing, but the hippo had the last laugh when a ball ricocheted off its head and struck one of the seamen on the leg with enough force to hurt though not to injure.

Their messenger came back in the afternoon, bringing with him a native guide and a soldier carrying a message from the Governor. Of more immediate interest was the basket of provisions, which included soft bread, wine and spirits: a banquet for men who had not eaten properly for a fortnight. The letter was reassuring: expressing the Governor's wish to serve them as best he could.

The following day, 29 September, they did what they could to prepare for their audience. 'It would have made anyone laugh to see us brushing up, to look as smart as we could before the Governor'. Then they embarked on what they believed would be the final stage of their journey. They headed south again. The land lay low and there was no difficulty now in spotting Sofala for it stood in the middle of the only grove of coconut palms along that stretch of coastline.

Two hundred years have seen considerable changes to the vulnerable coast due to the devastating cyclones that ravage the region, and modern Sofala bears no resemblance to the small harbour[77] which Dale sought, nor indeed to the settlement which the

Portuguese established at the end of the fifteenth century. By 1792 just one of the tree-covered islands that once protected the anchorage remained: Inhancato, or Sofala Island, stretching north–south. The rest showed as shifting sandbanks covered at half tide, and the only entrance for boats much larger than canoes lay between the northern end of the island and the mainland.[78] Even with expert pilotage, the small river up to the town was only navigable by vessels under 100 tons, for low tide left only 14 feet of water.

At 1pm they landed on the northern side of the river and got their first sight of the town from where they so confidently expected rescue to come. It was not encouraging. The small square fort of Portuguese stone,[79] with bastions at each corner, built by Pedro de Anaya, provided the focal point, fronting the river on one side and with a narrow creek running round it, so that at high tide it formed a fortified island. The rest of the town comprised a ruined church and various houses, giving the whole place a decayed feeling. The only vessel was a craft the size of an Indiaman's longboat but in the style of one of the Masulah boats used at Madras to cross the savage coastal surf, which lay above the high water mark. Sofala had never been quite the goldmine the colonialists had hoped for at the time of Dias, Vasco da Gama or Covilham, when they were making their first contact with East Africa and India. It was then a Moslem town, ruled by light-skinned Arabs – the mosque which had stood on one of the islands was burned to the ground by the Portuguese friar Jaoa dos Santos around the turn of the sixteenth/seventeenth centuries – and for a thousand years before the arrival of the Portuguese conquerors the Arabs had been trading gold. Local mines were exhausted, and less and less of the gold, now mined deeper in the interior, was flowing through Sofala. In addition, the climate took a heavy toll of the Europeans left, quite literally, to hold the fort for Portugal. Most of the Portuguese civilians who resided at Sofala when Dale arrived had been banished there, and many of the 40 or so soldiers who garrisoned the fort were natives or Afro-Portuguese.

The external deficiencies of the town were all but forgotten by the warmth of the welcome. They were escorted to the Governor's house and treated with every courtesy and kindness as de Souza recounted their story and asked his advice on how to proceed. Antonio Alberto Pereira told them not to worry about anything, but to enjoy the chance to recover from their ordeal at sea; yet for a time, and despite his heartiness, they were all individually conscious of a slight suspicion in his manner, as if he doubted their story. On a practical level, he requisitioned a house for them, and supplied them with clean clothes 'which were most gratifying to us, having worn our shirts six or seven weeks and become almost eat up with vermin'. As they washed, shaved and enjoyed the luxury of fresh cotton next to their skin, they were able to discuss their host's attitude, agreeing that he probably took them for French slavers in disguise, intent on kidnapping the natives and carrying them off to their ship, 'though our ragged and squalid appearance by no means justified any such apprehension'.

Once convinced that his guests were genuine – something which one of the civilian residents could have confirmed through knowing de Souza in Lisbon – the Governor broke unwelcome news to them. Only one vessel per year put into Sofala; they had missed it by a month and it would not be back until June the following year, a good eight months away. Worse, the north-east monsoon had set in, and there was no possibility of travelling up the coast by sea.

As they sat stunned, all plans in ruins, he began to suggest an alternative: an overland journey north to Sena, a town on the Zambezi among the sugar plantations from where they just might get through to Mozambique Island. He offered them guides and supplies, and if he had only presented the idea with optimism, they might have seized it. As it was, he appeared to have no faith in it himself, and was at pains to point out that it could take a long time to get beyond Sena.

They discussed it among themselves, but finally rejected the plan. Instead, their thoughts were on the boat they had spotted, a larger vessel than their converted yawl. If they could not sail north to Mozambique Island because of the monsoon, perhaps they could go south to Delgoa Bay where they were almost certain to meet some of the South Sea whalers. One or two of those would be sufficient to take the survivors off Madagascar and convey them to the Cape; but if that hope failed, then they could push on towards the Cape itself with a good chance of being picked up along the way. 'Many, I am aware, will condemn this as rash and foolish, but when the objective as well as the alternative is viewed, perhaps we shall stand excused.'

Chapter Ten

Tornado and
Tom-Tom

Dale's rapidly improving health made him impatient to resume the quest for a relief ship but when he broached the idea of taking the settlement's boat, the Governor declined to loan it on the grounds that it was Government property and he would have to answer for it. Next he claimed that it was worth the equivalent of £100, and therefore so valuable that they would never be able to repay the cost of it. Although of the candid opinion that the boat was in such a state that 'no one would have bought it for any other purpose than fire-wood', Dale offered him a bill drawn on the HEIC, security equal to an international bankers draft, but Pereira refused to accept it, evidently fearing that the Honourable East India Company was nothing better than a fly-by-night outfit which would refuse to pay up.

Isolated in his tiny mosquito-ridden outpost Pereira had two basic aims during his three-year tenure: to amass a fortune and live to enjoy it somewhere more congenial, and he had plenty of opportunity to effect the one and dream about the other. Relief from this tedious and self-obsessed life came only twice a year: first when the annual ship arrived, bringing coarse cloth from Surat in exchange for gold and hippopotamus teeth, and secondly when he went south to buy pearls on his own account. Dale estimated that, by the time his stint at Sofala was over, he could have made anything between £30,000 and £40,000. Such prospects, however, made him avaricious rather than generous.

Over conversation before dinner a day or so after their arrival he showed a marked interest in Wilton's watch and seals, remarking on the quality of English workmanship. The seals had the family coat of arms on them and as such were useless to him; the watch had been ruined by seawater during the escape from the *Winterton*, but the Governor then asked if any of them had one in working order. That put Dale on the spot. He did have a watch, but it belonged to the Purser who had loaned it to him for the journey. While the Governor examined it, Wilton and Dale conferred hastily and decided that, in the interests of getting hold of the boat, they should take the hint. Although he feigned embarrassment at accepting it, they were under no illusions about his delight for he played the same game more than once.

They had one final card to lay. De Souza was advised to explain just how rich and powerful the Company had become in India, and how generous it could be to anyone who assisted its servants at a time of need. Of that generosity, whether Dale knew of it or not, there was no better example to quote than that of the *Grosvenor*.

On 4 August 1782 the homeward-bound East Indiaman, *Grosvenor,* had struck a coastal reef some 750 miles from the Cape of Good Hope. After appalling hardships a mere handful of survivors eventually reached safety, and the Dutch Governor of the Cape, in addition to sending search parties into the desert, wrote to Warren Hastings, the Governor of India, at Bengal to inform him of the tragedy. Out of gratitude Hastings purchased a valuable diamond, had it set in a ring, and entrusted it to his Personal Secretary,

John Auriol, who was about to return to Europe. *Grosvenor* passed into legend, the subject of plays, novels and expeditions vainly seeking her fabled cargo. The ship that dropped anchor in Table Bay on 23 March 1784 while Auriol went ashore to present Hastings' ring was the *Winterton*, returning from her maiden voyage.[80]

At once the Governor's attitude changed. There was no more talk about bills or payment. He reminded them that England was an old ally of Portugal and declared it was his duty to provide all the assistance he could to her subjects; as for repayment, he was perfectly happy to rely on the generosity of the East India Company.

The boat was now theirs. An examination of their prize confirmed that she had been recently paid because they could see the new pitch, but whether she had been properly caulked, as the Governor claimed, remained to be seen. Like a Masulah boat she had no deck, nor were there the skills at Sofala to construct one that would keep out the water. The best they could contrive was to lay mats over thick bamboo canes so that they could move fore and aft and to hope that they did not ship more water than they could comfortably carry or bale out.

Whatever the boat's original rig, they decided that for their purposes she needed to be schooner rigged. When they opened up the sails they found that the coarse cotton had almost rotted, but they managed to adapt them; and they had to make do with the existing ropes. All in all, 'a parish fitting out, nearly as bad as on Madagascar'. On the other hand, thanks to the Governor's change of heart, they had a good supply of provisions, far more than they anticipated needing: six weeks salt and two weeks live.

On 12 October they boarded the new vessel which, in a burst of misplaced confidence, they named the *Happy Delivery*. They were now down to six men, for the Portuguese seaman had decided to remain at Sofala. The Governor had given them a small supply of spirits, wine and spices as well as a letter for the Governor of Cape Corientes in case they should put into harbour there. He went with them down to the water to wish them luck but along with the good wishes and alcohol went a warning to keep well out at sea, knowing from experience that the currents along the shore were treacherous.

The prospect of being within seven days of success sent them off in good heart; even when the boat started to leak heavily they were undismayed and simply put it down to the timbers having dried out during the weeks it had been laid up. Once the wood began to swell, the problem would all but disappear within 24 hours.

Far from decreasing, however, the leaks grew worse within 40 miles, and a freshening wind only compounded the problem by straining the boat until the pitch came away and what little oakum[81] there was between the seams worked its way out. Their suspicion about the caulking was confirmed. Although two men had to keep bailing constantly, their spirits remained high, for if the wind would just shift so that it was on the quarter they could sail 'large' with much less strain on the seams, the leaks would lessen, and they would make good progress. Unhappily for them, the wind refused to shift, the effort of bailing became too great, and that first evening, by common consent, they decided that the only thing to do was to put back to Sofala, just a day's run away.

Hardly had they changed course when the disobliging wind shifted until it lay dead ahead, making northward progress a true battle. Under no circumstances would they return to the original plan of sailing south to Delgoa Bay, 'for, perhaps, before we could have run half the distance, we might be stopped again, and not be able to reach any place: or, what was more probable, founder at sea'. The boat was too small and too unsound[82] to take the risk.

Night brought worse danger. They were sailing close to the wind, around 10 miles from the shore, when they found themselves among high breakers. It could mean only one thing: they were on a reef, and, in the darkness, there was no knowing whether they would find themselves grounded and smashed to sticks. Dale had to make a decision.

'A moment's thought determined us how to act: we were very

sensible our precious boat would not stay, that was above her ability; it was impossible to wear, that would have required the distance of a mile at least.'

'Wearing' and 'staying' were terms relating to changing direction, and how they were performed depended on the weather and the vessel's rig. With both manoeuvres impossible, and the sea crashing around them, they resorted to 'club-hauling', no mean feat given that they had only the one anchor and had to weigh it once the ship had swung round. Dale had the tiller, fighting to control the boat's head. Twice the force of the sea drove it so violently from side to side that he was knocked overboard. Either he was roped to the boat or luck was on his side, as both times he managed to recover.

It was quite enough to dissuade them from sailing by night again. The wind was set stubbornly against them and they had been warned of the dangers of getting close to the shore. From then on they moved only by day, and when the tide allowed, spending their nights aground in the shelter of the many broad rivers that flowed into the sea. Those rivers formed an intricate coastal network of waterways, creating low, swampy islands of tropical forest where, apart from the inevitable mosquitoes, the only creatures were hippos and a few monkeys.

One morning as they were waiting for the tide, three men appeared in a canoe. As concern for their diminishing food supplies had been growing they decided to take the opportunity of buying a few fowls. The natives pointed up a tributary of the river, said that their village was not far away, and requested a couple of the *Winterton* people to go with them. De Souza and one of the sailors volunteered and away they paddled.

All day the others waited, and as it grew dark their fears mounted. Thus far all the native people they had met had proved to be friendly, and Dale had felt no qualms at letting his comrades go off. But now, as night fell, they were worried. If the pair had not fallen victim to human malice they could have been attacked by hippos while in the canoe. Shared danger and a common purpose had formed a bond between them, and the four left in the boat passed a sleepless night.

Morning brought relief. The canoe returned with de Souza, the sailor and some fowls. Unable to get their provisions until late the previous evening they had spent a pleasant enough night with their native hosts. Once again they began the laborious task of creeping northwards, continually bailing out the water. Both de Souza and Wilton were falling ill; and two evenings later they lost one of the three seamen.

As they lay aground for the night, cooking dinner over a fire, they heard the sound of a tom-tom. Fascinated by the rhythm, and knowing there was nothing to fear from the local people, Thomas Adams decided to find the source. The others urged him not to be such a fool, particularly as dusk was falling fast. He took no notice of them; nor did he come back. The sound of the drum grew fainter then ceased.

At intervals that night they shouted his name, making all the noise they could in the hope that he would hear them and be guided back to the boat. For two days they waited. Then, accepting that the worst had happened to him, they set out once again; but this time they decided to follow the river, calculating that it must lead them to Sofala. Only Dale, Longster and the unnamed sailor were well enough to work the boat, and the task of manoeuvring at sea with such a contrary wind, while constantly bailing, was more than three men could manage. For 3 miles they followed the river between the trees, and for as long as it widened they felt optimistic of reaching Sofala or some other nearby settlement. Eventually, it started to narrow, and soon the trees formed an arch over their head. The air was close; shirts stuck to flesh. Green monkeys skipped and swung from branch to branch and hippos surfaced to breathe beside the boat. Dismayed to find they could go no further, they turned back and anchored on one bank of the estuary.

In the evening, at low tide, Dale, de Souza and a sailor walked

4 miles along the wood-fringed beach towards Sofala, looking out for potential hazards such as rocks. The two mariners had just decided that they would be able to work the boat up when a group of natives came up with totally unexpected news.

Thomas Adams had been found alive in the woods by some of their people and taken back to Sofala where he must have told the Governor of their decision to put back. Help was already on its way. In better spirits than for many days, Dale's party set off to take the news to Wilton and his companion. Their haste was increased not only by the need to get back before dark, but by finding elephant prints in the sand. Curiosity exceeding alarm, they used a piece of string to measure one of the larger prints, estimating it at more than 4 feet.

Dale and the sailor might be able to quicken their pace, but de Souza, wrapped in an old dressing gown brought from Madagascar over his shirt and breeches, was too weak and rapidly fell back, unable to respond to calls to hurry. With a sense of mischief as well as a genuine desire to reach the boat before dark, the other pair suddenly started gesticulating to him and shouting that there were elephants coming out of the woods. Without even bothering to look round, the usually indolent de Souza ran for his life, dressing gown flapping wildly, overtaking his companions who were all but hysterical with laughter. If he ever paid them back for the trick, Dale did not record it.

That night, 26 October, a tornado struck.

'I never in my life witnessed anything so awful: the elements together seemed conspiring to destroy us. The air was perfectly on fire, while the loud thunder struck terror, and the rain fell in torrents. It was lucky for us we were not at sea for we certainly must have been lost.'

Unable to keep a fire going, they huddled in the boat, unashamedly afraid of whatever wild animals might come up, and in the morning they found animal prints all round the vessel as it lay grounded.

Wilton's health was clearly worse than that of de Souza. Dale left him in the boat with one seaman and plenty of supplies while the rest of them took a small supply of bread and walked the beach as far as the south bank of the Sofala River which they reached around noon, only to find there were no canoes to take them over. A group of natives had set up makeshift huts and were also looking to cross. Dale's party tied a handkerchief to a pole and waved it in the hope of attracting attention on the northern bank, but without success. Their bread had run out; worse, they had no water, and the local men had none to spare, although they did give them a hut to sleep in. No canoes arrived in the morning, so they tied the handkerchief to a longer pole to make it more visible, and even stripped off so that their pale skins would identify them at a distance. The only food they had all day was a small skate brought by a fisherman, which aggravated their dehydration, and the knowledge that food and water lay just across the river made their thirst doubly hard to bear. Before they went to sleep they decided to return to the boat at first light.

While it was still dark they were disturbed by a musket shot from the other bank, the signal that help was at hand. The relief party came over with supplies and then set off to find the two left with the boat. In the morning, Dale's group were taken across the river and reunited with Adams whom they found in a wretched state.

The sound of the drum had drawn him quite a way from the boat, but he never did find out its source. Tired of walking, he turned back, only to become lost and disorientated in the darkness. Hungry, thirsty and exhausted, he lay down for the night, licking the dew of the grass, and prey to every mosquito in the vicinity. Next day he had bludgeoned his way frantically through the woods, tearing clothes and skin, until he ran into some natives who did what they could for him and then took him up to Sofala.

Later that day, the boat arrived, and the men were once more together, but under very different conditions. Gone was any pretence of hospitality from the Governor; he merely sent word for Dale and Wilton to make ready for an immediate departure. He was about to send letters to Quelimane, and they were to accompany his messenger.

At once de Souza went to see him to ask for assistance with supplies and other necessities for a journey of anything up to 300 miles. In view of their health they particularly wanted palanquins which, around Sofala at any rate, were simple hammocks suspended on poles and carried by two or four men. That request was peremptorily refused unless de Souza would pay for it. De Souza was willing to stand surety for the two officers but told the Governor 'it was extravagant to suppose that he should become personal surety for the seamen when it was so unlikely they could repay it'. Instead he offered Pereira a bill on the East India Company, but this time the the man would not accept it reasoning that it might take time to get it paid. By now the Governor knew that de Souza's family was of sufficiently high standing in India to make it easy for him to get unlimited credit at Mozambique Island, and this was something he could turn to his avaricious advantage.

The common currency of the region was not coin but cloth. Everything – food, transport, shelter – was paid for with varying lengths according to its perceived value. The Governor now expected de Souza to take as much of the commodity as possible and to give him a bill based on the local value, which represented a profit of between 200 and 300 per cent to himself. More than this, he also demanded interest until repayment, which infuriated the nephew of the Calcutta merchant.

'Do you think me a fool, or so little conversant in business as to comply with such terms?' de Souza demanded contemptuously, and the interview ended with angry words on both sides.

Fortunately for them all, de Souza's Lisbon acquaintance took them into his house for the night. More than that, he helped them procure some cloth for the journey using the few silver dollars they had brought with them. In addition to the cloth which was mostly blue and white dungaree – a coarse Indian calico – they took strings of small white beads, and variously sized rings of block tin. Everything was made into a small, easily portable bale, and to ensure they travelled light they disposed all unnecessary luggage, reserving little more than a spare shirt each so that they would never be dependent on native bearers. Wilton, however, packed a spare pair of shoes.

The Governor then sent for the two officers and, without so much as asking why they had put back to Sofala, reiterated his order that they depart for Quelimane with his messenger. With the Portuguese seaman as interpreter, they tried desperately to make him understand that they were sick, exhausted and in no state to set off within less than a day. In vain they entreated him for a few days in which to recover. He answered that he was supposed to be on his way to the Bazarute[83] Islands and had already delayed his departure by several days on their account. This cut no ice with Dale who was convinced that any delay was attributable to a fear of losing his boat rather than concern for his former guests. The conversation then came back to the subject of the palanquins.

'What do you think will become of those that walk?' they demanded. 'Or, do you imagine that, after sharing in so many hardships together we will thus meanly desert them?'

'If you expected conveyance for you all, why haven't you applied personally for it?' came his response. Prudence had held Dale's temper in check, but this was too much.

'You know very well,' he said through the interpreter, 'that we are unable to speak with you. We made our application by de Souza and it has been refused.' Dale's disgust was undisguised. 'An Englishman is not accustomed to sue twice for anything. If you don't choose to act alike by us, then we'll make it out independent of your assistance!'

Such loyalty left the Governor visibly unmoved.

'It is out of my power; and if I were to see de Souza begging for bread I would not give him a morsel!' were his last words, and both Dale and Wilton walked out indignantly. Afterwards he suffered either a qualm of conscience or a desire to ingratiate himself with the HEIC and sent them some cloth and beads which necessity forced them to accept with gritted teeth. Thus provided, on 29 October they set off on a journey which only three of them would live to complete.[84]

At Madras, concerns that the *Winterton* had not yet arrived were allayed by a man who had left the Cape on 10 August and who reported that because of the lateness of the season, she was proceeding directly to Calcutta.[85]

Chapter Eleven

Exhaustion, Malaria and Exposure

The black soldier from the fort at Sofala who was to double as their guide had made the journey to Quelimane before, albeit some years earlier. With him went four or five native porters with the provisions and textile currency, releasing Dale's party from the need to carry heavy loads in the heat. Although the monsoon had set in, the sky remained largely clear, and once they left the forested coastal strip of the province they would be out on the open grassland, exposed to the full force of a tropical sun.

During the first two days of the journey they kept relatively close to the coast, crossing the River Buzi by canoe. Word of their coming had gone ahead, and night of the second day found them ferried across the wide Pungue to a village where a hut had been prepared for them; but as they disembarked Dale put one foot into thick mud that sucked off his shoe. In the darkness all hope of finding it failed, and when later he unpacked his bundle, he had an unpleasant surprise: the spare pair of shoes he had brought with him from Madagascar had been left behind at Sofala. Such a mistake might have cost him dearly, but he and Wilton were lucky to have had feet of a similar size, and his friend at once came to the rescue with his spare pair. If Dale had regarded the prospect of walking 300 miles barefoot as 'an uncomfortable prospect', he would hardly have relished it in badly fitting shoes.

Next day they cut inland across a broad plain of savannah and wood.

'Some parts of it were very pleasant, and we often saw at a distance herds of wild buffaloes, very large. Little villages were scattered at 10 or 15 miles apart, but there were few inhabitants. Whenever we could, we endeavoured to reach one of these before night.'

At each village where they halted for the night the day's bearers were paid off with an arm's length or so of cloth depending on the length of the stage, and new men engaged for the following day.

They had long ago ceased to have any apprehension about the native people whose fair treatment of them was in marked contrast to that of Sofala's Portuguese Governor. Whenever they reached one of the scattered villages they were met by the men sitting in a row and clapping, before being shown by the Head Man himself to a hut which had been specially prepared for them. The same elder then sold them whatever provisions were available, usually water and fowls, and they paid him out of their stores. Wherever they went, prices were remarkably consistent: the equivalent of four to six strings of beads or an arm's length of cloth could buy a bird or a measure of flour. If the women approved the Chief's choice, all was well; if they did not, they demanded to see what else the white travellers had brought to trade and made their choice from that.

Once the transaction had been closed, one of the bearers turned chef for the evening, drawing the fowl, discarding the giblets, and cooking it for his employers. On one occasion, when the only food consisted of two rather small birds between the six of them, they decided to do their own cooking so that they could use the giblets as well as the flesh, and it was notable that the porters refused to eat any of the leftovers.

Dinner sometimes became a rousing affair, with the women dancing round a fire outside their guests' hut to the rhythm of the tom-tom under the dark African sky and the men gathering to watch. It made fine entertainment, but the crowd and the fire increased the heat around the hut, already intense due to the necessity of maintaining a fire inside to discourage the mosquitoes.

On 7 November, nine days after leaving Sofala they experienced their worst day. Settlements had grown more scattered, and they had spent the night in a dense wood with fires all round them to deter both insects and large predators. Dale comments:

'No village being near us, and having a long march in view before we could reach any, we set off early when the moon rose, about two in the morning. As the way we had to pass was very much infested with lions and tigers (sic) particularly, our guide desired us all to carry a lighted firebrand in our hands as the best means of defence, and the people with us had horns which they sounded as we went along, shouting loudly at the same time.'

As soon as they reached those stretches where they expected to find lions, the porters kept ominously silent. In single file the party moved along the path, torches breaking the darkness and apprehensive ears tuned to the heavy breathing of the unseen wildlife. To increase their undisguised fear, the guide occasionally took the wrong track, and nobody was sorry when dawn penetrated the trees. Wearily they took the opportunity of a rest, but while they were eating and drinking, the bearers abruptly got up and walked off. According to the guide they were simply refusing to go on any further unless they were promised more cloth than originally agreed.

The natives held all the cards: without expert guidance, there was no way out of the wood.

Out in the open the sun blazed down on the grass until the few streams they passed were scalding hot. Dale began to feel the first effects of sunstroke, and at one point passed out. When he recovered, he was all but too exhausted to keep up with his guide. Only the fear of being attacked by wild animals or dying of dehydration kept him on his feet until they halted at 5pm. Patches of flattened grass along the way was evidence of the recent presence of resting lions; the occasional acacia tree that punctuated the landscape often had a rough platform of sticks and mats on which passing travellers could rest in some degree of safety.

During the march the 'natives often amused us with the manner in which they kill the wild beasts', and Dale learned that of all the wildlife in that region the elephant was the most feared.

'Sometimes we met with a party of men going to hunt the elephant, armed with long spears and knives; and this appears the most likely method. It is extremely dangerous to be near them before sunrise. We saw one morning four or five prodigious large ones; they followed one another with slow pace and we could hear the cracking of the trees as they pulled down the branches with their trunks.'

If they had seen few native people over the last few days, they were to see none for the two days it took them walk the 40 miles to a tiny riverside settlement known locally as Macai which Dale estimated about 100 miles from Sofala. They reached it on 9 November; had their original plan worked out, they ought by now to have been back at Toleary with a ship.

Macai was no paradise in the 'miserable tract of country', but it was the home of the Portuguese superintendent of a certain Lady Donna Ignez who lived at Sena. Although Mozambique was a colony and the expatriate settlers were technically Portuguese subjects, some individuals from the sixteenth century onwards had concluded private agreements with local rulers and founded powerful landholding dynasties in their own right. Unable to persuade enough people to leave Portugal for a new life in their unhealthy African colony, the Portuguese crown leased out land at peppercorn rents, and even gave large estates to orphaned noblewomen. In whatever way she had acquired her rights, Lady Donna owned land from Macai to Sena. Her agent did what he could for his unexpected visitors and they rested three days at the village. When they resumed their journey on 12 November, their packs were carried by her slaves, and there was a palanquin for one of the seamen, almost certainly Adams who had suffered so terribly during his time lost in the jungle.

Dale is strangely reticent about the journey, except to say that some of them began to complain of illness. Exhaustion, malaria and exposure set in during the 100-mile walk up to Chirimgoura. Had the terrain been more demanding probably none of them would have made it, but it remained largely level, and the empty grassland gave way to cotton and even the occasional tea plant. At last they saw cattle grazing, and staggered into what was for that part of the world a significant Portuguese settlement. In addition to Lady Donna's resident agent, they found Signor Ignez himself, who responded with dismay to the news that they had been forced into the overland journey.

Now, at last, the help they needed was freely and generously given. Ignez dispatched one of his sons post-haste up to Sena to ask the Governor for instructions, and fed them all from his own table. Within two days of their arrival, they all became too ill to leave their beds, as if the sudden release from danger and the necessity to carry on at all costs allowed them to surrender to their sickness. Ignez's agent became doctor and nurse, and without his care they would all have died. How long it had taken them to reach the settlement and how many days or weeks they were actually there, Dale does not say.

Young Ignez returned with orders to send the six men up to Sena rather than down to Quelimane. Palanquins were collected – no one could walk – and they departed on 2 December. In four days they were carried the 70 miles or so north west to the Portuguese stronghold on the southern bank of the Zambezi.

❧❧❧

Flanked on three sides by swamp and on the fourth by the river, Sena, despite its unhealthy location, had been the site of a traditional African fair long before the Portuguese colonised and used it as a trading post and base for further conquest and missionary expeditions. Founded on uneven ground,[86] 'all hillocks and holes', the town had never grown along European lines with formal streets, retaining instead the layout of a village, and most of the houses were square edifices, built either from sun-baked bricks with tiled roofs of blue-tinged terracotta, or wattle and daub with thatch. Stone was the prerogative of the very wealthiest. Whitewashed walls provided a Portuguese flavour on the outside, and a cooling ambience within. At the north east end of the town a small, rectangular fort, also built of baked mud, with bastions and gun embrasures at each corner protected the settlement and commanded the vast river that flowed like silver rope work between low sandy islands, navigable from Tete down to the sea. Like the majority of Sena's buildings, the one church was simple in construction, along the lines of an old school in the Scottish Highlands, with gratings for windows and a clay floor. Across the miles of water rose the hills of the opposite shore, and beyond those the mass of Murumbala in which the Portuguese sent their slaves to search for gold. Gold dust, not cloth, was the currency of Sena, and what the Portuguese residents lacked in number they made up for in prosperity, wealth being judged by the number of slaves they owned.

❧❧❧

For Thomas Adams, Sena came too late: he died on the morning of their arrival, 6 December. Wilton and Longster were seriously ill. The living were carried to the house of the Governor and given what food and drink they could take. After de Souza had recounted their misadventures, they were moved to the house that had been got ready for their arrival, and dinner was sent to them. Shortly afterwards they received a visit from one of the richest men in Sena: Manuel Ribeiro dos Santos who owned various tracts of land along the Zambezi and possessed 800 slaves who mined gold in the hills, worked his land, or whom he hired out to other men. He spent a long time talking with de Souza, and that same evening, touched by their plight, he sent his slaves with palanquins to transfer them all to his own house.

'No one can rightly judge of what I felt on finding myself in a good room, and a comfortable bed to lie on, unless, like me, he had been buffeting about for four months, a stranger to almost every comfort. I could scarcely for a while believe the transition.'

Sunburnt, unshaven, emaciated and tattered, Dale was barely recognisable from the alert officer who had stared east from the quarterdeck of the *Winterton* a few months earlier.

Far from leaving them to the care of slaves or servants, Ribeiro constituted himself their carer. He washed and dressed them all, was always on hand to give them what medicines were available, and did his best to talk them over the ordeal they had been through. Nor were his friends slow to follow his example: they brought clothes, paid visits and wanted to help. The only doctor in Sena, a Frenchman, was another frequent visitor. He was not very skilful, but made it up, as far as he could, in attention: he began with bleeding and then gave bark.[87] I thought', recalled Dale with a wry smile, 'that he would have drawn me off like a pipe of wine, he took so much blood from me; but he said it was a common practice in such fevers.'

Seven days after their arrival, on 13 December, Thomas Longster became the second seaman to succumb. Then, on Christmas Day, Joseph Wilton, the young Fourth Mate who had been ill ever since the abortive mission to Delgoa Bay, lost his struggle for life. For Dale, that was the worst blow. Mess mates, comrades, just two years apart in age: the bond of friendship between them had only strengthened since leaving Toleary with such high hopes of success. Wilton had been so determined to go; had had such faith in Dale's plans.

Moved by Dale's grief, Ribeiro tried vainly to cheer him, urging him to share his Christmas dinner, and when the time came to take Wilton's body away for burial he invited various friends to attend and invest the occasion with the respect and dignity that the young officer deserved. Little is recorded of Wilton's background, beyond his service with the East India Company. He had been baptised at St Michael's, Dublin, on 9 June 1771 to William and Esther Wilton and gone to sea at the age of 12 on the HEIC's *Ponsborne*. The *Winterton* represented his fifth voyage, and his first and last as an officer.

Sadness at Wilton's death and memories of his own last Christmas at home with his family gave way to a new anxiety. From conversations with the French doctor, Dale had learned that the climate of Madagascar in what was now the rainy season was as unhealthy as anything in Mozambique; and only his physical weakness and the absence of any transport kept him at Sena, learning a little Portuguese, talking in French with the doctor and smoking small cigars made from tobacco rolled in dried plantain leaves. The men carried boxes of them, much as Englishmen carried snuff boxes, producing them to friends and guests. Pleasant and agreeable, the Governor continued to prove himself the antithesis of his opposite number at Sofala, including Dale in invitations to occasional chamber concerts in which one of his female slaves played second violin. And, to an outsider, life at the settlement had its funny side.

The palanquins of the rich at Sena, far more elaborate than the simple hammocks of Sofala, were status symbols as much as a mere method of transport, and Ribeiro was suitably proud of his. Dale witnessed a public day when the inhabitants all went in their best clothes to pay their respects to the Governor, and Ribeiro sported his deluxe model. Possibly the palanquin was better than the Governor's own: whatever the reason, the Governor demanded that he change it.

'It's mine and I shall use it,' retorted the landowner with spirit, and was promptly clapped into the guardhouse of the fort for two days. He bore no malice over the incident and continued on visiting terms after his release. 'I suppose these things often happen', decided Dale.

Shortly afterwards, Ribeiro left Sena for his estates down river at Chapenga, promising to meet his three guests there, and on the morning of 16 January 1793, armed with a supply of wine from the Governor, Dale, de Souza and the unnamed sailor said goodbye to the town that had opened its heart to them and where they had buried three of their comrades in as many weeks.

❧❧❧

The Zambezi flows at its fullest and fastest in January when the rainy season swells the tributaries. Too powerful to be checked by any tide, it sweeps down to the Mozambique Channel so that small boats can cover the 200 miles from Sena to the delta ports of Chinde or Quelimane in two days. It took only one for the travellers to reach Chapenga where they found Ribeiro waiting for them at his house on a hill overlooking the water. For two days they stayed with him, and he showed them round his estate where he grew timber for the big canoes used to transport cargo. Dale estimated he was sitting on a fortune, but, unconsciously comparing him with the Governor of Sofala about whom he was beginning to hear various unflattering comments, decided he was too generous to be ruthless in business.

They parted finally on the 19th and, loaded with good wishes, provisions and other supplies, eased themselves into the canoes waiting to take them on to Quelimane down the Rios Dos Boas Sinais,[88] the northern finger of the delta. Once on the water, Dale rapidly turned fretful: the canoes were so narrow that to change position without the risk of capsizing was impossible, and, in his opinion, the boat people wasted precious time, taking three days over a journey that might have been made in half the time, and forcing them all to sleep at the mercy of the mosquitoes that emerged at night. It was no longer a question of when he reached Mozambique Island but when he could get back to the shipmates and passengers he had left at Toleary more than four months ago.

Chapter Twelve

Fatal Fever

There were mixed feelings in the hearts of those who watched the yawl as it faded to a speck on the horizon. Hope rode high: those who had worked on the boat were skilled, she was well provisioned, and her officers were more than competent. Five weeks, they had estimated. Five weeks was more than enough time to cross that narrow sheet of water, explain the disaster to friendly Portuguese ears, and return with a vessel capable of taking them back to the Cape. In the meantime, while Toleary was not the most attractive village in the world, they had a roof over their heads and the protection of the King.

On the other hand, the yawl, re-rigged as she was with inferior materials, was a very small craft for such a treacherous stretch of sea; and with her had gone the two young officers on whose authority and leadership so many had been glad to rely. The King was sympathetic, but somehow they had to exist for the next few weeks, destitute as they were, on the charity of local people who did not all share their Monarch's humanity. Their little stocks of trinkets and silver were soon gone, leaving them nothing with which to buy food.

Since the break-up of the *Winterton* the local fishermen had spent a great deal of time diving on the reef at low tide to salvage the cargo, and in particular the 75 chests of silver once destined to pay the Company's soldiers and clerical staff. Despite the difficulty, they successfully recovered the greater part of the treasure, and four days after the yawl's departure they came to Toleary to present a proportion of their prize to the King. Attended by several hundred of his soldiers all bearing arms, and well informed as to what had been going on out on the reef, the King came out in state to meet them. Either by invitation or curiosity, the *Winterton* spectators witnessed a ceremony of dancing and musket firing, followed by the offering of the King's share.

What followed took them all by surprise. The King's first action after accepting what was due to him was to order a sum equal to about 25,000 dollars to be given to the survivors, and he assembled the people so that he could distribute it in person.

From the outset, Nathaniel Spens and William Dunn viewed the whole business with dismay. As servants of the HEIC they felt themselves responsible for the *Winterton*'s cargo; in their eyes, anything that came ashore belonged to the Company. Spens went up to the King and peremptorily told him that he had no right to give away the Company's property in the way he proposed.

The King dismissed his argument out of hand but with more courtesy than Spens deserved. It was not the Company's property: the silver had been salvaged by his people after the ship had been abandoned on his coast, and therefore belonged to him. In a direct rebuke to Spens, he observed that even if it was the Company's money, no better use could be found for it than the support of its servants. The sight of so much wealth, and the fear that they might be deprived of it, proved too much for many of the soldiers and sailors who broke ranks and seized whatever they could get their hands on. At once the King sent his soldiers to halt the scramble and recover as much of the silver as possible – which was certainly not the whole amount. He then gave Spens and Dunn the 25,000 dollars to distribute as they pleased.

With due regard for class distinction, the King had intended the passengers and the officers to receive more than the rest. When Spens and Dunn carried out the distribution the following day, the shares were inexplicably different. According to Dale, who would have been told after the event, it worked out at 80 dollars per soldier, 90 per sailor and 50 for each gentleman passenger. At a loss to understand the reasoning behind it, Dale wondered if Spens and Dunn were scared of the 'people' as he tended to call all the seamen and soldiers. Buchan put it at 10 dollars more for the sailors and soldiers, with 600 dollars between the ladies and 900 each for Dunn and Spens. Perhaps the most fortunate individuals were McKey and another fife player: they were rewarded with 300 dollars each, no doubt at the King's insistence. The King's share was safely buried. Afterwards, in the true royal tradition of not carrying money on him, he was often known to ask for a coin from those around him.

In Dale's mind, the actions of the two men in charge of the money amounted to nothing short of embezzlement, and he declared himself heartily glad to have been abroad when it took place.[89] The King's generosity and the unequal shares had an interesting effect. The soldiers and seamen were now financially superior to the passengers, and the soldiers and their wives in particular let the wealth go to their heads. Their prodigality led to a sharp rise in the price of essential foodstuffs for as long as the nouveau riche had money to throw around.

In the meantime, while they waited for Dale's party to return, the possibility of a chance ship putting in at St Augustine's Bay at any time had not been overlooked, and a rota was organised so that there would always be at least two responsible people there at any time. The Bay was a far more attractive area than Toleary: less sandy and more luxuriant, overlooked by the high, table-topped landmark of

Mont Mahinia (popularly known to English sailors as Westminster Hall), and watered by the Onilahy, or Dartmouth, river as it emerged from its forested valley to join the sea. By canoe the journey would have been simple, but the men had to walk, and in their debilitated state the full day's hike in the heat was as gruelling as any part of their journey to Toleary. Some of the sailors and soldiers, including the Boatswain, chose to make their permanent residence at the Bay; the rest preferred to remain under the King's eye where they felt safer.

Their respect for the autocratic young ruler never wavered. His generosity with bullocks waned in the face of his subjects' obvious disapproval, but never ceased; and however severe he might be with his own people – they watched the brutal execution of a physician who had, allegedly, caused the death of a royal relative – he was never less than courteous towards his guests. Like his subjects he had a drink problem, a failing that embarrassed Buchan, but however inebriated he got, he never gave the *Winterton* ladies any cause for alarm, and was always perfectly aware of his condition, telling them that 'Today drink speak, tomorrow King speak.'

He often came to talk to the women in their huts, and on one particular occasion one of his attendants asked him, in front of them, which he fancied most. The majority were very young, several extremely attractive. When the King expressed a choice, the attendant asked him why he did not make use of his royal power to obtain her. In fury, the king lashed out with his musket, felled the man, and had to be held back from shooting him. Because they had spoken in Malagasy, it was only afterwards that the girls understood what lay behind the sudden violence. It shook them at the time, but was reassuring in the longer term.

None of the King's subordinates ever took advantage of him when he was drunk, although one of the governors gave Buchan and friends to understand that he didn't think the King half the man his royal father had been. This man lived further into the forests and was an occasional and welcome visitor to his overlord's guests; on one occasion he and his wife arrived not long after the death of one of their children and he quietly requested people to avoid the subject as it would only distress her. Isabella Cullen would have understood.

If the King had a name, they never found it out and continued to call him the King of Baba. Like the Queen, some of the elders and subordinate governors had adopted royal or aristocratic English names, a trait common in the Indian Ocean, and the Governor of St Augustine's Bay went by the title of the Prince of Wales. When he died it was the occasion for two days of musket fire followed by the sacrifice of over 100 bullocks and a re-siting of his entire village at the Bay.

Absolute as the King's power was, major decisions were taken with his council of state, gathered under the shade of the great Tamarind tree at Toleary, where, unable to understand what was being said, the whites could only admire the fluent oratory. Away from the town they also witnessed a peacemaking ceremony with a neighbouring prince, observed a trial by ordeal leading to the acquittal of the accused, and heard the regular ritual that ensued when any of the natives became sick. On such occasions friends gathered at the invalid's door, singing loudly, clapping their hands and stamping on the ground. If the sufferer were someone of importance a drum and a conch-shaped shell increased the volume; and if the illness was grave, a bullock or two was sacrificed before being distributed among the friends. There was clearly some religious significance to the rite, but never did Buchan nor his comrades witness any obvious act of worship. What they did notice was that every man wore an 'owly' round his neck – a small leather bag containing a few crocodile teeth and pieces of wood. This was evidently a talisman to ward off danger; at night it was hung by the bed, and no man ever left his hut without it.

While waiting for the yawl to return, some of the *Winterton* people entertained themselves exploring the area around them, but they were not strong enough to go more than a few miles. Apart from that, there was little to do but collect food, cook and try to safeguard their limited possessions from theft. Occasionally their heartbeat was raised by a sound like a ship under sail, of the firing of guns at sea, but it inevitably turned out to be nothing more than the distant spouting of whales or their battles on the reef. 'It might have been thought that one disappointment at least would have guarded us from a renewal of such feelings, but it did not, for in our situation the reasoning faculties were no match for imagination', commented Buchan. As the first five weeks passed, hopes remained high, but gradually the fear that something grave had befallen their would-be rescuers crept in. The fragility of the craft, the limited provisions, and the lack of charts and instruments weighed on their minds.

They had been two months on the island when the King, aware that there was trade between Madagascar and Mauritius, and discovering that the French and the English were not such deadly enemies as he had supposed, one evening suggested the possibility of their being able to reach Fort Dauphin on the south east coast. Instantly spirits kindled like matchwood, as Buchan describes:

'None of us knew the least of the distance or of the country to be traversed: it had been a European settlement and that was enough. Mountains, rivers, forests, all obstacles were at once removed and Fort Dauphin seemed already open to our view. Our associate, Corporal McCoy, struck up…with more than usual glee on his fife, the favourite tune Over the Hills and Far Away.'

All they had to do was to send some of the fittest men along with a party of the King's soldiers, but the King was cautious: this had to be referred to his council for consideration. Their verdict dashed all hope: the council concluded that the rains should have begun up country and sufficiently swollen the rivers to make the journey impossible.

Well for them that the scheme was, as Buchan put it, 'knocked

on the head', for the journey over hostile ground and into the terri-
tory of even more hostile tribes would have finished them long
before they reached Fort Dauphin which the French had, in any
case, abandoned. Coming so hard on the heels of the failed return
of the rescue party, the disappointment was desperately hard to bear.
They had not entirely given up hope of Dale, but with every week
that passed, they grew more resigned to a long wait for a chance
ship. For one unnamed seaman, however, the shipwreck brought an
unexpected blessing in the form of a serious romance.[90]

Despite his poor health, Buchan was ready to take his turn at St
Augustine's Bay, and accordingly set off with Alexander Thompson
before first light. It took them all day and into the evening, and
when they finally made it, they found their accommodation consisted of a dirty hut with some rushes scattered on the ground. Buchan
developed a high fever which kept him at the Bay for a fortnight,
nursed by his friend, plagued by mosquitoes, and unable to derive
much pleasure either from the different scenery or the company of
those who had settled there. He was almost certainly suffering from
malaria, the disease which had taken as high a toll of would-be
colonists as the resistance of the local tribes ever since the
Portuguese and the French had attempted to exploit the island.
Only a canoe trip part of the way back and an overnight halt in a
native's hut enabled him to get back to Toleary alive.

The wet season had held off. Although they longed for rain to
freshen the air, revive the land and improve the muddy river which
was their only source of water, they were making a perilous wish:
water would have made the unhealthy coastline even more deadly in
the increasing heat. Already many of them were suffering from
malaria and other debilitating fevers: by mid-December the death
rate was rising inexorably.

'For those who could move out, the chief recreation was
crawling about in the cool of the morning and evening in the
vicinity of our huts and getting, if we could, during the heat

of the day, under the shade of a large Tamarind tree.'

The living, such as they were, had somehow to bury their dead comrades, and soon they became immune to grief and loss.

'With many dropping almost daily around none of us could with reason reckon on 24 hours of life but the survivors seemed generally to find some new store of hope to carry them on in their heavy journey. The symptoms of the fever that proved so very fatal were various both in its progress and termination, but a violent shivering followed by hot fits, much as a severe ague, was I believe most frequent, and what I chiefly experienced in my own case. An affliction of the spleen was also a prevailing malady but not attended with the immediate danger of acute disorders. Our complaints probably also increased by the extreme bad quality of the water. We had none but what we procured from the river at some distance which was generally so thick as to be a mixture of mud and water. I believe the precaution of boiling it was seldom adopted as we were not sufficiently aware of the poison we were taking. The sufferers sometimes lingered for a considerable time and gradually sunk. At other times death would be proceeded by a violent delirium of perhaps 2 or 3 days continuing. It did happen, but rarely, that the sick person died instantaneously, without having been apparently particularly ill. Recovery from one attack of the fever was no security against its recurrence but it was remarked that those who were naturally more robust and healthy when attacked were least able long to struggle against it.'

Few medicines had been saved from the ship. All Surgeon George Lillie could offer was compassion and encouragement. Like many of those who had embarked on the *Winterton* he was a Scotsman, so passionately homesick for his country that most nights he dreamed of her. His death at Christmas moved Buchan to tears. It was followed within a few days and in the same hut by his fellow country-man, Nathaniel Spens, four months short of his 26th birthday.

The young Scot, Isabella Cullen's nephew, had come from an old and proud family[91] which had fallen upon comparatively hard times after supporting the Jacobite cause. In 1788 his eldest brother had been forced to sell the ancestral estate of Lathallan and the family moved to Inveresk Manor, an elegant Georgian residence of warm stone in the highly fashionable district of the same name just outside Edinburgh. Initially Nathaniel, the third son, had enlisted in the Royal Navy as a midshipman[92] serving in HMS *Buffalo* and HMS *Fortitude* circa 1781. For whatever reason, he left the service and became a seaman in the Baltic Trade before joining the HEIC in 1784 as a midshipman in the *Rodney*. His middle brother, Archibald, had by then made a successful career for himself in the HEIC: it was he who had purchased the Manor, and it could well have been his influence that obtained for Nathaniel his midshipman's berth. Already an experienced sailor, Nathaniel was promoted to Third Mate after completing his midshipman's voyage, and subsequently to Second Mate on the *Melville Castle*. Then the advancement had stopped, and he remained Second on the *Winterton*, although too young for anyone to imagine his career had grounded.

Buchan, who could cry for Lillie's death, and who expressed nothing but respect for Dundas and affection for Chambers, offered neither obituary nor epitaph. Dale thought poorly of him, but would not speak ill of the dead in public. Perhaps Spens only fault was that, lacking leadership, he was too heavily influenced by William Dunn.

The King watched their decline in impotent dismay and with concerns of his own. He wished to visit another part of his kingdom, but was unhappy at the idea of leaving those under his protection to the depredations of local robbers. For their own safety, he advised them either to move down to the Bay or to go with him. Neither course was physically practical. Terrified of being abandoned, they fervently begged him not to go, and in the end, not for the first time, he yielded.

❯❯❮❮

By the middle of January 1793 more than 80 lay dead. Once-crowded huts were increasingly occupied singly, and there was no more keeping in touch with St Augustine's Bay. Those who had spent all their money in expectation of an early rescue either lived a wretched existence, dependent on the natives, or acted as servants to the more prudent. Their other option was to apply to Dunn for money and offer him a written bill for dollars which was to be repayable in Sterling in London. With only Lieutenant Brownrigg, William Dunn and John Moore left of the officers, there was no authority over the seamen, but there had also not been any repetition of behaviour likely to inflame the locals. Men and women wore the tatters of their European clothes and whatever simple garments could be made from the local cloth. Buchan acknowledged himself the proud possessor of two shirts – one of which had cost 10 dollars from a native after it had been stolen from him – a soldier's hat to shield him from the sun by day and the mosquitoes at night, a pair of coarse trousers and a piece of cloth for a blanket. He had even managed to retain possession of his precious seals.

Back in Scotland, on 14 January 1793, Christian Dundas, unaware that she had been a widow for more than four months, gave birth to the son, James, she had conceived shortly before her husband left Edinburgh to join his ship.

In terms of survival the men fared far worse that the women – not a single female had died since reaching safety. In addition to Spens and Lillie, death claimed Buchan's friend, Alexander Thompson, the Free Mariner; Samuel Hepburn, Mr Cameron (Mr C?), who might have been related to the London banker Donald Cameron – a substantial shareholder in the *Winterton*; Alex Bannermann, who had been George Lillie's assistant; William Lyne, whose sister never got over his death; one of the possible two Hamiltons; the man with the cork jacket; Mr Marshthorpe and George (de) Chiene. Those who remained alive crawled about or, if gone beyond that, lay on their rush beds a prey to natives who would sneak silently into their huts or even cut holes in the rush walls to steal anything to hand. Frustrating as it must have been, they found it more of an irritation than a cause for anger. Irresistible curiosity, not malice, was the besetting sin of their involuntary hosts, and their skill commanded admiration.

Chapter Thirteen

Dale's Deliverance

'A mere mud bank, the filthiest and foulest hole a man could put his foot into…' The river itself 'a great broad ditch of thin mud' was one description of Quelimane,[93] which lay about 12 miles from the sea. Hot, humid and about the size of Sena, the town usually lay well back from the river which at high tide during the wet season now crossed the sullen mangroves and reached almost to the houses. These were mostly of baked mud bricks, but the town boasted the obligatory small fort and the austerely imposing Cathedral of Nossa Senhora de Vibramento which had been completed just seven years earlier, dazzlingly white under the glaring sun. Slaves, ivory and gold were the main exports, and away from the river, coconut trees flourished. The Commandant was experimenting with indigo as a possible commercial proposition, knowing that the plant grew well along other parts of the coast.

John Dale and Thomas de Souza waited on Felix Umberto do

Silva Bandero, Commandant of Quelimane for the past 18 years, and presented him with a letter from the Governor of Sena which resulted in their being invited as guests into his house. Good food and fresher air than at Sena soon began to re-establish their health, and they found the resident Portuguese friendly and obliging, particularly a local merchant by the name of Andria Aveline. A small sloop had arrived at the port and was about to load for Mozambique Island; the master was ordered to take the three men as passengers, free of charge.

That raised a small problem. The master refused to allow the one remaining seaman from the yawl to eat with him and his passengers, relegating him to the boatswain's mess. The fact that everyone enjoyed exactly the same bill of fare did not reconcile the sailor to this demotion. Arguing that thus far he had travelled with his comrades on a democratic all-for-one-and-one-for-all basis, he refused to accept the master's conditions, preferring to remain behind in Quelimane.

On 31 January 1793 Dale and de Souza went aboard, along with 50 slaves, a man bloated with dropsy, and a priest who was being sent up to Mozambique Island in irons for some unspecified crime. The voyage took 13 days, during which time they were exposed to the rain and somewhat at the mercy of strong currents. They ran past the Island, lying low and close to the coast – possibly darkness or bad weather had made it impossible for the ship's master to spot the landmarks – and it took three or four days to regain it.

The approach to the port was difficult: the harbour lay in the shelter of Mossuril Bay, facing the mainland and a little less than half way along the length of the banana-shaped island from the north. Rocks guarded the southern entrance, and with a depth of only 4 fathoms larger vessels were forced to enter by the northern passage, taking them past the gleaming white chapel of Nossa Senhora de Baluarto and the vigilant sixteenth-century fortress of San Sebastiano that filled the north of the island in the shape of a pointed amoeba. The strong and unpredictable currents and the impossibility of entering the port without a fair wind provided lucrative work for the local Moorish pilot. Dale stored up memories of every anchorage he encountered: the information could be fed back to the marine cartographers who relied so heavily on the observations of mariners to improve their charts.

❀

On 12 February Dale and de Souza stepped ashore, entered through the elegant white stone arch of the Capetania and went straight to the Governor, Antonio Manuel de Mello e Castro, who held his full title of Captain General of the States of Mozambique directly from the Portuguese crown and was ultimately responsible for Sofala and the valley of the Zambezi from Zumbo to the delta as well as for the island of Mozambique and the mainland around it. He resided close to the harbour on the main square in an impressive neo-classical building of red-washed limestone with white detailing, which until the expulsion of the Jesuits in 1759 had been a convent and which suited the dignity of the office. Yet again they recounted the story of the shipwreck and their adventures, and Dale, in his capacity as an East India Company officer, appealed for Portuguese assistance.

De Mello was ready to help but in reality there were no Portuguese naval ships in port for him to requisition. If that came as a disappointment, Dale was equal to it, and with little more than his word of honour to trade on, he advised de Mello of his intention to charter a private vessel in the name of the HEIC. Since leaving Sofala he had met with nothing but help and kindness from the Portuguese colonists he encountered. Now he and de Souza were living as guests of one of the resident merchants who had been to England in his youth and retained an affection for the English, while de Mello, no less helpful, lent his authority to their plans.

Only two vessels lay in the harbour: a French slaver bound for Mauritius with her human cargo, and a small, 160-ton snow,[94] loaded and about to sail for Quelimane. De Mello requested the owner, a Hindu trader named Lacamichande Mootilande (?), to place her at Dale's disposal, telling Dale and de Souza to negotiate terms directly with the owner. With a rate of 7500 rupees agreed, the snow was duly unloaded and with the enthusiastic help of her Portuguese master Dale set about the difficult task of provisioning her.

❧❧

Mozambique Island might be the capital of Portugal's East African empire, but it was totally incapable of sustaining its own inhabitants. Even the most basic prerequisite for survival, water, was at a premium. With no springs to supply them, people had either to bring water from the mainland or rely on rainwater stored in cisterns, leading to a homogenised domestic architecture of white limestone houses with flat roofs; and without farms or market, individuals and families kept a few animals each. Everything else came in by ship from India, from Portugal or the mainland. There was little development: the north was taken up by the fort, the centre by the town, and the south was largely given over to stone quarries. Successive governors had actively hindered progress, devoting their energies to making their own fortunes. The majority of the population had no choice but to endure the privations: exiles, they had little hope of ever returning to Portugal, and, in an attempt to maintain the population, those who came voluntarily and then married were strictly forbidden to leave the island which measured a mere 2 miles long and ⅓ mile wide.

Dale chose his provisions thoughtfully. Rice, biscuit, rum, sugar, coffee and salted fish were the main items of food and drink. There was no salted meat available, so he bought salt and empty casks with which to preserve beef when he reached Toleary where beef was abundant. Anxious about the health of those he had left behind, he managed to get hold of a small box of medicines over which the physician in charge of the hospital ran an approving eye. Nor did he forget the King. If the man had lived up to his promise to take care of the survivors, a suitable gift was in order, and there was nothing the King would prize more than half a dozen flintlocks with a suitable supply of flints, balls and powder.

Reckoning that by now the survivors would be dressed in little better than rags, Dale also ordered a basic set of clothes – shirt, jacket, trousers and shoes – for each person, providing a sudden boost to the local economy. The master of the ship, clearly entering into the spirit of the mission, offered to purchase suitable clothes for the ladies, and did so 'very genteely' out of his own pocket. Whether the clothes were loaded with the rest of the stores, or left to await the return of the snow Dale does not say.

Dale's constitution was bearing up remarkably well; that of Thomas de Souza was not so good. With the Governor exerting himself on behalf of the *Winterton* survivors, and Dale's ship due to sail on 25 February, de Souza knew himself to be less vital to the rescue mission and booked a passage in the French slaver. This was neither indolence nor selfishness on his part. Mauritius was a regular port of call for ships going to and from India: the sooner he could get there, the sooner he could tell the HEIC of the fate of their ship. Dale entrusted to him the letter written and signed by the officers at Toleary on 11 September 1792, carefully detailing the circumstances of the wreck and the impossibility of saving any of the Company's property.

❦

Alarm bells were by now ringing in Madras and Calcutta. Nothing had been heard of the *Winterton* since she left the Cape of Good Hope, and after so long the worst had to be feared. Her failure to arrive was more than a disaster for those on board: as correspondence from the HEIC's Indian headquarters at Fort William, Calcutta, reveals, there were repercussions in India:

'The Govt. of Fort St. George (Madras) acquainted us in a letter dated 6th January that in consequence of the delay in the arrival of the Winterton and doubts of her safety they wished to be supplied with various articles of stationery for the use of the public office.' (Fort William, 8 March 1793)[95]

At Calcutta itself the authorities would draw from the situation a lesson on the wisdom of putting all their eggs in one basket:

'The Hospital Board requested that medicines consigned to the Presidency may be sent in the first four ships of the season as an accommodation that would be found extremely useful to obviate the risk of disappointment that would be suffered by the loss of any one ship as in the instance of the Winterton which contained the largest proportion of the medicines for Bengal.'[96]

❈❈❈

The French slaver reached Mauritius on 17 April. By that time, and unbeknown to both de Souza and Dale, events in Europe had taken an ominous turn. For France's neighbours, the French Revolution had reached a crisis with the execution of Louis XVI on 21 January.

'At home this killing of a King has divided all friends; and abroad it has united all enemies. Revolutionary Propogandism; Atheism; Regicide; total destruction of social order in this world! All Kings, and lovers of Kings, and haters of Anarchy, rank in coalition; as in a war for life,' declaimed Thomas Carlyle.[97]

The British Government, already paranoid about the possible spread of revolutionary fervour across the Channel, expelled the French Ambassador, effectively severing all diplomatic relations. On 1 February, war was declared, a war that would not only be fought on European soil and in European waters but which would soon extend to the colonies of the Indian Ocean as fast as ships could carry the news. Thus far the fate of those who had embarked on the

Winterton had been decided by the forces of nature; from now on, their fortunes would be inextricably linked to the course and conduct of the war.

❧❧❧

The instant that reliable news of the conflict reached Alexandria the British Consul, Baldwin, alive to the danger to the HEIC's interests, wrote a hasty warning. Baldwin

> '…was so anxious to promote the public service and so desirous to enable the Company's Government to derive every possible advantage from the communication that he declared himself responsible in his public character for the truth of the information, and assured them that they might act upon it with confidence, adding that all the British and Dutch vessels in the ports of France had been seized.'[98]

Baldwin's willingness to stake his reputation on his source paid dividends. His letter reached Fort St George, Madras on 2 June,[99] and Fort William, Calcutta nine days later, and was acted upon immediately. French ships in British ports along the coast of India were seized along with all the small factories,[100] and Colonel John Brathwaite was summoned to discuss the best way of capturing the troublesome French stronghold of Pondicherry which clung like a limpet to the coast south of Madras. By the end of July, he had 10,500 men, of whom just under a third were Europeans, ready to besiege the town.

❧❧❧

While waiting in Mauritius for his passage to India, de Souza found an American brig preparing to sail for St Helena and handed the officers' letter and list of survivors to her captain with instructions to see it forwarded to the Court of Directors of the HEIC by the first available vessel, and he also provided basic information to Captain Dennis of the vessel *Maria*[101] which was sailing for Bombay. On

2 May he himself embarked on the French ship, *Le Brutus* which was bound for Pondicherry.

❧❂❧

With de Souza gone, Dale finished his preparations. The original sailing date was delayed until 1 March, and that gave him time to see something of life on the island. He was not impressed, and could well understand why the wealthiest had houses on the mainland overlooking the island. The only social life occurred after dark when people either strolled about or took their chairs outside and enjoyed a smoke and a chat, and Dale met some interesting characters. Marine hazards and disasters were, unsurprisingly, a popular topic of conversation. He got to know a man who had been a passenger in that very Portuguese ship whose remains he had seen on the beach north of Toleary; the survivor told Dale that his captain had sailed to Mozambique in the ship's longboat, but by the time he returned only four weeks later many of the survivors were dead of fever. Dale was already looking at a delay of six months.

Another acquaintance was a young Moslem, one of the Governor of Anjouan's sons, who had also had found himself at Mozambique after his ship was lost. All he had left to his name were a few lengths of cloth saved from the wreck, but with typical Arab generosity to strangers in misfortune he insisted on sharing them with Dale. A Portuguese captain discussed with him the vagaries of the local currents, relating how he had left the harbour one night, steered northwards, and yet found himself at daylight 12 miles south of it. Such conversation may have dampened Dale's hopes, but it passed the time until 1 March when he at last sailed for Madagascar.

The 23-day voyage was tedious but uneventful, other than that he had ample opportunity to observe the retarding effect of the Channel currents on the vessel and speculate on their possible contribution to the wreck of the *Winterton*. Even the wind conspired to hold them back. As they lay at anchor some $2°$ north of St Augustine's Bay, Dale had his first sign that all was not well with those he had left at Toleary. Some canoes came up to them, and after a little persuasion the Madagascans came aboard. To Dale's dismay, one of them was wearing a European hat which, he was absolutely certain, must have come from the *Winterton* people. All his questions met with either incomprehension or a single, highly suggestive gesture: the native ran the edge of his hand across his throat. Highly agitated over the safety of his comrades, Dale assumed the worse from this mime. Later he decided that perhaps the native served some other potentate and feared he would be killed if he went with Dale to Toleary and fell into the hands of the King of Baba.

With a heavy heart John Dale endured the rest of the voyage down the coast until, on Sunday, 24 March, the captain dropped anchor in St Augustine's Bay and hoisted the Portuguese flag. There was no reaction from the shore. The ship fired a few guns, but it was a while before a canoe came out. When it did, Dale recognised John Slater, the Boatswain, although he was terribly wasted and sick. His news confirmed the Third Mate's worst fears: back in January, the last time he had heard anything from Toleary, the death toll had passed 80, and was rising at the rate of two or three a day.

Dale kept his thoughts to himself, but if he did not curse both the fatal missing chart and the governor of Sofala he was more than human.

The following morning he took the ship's boat up to the coast before Toleary and set off along the river to the village, carrying as much as he could by way of supplies. Six months ago he had helped bring the yawl down that same league of sandy ground, encouraged by the prayers and hopes of those left behind. Now he returned alone. Wilton, Adams and Longster lay in their graves at Sena; the other two seamen could be anywhere. De Souza, at least, should be safely on his way to Mauritius.

He stopped. The huts had come into sight. Men and women were dragging themselves towards him, wasted, sickly, skeletal, speaking his name in disbelief, calling him their deliverer. 'My abilities are unequal to paint the miserable state in which I found them.

Oppressed with mental affliction, their calamities were increased by the appearance of a contagious fever.'[102] As best they could, they followed him into the village to where the King sat under his tree on an unlikely throne: a chair washed ashore from the wreck. News that a Portuguese ship had been sighted at anchor had obviously reached him and he received the gift of muskets and powder courteously but without any sign that he knew his visitor; even when Dale explained why he had come he looked at him as if he were a stranger. It was the King's interpreter, Tom Bush, who made him understand that here was the man whom everyone had supposed long drowned, and then recognition dawned and he got up, flung his arms round Dale and wept with joy and relief. Seeing Dale's distress at the condition of his comrades, and thinking he was being held responsible, he told him: 'It was not the King of Baba who made the Englishmen die, but God. I supplied them with bullocks and rice...to make them live; but if God do this thing, who can help?'

Those who were too weak to move outside their encampment beyond the village had heard the wild musket fire, singing and shouting, without any reason to think that the native celebrations had anything to do with them. Buchan was lying down in his hut when Tom Bush put his head round the door, laughing and grinning, tormenting him with the promise that 'I would hear something that would make me too much glad'.

Incredulity greeted the news when Bush finally broke it to them in plain words and Dale himself arrived following his audience with the King. 'It was so improbable that we could for some time only with difficulty credit our own eyes'.[103] With equal amazement they heard something of Dale's adventures.

'The time seems long for so short a way,' concluded Buchan, 'but when one considers the numberless hardships they underwent, all cause of wonder will cease; and it will only remain for us to entertain a most grateful remembrance of their sufferings to which we certainly owe our preservation.'[104]

Chapter Fourteen

A Sail Astern

Dale organised the evacuation as quickly as he could, setting the fervent wish of the survivors to leave against the need to secure sufficient provisions. By the evening improvised hammocks had been rigged up and the ladies were being carried down to where the ship's boat lay ready to take them to St Augustine's Bay. Those men who were too ill to walk the 3 miles were likewise brought down to the shore and helped into the canoes that would convey them the same distance. The canoes were limited as to the number they could take, and the boat belonging to the little snow was proportionately small, so that it was the following day before everyone came together. The ladies were taken straight out to the snow and housed in the only cabin; the men remained on shore.

While waiting his turn, George Buchan briefly left his hut and returned to find one of the locals in the process of gathering up his pathetic bundle of belongings. 'I made a sort of expiring effort to save it by running at the thief who was probably scared of detection for he might almost have knocked me down with his little finger. I think, however, all was rescued.'

When he heard that Dale had organised clothes for everyone, William Dunn, still first and foremost the Company's man, was horrified at the expense, and told him that there was no possibility of the HEIC bearing the cost of any garments for the soldiers. If Dale went ahead with that part of the distribution it would have to come out of his own pocket; and Dale, already having to bear the loss on his private trade and the fact that his wages had stopped on 20 August 1792, was unable to see everyone provided for.

Although the rest of his comrades could barely wait to be quit of the place, one man discovered the power of love to be stronger than any fear of malaria and early death. 'One of our sailors, it would appear, discovered charms here which I could not, in voluntarily choosing to remain behind', recalled a baffled John Dale. Or, as a dispatch from Fort William was reported: 'having formed a tender connection with a young Madagascarian female, he preferred the arms of the jetty nymph to all the pleasure of returning to his former life and society'.[105]

For 10 days the snow lay at anchor while Dale and the crew of the ship salted beef and took on water. He had abandoned any plans of sailing for the Cape: instead they would return to Mozambique Island, get what medical help they could, and then proceed to India when a suitable ship became available. His decision to return had probably been made when he chartered the ship; had it not been, the condition of his companions would have forced it.[106]

On 3 April he gave orders to weigh anchor. More than 260 had survived the original shipwreck; only 130 remained alive to watch the island recede into the distance. Conditions on the ship were as miserable as those they had left behind. The men were quartered on the open deck while the women sheltered in their cramped cabin. Buchan commented:

'The passage to Mozambique happily did not exceed a week but having been exposed during that time frequently to heavy rains with a hot sun by day and the chill of night our many severe complaints were no doubt aggravated by these causes; and if the voyage had not been providentially short the effects would probably have proved very fatal.'

Only too grateful for their rescue no one complained, although during the voyage seven people died, two of them from the original complement of passengers. With a fair wind it took only eight days before the brig came round the fort and dropped anchor before the gate of the Captania and European civilization.

Dale and Buchan differed in their accounts of the treatment received on Mozambique Island. Seven years younger, inexperienced and sick, Buchan was desperately disappointed; John Dale, alive to the limitations of the place, and writing a semi-official report, was moved by the kindness of the people.

'I would be wanting in gratitude, as well as deficient in...truth...did I neglect at representing...the flattering reception we met with from the Governor and inhabitants of Mozambique who surveyed our forlorn condition with sentiments that do honour to humanity; prepared an hospital for our sick and vied with each other in every soothing attention to the ladies.'[107]

The Minister took Dale and Dunn into his house as guests, while Charlotte and Mary Bristow were invited to stay at Government House by the Governor's lady. During Dale's absence, de Mello e Castro had been succeeded by Diogo de Souza, Count of Rio Pardo (no relation to Thomas), who had arrived on 19 March and was as anxious as his predecessor to assist.

Buchan, however, was less than impressed:

'When we arrived the ladies were taken into the houses of different individuals and there was a house provided for the gentlemen. The Government advanced us money for our expenses…But we were badly situated, we were among a set of people who imposed upon us on all hands. Instead of our misfortunes attracting their particular attentions it rather seemed to occasion their neglect. For a day or two after we went there, many of the people from curiosity came to see us. But their kindness was too much forced and too unnatural to last. We were hardly ever after visited by a single person…Those who were very ill were sent to the hospital, but their treatment there was fully as bad as ours.'[108]

By contrast:

'I was more pleased', Dale wrote later, 'with the hospital than anything. I visited our people in it once or twice a day, and always found it neat and clean with constant attendance; they burnt a sort of berry which was very grateful to the smell.'[109]

Medical facilities, nonetheless, were limited. Although Buchan came to admit that Dale was probably correct in saying that the Portuguese did what they could for the sick, he stood by his view that they were seriously lacking in medical knowledge.

All they could do was bleed already weakened patients and give them sugar and water. Bitterly Buchan noted that during the two months they spent at Mozambique about 30 people died – a higher mortality rate than on Madagascar, but not necessarily worse than it would have been had they remained another two months at Toleary. The casualties now included the first woman, Miss Lyne. She had been ill, but she was still in shock from the death of her brother, William, and it took a great effort and a lot of tears before she could so much as ask Andrew Ramsay[110] how his brother, Henry, was doing. Shortly afterwards she died, along with the Fifth Mate, John Moore.

Moore's death left Dale as the only surviving officer, with the exception of Dunn, who was quick to assert his authority and share with Dale responsibility for the next stage of the rescue plan. There was still no Portuguese Government ship which could be pressed into service. An Indiaman was expected, but that was leaving too much to chance, so the Third Officer and Purser resorted again to bills drawn on the East India Company in order to charter a private vessel for Madras.

The ship was the 250-ton brig[111] *Joachim*, with a cargo superintendent by the name of Eusebio Francesco Suarez. She was hardly a thoroughbred of the ocean and her crew included four Indian seamen, known as Lascars, and one Sarang. The cost was a hefty 1600 rupees, bringing the total borrowed from the Governor to 5069 rupees, but however much Dunn would have liked to save the Company's purse, he must have known that beggars could not be choosers.

Two English whalers, the brig *Sally Ellis* and the *Mercury* attempted to enter the harbour by night from the north and without paying the 40 dollars pilotage charge. The following morning, the *Mercury* was on the rocks, while the other ship had had a narrow esape after striking and was only too glad to pay the pilot. The locals had a good laugh at captains who would risk life and livelihood for a mere 40 dollars apiece, but Captain Day of the *Mercury* was in serious trouble. Everything that could be salvaged from the ship was to be auctioned, but Dale doubted he got anything like the value, even though it represented equipment in short supply on the island. His problems were a little alleviated by finding fellow Englishmen on the island, and some of his crew decided to go with Dale. William Bowman/Beaumont, Robert Inglewight and Ben Hammond did not appear either in the Receipt Book or on the published list of the saved, but they were to be listed as being on the *Joachim*, making them likely to have come from the *Mercury*. The rest were to remain on the island with their Captain until the *Sally Ellis* returned from her next period at sea. Another person left behind under the protection of the merchants was Mrs Bellasis who was too ill to continue the journey.

❧

On 18 May, Captain Dennis and the *Maria* reached Bombay from Mauritius with the first news of what had befallen the *Winterton*, but it would be another three months before the facts were known in London. The worst, however, had already been feared, and *Lloyd's List*, 28 May 1793, published an ominous entry: 'Bombay 13th Feb.: No account of Winterton.' There were grim faces around the India House and dismay among the underwriters, shipowners, masters and merchants transacting their business in the coffee rooms at Lloyds in the Royal Exchange. The news posted out of London by mail coach; it spread along the Thames among the shipyards and the vessels at anchor, seeping by word of mouth through those water-front districts such as Southwark where seamen and their families lived. Although ships could be out of touch for months at a time, there were often 'speakings' at sea, when one ship would hail anoth-er and report the sighting at the nearest port. Nothing had been heard of the *Winterton* since she had left the Cape nearly 10 months earlier. Now it was clear she had never reached India. For Christian Dundas with her new baby, Agnew Talbot anxious for her son, Isabella Rowland with two members of her family on board, Lord Dalhousie with two brothers feared drowned and Alice Slater with her Boatswain husband at sea it was a terrible time. 'No account' could so easily mean 'foundered with all hands'.

❧

The authorities at Bombay Castle decided not to wait to see whether John Dale had succeeded in rescuing his fellows. With no East Indiamen in port, they hastily chartered the *Gloucester*, a 294-ton Indian-built vessel[112] and started to prepare her for a relief expe-dition. Owned and commanded by Robert Billamore, she usually engaged in local trade and transport between Indian ports, but she was newly built and sound and the government of Bombay supplied her with 'an ample store of provisions, wines, cloaths, and all sorts of necessaries that humanity could suggest'. On 2 June[113] she left for Madagascar.

❀❀❀

The HEIC policed its local waters with a small navy known as the Bombay Marine. Pirates and smugglers were its peacetime quarry, but whenever war broke out or was carried into the Indian Ocean the ships played an active role in defending Company possessions, sometimes alone, sometimes in concert with the Royal Navy. Now the vessels of the Marine cruised the Malabar and Coromandel Coasts looking for French ships to intercept. On 30 May the 18-gun brig *Drake* sighted one.

Le Brutus had been enjoying an uneventful voyage with Thomas de Souza at last able to relax. She had left Mauritius on 3 May, and 27 days later found her past Cuddalore and close to her destination. Her captain may well have been unaware that hostilities had broken out and surrendered to the *Drake* without so much as firing a shot for the honour of the flag; but for de Souza the capture was an advantage, taking him directly to Madras where he disembarked on the 1 June with his incredible story.

The press reported it in full at Calcutta, Bombay and Madras. Information could travel swiftly. De Souza's report dated 2 June at Madras, together with the letter written by the *Winterton*'s officers and the list of survivors and casualties among the officers and passengers, was reprinted across one and half columns of the *Bombay Courier*[114] on 13 June along with an advertisement for the latest edition of Johnson's *Dictionary*, a selection of births, marriages and deaths, and the account of how a drayman in London had horse-whipped a Frenchman for insulting a 'great personage'. The account was updated to include the three deaths in Sena but inaccurately listed both Mr Silk and William Coloquhoun among those who died in the wreck, and was, of course, written in ignorance of the rising death toll on Madagascar and Mozambique Island. Many of those who read the article must have assumed that their friends and relatives, originally supposed drowned to the last man, were alive and comparatively well.

❧

On 10 June the *Joachim* sailed from Mozambique Island with 85 survivors of the *Winterton* on board, plus the trio from the *Mercury*. They included Isabella and Margaret Cullen, Charlotte and Mary Bristow, Isabella Baillie, Lieutenant Brownrigg and 33 of his men, with just two cabins between them all. Although Madras was the destination, the immediate difficulties of provisioning at Mozambique caused them to put into Anjouan – popularly known to sailors as Johanna – in the Comoro Islands, a mere four days later, and there on the bustling island, they discovered the nearest thing to paradise since the Cape.

The Portuguese had driven the Moslems out of East Africa, but their influence had stopped there, and Anjouan remained a southerly Arab bastion, a favoured port of call and friendly towards the English. The general lethargy of the Portuguese gave way to flowing eastern robes and a zest for trade and hospitality; in place of the monotonous diet of Mozambique came a brilliant cornucopia of fruits and other food. Buchan admired their spirit and intelligence, and was suitably entertained by the waterfront characters who made a living from newly arrived ships and who had fallen into the same practice of adopting European titles that he had seen among the aristocracy of Madagascar.

'Nothing amuses a stranger more than seeing Dukes and Lords of every degree crowding on board…with their various testimonials and soliciting employment. The Duke of Y— has good lodgings; Lord M washes well; Lord L supplies good fruit and is honest in his dealings…We remained about a week, which most, I believe, passed very pleasantly on shore, getting accommodation in the different houses as best they could. The house I was in was comfortable enough, though small; and a good deal surrounded by walls: the same apartment answered for eating and sleeping, and was occupied by three of four of us. We relished much their curries, and an abundant supply of oranges and other fruits.'

It was a pity for the *Winterton* survivors that their health was so poor, otherwise they might have enjoyed exploring the interior of the island with its mountains and waterfalls and rich plantlife. Almost 'all the perfumes of Arabia', which Lady Macbeth thought unequal to the task of sweetening her bloodstained hands, could be made from the flora of Anjouan. Instead, Buchan's companions had to content themselves with the white sand and fresh breeze of the coast. Dale met up with his old acquaintance from Mozambique, the Sultan's son, who had made his way home and was delighted to greet Dale in proper fashion, loading him with presents of fruit. The Sultan himself had heard all about Dale's problems and, contrasting the size of the *Joachim* with the number of people she had to carry, suggested that it might be well for some of the *Winterton* people to remain on the island until an expected Indiaman arrived. Dale, already working on the necessity of stopping at Ceylon for final provisions, let the offer be known. Ten seamen plus John Jolly, a 17-year-old midshipman, took up the offer. The remaining 77 re-boarded their ship on 19 June for what they fervently hoped or fondly expected to be the penultimate leg of the voyage.

§✖§

News of war in Europe had reached St Helena, that vital speck of Britain in the mid-Atlantic, much earlier; and the Governor had taken immediate steps to safeguard British shipping. The two Royal Navy ships, *Thetis* and *Leopard* lay at anchor in the harbour as a motley convoy of India ships, whalers and French prizes gathered ready for escort to England. Three East Indiamen, *Talbot, Winterton* and *King George*, the last ships of the season, were missing, and the likely date of their arrival was so uncertain that Francis Hartwell, Captain of HMS *Thetis* was preparing to sail with what he had. Hostilities at sea had already erupted on a very small scale: at the very beginning of the month the *Thetis* had captured one French ship together with some useful correspondence from the Governor of Mauritius; and the ex-governor of Pondicherry who was opposed to the revolutionary regime in Paris was travelling under Hartwell's protection in the *Rose* to seek asylum in England[115].

On 15 June, Hartwell received de Souza's letter via the master of the American brig which had just dropped anchor. Now there were only two outstanding Indiamen.

❦

The *Joachim* had been at sea for a fortnight and, despite her inadequate sailing qualities, covered almost half the distance to Ceylon. At 8am on 7 July a sail was spotted astern, which the seamen among them put down for an English ship.

'A vessel supposed to be from England or some part of India was a very novel sight and imagination worked overtime: some longing for cheese and porter, others for the long untasted luxury of Port wine, while others again fancied a wish to know a little of what was passing in the world that we had been so long out of', wrote Buchan.

The last group was to be satisfied long before the rest.

The stranger was a fast sailer, making about twice the speed of the Portuguese tub. By midday she was less than a mile away and the Captain duly shortened sail in order to hail her, only to be greeted by a cannon shot to leeward, effectively an order to heave-to. For reasons best known to himself, he stood on, and a minute later a second shot screamed directly over the *Joachim*. At the same time the Tricolour, flag of the revolutionary republic of France, was run up.

This time the Captain took the hint and hove to. The French ship came alongside and sent on board four or five officers to examine the ship's papers. As a neutral ship, the *Joachim* was technically unaffected by the war but she was carrying English passengers and, as Buchan observed, 'I suppose we (miserable cargo as we were) were considered contraband goods.'

The French ship was *Le Mutin*, a 120-ton privateer from Mauritius under Captain Jean Mallet, one of the first to be fitted out after the declaration of war was known on the island. Under her original name of *Adonis* and under the command of Captain Joseph Auger she had sailed from Nantes on 29 November 1792, reaching Port Louis, Mauritius on 13 April the following year. There she had been converted to the 12-gun privateer *Le Mutin*. Mallet, who had arrived from France on her, along with his relative, Henri Mallet, was now appointed her captain. On 8 June he weighed anchor to begin his very first cruise.[116]

A privateer differed from a pirate ship in that her commander held a letter of marque from his government authorising him to attack the enemies of his country in time of war, while a pirate ship preyed indiscriminately and without legitimacy. Privateers were useful in that they were privately financed, bore all their own risks and thus assisted their country in wartime at no cost to the government. Prize ships were taken into service or sold along with their cargoes, and the proceeds shared among those with a stake in the enterprise. The rumour of a large Dutch East Indiaman in the area, undermanned through sickness and therefore highly vulnerable, had caused Mallet to sail from Mauritius ahead of the other privateers.

The little brig *Joachim* was hardly the sort of ship for which *Le Mutin* was actually searching, and stopping her had now left Mallet with a problem. The action, even if legally justified, would hardly augment his reputation: moreover, the court in Mauritius might well decide he had gone beyond his commission and order her release. On the other hand, to permit her to proceed to India was to advertise his presence in the area, alert the British and the Dutch to the

RIGHT: John Dale, aged about 14, by an unknown artist.
(Reproduced by kind permission of the Reverend Richard Adams; photography by Kitchenhams of Bournemouth)

MIDDLE: This romantic engraving purports to show Captain Dundas assisting one of the female passengers on to the poop just before the *Winterton* started to break up. From *Shipwrecks and Disasters At Sea* Volume 2, published in 1812. (British Library)

ABOVE: Surf breaks over the *Winterton* as the first rafts leave the ship during the afternoon of 21 August 1792. The ship's masts and rigging have been cut away and the kedge anchor continues to hold the hull broadside-on to the surf. This was originally printed in *A Narrative of The Loss Of The Winterton* by George Buchan in 1820, and it is likely that Buchan would have given his approval to the illustrations for his book. (Photography by Steve Cummings)

ABOVE: The last moments of the *Winterton*: as the poop floats free and John Dale's group cling to their raft, the remaining crew and passengers can be seen on the ship's starboard side. From *A Narrative of The Loss Of The Winterton* by George Buchan, 1820. (Photography by Steve Cummings)

RIGHT: The King of Baba and a Madagascan lady, and native women grinding corn. These illustrations, published in March 1793 in the *Gentleman's Magazine*, well before the news of the *Winterton* had reached England, were said to be the work of a young Englishman who had recently visited Madagascar and drawn the pictures from life. (Photography by Steve Cummings)

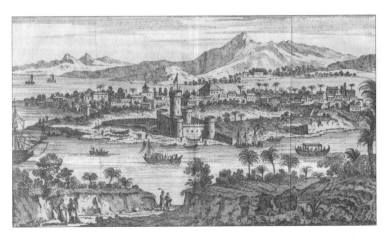

The Honourable East India Company's ship *Winterton*, painted c.1783 by
Thomas Luny (1759–1837). The painting shows three contrasting views of
the ship. (Reproduced by kind permission of Colin Denny)

Sofala, Mozambique, the Portuguese settlement on the Mozambique coast to
which Dale sailed in the yawl. From *Lo stato presente di tutti i paesi e popoli del
mondo* by T Salmon, Venice 1765. (Reproduced by kind permission of the
Centro Studi Archeologia Africana di Milano)

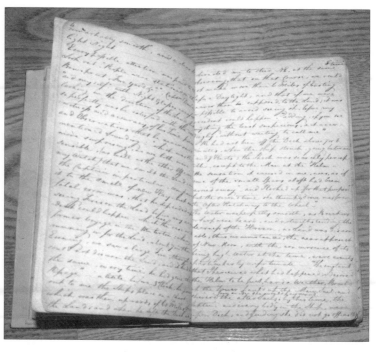

Entries from John Dale's journal. (Reproduced by kind permission of the Reverend Richard Adams; photography by Kitchenhams of Bournemouth)

A view of Norfolk, seen from Gosport, Virginia, where John Dale was held prisoner after the capture of the *Scorpion* by Rear Admiral Vanstabel. Aquatint. (National Maritime Museum)

Port Louis, Mauritius, from where the French privateers preyed on British ships and to which the *Winterton* survivors were taken after the *Joachim* became a French prize. The view is taken from the Champ de Mars, looking out to sea. Aquatint, 1813. (National Maritime Museum)

John Dale as a captain
c.1805 by James Nixon
(1741–1812).
Miniature.
(Reproduced courtesy
of Bonhams Auction
House)

George Buchan in later
life, by Sir John Watson
Gordon (1788–1864).
(Reproduced by kind
permission of Mr
Alexander Hay)

ABOVE: Captain Dale in the cabin of the HEIC's *Streatham*. (Reproduced by kind permission of the Reverend Richard Adams)

ABOVE RIGHT: A diver measures an encrusted cannon during Dr Robert Sténuit's expedition to survey the *Winterton* wreck in 1985 (see Appendix II). (Dr Robert Sténuit)

RIGHT: Removing some of the iron ballast to investigate the wreck. (Dr Robert Sténuit)

Shards of china reveal a glimpse of life on board.
(Dr Robert Sténuit)

The ship's cargo included copper packed into wooden chests.
(Dr Robert Sténuit)

A handful of Pieces of Eight – almost all that remained of the *Winterton*'s cargo of silver.
(Dr Robert Sténuit)

new threat, and weaken his chances of catching his real quarry.

The St Malo-born captain made his decision quickly enough. Despite the protests of her master, the *Joachim* was to be sent under one officer and a prize crew to Mauritius; and, to minimise over-crowding, 23 of the healthiest passengers, together with the Portuguese captain and four of his foreign crew, were to transfer as prisoners to *Le Mutin*. By choosing to take off only the healthiest, Mallet showed both prudence and a degree of compassion. Sick passengers would be docile, requiring less vigilance, and Mallet would have been reluctant to spare too many of his men. Of necessity, a privateer carried a much bigger crew than she required for herself: the extras were needed to board enemy ships and, once subdued, sail them into port. Mallet commanded some 70 men: if he boarded an Indiaman he would need most of them.

Buchan failed to mention who did the choosing or whether it was a matter of volunteers. The 20 comprised 16 soldiers, 4 seamen, Boatswain John Slater, Lieutenant Henry Brownrigg, and Third Officer John Dale.

The two ships remained alongside one another well into the evening while arrangements were being made, and those on the *Joachim* were 'visited by almost the whole ship's company exulting over the mighty prize they had made of a cargo of unfortunate invalids.'[117] Later, Buchan added: 'Our captors had certainly not much ground for boasting; but the best friends of the French will allow that this is a weak point, and that with them the passion is susceptible of being nourished on a very spare diet.'

At dusk the two vessels parted company, with the French prize-captain under orders from Mallet to make all speed to Mauritius. *Le Mutin* resumed her cruise, and whether devastated by events or merely resigned to yet another setback, Dale could at least say honestly, 'the distress occasioned by our accumulated misfortunes was, in a slight degree, alleviated by the polite attention of the French captain and his officers'[118] whose only fault was a propensity to boast.

As well as a crew which included nine officers and two surgeons, *Le Mutin* carried a total of 18 guns: two 8-pounders mounted on her forecastle, and ten 3-pounders made up her basic armoury, but she also possessed six 1-pounder swivel guns. She had the potential to cause trouble.

Chapter Fifteen

An Unexpected Friend

Alternately friendly and hostile to one another, the Dutch and British had been competitors east of the Cape for the better part of 200 years, and if by 1793 the Dutch East India Company – known by its initials VOC (Vereenigde Oostindische Compagnie) – did not operate on quite the same scale as its British counterpart, it was still a commercial power, holding the Cape, Ceylon and parts of the East Indies and meeting up with the French, British and even the Danes to buy tea at Canton. Their East Indiamen were magnificent vessels, typified by the 900-ton *Ceylon* laying to all intents and purposes sleepily at anchor in the midday heat of the Tuticorin Roads with her sails furled while her Captain discussed business and pleasure with the Cargo Superintendent of another Dutch ship.[119]

Launched in 1791 at the yard belonging to the Amsterdam Chamber of the VOC, the *Ceylon* was on her maiden voyage. She had sailed from Texel on 15 January 1793, exactly six months earlier, with a crew of 138 men, 89 soldiers and 2 passengers, spent the better part of a month at the Cape and reached Ceylon without any problems on 9 July.[120] Now she was anchored off Tuticorin, a small but important Dutch possession on the Indian mainland, famous for its pearls.

Sleepy she looked, even defenceless, but Captain Pierius Muntz of Harlingen was not a gentleman to be caught napping and he had her anchored on a spring,[121] primarily to help turn her round in the estuary when the time came to sail but also as a precaution. Two cables were run out holding the ship under tension rather than letting her ride at a single anchor or between both bower anchors. In those waters any ship had the potential to be hostile, and when the officer of the watch reported a vessel, probably two masted, in view Muntz took no chances. It might prove nothing more than an innocent merchantman out of Colombo, but he gave orders to clear the decks and prepare for action if required. Seamen scrambled to man the guns; soldiers hurried on deck to load their muskets. The unknown ship stood on, flying the American flag – no uncommon sight – and shaping her course directly for the Dutchman. That was enough for Muntz: he gave orders to sound the call to action stations, run up the national flag and give the smaller vessel a shot across the bows to make her heave-to well away from his ship.

Against a vessel of such size and potential armament, Jean Mallet and *Le Mutin* needed speed, surprise and luck. An unsuspecting, under-manned Indiaman with a sick crew and half her guns stowed in the hold was easier prey than one that was fully manned and alive to danger. With his guns run out, he ignored both the first and the second warning shot and closed in to lay alongside the *Ceylon*.

Muntz fired a third and final warning shot. In response, the Stars and Stripes were hauled down, and up went the French flag and pennant to end all doubt about the situation. At the same time a volley of canister crashed out from the 3-pounders and swivel guns on the forecastle of *Le Mutin*, and Dutch sailors and soldiers dropped, not all of them wounded. A furious Muntz cursed them for cowards, swore to shoot through the head any man who dared to duck down again, and, as the Frenchman came up to board, ordered his soldiers and gunners to fire.

They were at close quarters, too close for *Le Mutin* to manoeuvre. With a shuddering crack she caught her bowsprit against the Dutchman and when *Ceylon*'s guns opened up they smashed through the foremast and rigging, bringing everything down in a tangle of splintered wood, canvas and rope.

On the quarterdeck Muntz clenched his fist in satisfaction. The French would have to clear the forecastle before they could get back to their two powerful forward guns. No longer was he thinking of merely defending his vessel: the possibility of outright victory lay before him, and beneath the merchant navy uniform beat the heart of a de Ruyter. He bellowed orders to his officers and men, exhorting them to seize the chance and take the offensive without giving the French a chance to board.

Thwarted, Mallet let his privateer make leeway, firing as she drifted away from those heavy broadside cannon. Better to attack from behind, where the Indiaman's armament was lightest. His gunners fired at will, mostly loading case shot, and from the deck his men were strafing the *Ceylon*'s deck with musket fire and balls from the swivel guns.

'Cut the cable!' commanded Muntz, insensible to his own danger as the quarterdeck took the brunt of the French fire. Dutch muskets snapped out a steady reply as the soldiers fired and reloaded as fast as they could. Men fell around him, casualties from burning cartridges as well as musket and cannon balls. Two soldiers were shot dead on the poop; another was cut down by a cannon ball. As the urgent knives began to hack though the heavy hawser, strand by strand, a ball smashed through a seaman. Below on the gun deck, the crews were ramming home their shot.

A young midshipman stationed by the flag and shaking with fear watched the proceedings, saw several of his shipmates groaning on the deck in their own blood, and in a fit of blind panic started to haul down the Dutch colour as if anticipating an order to surrender. The instant Muntz saw what was happening he ordered it to be raised again, and the youth, in equal terror of his Captain and the enemy, fled to the shelter of a pile of crates and took no further part in the engagement.

As soon as the final strand of rope parted, the huge ship heaved and slowly turned, pivoting on the second anchor to display her portside to the Frenchman. The order to fire was given.

The broadside crashed out. For the likes of Dale[122] and Brownrigg it must have been a hair-raising experience, locked up below deck, able to hear but not to see what was happening and helpless against any ball that might smash through their quarters. Unaware that *Le Mutin* held prisoners, Muntz was demanding precision fire from his gunners, which meant that if they were not trying to bring down her remaining mast they were almost certainly aiming to hole her below the waterline. It was a long 15 minutes[123] for the captives.

The portside blast settled the matter. The damage was so great that Mallet had no choice but to strike the colour. From his quarterdeck the triumphant Muntz hailed his unexpected prize and demanded she lower a boat to send her Captain on board. There was no response from the French. Muntz ordered his men to fire again, and in a final demonstration of their expertise, they brought down the main topmast. The *Ceylon* swung out one of her own boats and lowered it for the Captain-Lieutenant to go across with an armed party, take command of *Le Mutin*, and fetch the French Captain and his two senior officers.

In the meantime the *Ceylon*'s other officers were taking stock of their own damage and casualties. Four men lay dead and 12 had been carried to the surgeon, some of them so seriously wounded that they were more likely to need the services of Johan Cluver, the ship's Chaplain. The Carpenter reported that two shots had breached the bow, and men were detailed to plug the more serious hole. Three shots had gone through the bulwarks of the quarterdeck and one through the bulwark top of the same. The rest of the damage consisted of musketballs lodged in the deck, masts and rigging. By the time *Le Mutin* had struck, the Dutch soldiers had fired 30 times each and exhausted their cartridges. The gunners had got through more than 50 balls.

Mallet came on board and showed his letter of marque issued by Anne-Joseph de Maures de Malartic, the Governor of Mauritius, as proof that he was no common pirate to be taken and hanged. Immediately Muntz demanded to know the whereabouts of other privateers that were ready to sail. This would be vital information for both the VOC and the HEIC. When his prisoner appeared to hesitate, Muntz reminded him that lies would leave him open to the laws of war. That concentrated Mallet's mind: he told his captor that there were another six or seven privateers at Mauritius and four naval ships of between 20 and 30 guns, but at the time of his sailing he did not know their plans. He volunteered the information that he had been hoping to fall in with a weakened vessel from Batavia, the Dutch headquarters in Java, and that there were not enough seamen to man the privateers because so many had been pressed by the navy to serve on the frigates bound for Pondicherry. In answer to an enquiry about his own casualties he claimed to have only four dead and eight wounded, some mortally, although Muntz suspected the butcher's bill might prove to be dearer. He ordered the rest of the prisoners to be handcuffed and rowed across.

On learning that *Le Mutin* herself had prisoners, Muntz gave instructions for them all to be released and brought over. Dale, Brownrigg and the Portuguese Captain found themselves not only free but among friends. Nonetheless, they were fair towards Mallet and his officers and assured Muntz that they had no complaints about their treatment on *Le Mutin*. Reassured on that point, the Dutch Captain duly put the French officers under arrest in his cabin rather than locking them up somewhere less comfortable. He dealt with his wretched midshipman by banishing him from the quarterdeck as an example to others, and concluding that such humiliation was sufficient punishment. It was not the boy's initial panic which angered him so much as the fact that he had gone and hidden himself afterwards.

Dinner at the Captain's table, with the French officers no doubt present, was a cheerful affair, as Dale describes:

'Our old allies[124] were happy in the opportunity of liberating Englishmen from confinement; and Captain Muntz insisted upon our partaking of a handsome entertainment on board the Ceylon, during which time I related the principal circumstances of our heavy and repeated misfortunes.'

Dale already had a story to dine out on, and did he but know it, his adventure was very far from over.

As soon as he could, Muntz wrote a report which his other guest, the super cargo from the *Zeenimph* carried to Tuticorin. Next morning he sent the dead ashore in one boat and all but four of the seamen and petty officers from *Le Mutin* in another. That quartet, three Danes and one Frenchman, had asked to sign on, and Muntz took them willingly, promising them wages of 12 florins a month. He had lost men in the action, good European seamen were hard to find that side of the Cape, and the four were able seamen and quartermasters.

Later, leaving his unexpected guests to enjoy another pleasant night's sleep on board, Muntz had himself been taken ashore with the French officers. The only man from *Le Mutin* left on board, apart from the four sailors, was a French clerk. The soldiers and seamen settled down with their Dutch fellows, while Dale, Brownrigg and the Portuguese Captain shared cabins with the ship's officers. Some of the crew may have been on shore leave.

In the middle of the night, a group of seamen, together with the French clerk, suddenly pointed pistols at the officers on duty and ordered them to consider themselves prisoners of war. What happened next is unclear from the report. Boatswain John Slater blundered into the scene or attempted to intervene, and was swiftly trussed up. Any attempt to get the *Ceylon* underway failed: there was hardly a breath of air to stir the sails. Thwarted, the rebels took to one of the ship's boats, moored alongside, and tried to make off.

A loyal party took to the Captain's gig and made after the deserters, undeterred by a burst of musket fire. Soon enough they caught up with them, and the whole ill-planned mutiny fizzled out. At best it was no more than a piece of opportunism, fuelled by the revolutionary zeal imported from the *Le Mutin* with the French clerk.

When Muntz returned in the morning, his Captain-Lieutenant was able to inform him that he had the mutineers under arrest, and he duly handed them over to the authorities at Tuticorin where their fate as criminals was unlikely to be as pleasant as anything facing the privateers.[125]

🎀

On the same day, 17 July 1793, Captain Robert Billamore in the *Gloucester*, chartered by the government of Bombay to rescue the *Winterton* survivors, dropped anchor in St Augustine's Bay only to find that everyone had been taken off two months earlier. Billamore stayed in the Bay for more than a fortnight, and although he did not make contact with the lovestruck seaman he heard that he was well. After leaving Madagascar he called at Anjouan and there picked up John Jolly and the seamen with him who had been taking full advantage of the warm hospitality of the people and the Sultan. Having no reason to suppose that the rest of the survivors were not safely at Madras, Billamore set a course for the Bay of Bengal.

🎀

During Dale's enforced cruise on *Le Mutin*, hostilities had been steadily worsening on the Coromandel Coast 100 miles south of Madras. Aboard HMS *Minerva* and assisted by the three Indiamen, *Mitford, Royal Charlotte* and *Warley,* Admiral Sir William

Cornwallis, brother of the Marquis, had blockaded Pondicherry in order to prevent seaborne supplies and reinforcements arriving from Mauritius.[126] Mallet had told the truth to Muntz; intelligence received at Fort St George warned Cornwallis that the French *Sybille* and three smaller frigates were bound for the town. The *Sybille* showed herself, but was chased off by the *Minerva* and never reappeared. Later, the British learned that she carried not just supplies but an artillery officer and 150 men. The capture of a small vessel with a cargo of shot and shells was another useful success.

Land operations were in the hands of Colonel John Brathwaite[127] who had been second in command last time the British had besieged Pondicherry and who had the advantage of intimate knowledge of the land and the town. He waited for Colonel Floyd to assemble sufficient troops and told him to make camp a few miles outside the walls. As reinforcements came up, Brathwaite ordered Floyd to occupy the strategic villages beyond the town, cutting off supplies, while at the same time offering protection to any villages within the French district that showed themselves friendly to the British. Satisfied that he had organised sufficient supplies of food and stores for his men, and that the artillery was well on its way, Brathwaite joined the army on 28 July and took operational command. By the 31st he had his whole army, including artillery, on the Red Hills. The force included the 19th Light Dragoons and 4th Native Cavalry, commanded by Colonel Floyd: the Royal Artillery, and the Madras Artillery; the 36th and 52nd Regiments and the 3rd Battalion Madras Europeans all commanded by Lieutenant Commander Nesbitt; the 72nd and 73rd Regiments, plus companies of the 1st and 2nd European Battalions under Lieutenant Commander Baird.[128]

A joint summons from Brathwaite and Admiral Cornwallis failed to bring surrender from Prosper de Clermont inside the city. Brathwaite did some reconnaissance along the south face of the fort, ascertaining that the combination of the French expansion since the previous siege, the contiguity of a branch of the Pannier river, and the probability of flooding, would make it impossible for artillery. Instead, he decided on a ruse. A house and garden on the riverbank about 1200 yards from the fort was turned into an apparent stronghold with gabions and fascines and invested with a party of troops. The French were deceived into thinking that here lay the point from which the British would advance, and accordingly they increased the firepower in that direction. Gradually Brathwaite tightened his grip from the northern coast, round the back of the fort and down to the southern coast, always maintaining his lines of communications. The town that he had helped to raze between 1761 and 1765 – only two Hindu temples survived – and which the French had spent nearly 30 years rebuilding was once more at his mercy.

Brathwaite allowed two of the Engineer Corps to reconnoitre at sea resulting in a plan to attack the north-east angle of the fort. From Cuddalore came supplies of rice and more gabions and fascines, courtesy of Kenworthy, the Company's Resident, along with additional boats.

By 10 August Brathwaite was just about ready to begin the attack.

> 'I therefore resolved that night to begin a battery on the west face of the fort, on a spot previously determined; it was to consist of eight 12-pounders, and two 8-inch mortars, and at a distance of about 800 yards was well calculated to enfilade the works of the north face of the fort against which our attack was directed, and to keep down the fire of them; and under cover of this battery which I expected to be ready in forty-eight hours, I meant to break ground...'

Things did not go entirely to plan: heavy rain made already damp ground impossible, and in the end Brathwaite attacked under cover of darkness on the 12th.

At daylight the French realised where the real attack was coming from and for several days concentrated their fire from the north works, causing significant casualties, including the Chief Engineer, while Brathwaite frantically tried to get the enfilading battery into operation.

❧

Further south, John Dale and his friends had said farewell to their Dutch host and finally succeeded in setting foot on Indian soil, most likely at Tuticorin itself. From there they travelled north west to the nearest British garrison at Pallamcotah on the River Tambraparni where they received a suitably warm welcome. Once news of their arrival became known in the appropriate quarters a boat was sent for them, and they sailed down-river and up the coast. The route took them over Adam's Bridge, the shoal that links Ceylon with India and forces all but small ships to go round the island. At Nagapattinam they fell in with the indefatigable little brig *Drake* whose captain took them on board, and on 19 August they joined Admiral Cornwallis and the *Minerva* off Pondicherry for a grand-stand view of the action and the armies camped up on the Red Hills. But for some of Dale's companions there was a sour end to their adventures. 'The few seamen with me', wrote Dale laconically, 'were pressed.' Buchan's editor felt compelled to add a footnote: 'Considering what these men had already gone through in the pub-lic service it is to be hoped and presumed that this was only done under an urgent necessity.' In time of war the Royal Navy was always short of men, and returning East Indiamen were frequently stopped in the English Channel and relieved of their seamen, exciting the wrath of the East India Company. Out in the unhealthy East Indies, mortality was high, and an outward-bound Indiaman brought a fresh supply of British sailors. The Indiaman's captain was then forced to hire local manpower for his homeward voyage, and the Company had to repatriate the Indian seamen.

The *Drake* did not stay long enough for Dale and Brownrigg to see Brathwaite's enfilading battery come into operation on 20 August. Nor, for that matter, did the French manage to hold out long enough for the Marquis of Cornwallis to appear on the scene. De Clermont capitulated on the 22nd, to the intense annoyance of his Lordship who had expected to be present at the surrender:

> 'I was very desirous of giving my personal assistance on carrying on the last piece of service that was likely to occur during my stay in India, and embarked on board a small French vessel that had been seized and armed in Bengal...By the great and meritorious exertions of the Government of Fort St George...and those of General Brathwaite and of the troops under his command...our batteries were opened against the place sooner than I had expected, and the mutinous and dastardly conduct of the garrison obliged the Governor to surrender the fort several days before my arrival.'

On 20 August the massive but reassuringly familiar fortifications of Fort St George came into Dale's view. The *Drake* hove to off Madras and the Indians in their Masulah boats came out through the surf to take off her passengers.

Madras was an unlikely site for a Presidency: it was not self sufficient – rice and other commodities had to be brought in – and the whole coastline was edged with a surf so violent that ships had to anchor 2 miles offshore; even the native Masulah boatmen were sometimes defeated. As a deterrent to the French and a first line of defence for the Company's riches further north in Bengal, it had justified its existence, and the original fort had been swallowed up by a huge citadel with every defensive feature known to military architects: curtain wall, bastions, ditches, lunette and counterway, barriers, palisades and counter-mined glacis. It was designed to house the Company's entire white population, but that population, including the Governor, Sir Charles Oakley, had demonstrated a decided aversion to inner-city life 'over the shop' and created, instead, a suburban idyll of elegant houses and gardens well away from the walls built at extortionate cost for their protection.

Given the level of luck that had attended them so far, Dale and Brownrigg might well have wondered whether they would be drowned in the very act of reaching the shore. But they made it, exactly 12 months to the day of the wreck, and walked into the Fort with its broad streets, open spaces and impressive (if architecturally impure) mix of Wren and Palladio – all columns, cupolas, pediments and corniced roofs. As well as the Company's offices, it housed a gold mint inside Fort Square, a pantheon, a mulberry plantation and an orphanage where around 150 girls in striped gingham dresses testified not only to the benevolence of the Company but also to the high mortality among their parents.

✹✹

On that very Tuesday, back in the London which Madras attempt-ed to recreate, *Lloyd's List* offered the first report of the wreck:

> 'The Winterton, Dundas, from London to Bengal, was lost on 20th August last on the Island of Madagascar. The Captain, Chief Mate, 40 seamen and 3 passengers lost.'

Captain Hartwell and HMS *Thetis* had left St Helena on 20 June and endured a miserable voyage made worse by the fact that the men had not tasted meat for five months and scurvy had set in so badly that Hartwell expected to send 50 of them to the hospital as soon as he reached Spithead. On entering the English Channel they had run into such a strong and unremitting gale that the whole con-voy had been dispersed, and not until 18 August did he heave to off the Isle of Wight without having regained sight of any of his charges. There he wrote his report[129] for dispatch to the Admiralty; and with it he enclosed all de Souza's lists and letters for forwarding to the India House.

The next day *The Times* gave more details including some names; on the 23rd it published in full the name of every person who had reached land alive, whether passenger, crewman or soldier, updated with the deaths of Wilton, Longster and Adams.[130] With the considerable benefit of hindsight it observed in an adjacent column: 'The Winterton, East Indiaman, seems to have been marked for misfortune from the moment she was launched...'

❦

John Dale's appearance in Madras might reasonably have been expected to generate considerable interest in the local newspaper despite the events at Pondicherry. Instead his name, unlike Brownrigg's, was not mentioned. On the other hand, while at the Presidency he wrote a report which was 'presented' to the Marquis of Cornwallis, perhaps after they had spoken together.

As copied,[131] the document ran to 28 pages of foolscap and was composed with infinite care. Dale gave credit to those who deserved it, played down his own part – and studiously avoided mentioning incidents that might portray Dundas, Chambers or even Spens and Dunn in an unfavourable light. As the only surviving officer his account represented the one authoritative account of what had happened, and, whatever his motives, he put loyalty to his fellow officers before all else.

Brownrigg rejoined the 75th, but the only soldier of that draft ever to find his name on the regimental muster was William Bowker who merited a footnote: 'This man Bowker embarked at Chatham on board the Winterton 26th April 1792 but being cast away afterwards he did not join 'till 20th November 1793.'[132]

Chapter Sixteen

From Maggots to Mauritius

'I cannot adequately describe the feelings of disappointment
we experienced when sentence was pronounced and our ret-
rograde movement commenced. We had got so near India
that we felt almost as if we were there…'

All the plans they had made, all the renewed anticipation of rejoin-
ing friends or family, or of starting a new life – all the sense of having come through an ordeal that had killed so many of their travelling companions: all were dashed in an instant. Eventually, 2 French
officers from the privateer and 10 seamen came aboard, and at 8pm
on 7 July the *Joachim* began to shape her new course for Mauritius.
Buchan's group had to reassure themselves that they appeared to be
in the hands of men who wished them no harm and who left them
their liberty. Whether their captors were quite so easy with the seamen and the remaining Portuguese officers who, if they could regain

control, might be in a position to work the ship, is speculation.

The Prize Master was what Buchan called an oddity: 'a short, shrivelled figure, with much more mercury in his heels than sense in his head. He bore visible marks of being what is called "up in years"…but did not like to acknowledge it'. He still had an eye for the ladies, and clearly enjoyed chatting up those in his care. In a spirit of teenage mischief, Buchan, who spoke adequate French, boldly dared to ask him his age in front of them. There was a sudden pause while the Frenchman reflected. Thirty-six! he announced 'to the utter injury of the best part of a quarter of a century', and, doubtless, a few giggles from the young ladies who formed his court. On another occasion, with similar flamboyance, he informed them that he had come pretty close to getting married when he was 16. His second in command was a sensible, steady character, making up for rough edges by obvious competence. The French seamen, by further contrast, had interpreted the revolutionary cry of liberty, fraternity and equality to mean that they were under no compulsion to obey any orders from their officers that did not suit them, and 'there was one continued wrangle and one continued disobedience'.

Buchan was in the grip of another malarial fit that left him hot, shaking and sick. As he hung over the ship's rail staring at the water, the old Prize Master came over to comfort him with the encouraging words: 'Mon ami, vous êtes fichu' (my friend, you are done for).

The good nature of the officers was the only positive aspect in an interminable voyage of six weeks instead of the anticipated three after the ship hit a persistent dead calm around the equator where the north-west monsoon meets the south-east Trades. The sails hung slack, and down in the bilges rice had got into the water, and had then swollen and rotted to give off a foul smelling gas. The ship had never been provisioned for such a long voyage, and was close to running short of salted supplies. Much of what little food remained was unfit to eat. 'The biscuit, like clockwork, moved of its own internal impulse, so full was it of maggots.' The only fresh food they could get hold of was fish caught by the crew, 'and an occasional shark was not unacceptable, though the meat is very tough…and its nature greatly repulsive'.

The *Joaquim* reached Port North West…as the Assembly had accurately but unimaginatively renamed Port Louis on receiving news of the revolution in 1790[133] – after nightfall on 16 August,[134] but perhaps Buchan's group caught a hint of mountains merging into sunset clouds before they settled to sleep. They would have been woken by the crew stumbling over them in the darkness as they hove to outside the anchorage, and if they had bothered to stand up they might have seen a few lights in the distance. For most of them, Mauritius came as a glorious surprise with the sunrise: a surf-ringed, palm fringed coastline of turquoise water, coral reefs, and pale sand, rising green and lush into 1000-foot jagged peaks of torn and twisted basalt. Right behind the town soared Le Pouce, a single dark pinnacle thrusting to 2500 feet out of a rock fist. Not as welcome a sight as Fort St George, but Jean Mallet had not done them such a bad turn.

With the morning came a procession of local bureaucrats and others with a vested interest in the ship. The cost of fitting out privateers was financed by the issue of transferable shares, and the value of such shares could, and did, go up and down on the basis of rumour and report. *Le Mutin* was owned by the influential Pitot family who were heavily involved in the privateer business. Had Mallet and *Mutin* been spoken at sea while shepherding a fat East Indiaman, shares would have risen sky high. A whisper of her capture would have made them worthless. The Portuguese ship was small fry, her human cargo a liability. Citoyen Pitot and his friends would not make a fortune from this exploit.

The *Joachim* was warped into the crowded inner harbour, and the *Winterton* people put their feet on *terra firma* for the first time in six weeks. For the soldiers and sailors freedom was almost certainly short lived. Some appear to have been sent as prisoners of war to a floating prison; others may have been sent to the hospital.[135] The passengers – and by logical extension their personal servants – fared better and spent the rest of the day as guests of an English family resident at the capital while the authorities tried to decide what to do about them. Buchan comments:

'It is not often that prisoners can speak in terms of almost unqualified gratitude of their reception in a hostile country; but so we were enabled, and so it is our duty to do so, in this case. The Government, and the society of the place, were then a good deal in the same state of disorder as prevailed in the parent country…But, not withstanding this state of things, it is to the honour of this island that their revolutionary annals were, as I have been informed, rarely stained by any particular acts of atrocity or violence.'

The island had a Governor-General in the shape of the recently appointed 62-year-old Anne-Joseph Hippolyte de Maures, Comte de Malartic, 'a fine old soldier with a very intelligent countenance',[136] who had taken over a year earlier, but his power was now limited. Like the National Assembly, this man, who had served with distinction with Montcalm in Canada and who would give his name to a town and a lake, was forced to look to the Jacobin Clubs for direction, but Mauritius was fortunate that the Clubs were less bloodthirsty and extreme than their Parisien progenitors. The most influential of them sent the English refugees a message that they did not 'make war against the unfortunate', and never deviated from that principle.

After all they had heard in England about the excesses of the Terror, and knowing now that the two countries were at war, the news took so much weight off the minds of Buchan's friends that they sent a small deputation to the Club to thank its members. Their speech delivered, they were then invited to be guests for the rest of the proceedings and 'departed the best of friends'. Those were Buchan's measured thoughts well after the event; the 17-year-old castaway was more forthright:

'But the misfortune was that les honnetes gens durst not show themselves, such an absolute sway had that worst of tyrants, the usurping mob, assumed. The Assembly ventured not to say yea or nay in opposition to a dictatorial club composed of the lowest of the rabble.'

Nor was he alone in that opinion.

He was correct in that not all the residents were so happy to see the Tricolour and Tree of Liberty, but they were at least allowed to live unmolested on their country plantations. One of them, identified only as Monsieur B-----R, an elderly gentleman who had served in earlier European wars, was particularly helpful to the *Winterton* people; however, the people to whom Buchan and some of the other young men were most immediately indebted were a group of American captains who found themselves detained in the harbour as a consequence of the privateer activity.

The Americans were about to become beneficiaries of the privateers' success. As neutrals, they had the freedom of the Indian Ocean at a time when the English and their European allies were fair game. Not only could they trade without hindrance: at the Port Louis auctions they could snap up English, Dutch and other captured ships. But on 4 June 1793, a day after learning about the outbreak of war, the French at Mauritius put an embargo on all foreign ships ostensibly to prevent a leak of information about their fleet which was apparently on the point of sailing from the island.

Thus, 10 or more American ships found themselves idling away the summer, to the indignation of their powerless captains, including Amasa Delano from Essex, Massachusetts. Something of an expert in South China waters, Delano had spent two years working for the East India Company before being paid off. At Macao, on the coast of south China, he came across a fellow American, James Stewart, owner of the whaler, *Eliza*, with a cargo of sealskins. For whatever reason, Stewart had parted company with his original captain and was attempting to do the job by himself – with conspicuously little success, in Delano's opinion. Delano advised him to sell his cargo in Canton where the demand for sealskin was highest, helped him out of trouble of his own making with the Chinese Customs, and then asked a Dutch friend at Canton to assist Stewart in finding a cargo for the *Eliza*.

Vann Brann agreed to load a cargo of his own, but stipulated that the experienced Delano should take command, and when the *Eliza* sailed she was bound for Ostend with a hold full of sugar. The old whaler sailed like a bathtub, even in the best of conditions, and they had only unfavourable winds in dangerous waters. Under a lesser captain than Delano she would have been lost on the treacherous shoals, or captured by Malay pirates as Delano recounts.

'A fleet of prows came out of a small bay on the north-east coast of the island [Sumatra]. They passed across my fore foot, at the distance of a mile and a half, sailing in a line one ahead of another, with the wind directly after them. As soon as they had passed our bow, they hauled under our lee, and formed nearly a semi-circle around us. This manoeuvre did not please me, and I ordered two 6-pound guns to be fired with round shot at the foremost prow. This was done, and repeated a few times, when the Malays altered their course, and left us free. I have no doubt that they had bad intentions toward us. Had we not fired at them in season, and, as I have reason to believe, hit some of them, we should no doubt have found ourselves in trouble from their treacherous attacks and manoeuvres…I have long been convinced that a ship, not strongly armed, should never let a Malay fleet of prows approach very near. Fire as soon as you can reach them, even if you are not near enough to do them any injury.'

The *Eliza* had leaked badly throughout the voyage and rather than see the cargo dissolve and the crew collapse from exhaustion at the pumps Delano put into Mauritius for repairs. Only after they had dropped anchor were they informed that they would be unable to leave. Now he and Stewart were in a delicate position. They and their ship were American, and therefore safe from arrest; but the bill of lading which Delano carried quite literally close to his chest showed that her sugar was partly Dutch owned and could therefore be seized. Holding his nerve he quietly unloaded his cargo and set to work examining the ship.

Delano was shrewd but good-hearted, keen to share his experience with other captains and generous enough to have taken pity on Stewart. The pair of them hospitably offered Buchan a berth during his early days on the island until suitable accommodation could be found on shore, and they entertained some of his comrades on board, including John Hamilton, the young writer destined for the Bengal Presidency.

Hamilton's health had suffered on Madagascar, but no more so than that of the others and Buchan was not unduly alarmed to hear him complain of a sore throat one Friday. While aboard the *Eliza* he began to grow worse, and by the early hours of Sunday morning those around him realised his condition was serious. He 'suddenly put out his hand to Captain D----- saying "goodbye; I am gone," and shortly after expired'.

The American commanders ensured that Hamilton received a dignified funeral, manning their ships' boats and accompanying the body across the harbour to the cemetery.

The mourners included the handsome and dashing young Jacob Crowninshield from the Massachusetts port of Salem, commander of the ship *Henry*.[137] The second son of Salem captain George Crowninshield, Jacob, like his four brothers, had commanded his first ship by the age of 20, and in 1791 he had made an extremely profitable voyage for his father-in-law, the shipping magnate Elias H Derby, America's first millionaire. Derby had been the first American to challenge the Anglo–Dutch mercantile domination of the Indian Ocean, and his captains combined commercial astuteness with first-class seamanship.

On 22 January 1793 Crowninshield and the *Henry* left Salem bound for India, called at the Cape where he took on some cargo from another Salem ship, and reached Mauritius in May. There he sold a variety of cargo that included 20 hogsheads of tobacco, the same quantity of codfish, 101 cases of gin, 90 boxes of Malaga raisins, 108 men's saddles, 398 pairs of shoes, 8 casks of brandy and nearly 3000 feet of pine boards. As he informed the Tribunel, he planned to sail on to Bengal on 20 June but the *Henry* was caught by the embargo.

Nathaniel Silsbee, another of Elias Derby's young Salem captains, also found himself trapped. Although just 20, he was in command of Derby's new vessel the *Benjamin* and having heard about the war he put into Mauritius, sold his cargo for a good price, and traded paper dollars for Spanish silver. It was a shrewd move, for although he, too, fell foul of the embargo, his silver began to appreciate dramatically during his detention.[138] Other American ships included the *Cleopatra* (Captain Campbell, Calcutta–Ostend), the *Aurora* (Captain Meek, Calcutta–Salem), the *Betsey* (Captain Page, for Rhode Island), the *Vigilant* (Captain Murphy, Salem–Ostend), the *Union* (Captain Rich, Calcutta–Ostend), and – last to be detained – the *Abigail* (Captain Jenks, destination unspecified).[139]

❦❦❦

Hamilton's appears to have been the last death among the *Winterton* passengers for whom the Mauritius climate did more good than any medicine. Although the winter was giving way to spring and the temperatures were rising, it was a more healthy place than anywhere they had visited since leaving England apart from Anjouan. 'It is a most delightful island, anything in world will grow in it,' Buchan enthused, and with reason.

The Dutch, who first colonised the island in 1598 named it after their Stadtholder, Maurice of Orange, and, after clearing some of the tropical rainforest, introduced coconuts, bananas and oranges. They also planted sugar cane in order to provide their disgruntled troops with a supply of arrack, and began to cut down the ebony trees for export. As well as the flora, they introduced alien fauna such as pigs and dogs which, together with human depredation, caused the extinction not only of the dodo but also tortoises and the solitaire, another large, flightless bird. By the time the price of ebony dropped, the coastal supplies of the tree were finished, and it was uneconomic to cut and transport timber from higher up in the interior. In 1710 the Dutch abandoned their colony for the second time, and although the French claimed it five years later and renamed it the Ile de France it was a few more years before they really began to establish themselves. Under Labordonnais, a man who loved the place and knew how to govern well, the island prospered, attracting willing white settlers who enjoyed the climate and a life of ease. In 1767, with the liquidation of the French East Company, the French crown took over Mauritius and, as well as a Governor, they appointed an Intendent by the name of Pierre Poivre.

Poivre was an avid botanist who had collected specimens as far afield as Ceylon and China: he brought spices including nutmeg, cinnamon and pepper to the island, and found they grew well. He even founded magnificent and enduring botanical gardens; small wonder that the *Winterton* people, sharing the local easy living – the work was done by around 50,000 slaves who were specifically exempt from the doctrine of 'liberty, brotherhood and equality' – had little to complain of. Even when the French Government in Paris abolished slavery in 1794, Governor-General Malartic, in many ways a conservative and a moderate, backed his people in refusing to recognise the decree. Port Louis was a rich and prosperous town with stone buildings, cobbled streets, warehouses and the industry to support the population; it could stand comparison not only with the ports of the East, but with some of those in Europe. Once freed from the restriction of rule by the French East India Company in 1770 it had quickly become the most important French harbour east of the Cape of Good Hope, and its own merchants and shipowners pursued a lucrative trade around the Indian Ocean.

Since arriving at Port Louis all those caught by the embargo had gone through the official hoops of interrogation and sworn statements in front of lawyers declaring who they were, what they had been doing, and what events had led up to their enforced visit to Mauritius. Like Silsbee, Crowninshield had appeared before the Tribunel on 16 June, and Theodor Diniz, second in command of the *Joachim*, was given the services of an interpreter to make his declaration on 19 August. There was nothing sinister about the French proceedings: this was not Paris where merely to be brought before a tribunel was to be found guilty of some capital offence. But it was all delay, and protests were heard politely by deaf ears. The castaways' situation was different. There was a sense that if some way could have been found to send them on their way to India without compromising what the authorities considered their national security, they could have taken it. But Mauritius was strategically important to the French war effort, as the British themselves had earlier acknowledged: 'As long as the French have the Ile de France, the English will not be masters of India', complained William Pitt the Elder back in 1761.

Towards the end of September came the distinct possibility that the embargo would be lifted. The French fleet was at last about to sail, almost four months late, theoretically removing all barriers to the movement of neutral ships. William Dunn, the *Winterton*'s Purser and now the Company's representative, took the opportunity to write to Thomas Morton at the India House, outlining what had happened since John Dale's last letter. He went on:

'We have already heard by an American vessel that arrived here on the 15th inst. from Madras that the privateer that took us was captured by a Dutch ship of Ceylon and carried into that island. Sir Charles Oakley was informed of our situation and has wrote to M. Malartic the Gov. of the place requesting his attention to us and that he would permit us to proceed to India by the first opportunity, which he promises to do. We mean to take our passage to Bengal in an American ship which will sail at the end of next month. At the present there is an embargo on all foreign ships in the port, but I hope that by that time it will be taken off.

'A convoy sails for France from this island by whom I embrace the opportunity of writing to you. I enclose you lists of the ship's company, passengers and militia knowing how anxious the friends of those who had connections on board Winterton will be to hear of her fate. I am, sir, etc, William Dunn'[140]

Two days later he went before the Tribunel to offer a formal account from the English perspective. He spoke through an interpreter, Dominique Bonniface, starting right from the moment when Dundas had decided to take the *Winterton* up the Mozambique Channel, going into minute detail about the wreck and explaining how they came to be on the Portuguese ship. He may have believed that this was the last formality and that real progress was being made in speeding up their release, but in the event, all hopes of sailing in October were dashed when the French agreed to only a partial relaxation of the embargo. Vessels bound west of the Cape of Good Hope could leave, but not those headed for India and beyond. That decision led to the inescapable conclusion that those in government were principally concerned with keeping secret the activities of the privateers which were fitting out and in which they had shares. While the 23-year-old Jacob Crowninshield fretted, made fruitless petitions to the Assembly and thought seriously about abandoning India and taking a cargo to Europe, the harbour came to life as other captains prepared to sail. Delano and Stewart had managed to unload their sugar and gradually sell it, but to repair the *Eliza* was to throw good money after bad. When the captured Dutch East Indiaman *Hector*, 60 guns and newly built, came up for sale they sold off the *Eliza* and put their money into the Indiaman.

Andrew Ramsay, elder of the two young brothers who owed

their life to the soldier who single-handedly got them safely to the shore of Madagascar, made the decision that there was no point in going on to India while so sick. At least one of the American ships was bound for England, and he had no difficulty securing a passage home. The rest of the group chose to carry on waiting at Port Louis. The alternative: to go west to the Cape and seek a passage to Madras or Bengal on an outward bound Indiaman or neutral vessel, was distinctly unappealing. They were by now staying with local families and finding that, provided they did not start thinking of India, time did not hang heavy on their hands. Although they were all subject to recurrent attacks of malaria, the island air was much healthier than that of Madras or Calcutta at the same season and the French continued universally hospitable. One resident, a Monsieur Dubuc,[141] apparently took up their cause, but nothing came of it.

Dubuc had the reputation of a professional duellist, although they saw nothing of it themselves. What they did witness was a duel fought with pistols between two 14-year-olds. Buchan, himself only 17 at the time, called them 'little boys'. The young men played their parts with perfect sang-froid; their seconds, who were much older and who appeared outwardly happy to sanction the affair of honour, conveniently neglected to put balls into the pistols. Actual blood-shed was avoided, but both combatants had gone to the Champ de Mars with every intention of killing one another.

🍂

Besides Andrew Ramsay, two other survivors were already on their way home: John Dale and Midshipman John Jolly. The latter had reached Madras on 13 September after being picked up by Captain Billamore's otherwise abortive relief expedition, and neither he nor Dale had any cause to stay in India which, after all, had never been their final destination. Following the fall of Pondicherry there were dispatches and trophies to be sent back, and the Company's *Scorpion* was lying off Madras waiting for Captain Oakes RN and George Brathwaite of the 72nd Highland Regiment to embark. George had acted as his father's Aide-de-Camp during the campaign, and to him was entrusted a letter from the Marquis of Cornwallis, the report of the campaign written by his father, and a collection of 10 French flags comprising the Fort's own standard, two standards belonging to the Regiment de Bourbon, two colours carried before the Governor, four banners bearing the motto: 'Discipline et obeissance a là loi',[142] and the banner of the National Guard proclaiming: 'Le Peuple Francais – La Liberté ou la Mort'.[143] By sending the dispatches by his son, General Brathwaite was not merely bringing the younger man to the notice of those with the power to further his career, he was also putting him in line for a windfall of £500, the usual sum given to the bearers of good news.

Either independently or together, the two mariners booked their passages home at the Company's expense, and *Scorpion* sailed from Madras on 20 September.[144] She was a bigger vessel than the *Drake*, three masted, square rigged, more heavily armed, and carrying a complement of 45 European officers, petty officers and seamen; possibly she had Lascars as well. Captain William Selby, like the Governor who dispatched him, was well aware that he would be sailing in dangerous waters and that he would not be safe until he reached port on the English coast.

Chapter Seventeen

Pleading with Tears

The Anglo-Indian boy who acted as a servant to Captain William Selby enjoyed himself eavesdropping on the dinner-table conversation. He had heard his Captain's yarns, many times, but the rest of the company had a whole new stock of exploits to retail. Assuming that John Dale dined at the Captain's table, his adventures over the past year and a quarter were more than sufficient to astonish the rest, while Brathwaite knew every detail of the Pondicherry campaign, and Lieutenant McKenzie of the 71st and Captains Oakes and Manning RN had their own anecdotes.

Among Selby's own officers was a young Acting Lieutenant by the name of Robert Deane who had entered the Bombay Marine in 1791. After a year as midshipman he had been given command of an armed Pattamar, the *Deriah Dowlut,* in which he zealously quartered the Malabar coast hunting for pirates and discouraging pepper smugglers before joining the *Scorpion* a couple of weeks before she

sailed for England. Brave and enterprising, he stood on the thresh-
old of an eventful career in the Company's marine.

While time ticked by on Mauritius, the *Scorpion* ploughed across
the Indian Ocean with a strong lookout on duty but without meeting any privateers from Mauritius. She put into St Helena[145] with
her news and to take on supplies, before sailing north towards the
heavy grey seas and freezing winds of the grim North Atlantic winter. By January 1794 she was only a fortnight or so from the English
Channel.

❀

Dunn and Schwartz, the Portuguese cargo superintendent, appeared
again before the Tribunel at Port Louis on 19 November with a
petition against Citoyen Pitot who represented the shareholders of
Le Mutin. Dunn stated that he wanted his friends to sail on the
Joachim if she was allowed to leave at the lifting of the embargo;
alternatively they would take the first ship for India. Again nothing
happened.

Then, unexpectedly, on the last day of November, the Assembly
proclaimed that foreign ships were free to go.

Two factors lay behind the announcement. A country ship, the
Princess Royal, was captured and brought into Port Louis, and
papers found on her demonstrated that the British knew sufficient
information about the privateering activities to make the embargo
all but superfluous. Then one of the detainees came up with a plea
to which their hosts were not immune. Whatever might be happening in Paris, the National Assembly at Port Louis had not forgotten its good manners, or the French tradition of gallantry.
Isabella Cullen and Charlotte Bristow went in person to the
National Assembly and begged to be allowed to leave. Isabella's
matriachal authority, Charlotte's youth and Anglo-Indian beauty,
and a display of feminine tears – whether spontaneous or else carefully calculated to wring the hearts of the delegates – triumphed
over bureaucracy. The astonished and appreciative Jacob

Crowninshield, wrote to his father on 1 December:

'I am happy to inform you that the embargo for India is at last taken off, this was done yesterday in consequence of some English ladies that have been shipwrecked going in person to the Assembly and pleading with their tears the cause of justice and humanity. All the petitions that I had sent in before had no effect till this method happily succeeded. There are five of these ladies that were passengers on the Winterton that was cast away about two years ago on Madagascar, and since which they have suffered every hardship except death itself. They were brought in here by a privateer some time ago and are now engaged to go with me upon the Henry to Bengal, where are all their friends and connections.'

He added, as if to justify his chivalry to his hard-headed and ambitious father: 'They are of the best families, and some of them very rich, particularly the two Miss Bristows.'

His plan was to sail on 3 December; the day before that he wrote again to his father:

'I have at last obtained permission to set sail for India…I am in hope to get away tomorrow. As for myself, I may with propriety say that I have been ready for this six months past, so that nothing will prevent the ship's going on that day but the ladies passengers not being ready – or our being stopt by the …(?). This is not impossible, I could expect anything from them that it is possible for the worst of men to be guilty of.'[146]

Newly self-liberated from colonial status, the Americans were generally supportive of the French Revolution, but not when it interfered with the right of ambitious entrepreneurs to make commercial fortunes.

Crowninshield's last-minute fears were unjustified: his passengers came aboard – Buchan had to be carried as he was once again racked by malaria – and the *Henry* sailed unmolested on 4 December. They were not sorry to leave when they did as something of a riot had broken out in the town. A shortage of provisions, which had already led to steep price increases and even problems with fitting out the privateers, was blamed on monopolies and profiteering. An angry mob marched on Government House and erected a gallows in front of it. No real harm ensued, but the fear, particularly among the people with whom the *Winterton* survivors were lodged, was unnerving.

The voyage was not without incident: the ship's fireplace was sited next the to mainmast, with the mainsail just above it. The wooden frame caught light; flames flared up towards the canvas, and but for a quick-thinking passenger the results could have been catastrophic. Otherwise, with good company and an assurance of safety, everyone enjoyed themselves. On Thursday, 16 January 1794 they hove to off Madras with enough news to justify a special edition of the *Madras Courier* that same afternoon.

The article listed the passengers, not all of who were from the *Winterton*, and gave detailed information about the state of affairs on Mauritius and the strength and intention of the French naval vessels as well as the privateers. The capture of the *Princess Royal*, already reported, was confirmed, together with news that she had been sold at auction.

Not until the following day did everyone land. The *Courier*, in its regular edition, announced: 'This morning Mrs Cullen, Miss Cullen, the Miss Bristows, and Miss Baillie landed from the Henry and had the happiness of setting foot on friendly ground and finding post tot naufragia – portum'.

For some the adventure was finally over. Assistant Surgeons John Field McLean and William Coloquhoun joined the Corps of Surgeons, and as soon as he was well enough Buchan took up his post as a Writer. Henry Ramsay just needed to get home to England to find another ship on which to continue his marine career.

Like Dale, Buchan wrote an account of his experiences, and he, too, conveniently left out anything that might cast a shadow on the names of the *Winterton*'s dead, as if there was a tacit conspiracy to shield them from blame. His report was longer than Dale's and contained several sections of thoughtful observations on aspects of Madagascar and its people.

On 20 January, the *Henry* sailed for Calcutta. The correspondent of the *Courier* noted: 'We much fear they will experience a tedious passage as the Henry was in sight and scarcely abreast of the North Roads on Wednesday'.

Tedious it might have been, but at least it was uneventful.

Calcutta was the Company's Indian headquarters, 100 miles inland up the russet Hooghly River with its dull sandbanks and the thick border of jungle that followed its meandering course. Even at Calcutta the river stretched twice the width of the Thames in London, but for big ships it was navigable only as far as Diamond Harbour, and small vessels had to be professionally piloted or towed with great care up the remaining 50 miles. Those who had made the journey before waited impatiently for the river to make that final turn and reveal first the fort and then the town.

Fort William might be smaller than its counterpart at Madras as it existed to defend rather than shelter the town, but it represented the art of fortification raised to perfection in the form of an octagonal Vauban fort. It had cost the Company £2,000,000 to build in the years after 1765, and could even impress a Frenchman.

'Fort William, the finest fortress that exists out of Europe, presents itself immediately to the sight which it astonishes by the grandeur and splendour of the buildings that are seen above its ramparts. The houses which form the first front are so many magnificent palaces, some of them having a peristyle of four and twenty pillars. All these structures, disposed in an irregular line through a space of more than a league form an inconceivably striking prospect' wrote de Grandpre.[147]

And nobody who saw Calcutta was anything but awed and dazzled by this eruption of Georgian elegance and flagrant extravagance within the jungle of Bengal.

Most of the white civilians who lived there enjoyed a lavish lifestyle of houses, gardens, carriages and entertainment paid for by high salaries or large loans and made possible by cheap labour. But it came at a cost. For every young man who survived both his journey to and his time in India, maybe nine died.

Jacob Crowninshield put up at the house of Fairlie, Reid and Co., landed his cargo and advertised his wares in the *Gazette*. His unlikely cargo was made up in part of a quantity of French claret, a 1783 vintage Madeira, paintings including a Venus by Sir Joshua Reynolds, 16 pairs of 'magic prints', jewellery and a collection of musical instruments – two bass violas, a pair of bassoons, two clarinets, four trumpets, two violins and a guitar.[148]

❧❧❧

Crowninshield's career was meteoric. He went on to transport to New York the first live elephant ever to set foot in the USA before giving up the sea in favour of business and politics, and in 1802 he was elected to the House of Representatives. Five years later and against Crowninshield's own wishes, Jefferson appointed him Secretary of State for the Navy although he did not actually take on the responsibility. In 1808, while giving a speech in Congress, he collapsed with a haemorrhage and died, aged 37.

Nathaniel Silsbee turned his silver dollars into coffee and spice, reached the Cape, off loaded that cargo on to other ships bound for Salem, took a new cargo back to Mauritius, and by the time he returned to Salem he had made a healthy profit for Elias Derby and set himself up on his commission. Like Crowninshield, he swallowed the anchor at a young age and went into politics. Amasa Delano and James Stewart were less fortunate with their huge East Indiaman, but Delano went on to continue a maritime career so colourful that it reads like a very improbable fiction.[149] The two men had made a great impression on Buchan who expressed a fond but faint hope of hearing news of them while acknowledging it was unlikely that his account would ever come to their eyes.

🦋

Isabella Cullen and her friends used their time on the *Henry* to advantage. Uppermost in their minds as the ship came up the Hooghly was gratitude, and a resolution that the parts played by two men should not go unrecognised nor unrewarded by the East India Company. The effusive letter to Sir John Shore, Cornwallis's successor, was written at Calcutta on 21 February a few days after they had landed and been reunited with Thomas de Souza, but the tone and content must have been discussed on the ship while they were all together, and it dominated the front page of the *Calcutta Gazette* of the 27th.

> 'We the undersigned…glowing with gratitude to those whom, next to Heaven, we are indebted to for our preservation and delivery, presume to address the Honourable the Governor in Council, to solicit such marks of favour and attention from the Government to our benefactors, which, whilst they shall in some degree discharge a debt we can never pay, will perpetuate the remembrance of deeds of humanity…'

After sketching the story of the wreck, the writers paid tribute to the King of Baba.

> 'It is unnecessary to take up your time with detailing the steady conduct, the uniform tenderness to the sick or the universal benevolence of this wonderful man. Habituated to intoxication and to acts of savage violence towards his own people…to us he was invariably gentle and humane…even in cases when the intemperance of our people and their viola-

tion of the laws of hospitality exposed us all to immediate death from his enraged subjects...'

After several more paragraphs, they turned their attention to one of their own.

'We presume, however, to encroach a little farther on your time, to mention one other person to whose indefatigable exertions...we more immediately owe our lives.

'Mr Dale, third officer of the Winterton, who, after enduring great hardships in his passage in an open boat to the coast of Africa and in a march of 300 miles by land, during which almost all his companions died, and he experienced unparalelled distress, returned to the scene of misery at Madagascar for our relief and deliverance. We are well aware how totally unneccessary it is to make any appeal to your feelings on behalf of this young man; still we trust you will forgive us, if we solicit and ardently entreat, that you will be pleased to point him out to the Honourable Court of Directors as meriting some very strong mark of their attention and support.

'We have only now to beg that you will also pardon this address, however irregular, from the motives which have dictated it. We have conceived it due to ourselves, and due to posterity; which, although it is only signed by such of the survivors as are now in Bengal, still we confidently believe that the feelings of all our unfortunate companions, wherever they may be, are in full accord to the prayer of this address.

'We have the honor to be, with the most profound respect, Sir, your most obedient servants:
Isabella Cullen
Margaret F Cullen
Charlotte Bristow
Mary Bristow

Isabella Baillie
William Dunn
Suetonius McGowan
John Gordon
Thomas de Souza

Their sense of indebtedness to Dale did not end with the letter. A large silver jug, suitably inscribed, later bore tangible witness to their gratitude.

Freedom of the press was not a feature of the Company's rule. The letter would not have been made public if Shore had not intended to act on it. A copy was duly sent to the India House for consideration by the Court of Directors, but it would be a long time before either John Dale or the King of Baba knew anything about it. By then, the rest had dispersed. Isabella and Margaret travelled on to Sarnat to join William, and the other three girls remained at Calcutta to enjoy the social life with their families. Appointed Ensign and with his allowances backdated to the date of the wreck, John Gordon joined his brother-in-law, Major William Neville Cameron in the Bengal Engineers[150] along with Suetonius McGowan.

Few of those who lived to see India were in the best of health. Buchan ended his narrative by claiming that everyone quickly put the past behind them and got on with life, but the reality was different for each of them. Some were to live into old age; others had just a few months left.

❈

Meanwhile, events in France were shaping up to intervene yet again in the life of John Dale.

The first years of the Revolution had not been easy. Internal revolts, administrative disintegration and war with her neighbours all threatened to throw France into deeper chaos. Many experienced officers in the army and navy had gone into exile, unwilling or afraid to serve the regime; and yet somehow the fledging republic had not only survived but repulsed her enemies and begun to regain order at home. By the end of 1793 a young Lieutenant Colonel Bonaparte had retaken Toulon, handed over to the British by royalist sympathisers; and at Brest the Representative of the People, Andre Jeanbon Saint-Andre, with the physical and psychological help of a guillotine, had restored the key Breton port to something of its former discipline and usefulness. But by the end of that year disaster had struck.

The harvest failed. France faced famine and with it the prospect of riots, counter-revolution and invasion. Somehow, the Government had to buy sufficient grain from abroad to keep stomachs full, heads high, and armies in the field. With every country on her borders hostile, the National Convention looked to the one nation whose own recent struggle for independence had given her a natural sympathy with the French ideals and which produced sufficient grain to meet her need: America.

There was just one problem: the British navy would intercept any fleet of laden merchantmen making for the coast of France. Saint-Andre was entrusted with ensuring that a grain fleet reached home safely.

The French were short on Admirals, but a former merchant officer had found himself promoted from Captain to Rear Admiral in November 1793. Pierre-Jean Vanstabel (1744–1797) from a Dunkirk seafaring family had 20 years' experience behind him when he became an auxiliary officer in the French Navy. In 1781 he was off the English coast in the little cutter *Rohan-Soubise* when he encountered the British privateer *Admiral Rodney*. During the one-hour engagement, Vanstabel was shot twice in the throat but, after getting himself patched up, continued to give orders until the *Admiral Rodney* capitulated. Promotion continued, until by 1793 he was a Captain.[151] He now found himself charged with the task of leading a squadron of men-of-war to Chesapeake Bay in order to protect that convoy of up to 130 merchant ships many of which were currently loading grain in the ports of Virginia under the command of Captain Emeriau.

Saint-Andre either had a fine grasp of naval realities or he was taking good advice. Once Vanstabel was homeward-bound with the convoy in the spring of 1794 it would be necessary to ensure that the British fleet never got within striking range. Another Rear Admiral was needed, and Saint-Andre had chosen the former frigate captain, Louis Villaret de Joyeuse, who swiftly dropped the aristocratic particle from his name to become plain Villaret-Joyeuse. He was to go out to meet Vanstabel and, if necessary, keep the British fleet occupied while the convoy reached port. As an incentive, Saint-Andre promised him an audience with the guillotine if he failed.

Across the Atlantic in Norfolk, Virginia, the British Consul, Colonel John Hamilton gloomily watched the French merchantmen in the half frozen, shallow waters of Chesapeake Bay. No admirer of the Americans, Hamilton believed that only the fear of backing the losing side prevented Congress from entering the war on the side of France. On 6 January he wrote home to Lord Grenville:

> 'The situation of the country is very critical. They are not pleased with Great Britain, they are at enmity with the French minister and greatly divided among themselves. What will be the event, time only can discover, but it is my opinion that nothing but the success of the combined armies and fleets will keep this country in peace...About thirty large French ships are now here richly laden...I believe about 30 large French ships are loaded at Baltimore with flour and under a convoy of the ---------- of 40 guns and three frigates...They have been detained by the frost but as the weather is at present very fine I think it will open the Bay.'[152]

Towards the end of December 1793 Vanstabel had left Brest with his squadron including the 80-gun *Tigre*, *Jean Bart*, 74 guns, and *La Charante*, *La Semillante* and *La Concorde*, all 40-gun frigates. On board the flagship was a minister with a sum reported to be in the region of 1,000,000 dollars to pay for the supplies. The activity of the French had not gone unnoticed. On 17 January *Lloyd's List* reported that six French frigates had been cruising in the Channel for some days past, and that many ships were being taken. When Captain Hewison of the *Pomona* reached Leith he brought news of the capture on New Year's Day of the *George,* a Liverpool-based merchantman bound for Africa, taken off Finistere. She would be taken on to America to boost the capacity of the grain fleet, along with any other vessels unlucky enough to cross Vanstabel's course.

On 12 January 1794 the squadron sighted a small, armed ship heading towards the Channel. The HEIC's *Scorpion* did not stand a chance.

Chapter Eighteen

A Floating Prison

Any resistance Captain William Selby put up was token. More likely, he tried to run and was overhauled. The capture of the dispatches was a cause for celebration, for they included the French flags taken at Pondicherry. The British would not have the satisfaction of putting those on display.

For the second time in a matter of months Dale found himself transferred as a prisoner on to a French ship, this time the frigate *Semillante*, and her officers were not as civil as those of *Le Mutin*. Nor did Rear Admiral Vanstabel intend to send his prizes and prisoners home to Brest: the *Scorpion* was going to augment the grain fleet, and the enlarged squadron continued across the bitingly cold North Atlantic. The *Scorpion*'s complement had been split up, with the naval and army officers on *Le Tigre*.

Two hundred miles long, with a ragged tidal shoreline of well over 100,000 miles Chesapeake Bay stretches from Havre de Grace in Maryland down to Norfolk, Virginia, collecting the water from the web of rivers that irrigate the wooded coastal plain. For the early colonists its shallow fertile water provided food – the name means 'Great Seafood Bay' – and harbours safe from the Atlantic storms. Norfolk held the key to the water-gate, and during the War of Independence, a British fleet under Lord Dunmore celebrated New Year's Day 1776 by bombarding the town and destroying a large part of it. Colonial troops then marched in and razed what survived in order to prevent the British from occupying such a strategic position. The only building to survive was the church, with a cannonball embedded in one of its walls. Not until 1783 when the blockade was finally lifted could the people of Norfolk start to rebuild their maritime town, and by the time the French ships arrived to load their vital cargo, only a few brick buildings had been completed. The British Government, moreover, now refused to see the US trade with French colonies as a neutral act. Those ships engaged in it were stopped and searched for British seamen; they were as liable to be seized as any declared enemy's vessels.

Little wonder that Norfolk, with all its recent memories and present grievances, appeared to John Hamilton to be so anti-British and so pro-French. He wrote home that a French corvette had arrived with pamphlets on the subject of equality and liberty in order to put more strain on US neutrality. A big West Indiaman, *Friendship*, had been taken by French privateers off Charleston and sent into Norfolk.

'This coast is again lined with privateers, and two frigates are just come to anchor in Hampton Roads, L'Embuscade and La Normande which I am informed are to be loaded with flour, and to join the convoy to the ships loaded and loading here and at Baltimore. And the whole of the French ships now...are ordered to be got in readiness and proceed to sea under the convoy of four 40-gun frigates and six or eight armed ships, and that in the passage they are to be met with in a certain latitude by eight or ten sail of the line from France.'

For Hamilton, nothing short of serious gunboat diplomacy would cow the French, impress the Americans, and restore the pride of his own nation which was continually being insulted by the blatant French bias.[153] This concern for national prestige went hand in hand with his personal ambition, expressed to Nepean, to be appointed Consul General of the Southern States.

❧✳❦

La Charante detached herself from Vanstabel's fleet and Hamilton saw her arrive at Norfolk on 11 February a little ahead of the others, having made the run from Rochefort in 50 days. The rest were in the Chesapeake. 'They consist of one ship of 80 guns, one of 74, two frigates and two sloops of war. It is said that two seventy-four gun ships, a part of this squadron, are sailed for New York.'[154]

Nine days later Hamilton reported that the French were repairing rigging and it looked as though they would be ready to sail in 10 to 15 days. By now he was aware of the capture of the *Scorpion*, although he had not actually seen her.

'The French fleet on their passage captured the Scorpion packet belonging to the Honorable East India Company, she was charged with dispatches for the Government mentioning the capture of Pondicherry and Carricall by the British. The Fleet also captured the ship George of Liverpool, Captain Thomson.'

Hamilton was informed that the French were holding a number of British officers and seamen, but he was not allowed to visit them. On 15 February, Dale wrote to him, and there is a hint of desperation in his letter.

Sir,

My situation will I hope excuse the liberty I take in troubling you with this, as I look upon it as a duty incumbent upon me, to take the earliest opportunity of informing the public of an event, which from its magnitude, must sensibly affect many families in England. I shall therefore with your leave, just mention the particulars. I sailed from the Downs May 2nd 1792 Third mate of the Winterton (in the service of the East India Company) and on the 20th August following the ship was wreck'd on the Island of Madagascar. The people sav'd to the number of 230, were, after being seven months on the island before they were relieved, reduced by sickness more than half, amongst those who perished were many passengers, the Captain, and every officer but myself. The survivors proceeded onto Madras and on the way we were taken by a French Privateer from the Mauritius who sent the greater part of us there, reserving me with about 20 more on the privateer, which was afterwards captured by a Dutch ship, in one of the ports of India, from whence I arrived at Madras, a twelvemonth after the loss of the ship.

The Scorpion being then under orders to sail for England with dispatches, I obtained a passage in her, and was taken by the French Squadron now lying here.

I have reason to think, that no authentic account has yet reached London of the above, and I need not mention the consequence it is of to the court of directors, as well as to those individuals who must be anxiously waiting the fate of their relations and friends who were in the Winterton.

Your interference in my behalf will greatly oblige,
Sir,
Your most Obdt
Humble Serv't
John Dale
On board La Semillante, Hampton Roads Feb 15th 1794

Dale's letter reached Hamilton while he was writing to Henry Dundas in London. The Consul was doing his best for his nationals, but with little apparent success.

'I have endeavoured to procure their release from the Admiral and French Consul but whether I succeed or not am uncertain. They observe great secrecy, not even permitting their good and faithful allies the Americans to go on board. The Scorpion prize ship is come into harbour to load with flour.'

Once more he repeated his mistrust of the Americans. He allowed that President Washington was sincere in his neutrality, but felt that the individual States were so sympathetic to the French that their public bodies were prepared to offer active support at the risk of breaching that neutrality. The British needed to keep a watchful eye on them, he warned Dundas, 'for rest assured nothing but the success of the combined armies and fleets have deterred them from waging war against Great Britain and her allies.'[155] To that letter he appended a note that the Americans were holding feasts for the French and allowing them to parade the Tricolour and that other symbol of the Revolution, the Tree of Liberty; furthermore, he noted that some Americans were going out to the French West Indies to fit out privateers. He also enclosed Dale's letter.

The English prisoners were having a wretched time on the French ships. Not only was the weather freezing, but their captors had little regard for their health or their rights. Attempts to write to Hamilton were frequently frustrated, and as Phineas Bond, the British Consul at Philadelphia, later wrote indignantly to Grenville:

'In the predicament of prisoners who could not resent affront, as they were constantly assailed by the grossest abuse of our most gracious King, and of his ministers and of all that Englishmen hold sacred. Nor were they excused even from personal insult...They were stripped of many valuable things, deprived of little articles of furniture – of presents, and even of family letters which they had in charge for their friends. I have also represented the contravention of the positive directions sent by the French Consul to the French rear admiral in respect to our seamen who were distributed among the merchant ships – that many of these unfortunate people who were afflicted with the scurvy had been confined on shipboard within the shores of Virginia from the period of their arrival, destitute of those refreshments and means of recovery which they might have obtained upon land, and for want of which many fell victim to the scurvy. Others by being confined on board died of a putrid fever which raged upon two of the line of battle ships. The very few who had been permitted to go on shore had been so long confined that there was no hope of their recovery.'[156]

The British had taken the Island of Martinique, and in February 1794 marines seized all American ships, imprisoning their crews in even more appalling conditions than those suffered by the British in the Chesapeake. An outraged Congress demanded that something be done to save the country's merchant marine from extinction.

By 6 March, 89 French merchantmen had completed their loading and were ready to sail. The eastern coastline prickled with masts and spars; even the warships were taking on grain. It said much for the US harvest of the previous autumn that they could afford to export such a vast quantity. Hamilton continued to watch the operations with anxiety, repeating his fears of America entering the war on the side of France, and spinning impractical plans to enlist the help of royalist sympathisers in America to fight for Britain. Then, on 26 March, Edward Thornton, the Consul at Baltimore, sent an express warning that Congress had passed a 30-day embargo on ships but that it would not come into force until after the French had left. That panicked Hamilton who had placed local orders for some pilot boats for Admiral Jervis out in the West Indies. He was now more convinced than ever that the Americans were looking for an excuse to declare war. Two days after Thornton's note he fulminated by letter to Grenville:

'I have frequently asserted to your lordship the diabolical inclination of many of the people of this country to bring on a war by spreading malicious reports of pretended violations of the neutrality'.

At this time the 32-gun frigate HMS *Daedalus* was in port and when she fired a salute two of her guns were alleged to be loaded with grapeshot which hit the town. The authorities produced examples of the offending shot, but when it proved to be of a different weight to that carried on the *Daedalus*, the Mayor went away satisfied that the accusation was false and mischievous. A diplomatic incident was avoided, although Hamilton sent a complaint to the President[157] on the grounds that the French were trying to cut out the frigate and provoke her officers.

❧❦❧

Renamed *La Ville de L'Orient*[158], and given a French Captain by the name of Volet with a crew of 14,[159] the erstwhile *Scorpion* was loading flour, while at the same time George Washington was watching the progress of the Anglo-French war with concern. Warships from both countries were free to come in and out of ports such as Norfolk, and it did not take much imagination to envisage the war spilling into his waters. The old earthwork fort at Norfolk had been useless during the War of Independence. On 20 March he ordered the construction of a new fort that would allow America to defend the Bay.

Hamilton liked to think that his representations to Vanstabel at last bore fruit. More likely, the impending departure of the French convoy caused Vanstabel to agree to the release of his British prisoners. From *Le Tigre* young Captain Brathwaite informed the Consul on 1 April:

Dear Sir,
General Vanstabel has given me permission to acquaint you that
he has been pleased to agree to our immediate enlargement upon
Parole. I have therefore to beg you will be good enough to send
two pilot boats to the Tigre to receive the general orders for our
conveyance, and that of the other British Officer, prisoners of
war on board the French Squadron.

PS The General desires you will prepare a receipt according to the
following list, engaging that officers of a similar rank may be
exchanged on the part of the British and to prevent loss of time the
General desires that this receipt may accompany the pilot boats to
be delivered to the General after our entry on board the pilots.

Suddenly Vanstabel was in just as much hurry to free his prisoners
as they were to get ashore. Brathwaite listed the men concerned:

His Britannic Majesty's Officers

Captain Oakes	Royal Navy
Captain Manning	Royal Navy
Captain Brathwaite	His Majesty's 72nd Regiment
Lieut. McKenzie	HM 71st Regiment

Officers of the Hon. The East India Company

Captain Selby	commanding the	Scorpion
Lieutenant Hewitson		ditto
Lieutenant Sefton		ditto
Messrs George Budden	Surgeon	ditto
Robert Dean	Act'g Lieutenant	ditto
John Aickenby	Midshipman	ditto
John Casey	ditto	ditto
Dale	officer of the Winterton passenger on board	ditto
Jolly	Midshipman ditto	ditto

Merchant Officers

Archibald Thompson	Commander of the ship George, Liverpool	
Henry Booth	1st Mate	ditto
Jn Latham	2nd Mate	ditto
Thomas Fraser	3rd mate	ditto, sick on shore
John Rae	Surgeon	ditto
Richard Bryan	Commander of ship Sally, Bermuda	
Smith	Supercargo	ditto
Pitt	passenger	ditto
Joseph Hinton	Commander of the Sloop Bermuda	
Thomas Fraser	Lieutenant	ditto

Alexander Macquere, servant to Captain Brathwaite
A Black and half-caste boy, servants to Captain Selby

The following day Hamilton enclosed the required receipt, guaranteeing that the appropriate number of French prisoners would be freed. With it he sent a blank receipt for the release of any and all private seamen. Sir Charles Knowles Bt, Captain of the *Daedalus* also agreed in writing to make immediate application 'to the Lords Commissioners of the Admiralty of Great Britain for the liberation of a like number of French Officers who may be prisoners in Great Britain of similar rank'.[160]

Dale and his companions were free at last, but it was not until 11 April that they were issued with passports, and even then the four Royal Navy and army officers were complaining to their Consul that their swords had not been returned to them. Not that the passports were of any use, as Congress's embargo meant they could not get a passage home. Hamilton was trying to protect the three pilot boats under construction, putting two of them into the name of a friend and refusing to accept an American apology for taking over the third while under the misguided impression she had been running information to the West Indies. At the same time, Captain James Leslie of the *Friendship* was protesting to the harassed Consul that the French vessel which captured him and his valuable cargo was not legally a privateer with a letter of marque.

On 15 April the precious convoy finally sailed under its heavy escort. Every free space on every ship, whether merchantman, frigate or ship of the line, was packed with grain and flour. Now they had to cross the North Atlantic and trust that Villaret-Joyeuse would be able to see them safely home.

After borrowing money from Hamilton, Brathwaite's party left Norfolk and made for Philadelphia where they waited on the Consul and complained to Phineas Bond about their treatment. Bond was already working on behalf of some seamen on another ship who were not only being half-starved and deprived of clothing but who were kept in irons at night: this was just another instance of the French ignoring the directions of the French Consul.

It is reasonable to suppose that they all travelled together. Once the embargo, which had already been extended once, was lifted they were at last able to book passages for England. By that time, Vanstabel's convoy was nearing home and the whole of the French Navy was under orders to protect it. A third Rear Admiral, Joseph Marie Nielly had left Rochefort and was cruising some 300 miles west of Belle Ile, ready to reinforce Vanstabel as soon as his convoy came into sight. Villaret-Joyeuse's fleet of 26 ships of the line had slipped out of Brest and positioned itself to be between the convoy and the British. Admiral Howe, with a very similar force, encountered the French 430 miles west of Ushant on 28 May, but largely due to poor visibility the full battle, the first of the war, was not fought until a few days later. Although the British had the better of the action, they totally failed to prevent the vital convoy reaching Brest, and the battle's popular British name of The Glorious First Of June, bestowed on it by the playwright Sheridan, rather reflects the brilliant sunshine in which it was fought than the result of the actual combat. Villaret-Joyeuse had commanded with Saint-Andre breathing down his neck until the Representative of the People found an excuse to hide himself below deck, and he was in no doubt about the outcome: the French had lost a few old ships, but he had kept his head.

❦

By 18 July Captain Brathwaite was putting up at the highly rated Gunter's Hotel in Jermyn Street, London, and writing with a mixture of indignation and appeal to Edward Nepean at the Admiralty.

> 'I am sorry to add that on the 12th January last we fell in with and were captured by a French squadron...where after being detained 54 days on board their ships...we were constrained to remain two months in America and to travel at a considerable expense...to Philadelphia. I therefore flatter myself Government will be pleased to take into consideration my sufferings as a prisoner on board the French Fleet, and the heavy expenses I have been understandably put to by returning to my own country, and therefore extend to me the gratuity of £500 which has usually been granted to officers coming home charged with similar news of importance.'

The officers of the *Scorpion* had either returned more quickly or reported to their employer with greater haste, for on 9 July they were cleared of all blame for the capture of the *Scorpion* at a meeting of the East India Company's Court of Directors. The following day Captain Selby requested that he and his officers should continue to be paid until they returned to their stations, and that was followed by a petition from his officers to be allowed to go back to India on one of the current season's ships and that their accommodation on board should be in line with their ranks. The HEIC agreed to pick up the bill for the money they had borrowed from Hamilton, but Robert Deane never recovered financially from the loss of the personal property confiscated by the French.

Two years and two months after he had sailed from England, John Dale announced his return on the 11 July and that he awaited the Court's orders: in other words, he wanted to know if they had a ship for him. The wishes of the *Winterton* passengers at Calcutta had already been communicated to the Directors who had considered the issue, and the response to Dale's letter was swift:

'In reply to your letter of yesterday I have to acquaint you that on the 20th of last month the Court of Directors resolved to present you with the sum of 200 guineas in consideration of your particular exertions in behalf of the unfortunate sufferers by the wreck of the Winterton, and the very uncommon hardships and misfortunes you experienced. A warrant for the above sum now lies ready for payment in the treasury which may be received either by yourself or any person you may empower to receive it, or by letter of Attorney...I am...W. Ramsay, Secretary.'[161]

Chapter Nineteen

Births, Marriages and Deaths

Counting the two unnamed seamen who had remained in Mozambique, the love-struck sailor at Toleary, Thomas de Souza in India, and John Jolly with his group at Anjouan, and excepting the trio who were probably from the whaler *Mercury*, 91 men and women appear to have been alive at the time of the *Joachim*'s capture. The only subsequent death to be recorded was that of John Hamilton, but some of the soldiers and crew could have died in captivity on Mauritius, and Midshipman Charles Moray's name is missing from the list of those who reached India. Just one soldier, William Bowker, ever appeared on the Muster Roll of the 75th Regiment.

Some went on to serve together, others found themselves in more scattered posts; the marine officers came and went with the monsoons; balls and concerts at Calcutta brought old acquaintances together; newspapers at the three Presidencies reported births, marriages and deaths, arrivals from and departures to England; and well-travelled gossip at third or fourth hand revived memories of names and faces. A novelist could have woven a love story into the narrative; but there is no record of marriages between those who survived the shipwreck and reached India.

Isabella Cullen, who had lost her elder daughter and found herself responsible for the young women wrecked with her, spent only a few years in Sarnat where she gave birth to three sons, Archibald, Robert and William, before returning to England where another son, John, was baptised in London in 1799. Meanwhile, back in India, her husband William rejoined the army as a Captain in the same year, becoming Lieutenant Colonel of the Scots Brigade in 1801. By the time of his death on 10 April 1807[162] he was commanding the regiment. Isabella never remarried but survived him by many years, dying at Edinburgh on 25 May 1842 at the impressive age of 82.

After her mother's departure, Margaret Cullen remained in India, and at Madras on 8 August 1800 married John Locke, son of the Captain of the East Indiaman *Marquis of Wellesley*.[163]

The year 1795 saw two 'Winterton' weddings. Less than a year after her arrival at Calcutta, Isabella Baillie married Major Innis Delmaine of the 16th Bengal Infantry at Cawnpore. She was considerably younger than her 35-year-old husband but after his death in 1814 she remained, like Isabella, a widow and died at Barrackpore on 6 September 1835.

Robert Hyde Colebrooke, a Lieutenant in the Bengal Infantry had been enjoying a busy career surveying the coast between Madras and Bengal, the Andaman and Nicobar Islands and, under battle conditions, Mysore. In 1793 he found himself in charge of the Surveyor General's Office. Workaholic though he was, he noticed the arrival into Calcutta society of Charlotte Bristow, almost half his age. In 1795 they married. It was a good match for both of them. Her father was rich, respected and influential; the bridegroom, although illegitimate like Charlotte herself, came from a wealthy and privileged background. His father had been an Ambassador, one of his uncles had been Chairman of the HEIC, and his cousin Henry was becoming an authority on Sanskrit. Despite the demands of his surveying and his decided preference for working on location rather than in the office, Colebrooke and Charlotte managed nine children before, in 1808, he sent her and the children on a visit to England – he himself had never taken home leave. They did not meet again: while surveying the Ganges Plain he contracted dysentery and died that same year. Charlotte eventually returned to England, dying at Bath on 2 July 1833. No records of her sister's life have come to light.

Henry Quinn Brownrigg[164] gained promotion to Captain in the 75th in 1795 and died on 13 November 1809 at the age of about 55. He and his wife Maria, née Bowles, left no children. His brother Robert became Governor of Ceylon and was rewarded with a Baronetcy.

Fate dealt very different hands to the two Assistant Surgeons. William Coloquhoun served in the 4th Mysore War, distinguishing himself at the capture of Seringapatam in 1799[165]. He was appointed Surgeon in 1801 and a Superintendent Surgeon 16 years later. In 1818 he took the name Coloquhoun Stirling,[166] and, among his other appointments he was Surgeon to Sir John Malcolm's mission to Persia. In March 1831 he retired, dying on 21 March 1842.[167] By contrast, John Field McLean did not survive even a full year in India. On 15 August 1794 he died at St Thomas's Mount, Madras. Perhaps he never recovered enough from the ordeal to begin the career for which he had been trained.

A successful career could have awaited Henry Ramsay, the young Scots midshipman for whom the *Winterton* voyage had been a baptism of fire. He returned home on the Indiaman *Woodcot*, his health more damaged than his enthusiasm, and quickly went back to sea as a midshipman on the *Berrington*. His anxious mother, Elizabeth, the Dowager Lady Dalhousie, wrote plaintively to the Captain:

'I have been Most Unluckie having Wrote you twice under cover to my son, Which I'm convinced has Never reached him. Indeed, Sir, I looked on Henry's getting into your Ship as a piece of singular good fortune, and I hope you will take him under y'r Immediate Protection…I trust you'll take very kindly to My Dear Boy; he is of a very Shy Temper, but you'll find him with real good Dispositions, His profession has been altogether his own choice. When you are better Acquainted, may I request You Would Write me a few lines and say how he goes on and how his health is, it's (?) his misfortunes in the unfortunate Winterton. His first Voyage, I think, hurt his constitution very much. May I also beg you'll supply his wants, take his bill for any money he needs. Dalhousie or I will most gratefully acknowledge it…Make Henry write me every opportunity.'[168]

Did Henry actually receive the missing letters and quietly dispose of them rather than suffer the embarrassment of having his Captain think him in need of a nanny? He may not have been quite the shrinking violet of his mother's imagination. After one voyage as Fourth Mate on the *Lord Hawksbury* he appears to have got stuck as Second Mate, serving in that capacity on both the *Tottenham* and the *Duke of Montrose*, and in June 1805 he resigned at Madras. He later signed on as Second Mate of the *Nottingham*, only to become involved in a duel in China with another marine officer and was wounded in the head. Despite a trepanning operation performed by Dr Home, he died on 24 July 1808 at the London home of one of his brothers, William.[169]

The death of Henry was a terrible blow to his sensitive brother Andrew, for whom India was never less than an endurance. The Court of Directors had allowed him to remain at home until he had recovered from the effects of the wreck, and then he went out to India as Assistant to the Collector of Midnapore. The following year he travelled to Jungapore as Assistant to the Commercial

Resident whom he succeeded in 1804. In January 1800, aged 23, he married Rachel Cook. There were no further promotions, and Andrew became desperately bitter about being passed over, blaming Lord Minto for treating him disgracefully. In a letter to his brother, George, the 9th Earl of Dalhousie, in 1813, and clearly distraught at the death of another relation, he wrote:

'To me her loss will be severely felt, for excepting yourself, she was the only relation I had left who seemed to take any interest about me. The last five years have indeed fallen cruelly hard upon me, and the loss of almost everyone who cared about me, added to the unjust and harsh treatment I have met with from government, has thrown a melancholy over my spirits which makes me indifferent to future events...I was glad to find you had spoken to Lord Melville about Lord Minto's conduct to me, but I hope this is the last time you will lay yourself under any obligation on my account...and never more will I expect promotion. I shall at least, in that case, not be disappointed'.[170]

Not until 1829 did Andrew return home. Three years later he was awarded an annuity by the HEIC, and he died on 2 April 1848 just short of his 72nd birthday.

Ensign John Gordon of Embo joined the Bengal Engineers and was promoted to Lieutenant in 1800. On the death of his father at the end of November 1804 he succeeded to the Baronetcy for a few brief weeks, dying unmarried at Penang before the end of the year aged only 28. His fellow cadet, Suetonius McGowan died even younger in 1798 at 23 and was buried below the fort at Chunar. A couple of years earlier his father, the former NCO, had reached the rank of Colonel.

William Dunn made just one more voyage for the Company before disappearing from view. In June 1795 Janet Carmichael, widow of the Carpenter's Second Mate, John, wrote to the pay office at the India House asking them to pay her late husband's outstanding wages to Dunn. On 15 July £4 was paid to a Mr Dicky of Flore Street, Bedford Square for Dunn to pass on to her.

Midshipman John Jolly, who had ended up with Dale in the *Scorpion* at Norfolk, never made the grade. Born in London in 1776, he had spent a year as a seaman in the Turkish trade before joining the *Winterton* for that fateful voyage, and after his return to England he continued as a midshipman. Although presented as Fourth Mate for the *Lord Macartney*, his appointment was turned down and in February 1796 he was dismissed from the service. Whether he had found it impossible to get to grips with navigation, or his character was seriously flawed is not recorded.

Several of the seamen came back to England to collect their outstanding wages over the years that followed. Along with Dale himself, Thomas Osborne, Joseph Smith and Thomas Campbell all signed the wage book during July 1794;[171] James Berwick, May 1795; William Foster, January, and John Herring, December, collected in person during 1798, but it has to remembered that a number of crew members had given authority for others to receive money on their behalf. Boatswain John Slater's wife, Alice, took care of the finances for several of the crew.

The success of the French privateers based at Mauritius had led to a large number of crewmen from the captured prizes being held in a floating prison. In 1794 the list of names, mostly Dutch and English, included two known to have been on the *Joachim*: William Beaumont/Bowman, and John Kindrain (the name is spelt variously). The name Joseph Carr also appears, but there is no proof that he is the Carr from the *Winterton*. There were other, unnamed, English sailors at the island's hospital.

Too sick to work again, Henry Rozier, a quartermaster, received a pension of £4.16.0 a year for life, and life pensions were also granted to Ann Chambers, the First Mate's widow and Elizabeth Dowdall, widow of one of the quartermasters who had died before leaving Mozambique. Eventually, even the Carpenter's wife, Isabella

Rowland, had to apply. William's good sense at the time of the wreck and his hard work on the yawl at Toleary had saved many lives: he deserved better than an early death.

The East India Company did not forget its debt to the King at Toleary. John Dale and William Dunn wrote a gentle reminder to the Court of Directors in the spring of 1795,[172] but it was not until October 1798 that the ship *Drake*, the same as had taken Dale up to Madras, left Bombay for Madagascar with suitable gifts. A message was sent to the King who had gone inland, and he duly returned to receive Captain Bond in state, using the knees of his wives as a throne.

He found it hard to grasp either why the Company felt itself in his debt or why Captain Bond should have made such a long voyage when he, Bond, had no ties of blood or friendship to any of the *Winterton* survivors. Eventually they made him understand how the Company viewed the situation and he accepted not only the gifts but an invitation to inspect the *Drake*. After being rowed out to her he mounted the back of one of his chiefs and was carried up the ship's side. When his visit was over, he returned to the boat in the same way.[173]

When last heard of, the anonymous crewman who chose love on Madagascar had reportedly lost his reason.

Captain Mallet of the privateer *Le Mutin* was released by the Dutch and soon returned to Mauritius and resumed his career, this time on the *Revanche* under Captain Claude Dubois, on 27 March 1794. He took the prize ship *Endeavour* back to Port Louis, and in 1797 was appointed Lieutenant of the *Amphitrite* but the cruise ended in disaster when the ship was wrecked off the western coast of Madagascar. Once again he returned to Port Louis, and served as an officer on *La Confiance* under the orders of that most celebrated corsair, Robert Surcouf, returning home to France after the Peace of Amiens brought a temporary halt to the war. It is said that he was captured in 1803 by the British while trading along the coast of Guinee but that he escaped and was last heard of making for Brazil.

❧

Despite all he had suffered, George Buchan was able to take up his first appointment at Madras as an Assistant in the Military, Political and Secret Department where he was also useful as a translator of French. Subsequently he became Paymaster to the expedition which captured Malacca from the Dutch and he spent a couple of years at the new possession before making a brief return on business to Madras in September 1797. With November fast approaching he knew he had to leave India promptly if he was to get back to Malacca before the storms set in and ships were unable to approach the Coromandel Coast. Unfortunately for him, he was late departing Fort St George, and from the Masulah boat that took him through the rain and surf he was dismayed to see his ship sail without him.

As a result of his drenching in the open boat he contracted a fever, but dared not put off his departure any longer and finally embarked on a small and ominously unstable vessel of just 100 tons with only one cabin for eating and sleeping. Had they run into storms, the vessel would have capsized; instead they were faced with calms and contrary winds until, after three weeks at sea, they were still in the Bay and running short of water and food. Sand from the ballast had got into the pump, and the captain sensibly decided to put back to Corin, one of the very few relatively safe harbours along the coast at that time of the year.

Although they sighted land the same day, they were to the south of their destination and unable to make any progress northwards. A change of wind, violent but favourable, raised hopes which were soon dashed by the discovery that there was 6 feet of water in the hold and that the vessel had sprung a leak beyond the power of the pump to stem. Although afraid of foundering, the captain was even more fearful of getting near the treacherous coast at night, and decided to remain at anchor and try to keep the ship afloat until the morning. There were 24 on board, including 15 Lascar seamen, the master and the owner, plus the owner's pet spaniel; and everyone, sailor or passenger, took his turn either at the pump or at baling out the water. It was a fraught night as the water continued to rise until it reached the cabin itself. Buchan was one of those detailed to man the pump, and in two hours they had lessened the depth by 6 inches. After that they managed to hold it steady until 5am when the pump spear broke, and in the short time it took to fit another all the hard work had been lost. The weather had worsened, the ship was awash, and once the second pump spear broke an hour later, they had no option but to cut the cable and try to get as close to the land as possible before the ship foundered.

Even in that they were disappointed. The ship was so waterlogged that she could barely move, and all that was left to do was to lash together some rafts and lower the ship's boat, a small two-oared craft.

'Happily there was no scramble and all who seemed desirous to get into the boat did so, and the number was altogether 10 or 11 including the owner of the boat , the master and his chief officer, the writer of this and 6 or 7 natives which completely filled and loaded the boat. We had not left the vessel more than a quarter of an hour when she sank. We proceeded towards the shore, but, on coming near, an insuperable barrier seemed to rise before us in a very high surf which it appeared altogether impossible for any ship's boat, and still more so for such a one as ours, to cross. We accordingly stood out again from the land to get away from the heavy swell that was driving on the shore and rowed before the wind and current southward in the distant hope that we might fall in with some vessel or come in sight of some village from whence assistance might be had. We were all greatly reduced from the long continued exertion, having tasted nothing since we left the vessel…and not having a morsel of bread, a drop of water or any sustenance with us.'[174]

Once again Buchan found himself in the same predicament as five years earlier; and there was another similarity. The owner's spaniel had joined his master in the boat, and Buchan found himself thinking back to the *Winterton* and the pig whose blood he had drunk as a last resort. 'I remember contemplating with some satisfaction the probability of our being enabled to turn our poor dumb companion to a very useful purpose.'

For five hours they drifted, close enough to the shore to see and be seen, but the local Indian villagers were in no position to help them. Suddenly the sun came from behind a cloud and struck on a long, low reef of black rocks on which the sea smashed. They were heading straight for it, with no hope of clearing it.

'There were not fewer than 8 or 10 broken surfs rising to a fearful height and following each other in rapid succession, and seeming ready to engulf any boat that approached…In this desperate dilemma a short pause ensured while we considered for a moment what was best to be tried. The time for deliberation was indeed not long for we had drifted within a few yards of the dangerous reef and a few moments more must have been decisive. In this state of things the attempt to cross the surf had now become our only though very hopeless alternative, one that appeared more a sort of expiring effort than anything. The resolution being made to take the plunge we made the best preparations we could for the guidance of the boat…and having so done we rowed for the breakers. By a striking Providential interference at that moment, to us so very critical, a short lull ensued and we were able without material interruption to get about half way through the surf. It then resumed its threatening appearance but wonderful was it to ourselves to find that our little boat, instead of being overwhelmed by the towering waves, rose on the top of them and in this manner were we tossed from one to another so that none broke over us until we were close to the shore which we at length to our very great satisfaction reached after experiencing a very wonderful deliverance. The master of our late vessel who managed the vessel's helm steered with great skill but no human skill could possibly have availed if we had not, unknown to ourselves, been guided by an infallible pilot'.

Buchan, like the spaniel, survived to resume his duties, this time as Sub-Secretary in his old department but was shortly devastated by news that his youngest surviving brother, Robert, only 15 years old, had been lost overboard while on a voyage to China as Sixth Mate on the East Indiaman, *Arniston*.

By October 1801 he was Secretary in the Military Department and less than two years later he became Chief Secretary in the same, rising to Private Secretary in 1809. His health, which had never fully recovered from the wreck of the *Winterton*, forced him to plan his return home that very same year. By coincidence, Dale was at Madras with the *Streatham* at the same time, but for whatever reason Buchan booked his passage on the *Lady Jane Dundas*, thus avoiding another unsought adventure. When asked to postpone his departure for a short while to clear up some further business, he reluctantly but fortuitously agreed to do so. The *Lady Jane Dundas* sailed without him, only to founder with all hands after parting with the fleet off Mauritius on 14 March 1809,[175] while he returned safely to England in 1810 on one of the Company's fast packets. Three times he had escaped drowning: small wonder he believed so firmly in providence.

Buchan never married but returned to his family seat at Kelloe as the last surviving brother, for Henry had died in 1805 aged 26, and shortly after his return his 19-year-old sister Elizabeth died. The family's house on Adam Square in Edinburgh, which had once belonged to the great architect himself, had been sold many years earlier. He had evidently kept in touch with John Dale, and some time before 1820 they met up, at which time Buchan told his friend that he was considering writing about the shipwreck which had thrown them together. Short accounts of the wreck based on Dale's narrative had already appeared in print, but Dale now loaned Buchan his private manuscript, a volume he had never intended for publication, and Buchan's book was published in Edinburgh in 1820. Whether at his friend's request or at his own discretion, Buchan was careful to avoid strong criticism of the ship's officers.

Despite his impaired health, George Buchan managed to outlive everyone else from the ship, although, to be fair, Isabella Cullen achieved a greater age. His memorial tablet in the little church at Edrom reads:

'George Buchan Esq of Kelloe who died at Kelloe on 3rd January 1856 aged 80 years. He was formerly Chief Secretary to the Government at Madras but for many years he had resided at his family seat, occupying himself with the duties of a country gentleman and magistrate.

'Zealous for every good work for the service of God and the benefit of mankind, his active benevolence and munificent bounty endeared him to the poor, while his rare mental endowments, his high-toned principle and consistency of character obtained universal respect and esteem.'

Chapter Twenty

The Captain's Tale

When Donald Cameron's *Earl of Oxford* sailed for Calcutta in February 1795 it was with John Dale as Second Mate. Given that the *Winterton* had not even completed her outward run, Dale had made only one trip as an officer, and then he had been merely Sixth Mate, hardly more than a midshipman. He had never been to China as an officer, which was a prerequisite for any mate with his eyes on the quarterdeck.

The *Earl of Oxford*'s voyage was unmarred by mutiny, privateers or reefs, and the ship returned safely the following August, after which Dale was promoted to Chief Mate on the *Earl Talbot* under Captain Jeremiah Dawkins, which left Portsmouth in March 1797 bound for Madras and China. As on the previous voyage, the East Indiamen now sailed in convoy and with a Royal Navy escort as far as Madeira. The strength of their armament exempted them from the obligation to sail in an escorted convoy, but in practice they chose to do so. The few ships actually owned by the HEIC, as opposed to being chartered, were not insured and had little choice in the matter.

Once a commander had accepted Royal Navy escort he had to defer to the authority of the senior naval officer, for whom convoy duty was at best a bore relieved by excellent dinners at the various captains' tables and at worst a nightmare. The choice of route was always an unsatisfactory compromise, especially when the naval officers often had little or no experience of Indian waters, and the India captains considered themselves at the very least equal in rank to the men who were in authority over them. Add to that a degree of naval envy at the apparent wealth of these merchant officers and a mounting frustration at the way they either dawdled at night or else found ways of leaving the convoy, and the navy's irritation becomes perfectly comprehensible. A frigate in charge of a fleet of Indiamen was a sheepdog herding a flock of wilful sheep.

Outward bound, Captain Dawkins fell ill, and on 10 July 1797, a day after reaching Madras, he died. Only just into his first voyage as Chief Mate, John Dale was given an unexpected 28th birthday present: the temporary command of an East Indiaman, and not just any old East Indiaman. The huge *Earl Talbot*, all 1428[176] tons of her, was on her maiden voyage. By a stroke of irony, the Company had finally abolished the custom of buying and selling commands, whether by the captain or his widow, and Dale could not bank on getting a ship of his own. The plum which had fallen into his lap was not quite ripe but still delicious. He could afford to stretch out in the round house or walk the quarterdeck and dream. From Madras he took the *Earl Talbot* via Penang and Malacca to Whampoa, the European anchorage for Canton, and the ship spent Christmas loading tea, moored in company with the other magnificent vessels of the China fleet and the merchantmen of other nations. It was his first visit to China since his days as a seaman on the *Valentine*; it was also his last. In January 1798 the China fleet sailed for home, calling at St Helena on the way, and in the October Dale reached the Downs.

He had brought the *Earl Talbot* home in one piece, to the undoubted relief of William Moffat the ship's husband. Even ships in convoy could come to grief in storms or when separated from the others. Now all Dale could do was to wait and hope. There were plenty of other first mates in line for promotion; every one of them by definition more experienced than himself. He was living in London, in Upper Norton Street, part of a large modern development in Marylebone, subsequently demolished to make way for St Pancras Station, catering largely for the middle classes who had business in the city but who were not yet ready to aspire to addresses at Clapham Common or Bedford Square.

Dale did get his Captaincy,[177] but not the *Earl Talbot*. Instead, he took over another of Moffat's ships, the older and smaller *Lord Thurlow*, which at 800 tons was not dissimilar to the *Winterton* and which had already made four voyages for the HEIC. There had been a time when four voyages was the normal contract, but now ships were making more, protected from the Teredo worm by copper sheathing, and there was prestige and potential profit for a captain in a regular East Indiaman. The vessels of the China fleet were larger than the regular ships because they were not required to negotiate the Hooghly River in order to call at Calcutta. In hindsight, Moffat might have wished he had given Dale the *Earl Talbot* which was once again bound for Canton. After the China ships had left the convoy she was lost with all hands in 1800, probably on the infamous Paracel Shoal. The *Lord Thurlow*, on the other hand, enjoyed a safe run to Madras, leaving Portsmouth in April 1801, reaching Madras in August along with the China ships and the *Princess Charlotte*, and giving Dale his first proper taste of what it meant to be a Commander in the service of the HEIC.

The Company valued its captains highly, often referring to them as 'Commanders' as if to indicate their superiority over other merchant captains, and a Commander was ranked alongside a Colonel in India. The guns of the Presidency forts saluted the arrival of his ship, and when the great man himself went ashore he was welcomed with a 13-gun salute and a guard of honour. A prosperous captain kept a house and carriage at Calcutta, living ashore in great style when in port, and it was hardly surprising that, as a class, HEIC captains had a reputation for wealth and a self-importance somewhere between pride and arrogance. At Madras, far less prestigious than Calcutta, Dale could well have stayed as a guest with acquaintances, perhaps even with George Buchan who looked upon him as a friend and who was definitely at his office at the time for on 19 August he announced news of the 1801 Act of Union in the *Madras Courier*. The arrival of the fleet meant news from England, social and political, letters from friends and families, more troops and new civilian faces. A ball, advertised in the *Courier*, was held before the ships sailed – an ideal time for the Presidency's bachelors to make themselves known to any single women who had arrived that season.

There is a gap of three years between Dale's first two voyages as a Captain. At some time between his return from India and April 1803 he went to Llandrindod Wells to take the waters. Although not nearly as large or as fashionable as Bath, Llandrindod had become a popular spa town ever since an entrepreneur from Shrewsbury had leased several large houses, turned them into hotels, and advertised heavily. The publication of a paper by an influential German doctor endorsing the medicinal virtues of the local water only increased its appeal. Whether Dale went for his health or for social reasons is not clear, but while staying there he made the acquaintance of Thomas Thomas of Llanbradach who was to become both friend and brother-in-law. This gentleman was paying his addresses to the elder daughter of Thomas Jones, the Welsh artist who lived at Pencerrig House just down the road at Builth Wells, and he invited Dale to go with him to meet the family.

Jones had studied in London under Wilson and established himself before doing what many young artists did by travelling to Italy. While in Naples he had taken up with Maria Moncke, a Danish widow and Catholic convert. Two daughters had been born to them before the deaths of his elder brother and then his father brought

Thomas Jones back to London with the irregular family of which his parents – both strict Dissenters – were unaware. He made haste to marry Maria and then took up permanent residence at the family seat. His daughters, Anna Maria and Elizabetha Francesca remained in London for some years to be educated, and then came home to Pencerrig.

That the two girls were illegitimate was no secret in the district. Long after their deaths someone claimed that neither they nor their mother, who died in 1799, were accepted everywhere, but Jones came from a line of highly respected and wealthy local landowners, and Thomas Thomas certainly did not cavil at Anna's irregular birth. The father might 'be a little stunted man, as round as a ball, the truest Welsh runt',[178] as a friend once described him; the daughters, however, were local beauties, and Eliza with her large eyes, cupid's mouth and waist-length curls caught John Dale's attention.

In 1803, Thomas Jones died, leaving his extensive lands to his daughters. As the elder, Anna gained Pencerrig; Eliza inherited Llandrindod Hall and Trevonnen. Each girl was worth an impressive £4000 a year, an income sufficient to send Jane Austen's Mrs Bennet into raptures. On 11 April 1804 their uncle David, Rector of Gladestry, had the pleasure of performing a double wedding ceremony when Anna and Thomas and Eliza and John walked down the aisle of the Parish Church of Llanelwedd.

The Thomases went to live at his family estate of Llanbradach, and the Dales moved into Pencerrig which was smaller than Landrindod Hall and larger than Trevonnen. In any case, both of Eliza's properties had tenants. At about the time of the marriage, Nixon, Limner to the Prince Regent, painted a miniature of Dale in his captain's uniform.[179] The portrait in its gold case containing a lock of hair has all the hallmarks of a love token given to his young bride. He appears a little older than his years, very much the assured captain and with none of the self-consciousness apparent in the earlier portrait.

During the latter part of that period, Dudman's Deptford yard was busy building a ship for one of the new leaders among East India husbands, Richard Borrodaile. She was to be named the *Streatham*, and she was already earmarked for Dale who would become one of her shareholders. At 800 tons she was a regular Indiaman, and presiding over the Captain's table, Dale must have been proud of her. Clearly he was prospering, and that was not always the case when ships sailed in convoy, arriving together and disgorging a glut of articles. Successful commanders – and there were many who made very little or even sustained losses – reckoned their success in thousands rather than hundreds of pounds. £4000 in the India trade was a fair estimate of a good profit on a single voyage; quite exceptionally, ships trading to China could make their captain as much as £12,000. As well as his private trade, a captain also kept the money paid by passengers for a seat at his table, and while strict rules governed the amount to be paid for a berth by those travelling on company business, the rest was by negotiation.

In May 1805, while the *Streatham* was fitting out, Eliza gave birth to a daughter, Eliza Agnew, at their Marylebone home.[180] Her husband sailed for Madras and Calcutta on the *Streatham*'s maiden voyage from Cork at the end of August that same year, in convoy. The Trafalgar campaign was over before the ship left England but that did not mean that the oceans between England and India were any less dangerous. *Streatham* called at Madeira, San Salvador and the Cape, before reaching Madras in April 1806, and Penang in June. Dale sailed up the Hooghly to Diamond Harbour in the July and, after visiting other ports, returned home by way of Madras, the Cape and St Helena. During the voyage he had purchased gifts for Eliza including china and fans, engraved with their joint initials, in anticipation of a reunion that would never take place. His daughter died on 15 May 1806, and her mother followed five weeks later at Clifton, the Bristol Spa where she had gone, probably with her sister, to take the waters. For four days a team of four horses solemnly drew her coffin home to Pencerrig. Mother and daughter were buried in the Jones's vault at Llandrindod Wells.

Possibly a letter from Thomas or Anna reached Dale before he arrived home in England. Otherwise it may have fallen to one of the ship's owners, or a friend at the India House, to break the news when he disembarked.

Dale inherited his wife's estates, but did not return to live in Wales. Instead, he let Eliza's uncle, Middleton Jones, and his wife move into Pencerrig. In 1807 his sister-in-law, Anna, died, and Pencerrig passed to her baby son – who was himself to die tragically young in 1810. The lands of Thomas Jones had passed out of the family and into the hands of his two sons-in-law. In 1808 Dale went back to sea.

In wartime, all merchant captains faced the problem of keeping their ships fully or even adequately manned at a time when the Royal Navy both at home and abroad would frisk every merchantman and press as many of her seamen as it liked. Dale's 1808 voyage took him via Madeira, Rio de Janeiro, Diamond Harbour and Kidderpore, and by the time he left Sauger, homeward bound, on 24 February 1809, his crew consisted of 44 British, 33 Chinese, 40 Lascars and 16 from other nationalities. There was nothing intrinsically wrong with non-British seamen, other than that the Lascars suffered in the north European winter, and that most foreigners – as the *Streatham's* Captain was about to find out – were understandably reluctant to lose their lives in another nation's war. Well for George Buchan that he had not chosen or been in a position to travel with his friend.

Escorted by HMS *Victor*, the *Streatham* sailed in company with the *Europe*, the *Monarch* and the *Lord Keith*, and she flew the Commodore's pennant to indicate that her Commander was the senior marine officer. The *Monarch* sprang a serious leak and since repairs at sea were ineffectual, Dale gave her permission to leave the convoy on 20 May.[181] Five days later, their escort left them, and on the last day of the month the three vessels – only two of them regular Indiamen – found themselves due south of Calcutta and some 750 miles south east of Madras, not far from the Andamans.

Lurking in the waters was *La Caroline*, a 68-gun frigate which had been something of a thorn in the side of the British. She was just one of four now based at Mauritius with orders to disrupt British shipping, and her presence in the Bay of Bengal was not by chance: she was acting on reliable information passed to her by the captain of an American vessel. At dawn her lookout sighted 'a strange sail' soon identified as the three Indiamen steering NNE 'under a press of sail', proving that John Dale was not taking his time. The watch on the *Europe* was similarly awake, spotting the frigate at just before 6am. Captain Gelstone promptly ordered the hammocks to be stowed and the decks cleared for action, although in those early moments he fully expected to find that the vessel would turn out to be HMS *Victor*.

Steadily and relentlessly *La Caroline* came on; whatever flag she was flying, it was not the Tricolour because she only hoisted that when at close range, accompanying the action with three cheers for the Emperor, by which time not one of the Indiamen could have doubted what she was. The *Europe* was by far the closest – a good distance separated her from the *Streatham*, and *La Caroline* picked her off first. The battle began at 7am when the Frenchman fired a mixture of round, grape and bar shot, designed to cripple rather than sink the merchantman. Gelstone returned fire briskly, his men reloading as quickly as they could, and for more than 20 minutes the *Europe* stood her ground, though her rate of fire went down, two men were killed and her rigging was torn apart. Many of her crew earned their Captain's praise for their courage, but the unfortunate Lascars were 'only in the way'.

With the *Europe* incapable of flight, *La Caroline* wore round under her victim's bows and, after another burst of raking fire, ran down to leeward of the *Streatham* with her starboard guns loaded and her gunners under orders not to fire until they were within musket shot. For an hour[182] the two ships exchanged fire. Well into the engagement Dale's gunners came close to killing *Caroline*'s Captain, Lieutenant Jean-Baptiste-Henri Feretier.

'I had', wrote the French Captain, 'the misfortune to lose my Master...who was a most excellent officer; his head was shot off by a cannon ball as he stood by me on the quarterdeck, the same shot carried off half my hat and wounded me slightly in the cheek.'[183]

Streatham was not badly damaged, but, like her consort, had problems maintaining a rate of fire that would tell against her more heavily armed and quicker opponent.

Dale told Eglinton Maxwell, his Chief Mate, to go below

'...to encourage the people at the guns, he returned shortly to inform me that the Chinese and Portuguese who were stationed on the gun deck could not by any exertion of the officers be kept to their quarters, deserting as fast as they were brought back, and that our firing was almost exclusively maintained by the Europeans.'

Despite her crippled condition the *Europe* attempted to rejoin the action, and the *Lord Keith* managed a brief intervention before two broadsides from the enemy induced Captain Peter Campbell to take flight, much to the disgust of the French.

Unable to continue his defence of the ship, Dale gave the order to haul down the pennant, and *La Caroline* returned to the attack on *Europe*. With several hits on the larboard side and water rising in her hold, the *Europe* made a hopeless attempt at escape before she passed to leeward of the *Streatham* and hailed her, asking if she had surrendered. That was enough. Gelstone, too, hauled down his colour.

For two days the French were busy repairing the *Europe* and getting the *Streatham* into a condition to mount her guns. In all the drama and danger, Dale had no time to think of anything but the job in hand; now, as *La Caroline* set course for Reunion Island with the two Indiamen following under French crews, he must have reflected wryly on two other India captains: Nathaniel Dance who had earned his knighthood through his successful defence of the

India fleet, and Pierius Muntz who had refused to strike to *Le Mutin*. But Dance had had a full fleet under his command, and Muntz had only had to deal with a small, lightly armed privateer, not a fast, highly manoeuverable frigate who mounted almost as many guns as the *Streatham* and the *Europe* together.

For close to four months Dale and Gelstone languished as captives on shore, with their ships at anchor in the harbour of St Paul. The capture of the two vessels was a major blow not just to their pride but to their hopes of a profitable trip. Insurance might recompense them for their actual losses but it would not bring them new ships to command nor make up for theoretical profits.

The only spark of consolation came from the fact that the French had not yet taken the Indiamen to Mauritius where they and their cargoes could be sold. Instead, the cargoes, consisting largely of silk valued at £500,000 had been unloaded and placed in warehouses, and along with the *Grappler* and *La Caroline* the two ships now formed part of the defences of the only useful harbour on the island.

The naval activities of Sir Edward Pellew in the Indian Ocean had hampered the French to such an extent that insurance premiums had dropped considerably, but since the arrival of *La Caroline* and her companions an unacceptable number of ships had been taken, many of them East Indiamen. The capture of the *Europe* and the *Streatham* proved to be the the final straw. In August the Royal Navy at last turned its attention to the islands of Mauritius and Reunion.'[184]

'...being joined by the Nereide, Otter and Wasp schooner, having on board a detachment of the 56th regiment, and of the 2nd regiment Native Infantry, amounting in the whole to 368 men, under the command of Lieut.-col. Keating, and the Sirius having joined, we proceeded at dusk, on the evening of the 20th, for the Isle of Bourbon. The force intended to be landed were, the detachment of his Majesty's and Company's troops, reinforced by the marines of the squadron, and a party of about 100 seamen from this ship and the Otter, under the command of Capt. Willoughby, whose zeal induced him to volunteer the command of so small a party. As secrecy and dispatch were essential to the success of the Expedition, the whole of this force, amounting to 604 men, were embarked with five additional boats on board the Nereide, Capt. Corbet, who from his perfect acquaintance with the coast, as well as his known skill and activity, was intrusted (sic) with this important service. – On our approach towards the bay of St Paul's, to prevent suspicion, the Nereide preceded the other ships; and being anchored close to the beach, the whole of the detachment were landed with the greatest celerity, without any alarm being given to the Enemy, and proceeded towards the batteries, which were successionally stormed and carried with the greatest gallantry, and several of the guns pointed on the ships in the roads. In the mean time the squadron stood into the bay, and according to the plan agreed upon, when the movements of the troops enabled them to act, opened their fire on the shipping, which was warmly returned by La Caroline frigate, the Indiamen, her prizes, and those batteries which, from their distance from the first point of attack, were enabled to continue their fire; but these being finally carried, our ships prepared to anchor, and the Sirius having already taken a close raking position a-head of La Caroline, they found it necessary to surrender…The squadron having anchored in the Roads close off the town of St Paul's, immediate exertions were made to secure La Caroline and the rest of the shipping, whose cables being cut had drifted on shore, and they were hove off without material injury.'

The *Streatham* and the *Europe* were once again under the British flag; their cargoes and captains were still in French hands.

'On the morning of the 22nd we could have but little communication with the shore, on account of the surf on the
beach; but we observed the Enemy collecting on the heights,
and in the afternoon they appeared in force, advancing to the
town from St. Denis, upon which it was considered advisable
by Lieut.-col. Keating and myself, to destroy the stores containing the public property.'

Some fine judgement had to be exercised. Having retaken the
Indiamen, they knew that the cargo was on shore, and at all costs
they wished to avoid damaging it.

'From the state of the surf on the beach, the marines were
selected for this service, with a small party of seamen: and
Capt. Willoughby again volunteered his services on the occasion. The Lieut.-Col. himself accompanied the party; and a
large and valuable magazine, the only one we could ascertain
to be public property, was fired, and the party re-embarked
without loss.'

The magazine, however, contained silk valued at £500,000, some or
all of it taken from the two Indiamen.

'On the morning of the 23rd, the troops, marines, and seamen, all in boats, were in readiness to land under cover of the
Nereide, when we were informed that the Enemy, under the
command of Gen. de Bruleys, had retreated to St. Denis in
the night. The Commandant St. Michael being disposed to
negotiate, the Lieutenant-col. and myself agreed to sign the
terms...since which time the troops and seamen have been
actively employed in shipping the property found in the public stores, consisting of provisions and some ordinance stores,
and a part of the cargoes of the captured Indiamen, which
had not been fired at the same time as the others...the car-

goes of the Indiamen alone being valued by them at 3,000,000 of dollars. – As the Captains of the captured Indiamen were found in this place, I have replaced them in their former situations, with such of their people as we can collect, and are fitting their ships for sea.'

On the same night, Dale returned to his cabin and recommenced his log book as though nothing untoward had happened. He recorded that there was damage to the tiller and that the Captain of HMS *Otter* had obligingly loaned his carpenter to make the repair. When the *Streatham* sailed, it was in company with HMS *Otter*, the *Grappler* and *La Caroline*.

The following year, the Royal Navy took Mauritius with some help from the HEIC's Bombay Marine including Robert Deane, the former Acting Lieutenant of the *Scorpion* who was by then a captain himself.

Just as any naval commander who lost a ship was automatically subject to a court martial, so the commanders of East Indiaman faced a court of enquiry, which might blame or vindicate them according to the circumstances. Dale and Gelstone came through with their reputations intact, but they had sustained significant losses. James Thomas and John Mortlock,[185] both with financial stakes in the ship or her cargo, suffered badly over the incident, and by extension, Dale, with his hefty shareholding, cannot have emerged unscathed.

By the time of his next voyage, Dale was probably engaged, because on 3 September 1812, just two months after his return from a voyage to Diamond Harbour and Madras, he married for the second time, aged 43.

Back in 1777 the City of London had witnessed an important marriage when Frances Cattley married her first cousin, Stephen. The Cattleys were bankers and merchants, influential in the City and important in the trade with St Petersburg; and, irrespective of any question of love, this marriage kept a great deal of money within the one family; indeed, three of Frances's younger sisters married other Cattley men. Frances and Stephen produced nine childen, and it was the third child, Frances Bode[186] Cattley whom John Dale married, at All Saints, Wandsworth. Already 27, she had been living with her widowed mother on Clapham Common, a highly desirable address for the middle classes who had made their fortunes but still wished or needed to be within reach of the City. Successful East India captains were good catches for a wealthy mercantile family.

Early in 1813, Middleton Jones, the brother of the late Thomas Jones, suddenly claimed that his nieces were never legally entitled to inherit their father's lands as both were born out of wedlock and the land was entailed on legitimate issue. Both Dale and Thomas contested the claim vigorously. Thomas evidently proved that there was no such strict entail on Pencerrig, but Dale was not so lucky. His late wife's birth certificate, issued in Naples, certainly implied that her parents were married, but the London marriage certificate of Maria Moncke and Thomas Jones described the latter as a bachelor, and neither correspondence with the Church in Italy as late as 1820 nor even a journey in person to Naples could give him the proof of his wife's legitimacy that he needed to satisfy the entail.

Just before judgement was given in favour of Middleton Jones in August 1813, Frances Dale presented her husband with a daughter. Jane Frances was baptised at the Wandsworth church where her parents had married. More children followed: Louisa Anne in 1814 and John Andrews[187] in 1816. Dale had passed up two HEIC voyages, handing command of the *Streatham* first to Peter Grant and then to Charles Mortlock who had been his Second Mate in 1805. The right to forgo voyages was a prized perk for captains who were doing well because the man who commanded in their stead would have paid for the privilege. And Dale had been doing well: he had just bought almost £7000 of shares in the ship.[188] He moved to Norfolk Street, which ran down to the Thames from the Strand and where Coleridge lived until 1816. The road had come into being after the Duke of Norfolk made leases on his lands in 1682, and there was said to be a Roman Bath in the cellars of one of the properties.[189] The loss of the Welsh revenues and the sheer cost of trying to prove his claim, was to prove a serious blow to his prosperity.

In March 1817 Dale went back to sea for a final voyage, returning to find that Frances had given birth to their fourth child, George Dundas. 1819 saw the birth of Alexander Forbes who died before he was two, and in 1822 their last child, Katherine Rose was born. By now the family had a London home in Sloane Street, Chelsea, and a house at Speen, just outside Newbury.[190] East India captains rarely had the sea in their blood: they may have enjoyed their time, but their ambition was to make a fortune. John Dale was not to become one of those ex-mariners who paced the cobbled streets of an English port or gazed out to sea from the harbour wall wishing they were back on the quarterdeck. Good seaman though he undoubtedly was, the undulating Berkshire countryside appealed more to him in his retirement than the rolling waves, and times had changed since he first went to sea. By the time he retired there was a regular steamship service across the Irish Sea, and in 1825 the auxiliary paddle steamer *Enterprise* made Calcutta in 115 days, under steam power for well over half of the voyage. She, too, had been built at Deptford, and disappointing as her performance had been, she was the herald of a new era.

Few details of Dale's private life have survived, but he did purchase a Royal Worcester dinner service of white china with a blue rim and additional gilding. The service was embellished with a lion demi rampant in gold, a heraldic device to which the family does not appear to have had any right.

On Christmas Day 1823 Frances passed away, aged 38. Their eldest child was 10 years old; their youngest just 21 months. John himself died on 8 March 1827 at the age of 57. Buried with them at Speen is their son, Alexander, and Dale's half-sisters. Neither of the surviving sons married, and neither followed their father to sea. George Dundas Dale turned out to be the black sheep of the family and retired in unspecified disgrace to Cumberland. John Andrews became a scientist of some small note: his major contribution was to recommend the use of gutta-percha to insulate the Transatlantic cable, but he was a diffident man, even unwilling to take up the offer of a place on the *Great Eastern* when she made that cable-laying voyage. Of the girls, Louisa Anne died a spinster, and Jane Frances and Katherine Rose both married local clergymen; all were brought up at Speen by their maiden Talbot aunts.

The modern town of Newbury is gradually gaining on Speen, but the church where John and his second wife are buried stands in a tranquil valley still closer to their time than to the present. The tomb is overgrown and the inscription on the top has weathered and flaked away. His name is hidden in the grass, but he lies in an English churchyard while many of his companions from the *Winterton* left their bones in the sea or the foreign soils of Mozambique, Madagascar, Mauritius and India, too many of them in the anonymous graves which their dying comrades struggled to dig for them at Toleary.

Appendix I

Lists of Crew and Passengers of the *Winterton*

List of Crew on board the *Winterton*

The following list is compiled from the Receipt Book at the British Library (L/MAR/B 451 G), the report in *The Times* originally compiled by the surviving officers, and the list of those on board the *Joachim*. There are some discrepancies. In particular, *The Times* report states that 87 crew survived the initial wreck and that 16 seamen, the Captain and the First Mate died. Add the three who died at sea prior to reaching the Cape, and the initial ship's company stands at 108. However, the three sources suggest a total of 122, which may be partially explained by errors in the officers' letter, by men having left and joined the ship at the Cape, and by the addition of three men from the wrecked whaler at Mozambique.

Names in **bold type** are listed in the Receipt Book as having received two months wages in advance. This list was compiled over several days shortly before the ship sailed and would have been sent back to India House. Subsequently a second list was made in London, also in the Receipt Book, detailing further payments to spouses, persons nominated to receive wages for individual crewmen, or to the crewmen themselves when they returned. This list was annotated when the first report of the ship's loss reached India House in August 1793, and thereafter as information about the survivors came in. Names in ordinary type are of men who appear in this second half of the Receipt Book but who did not feature in the first list. A * denotes that the person concerned also appears in the list of saved as printed in *The Times*.

Names in *italic* appear in the list of saved but do not appear in the Receipt Book. It is possible that these men joined the ship at the Cape.

The Times report contains errors in names. For example it shows Wm Longster as a Quartermaster, while the Receipt Book states *Thomas* Longster, Quartermaster. However, the postscript noting his death gives his correct first name. Dates are written day/month/year.

Name	Position	Monthly Wage	Notes
Abbot James*	Seaman	£1.6.0	
Adams Thomas*	Seaman	£1.6.0	Served on 3rd voyage. Died Sena 6/12/1792.
Allgrove George			Drowned.
Alston John	Seaman	£1.6.0	Drowned.
Anderson William*	Seaman	£1.6.0	Died after the wreck, but listed as on the *Joachim*.
Atkinson John	Seaman	£1.6.0	Died 3/4/1793 on Mozambique.
*Arthur William**	Midshipman		
Bacon Thomas*	Seaman	£1.6.0	Survived the wreck.
Baird Thomas*	Seaman	£1.6.0	
Bannerman Alex*	Surgeon's Mate	£2.0.0	Died after the wreck.
Bates James*			Saved.
Bathgate Charles*	Steward	£1.10.0	Died after the wreck.
Berwick James*	Seaman	£1.6.0	On the *Joachim*.
Biggins John*	Seaman		
Bishop Robert*			Survived; paid 6/5/1794.
Blisset James/Thomas*	Seaman	£1.6.0	On the *Joachim*.
Bowman/Beaumont William	Seaman	£1.6.0	On the *Joachim*. Held in the floating prison at Mauritius 1794. Probably from the whaler *Mercury*.
Bristow Charles*	Cook	£1.10.0	

Name	Position	Monthly Wage	Notes
Campbell Thomas*	Seaman		
Candlar/Kindler/ Kindrain John	? Boatswain's Servant	£1.10.0	Wages paid to Alice Slater. His pay seems too high for a mere servant. On the *Joachim*, and a prisoner at Mauritius in 1794.
Carmichael John*	Carpenter's Second Mate	£2.0.0	On 20/6/1795 Janet Carmichael wrote to the Pay Office at the India House asking them to pay outstanding sums to William Dunn for her late husband. On 15/7/1795 £4 was paid to Mr Dicky of 6 Flore Street, Bedford Square for William Dunn to pass on to the widow.
Carr Joseph*	Seaman	£1.6.0	Survived the wreck.
Casper Peter	Seaman	£1.6.0	
Chambers Charles	First Mate	£5.0.0	Drowned.
Collier Charles*	Seaman	£1.6.0	Survived the wreck.
Connolly Michael*	Seaman	£1.6.0	Survived the wreck. On the *Joachim*.
Cross John*	Seaman		
Curry William*	Seaman		Survived the wreck.
Dale John*	Third Mate	£3.0.0	Survived. On the *Joachim*. Paid 22/7/1794.
Davidson Robert	Seaman	£1.6.0	
Deane Thomas*	Seaman	£1.6.0	Survived the wreck. On the *Joachim*.
Delaney James	Seaman	£1.6.0	Survived wreck; died later.
Dickson/Dixon* Francis	Seaman	£1.6.0	Survived the wreck. An Ann Dixon was awarded a pension in 1795 but here is no proof that her husband was Francis Dixon.
Dionard Antony*	Butcher*	£1.6.0	Survived wreck; died later.
Dow David*	Second Mate's Servant		Survived the wreck.
Dowdall Henry*	Gunners First Mate	£1.10.0	Survived the wreck; died later. In 1797 his wife received a pension for one year.
*Dulsay James**	Quartermaster		

Name	Position	Monthly Wage	Notes
Dun(n) William*	Purser	£2.0.0	Survived. Reached India via the *Joachim* and Mauritius. Paid 11/2/1795.
Dundas Daniel*	Gunner	£2.5.0	Survived the wreck; died later.
Dundas George	Captain	£10.0.0	
Fairhead William*			Survived the wreck.
Foster William*	Seaman	£1.6.0	On the *Joachim*. Paid 7/1/1798.
Freeman Henry*	Seaman	£1.6.0	Survived the wreck.
French James*	Seaman	£1.6.0	Survived the wreck; died later.
Garratt Thomas			
Geddes John*		£1.3.0	Survived the wreck; on the *Joachim*.
Griffin James	Seaman	£1.6.0	
Hammond Ben			Although not mentioned in the Receipt Book or *The Times* he is reported on the *Joachim*, so is presumably from the whaler *Mercury*.
Handling Edward	Bosun's Mate	£1.10.0	
Hayes James	Seaman	£1.6.0	
Herring John*	Survived.		On the *Joachim*. Paid 11/12/1798.
Higgins James	Captain's Cook	£3.0.0	Died at sea 7/7/1792.
Hill James*	Seaman	£1.6.0	Survived the wreck. On the *Joachim*.
Howard John	Gunner's Servant	£0.15.0	
Hughes John	Poulterer	£1.6.0	Drowned at sea 26/5/1792.
Inglewight Robert			Although not mentioned in the Receipt Book or *The Times*, he is reported on the *Joachim* so is presumably from the whaler *Mercury*.
Irlam Nathaniel*		£2.0.0	Survived the wreck.
Jolly John*	Midshipman	£1.6.0	Survived.

Name	Position	Monthly Wage	Notes
Knox Andrew*	Seaman	£1.6.0	Survived the wreck. On the *Joachim*.
Lilburn Robert	Cooper	£2.10.0	Died.
Lillie George*	Surgeon	£3.0.0	Died Christmas 1792, Toleary.
Long Thomas*	Boatswain's Mate	£1.10.0	Survived. On the *Joachim*.
Longster Thomas	Quartermaster	£1.10.0	Survived the wreck. Died Sena. *The Times* calls him *William* in the list.
Mackie Thomas			Drowned.
Manuel Lewis	Seaman	£1.6.0	Died at sea 4/6/1793.
Marshall Thomas*	Captain's Servant	£1.3.0	Survived the wreck; died later.
Martlin?			Survived the wreck; died later.
Mather John*	Seaman	£1.6.0	Survived the wreck.
Mayslen John*	Armourer	£1.10.0	
McDonald Hugh*	Surgeon's Servant		Survived the wreck.
McNaughton John*	Seaman	£1.6.0	Survived the wreck.
Moore John*	Fifth Mate	£1.10.0	Died at Mozambique. Letters of Admin., granted to Abraham Moore.
Moray Charles*	Midshipman Coxwain	£1.10.0	Survived the wreck. On the *Joachim*.
Newall Robert *	Midshipman	£1.6.0	Survived the wreck; died later. *The Times* calls him *Thomas* Newall.
Newton Thomas*	Quartermaster		Dead. *The Times* calls him *Patrick* Newton.
Nimmo Robert	Seaman	£1.6.0	Survived the wreck.
O'Bryan Peter*	Seaman	£1.6.0	Survived the wreck; died later.
Oliver George	Seaman	£1.6.0	Dead.
Osborne Thomas*			On the *Joachim*. Paid 18/7/1794.
*Paddington G**			
Patterson David*	Seaman	£1.6.0	Survived the wreck.

Name	Position	Monthly Wage	Notes
Patterson Robert*	Seaman	£1.6.0	Survived the wreck.
Piercy Daniel*	Quartermaster	£1.10.0	Survived the wreck; died later.
Pindar George	Seaman	£1.6.0	
Ponson Matthew*	Carpenter's Assistant	£2.10.0	Survived the wreck; died later.
Porter/Porteus David*	Seaman?	£1.6.0	Survived the wreck. On the *Joachim*. Died later?
Ramsay Hon. Henry*	Midshipman	£1.6.0	Survived. On the *Joachim* On *Le Mutin*?
Roach Francis	Seaman	£1.6.0	Drowned.
Robertson William*	Seaman	£1.6.0	Survived the wreck.
Rogers James*	Seaman	£1.6.0	Survived the wreck; died later.
Rowland James*	Carpenter's Mate	£0.15.0	Survived the wreck.
Rowland William*	Carpenter	£3.10.0	Survived, and was on the *Joachim* but must have died by April 1797 when his widow was awarded a pension.
Rozier Henry*	Quartermaster	£1.10.0	Survived. On the *Joachim*. Awarded life pension as unfit to work.
Sinclair John*			Survived the wreck.
Slater John*	Boatswain	£2.16.0	Survived the wreck. On the *Joachim* and *Le Mutin*.
Smith Joseph*			Survived the wreck.
Smith Rayner*	Caulker's Assistant	£2.0.0	Survived the wreck; died later.
Smith William*	Seaman	£1.6.0	Survived the wreck.
Somers William	Seaman	£1.6.0	
Sowerby John*	Seaman	£1.6.0	Survived the wreck; died later.
Spens Nathaniel *	Second Mate	£4.0.0	Died Madagascar c. New Year 1793.
Stevens Jeremiah*	Caulker	£3.0.0	Survived the wreck.
Stobs Matthew			Drowned.
Taylor John	Seaman	£1.6.0	
Templeman Thomas	Seaman	£1.6.0	Drowned.

Name	Position	Monthly Wage	Notes
Thompson Samuel*	Gunner's Mate	£1.10.0	Survived the wreck.
Thomson John*	Seaman	£1.6.0	Survived the wreck.
Thomson Robert	Seaman	£1.6.0	
Travers John			
Troy/Tory Thomas*	Seaman	£1.6.0	Survived the wreck; died later.
Turner Henry?			
Underhill James*	Captain's Steward	£1.10.0	Survived the wreck; died later.
Wallis Thomas*	Midshipman	£1.6.0	Survived the wreck; died later.
Ward James*	Seaman	£1.6.0	Survived the wreck.
Watkins William	Seaman	£1.6.0	
White Henry	Seaman	£1.6.0	Died at sea 12/7/1792.
*Williams John**	Seaman		
Wilton Joseph William*	Fourth Mate	£2.0.0	Died at Sena 25/12/1792.
Wood Samuel*	Seaman	£1.6.0	Survived the wreck. On the *Joachim*.
Wrightman James	Seaman	£1.6.0	
Young Alex*	Cooper's Mate		Survived the wreck; died later.

The only men whose survival is certain are those few who actually returned to London to sign for their wages, who received a pension, or whose career can be traced: Bishop, Dale, Dunn, Foster, Herring, Jolly, Osborne, Ramsay and Rozier. In 1797 Isabella Rowland received a pension, but there is no knowing how long had passed since William's death, or even if his death was as a direct result of his ordeal.

According to *The Times* 16 crew members plus Dundas and Chambers drowned in the actual wreck. The only certain victims are Allgrove, Alston, Lilburn, Mackie, Newton, Oliver, Roach, Stobs and Templeman. A further 12 men are unaccounted for and must be presumed either dead or as having left the ship at the Cape: Pindar,

Casper, Davidson, Garratt, Handling, Hayes, Howard, Somers, Taylor, R Thomson, Travers and Wrightman.

Twenty-two men reported as having survived the wreck, but there is no clue to their fate. Ten were left with John Jolly at Anjouan and were collected by the *Gloucester*. Two must have gone with Dale (although none of them has a remotely Portuguese name).

List of the Soldiers saved from the Wreck

The source is again *The Times* of 23 August 1793. Given the discrepancies between the names of the passengers and crew listed in the same article and other sources, this list must be treated with caution. Name spellings were far from standardised, and by the time the handwritten list had spent a year travelling between Madagascar, Mozambique, Mauritius and London it could well have been somewhat fragile. The printers may simply have done their best.

Surname	First name	Rank
Adams	John	
Anderson	Michael	
Aspley	Robert	
Audney	Alexander	
Barlow	Thomas	
Barrett	Robert	
Baylie	Francis	
Booker/Bowker	William	
Burnett	Not known	Corporal
Burrows	William	
Campbell	Faulix	
Campbell	Kenneth	
Campbell	George	
Cassell	Stephen	
Caswell	Samuel	
Chouch-an	George	

Surname	First name	Rank
Clark	John	
Connolly	Archibald	
Cooper	Samuel	
Cousins	Spencer	
Craig	Thomas	
Crosby	Edward	
Deacon	unknown	Corporal
Donnerland	Bryan	
Elder	David	
Ellis	John	
Everton	Luke	
Faulkener	James	
Ferguson	James	
Giddins	William	
Goose	Thomas	
Grainger	George	
Gwilt	Orlando	
Haddock	Thomas	
Hardy	William	
Hartley	James	
Hatcher	Richard	
Hays	George	
Heath	Matthew	
Hewitt	John	
Hillier	Thomas	
Hogg	James	
Hollier	Samuel	
Hughes	William	
Hunt	Not known	Corporal
Hutchins	James	
Johns	William	
Jolly	William	
Kelly	William	
Lansdown	Samuel	
Kidder/Tidder	John	
Leslie	William	
Lewis	David	
Lowmon	William	
Lynch	Richard	
MacGarth	Robert	
Mansfield	Alex	
Marshall	John	

Surname	First name	Rank
Marshall	Edwards	
McDonald	William	
McFarlan	Norman	
McGregor	Charles	
McKey	William	
McKilltop	John	
McKinsie	John	
McLauchlan	William	
McNeill	Duncan	
McPherson	George	
McTairsh	Not known	Sergeant
McUshett	Not known	Sergeant
Moore	Samuel	
Moore	John	
Moore	David	
Morris	Jeremiah	
Patten	Timothy	
Ramsay	William	
Reilly/Relly	Thomas	
Reynolds	John	
Richards	Oliver	
Robertson	Thomas	
Rose	Not known	Sergeant
Russell	Not known	Sergeant
Scott	Isaac	
Scrivener	William	
Smith	George	
Strat(t)on	William	
Tyson	Thomas	
Waghorn	Henry	
Watson	John	
Welsh	John	
Wilson	John	
Wilson	James	
Wood	Samuel	
Woodnott	Abraham	
Young	John	
Young	James	

List of the Passengers on the *Winterton*

The primary source for the passenger list is *The Times*, but it does not give first names. Buchan and Dale rarely mention first names, and so positive identfication of a number of passengers is either impossible or a matter of conjecture. Tracking those who survived to serve the Company – or those who married into it – is much easier.

Drowned signifies lost in the break up of the *Winterton; died* implies dying before reaching India.

Baillie	Isabella	Baptised 1781 aged 3. Died 1835.
Bellis/Bellas/Bellasis	Mrs	Identification and ultimate fate uncertain: remained on Mozambique Island. Possibly Sarah (née Williams) who had married Ensign Joseph Bellas in 1785.
Bristow	Charlotte	1776–1833.
Bristow	Mary	1777–? Survived.
Buchan	George	1776–1856. Writer for Madras.
Collier	Charles?	Free Mariner. Died some years later in a shipwreck.
Cullen	Isabella	1760–1842.
Cullen	unknown	c.1780–1792. Drowned. Referred to only as *Miss Cullen*.
Cullen	Margaret	c.1782–? Survived.
De Chiene/ Chiene	George?	Died, probably on Madagascar.
Frazer	Thomas?	b.1775. Writer for Madras. Identification uncertain, but as he was not on the *Joachim* when she was captured he must have died earlier.
Gibbs	Robert	Free Mariner. Survived.
Gordon	John	1776–1804. Cadet.
Hamilton	John	Writer for Bengal (Calcutta). Died on Mauritius. There may have been two writers named Hamilton aboard: the other was destined for Madras but must have died.

Hepburn	Samuel	1776–? He had been appointed a Writer, but if this is our man, a note at the OIOL (source unknown) states he died at sea in 1794.
Lyne	William	1772–1793. Cadet. Died on Madagascar.
Lyne	Miss	Sister of William. Died 1793 on Mozambique Island.
Marshthorpe	Not known	Died.
McGowan	Miss	Sister of Suetonius. Drowned.
McGowan	Suetonius	1775–1798. Cadet.
Percival	Not known	Died.
Ramsay	Andrew	1776–1848. Writer for Madras. Survived.
Silk	Not known	Survived.
Souza, de	Thomas	Survived.
McLean	John Field	Assistant Surgeon. Survived.
Coloquhoun	William	Assistant Surgeon. Survived.
Thompson	Alexander	Free Mariner. Died on Madagascar.
Cameron	Not known	Died.
Alderson	Not known	Died.
Robinson	Miss	Drowned.

Survivors Alive at the Capture of the *Joachim*

The source is the list which appeared in *A Narrative Of The Loss Of The Winterton On Her Passage To India* (1796 London, printed by C Whittington for B Crosby, No. 4 Stationers Court, Ludgate Street, 6d). Again, there are mistakes, such as calling Margaret Cullen *Mary,* and among the names must be the men from the whaling ship.

Bound for Bengal
Mrs Cullen
Miss Mary Cullen
Miss Bristow
Miss Mary Bristow
Miss Baillie
Mr Hamilton
Hon. Mr Ramsay
Mr Gordon, cadet
Mr McGowan, native of India

Bound for Madras
Mr Maclean, surgeon
Mr Coloquhoun, surgeon
Mr Buchan
Mr Collier, free mariner
Mr Silk, ditto
Mr Gibb, ditto

Crew
John Dale
William Dunn
John Slater, boatswain
William Rowland
Henry Ramsay
Charles Murray/Moray
Thomas Long, boatswain's mate
Henry Rosier, quartermaster
James Hill, baker
J Blisset, capt's cook
David Porteous

Ben Hammond
William Anderson
James Herrig
James Berwick
Michael Connolly
Sam Wood
Thomas Dean
Andrew Knox
William Beaumont
Robert Inglewright

Servants
J Geddes Capts
T Osborne, 1st mate's
William Foster
J Kindrain
Ja. Rowland Carpenters's

Lieut Brownrigg of 75th plus 33 recruits, 1 woman, 1 child

Appendix II

The Search for the Treasure

Winterton soon faded from public interest, eclipsed by the naval and military engagements of the French Wars. During the nineteenth century mass emigration to America and Australia provided a new crop of maritime tragedies; Europe marvelled at the courage and discipline of the soldiers on the troopship *Birkenhead* who stood to attention as their ship sank in shark-infested waters while the women and children took to the lifeboats; and *Forfarshire* gave the nation a heroine in the form of lighthouse-keeper's daughter, Grace Darling. Despite the terrible shipping losses – naval and merchant – of two world wars, *Titanic* dominated the twentieth century, and *Winterton* was relegated to a passing mention in a few specialist books.

But in one quarter at least she lived on. No wreck with such a cargo would ever be forgotten in diving circles. As soon as the internationally famous marine archaeologist, Dr Robert Sténuit, founder of the Groupe de Recherche Archeologique Sous-Marine Post-Médiévale, read her history he was enthralled. 'When it comes to shipwreck tales, the ships lost by the East India Companies are in a class of their own,' he wrote. 'But this story is a classic among them.' He was moved by the quiet heroism, the dignity, suffering and courage of both men and women; and he was pardonably excited by the treasure she had carried:

'More than 8 tonnes! There were more than 8 tonnes on board the *Winterton*. 262,000 troy ounces precisely, which is to say 8135 kilos of silver or 289,629 pieces of eight, packed in 75 chests of 107 kilos apiece. The first time that I read the story – 20 years or more ago – I swore that one day I, myself, would find that wreck.'[191]

That day came in 1985 when, having secured the active co-oper-
ation of the Madagascan authorities and assembled his team from
GRASP and COMEX, Sténuit embarked on an expedition to the
island. Their vessel was the COMEX ship, *Soleil d'Orient*, superbly
equipped with three magnetometers to locate wrecks, two airlifts
and a prop-wash to uncover the site, and a 3½-ton crane for lifting
heavy objects. As well as comfortable accommodation she also
boasted a dark room, art studio and conservation room. *Winterton*
was not the team's sole quarry, and they had already spent several
months on the east coast before moving round to Tulear, the only
port along that stretch of the south-west coastline. Despite all he
had read, Sténuit was convinced that anything between 1 and 4 tons
of silver remained on the ship, inaccessible to the native fishermen
but well within the reach of modern divers with their sophisticated
technology.

The latitude given by Buchan was 23°30', 63 miles north of St
Augustines Bay, itself 6 miles long. Armed with a modern French
chart and Buchan's description of the reef, Sténuit calculated that
the wreck site had to be around 22°27' South, give or take 6 miles.
Before beginning work with the magnetometer he went out in the
Zodiac, one of two inflatables, and made a preliminary dive on the
exterior edge of the reef. There was a heavy swell, the conditions
were far from ideal but not, they felt, too dangerous for experienced
men.

One moment he was in 3 metres of water on the edge of the reef,
with 10 metres of visibility; the next, everything went black with a
cataclysmic crash. For several seconds, and they were long seconds
even for a diver of his experience, he was in utter darkness; then suddenly the sea turned into boiling foam, more air than liquid. A huge
roller had passed overhead, breaking on the reef in a savage crescen-
do of white water.

When he finally surfaced, in deeper water away from the reef,
there was no sign of the *Zodiac* or the three companions he had left
in her, but the diving gear scattered on the seabed was graphic proof

that she had been overturned. He knew exactly what had hit them; it is called a 'rogue wave' and is all the more dangerous for its unpredictability. All he could see now were massive mountains of grey water bearing down on him and lifting him like a cork. He dived under, and swam further out to sea before surfacing, and at last spotted the *Soleil d'Orient* like a red stain ³/₄ mile away to the north. Stripping off his diving suit he swam as powerfully as he could, but far from approaching the ship, he felt himself dragged further south by the current.

Just in time, for his strength was ebbing, he was picked up by the second inflatable which had just plucked another man out of the water. As the *Zodiac* had capsized, her equipment had been flung about, and a cylinder had struck the second diver causing broken ribs and some unpleasant cuts. The other missing pair, one of them a Madagascan naval officer, were eventually found at a distance on the reef, righting the *Zodiac* with the help of a group of local fisherman. It had been a nasty taste of what the *Winterton* people must have suffered.

Five days went by before the sea was calm enough for work to resume, and then they set up the magnetometer. It consisted of a torpedo-shaped 'fish' towed underwater behind the research vessel, sending information on the intensity of the local magnetic field down the co-axial cable and back to the ship. Any anomaly, such as the iron hull of a modern vessel or the iron cannon and ballast of an older ship, would show up on the on-board recorder. The GRASP/COMEX team made a number of parallel runs up and down their chosen area, eyes glued to the stylus. And they found something. A second pass, 50 metres east, confirmed the anomaly. Sténuit was first into the water.

'It was a shipwreck. A wreck spread out everywhere. Huge iron cannons, of the right period, an enormous and typically English anchor, triangular in shape, hundreds of iron bars. Pig iron, used as ballast in warships and East Indiamen as raw material in international trade, was mixed with mountains of cannon balls. This first glance was enough to make up my mind. This was indeed our *Winterton*.

'All the same, I had to make certain that all the objects lying here were compatible with what we knew of the ship, and nothing was incompatible. The debris was amazing. Everywhere there were pieces of copper leaf (the HEIC used it to sheath the bottoms of their ships to protect against the Teredo worm in tropical water), and hundreds of the little round-headed copper nails, which were used to fix the copper leaves to the wood. I could also see occasional piles of conglomerate, green to grey. Some had the shape of the base of the wooden chests in which the copper cargo was carried, exactly as described in the Company's Commercial Ledger; and the ultimate proof was that there were the flints, large, medium, and small, scattered in their hundreds in the sand and in the holes.

'But as ill luck would have it, that same morning, just as we were about to make a second dive, an enormous swell came down on us from Durban. In just an hour the site became unapproachable, and the *Soleil d'Orient* had to run; we wouldn't have fancied diving even if our lives depended on it.'

He did not need to find the ship's bell: she was clearly an Indiaman, British, and, with the exception of her distance from the shore, pretty much exactly where the *Winterton* was known to have been wrecked.

Days went by before they could go down again, and when they did it was necessary to cling on in order to stay in place. One of the team wrapped his legs round a huge mortar ball and set to work. There were several of those mortar balls,[192] with diameters of between 25 and 32.5 centimetres; they were not listed on the cargo manifest but could have come under a general heading. Another surprise came in the shape of some big, cast iron cylinders found around a large gear that measured 1.25 metres long by 65 centimetres diameter. There were teeth at both ends and a central axle. Sténuit speculated that it might have been destined for a sugar mill.

Sténuit's excavations were interrupted by the discovery of the first piece of eight. It lay flat on a rock, anchored only by the vegetation, and when they carefully prized it loose it left behind its imprint in reverse. The metal was eroded: they could make out only the first three figures of the date: 178-. That was significant: it ruled out any ship lost before 1780.

While first studying the manifest Sténuit had been surprised to find anchors listed among the cargo for they were large, bulky objects, surely uneconomical to transport as cargo. But on the bottom he learned the HEIC's answer to the problem: anchors were fabricated and transported in pieces for assembly in India.

That same day they found a further 14 pieces of eight. 'I have found them by the thousand, in many other wrecks, over the years, but each one gives me the same pleasure every time.'

The search was hampered, however, by the huge quantity of pig-iron ballast which was soldered together by its own rust making it impossible to look beneath it. Elsewhere, the rocks were carpeted by a layer of living material, mainly sponges, beneath which the crevices and holes contained nails, flints, shards of china, broken scraps of navigation equipment and fistfuls of silver pieces. Every evening they carefully updated their plan of the wreck with the details of their finds, building up a picture of where particular objects were concentrated.

Despite their best efforts and equipment, they were not getting very far and it was impossible to predict when the heavy swell would appear to disrupt their activities. Twice the *Zodiac* was overturned by breaking rogue waves and tossed across the whole reef with the half-drowned divers desperately clinging on to her. At the end of the first month what had been merely bad weather gave way to storms and it was back to Tulear to repair the damage. Eight days of delay went past before they could get back on site.

'There are two schools of thought about working in a big swell. Some prefer to hook their legs round a cannon or an iron ingot (the advantage of the ingot is that you can take it with you wherever you want to work). Of course, every 10 or 15 seconds the raw power of the swell will try to double you up forwards only to try to snap your spine backwards immediately after. You resist with your abdominal muscles, and occasionally ask yourself if your body will hold or break. Other divers like to buckle 30 kilos of lead weight round their waist, despite the fact that you can see them thrown back and forth all the while.'

In the end they resorted to dynamite: small charges carefully set to displace the masses of rusting iron without damaging the wreck site. A difficult business undertaken with care not to injure the divers or alarm the fishermen who, like themselves, were profiting from any break in the weather. The explosions uncovered a few coins, but nothing to indicate that they were close to the treasure. Then Sténuit made a discovery: a large piece of copper sheet bent very deliberately at right angles.

The most feared hazard on a wooden ship, particularly one carrying powder, was fire, and the powder magazine of an East Indiaman was lined with copper. No iron was allowed for fear of sparks. The discovery was significant because the ships carried their treasure in a secure place usually the powder magazine or the spirit store which were locked and guarded.

Sténuit took great care with the charges. Two were placed beneath a solid mass of eight rusty ingots to send them up vertically while a third charge was laid to the side to push them out of the way. He was convinced that the silver must lie just below. It was a textbook explosion, but instead of the thousands of silver coins, all he found was more iron, and, below that, the rocks. What he could not know[193] was that the officers had shifted the silver into the lazarette in order to trim the ship during their efforts to get her off the reef, which was one reason why in the final hours seamen were able to help themselves with impunity. It might have made it that little easier for the King of Baba's subjects to salvage.

For three days the weather remained calm, an opportunity to photograph in clear water and to sift through the debris without the need to cling on. Dr Sténuit set up more charges, but all in vain.

When the weather deteriorated the team accepted that the only silver left on the *Winterton* was the odd handful they had found.

'Once again I had to take off my hat to the tenacity of those divers of long ago, to their professionalism and their technique, however primitive. As for our fears of causing the ruin of professional coin dealers by flooding the world market with pieces of eight, those were happily laid to rest.'

There was one other quarter in which *Winterton* had never been forgotten: the people who lived alongside the reef and fished in its lagoon, whose ancestors had risked the surf and the dangers of being crushed or trapped while diving in the battered hull. They still wear their memories of the unlucky East Indiaman in the form of much-prized manilla-shaped good-luck bracelets.

Notes

Prologue

1. Dale/Whittingham 1796.
2. An optical telescope with a large diameter eyepiece and lens, designed to admit as much light as possible, thus making it useful at night. It produced an inverted image.
3. Dale claimed that his birthday was on 29 August but may have confused it with his baptismal day.
4. £3.50.

Chapter One

5. Barnard. No evidence exists as to which of the two yards built *Winterton*, but the balance of probability favours Deptford Green.
6. Although Captain's Servant appears a low rank, it was considered to be a suitable position for a young gentleman looking to rise in the marine service. Captains routinely signed on their relations as seamen or servants as a route into the officer class.
7. The late Sir Thomas Rumbold Bt, a former Governor of Madras, had been one of the shareholders until his death. Many East Indiamen were named after their shareholders, particularly those with titles.
8. Buchan 1820.
9. Years later, Captain Dance would gain both revenge and a knighthood when, as Commodore, he successfully defended the HEIC fleet from attack by the French Admiral Linois in *Marengo*.
10. NLS ADV.MS 80.7.2 f40+.
11. See Appendix I.
12. Wilton is very possibly related to the sculptor Joseph Wilton.
13. *House of Forbes*.
14. OIOC L/MAR/B Log of the *Winterton*, 3rd Voyage.
15. Cook: Only in exceptional circumstances did the Company issue chronometers to commanders. The fact that most commanders used chronometers made by John Arnold is not a sign of bulk buying but the consequence of the Hydrographer, Alexander Dalrymple's unambiguous preference for Arnold's design over that of competitors such as Earnshaw and Barraud.
16. Arguably two chronometers are worse than one. Unless they both keep time identically, on which one should a captain rely? Once chronometers became plentiful and less expensive it was the practice to carry five.
17. OIOC L/AG/1/6/20.
18. WO Muster Rolls, 75th Regiment.
19. At that period regiments were often raised for a particular purpose and could subsequently be disbanded. After the American War of Independence the British army had been reduced in numbers of men and regiments, but King George III now agreed with the Company on the need to strengthen the forces in India. Although the Company would have preferred, for financial reasons, to raise its own units a royal warrant to raise 4 new regiments of 10 companies and a

grenadier company each had been issued on 12 October 1787. Abercrombie, based in Stirling, found it hard to recruit in Scotland and had been sent into England for the purpose, looking to persuade discharged sailors and men in prison for civil offences to take the King's shilling. The 75th eventually became the Gordon Highlanders. J SAHR 1974.

20 OIOC Minutes of the Court of Directors of the United HEIC 29 June & 22 August 1787.

Chapter Two

21 The *Memoirs of William Hickey* are an invaluable example of a young man who outlived his scandalous teenage years and became a respected attorney in India before returning to England.

22 Buchan 1820.

23 In 1774, after intervening to stave off the Company's financial collapse, the Government had effectively part-nationalised the HEIC with the establishment of a Board of Control to regulate its operation. In 1792 Henry Dundas was President of this body.

24 OIOC L/MAR/C529.

25 NLS ADV.MS 80.7.2.f66.

26 If his regiment was disbanded or reduced in number, an officer could go on the half pay rendering him eligible for call up should the army need to expand, as happened during the Napoleonic Wars.

27 An indication of his wealth is that, when he married legitimately, he was able to settle £40,000 on his wife.

28 In *Honourable Company* Margaret Bellasis mentions the loss of the

Winterton, but without suggesting a family connection, and she names no one who could be identified with this passenger. Her name is spelt variously as Bellasis, Bellis or Bellas. One candidate is Sarah Bellas née Williams who had married Ensign Joseph Harvey Bellas in India in 1785.

29 OIOC J/1/14/f139. The most likely Hepburn is Samuel Hepburn, baptised 17/8/1776 at Temple, Midlothian, Scotland, the son of to Robert Hepburn of Clerkington. An unattributed note states he died at sea 1794, which may be just anther inaccuracy.

30 If he is the Thomas de Souza buried at Calcutta Cathedral in 1827, aged 64, he was 29 when he embarked on the *Winterton*.

31 *The Times* 30/4/1792.

32 NLS ADV.MS 80.2.63.

33 Buchan 1820.

34 Dale *Journal.*

35 OIOC B/4/322. Madras Letters Board, Political Dept 27/10/92.

36 See 21.

37 Dale 1793.

38 ibid.

Chapter Three

39 Buchan 1820.

40 Dale *Journal.*

41 Buchan 1820.

42 ibid, quoting Dale.

43 OIOC L/MAR/B Log of the *Winterton*, 2nd voyage.

44 Dale 1793.

45 Unpublished thesis of Dr Andrew Cook of the Dalrymple Society.

46 Thomas Luny's painting suggests the ship carried 38 guns, 26 on the gun deck, the remainder on the

upper deck abaft the mainmast. In practice, she carried the basic battery of 26.

47 Buchan 1820.

48 Findlay's *Indian Ocean Directory*.

49 The ship had at least six quartermasters: Daniel Percy, Henry Rozier, Thomas Longster, Thomas Newton, Patrick N --- and James Dulsay. Newton died in the wreck and may well have been the petty officer alluded to.

50 *Loss of the Winterton* published in *Shipwrecks and Disasters at Sea*. This is one of several printed versions of John Dale's account shortly after the events and is the most accurate.

51 Buchan 1820.

52 *Loss of the Winterton* published in *Shipwrecks and Disasters at Sea*, apparently quoting Dale.

Chapter Four

53 Buchan's contemporary MS goes for the former explanation; his later book cites the tide as the reason.

54 Buchan 1820.

55 Dale's *Journal* refers to the Fourth, Fifth and Sixth mates, but *Winterton* did not carry a Sixth Mate. It is possible that the young midshipman and Coxwain, Charles Moray was with them, but it may just be an error of memory. His contemporary account refers only to the three of them.

56 Dale quoted in Buchan 1820.

57 The man is not identified but must be from among Patrick N---, James Dulsay and Daniel Percy.

58 Buchan's editor seems to think that the three officers must have worked in secret lest their raft be seized by others, yet from the narrative itself

it is clear they were working on the upper deck in full view of everyone.

59 Buchan 1820.

60 ibid, quoting Dale.

Chapter Five

61 That is Dale's conjecture, reported in his *Journal* and based on the fact that he had seen the women and Dundas on the poop before he left the ship.

62 Buchan 1793.

63 Buchan 1793.

64 Buchan 1820.

65 Article in *The Gentleman's Magazine of* March 1793, dated 5 September and said to be the work of a young Englishman. Although the date of 5 September (1792) fits, it cannot be by one of the *Winterton* survivors because news of the loss of the ship did not reach England until August 1793.

66 Despite the proximity to Africa, Madagascar was settled by Indonesians around 700AD. There were also Arab and African influences.

67 Dale *Journal*.

Chapter Six

68 He could be Mr Cameron, William Coloquhoun or George Chiene the Free Mariner. Buchan rarely identifies his fellow travellers except by the surname initial.

69 Mangroves are any tree which sends out aerial roots, and can be found in arid, sandy coastal conditions as well as in the swamps with which they have become popularly synonymous.

70 Findlay.

Chapter Seven

71 This is the title that Buchan and

others gave him, but Baba means *father* and rather describes his relationship to his people. *Dean* was the title frequently used for the most important man in the district, but through contact with European ships the idea of royal titles was known around St Augustine's Bay and imitated.

Chapter Eight

[72] Mauritius.

[73] Dale *Journal*.

Chapter Nine

[74] Dale *Journal*.

[75] Buchan 1820 quotes it as 30° South which is clearly impossible; Dale's 1793 MS clearly states 18° South.

[76] Only two, Longster and Adams, were ever named.

[77] Denis Montgomery in *Aquatic Ape, African Eve* published 1999 on the Internet quotes speculation by archaeologist Paul Sinclair that the location of Sofala as an Arab Swahili trading port may have changed several times due to cyclones before the Portuguese established themselves.

[78] Horsburgh's 1826 East India Pilot.

[79] The stone was brought in the form of granite ballast; one ship sank in the Tagus even before leaving Portugal. The remains of the fort were washed into the sea in 1905 when a cyclone struck.

Chapter Ten

[80] *The True Story of the Grosvenor, East Indiaman, wrecked on the coast of Pondoland, South Africa, on 4th August 1782*, Percival Robson Stuart

Kirby. Published 1960 by Oxford University Press, Cape Town.

[81] Oakum was obtained by picking old rope, an unpleasant task sometimes given to convicts on land. At sea it was all part of a seaman's duties. It was used to fill the gaps between the planks, which were then sealed with pitch: caulking.

[82] The term 'seaworthy' and its opposite encompasses more than the condition of the ship – it also includes the competence or otherwise of the crew. The *Happy Delivery* was, therefore, unsound rather than un-seaworthy.

[83] The Ilha do Bazaruto lies close to the mainland at Santa Carolina, south of the Save River.

[84] The decline of Sofala continued. In 1812, HMS *Nisus* called at Sofala, and the ship's doctor, James Prior, noted that there remained only a solitary Portuguese resident and a few black troops (Empires of the Monsoon, Richard Hall; Harper Collins 1996).

[85] OIOC E/4/322 Political Dept. 27/10/1792.

Chapter Eleven

[86] Stewart, *Zambezi Journal*.

[87] Quinine, obtained from tree bark: the classic treatment for malaria.

[88] River Of Good Signs, as it was named by Vasco de Gama.

Chapter Twelve

[89] Dale *Journal*.

[90] *The Gentleman's Magazine* April 1794, quoting the *London Gazette* in turn quoting information from Fort William dated 8/10/1793.

91 Thomas Spens of Lathallan married Margaret Hope, daughter of Sir Archibald Hope of Craighall by his second marriage. He died in 1783, succeeded first by his eldest son. Thomas and then, in 1800, by his second son, Archibald. Nathaniel and his brothers were, therefore, nephews of Isabella Cullen who was Margaret's step-sister.

92 OIOC L/MAR/C series.

Chapter Thirteen

93 Horace Waller in 1862, reported by James Stewart in his *Zambezi Journal*, published by Chatto & Windus 1952.

94 Snow: a two-masted, square-rigged ship.

95 OIOC E/4/52 Bengal dispatches.

96 Ibid E/4/53 dated 30/11/1793.

97 Carlyle: *History of the French Revolution*.

98 PRO WO1/356/58589 Marquis of Cornwallis at Madras 16/9/1793 to the Rt Hon. Henry Dundas.

99 Colonel Brathwaite, whose report was enclosed with Cornwallis's letter, claimed that he was summoned to Cornwallis on 1 June; while the subsequent experience of Thomas de Souza implies it had been known as early as 30 May.

100 Factories: foreign trading stations, as opposed to *manu*factories.

101 *Bombay Courier* 18/5/1793.

102 Dale 1793.

103 Buchan 1793.

104 ibid.

Chapter Fourteen

105 *The Gentleman's Magazine* April 1794.

106 At the time of parting, Dale and de Souza may have had a slightly different intention, i.e. of getting their people to Mauritius.

107 Dale 1793.

108 Buchan 1793.

109 Buchan 1820 quoting Dale.

110 By implication.

111 A brig: a two-masted vessel square rigged on both masts.

112 *Bombay Country Ships*, Anne Bulley, Reference 382.094, IOLR. These country ships were built to European design from Malabar teak, which was superior to English oak, particularly in tropical waters. The builders were also excellent craftsmen, so despite strong opposition during the last quarter of the eighteenth century more shipowners were inclined to look to Indian yards. The latter received a boost during the Napoleonic period when the Royal Navy's demand for ships and a shortage of oak forced merchant owners to source from abroad. Eventually even regular East Indiamen and warships were built at the famous Indian yards.

113 *The Gentleman's Magazine* April 1794.

114 There are no extant copies of the *Madras Courier* at the time of de Souza's arrival, but the Presidencies' newspapers freely copied material from one another.

115 PRO ADM1/1910. Letter from Captain Hartwell to the Admiralty dated 18 August 1793.

116 Toussaint, Auguste, former Director of the Archives of Mauritius.

[117] Buchan 1793.

[118] Duncan's *Mariners Chronicle*. The account, though clearly based on Dale's own writing, is so seriously flawed at its conclusion that it is unwise to rely on any statements unless corroborated elsewhere. This particular assertion is confirmed, which is more than can be said for the final paragraphs of the account.

Chapter Fifteen

[119] Nationaal Archief Den Haag, 1.04.02 VOC, inventory number 6836. *Account of what had happened on board of the VOC Ship Ceylon on 15th July, laying in the estuary of Tutukoryn* – written by Pierius Muntz to W J Van de Graaf, Governor and director of the Island of Ceylon and Coast of Madura and dependencies.

[120] Nationaal Archief Den Haag.

[121] There were various ways of setting up a spring. Everything depended on the situation: tide, prevailing wind, geography, etc. Sometimes two anchors were used, one from the bow and one from much further aft; alternatively, the ship rode at a single bower anchor with a cable run out from further aft and secured to the riding cable.

[122] Dale was running short of pages in his notebook, and gives only a couple of lines to the engagement.

[123] Dale's estimate. With the use of the paper cartridge and a properly maintained flintlock, a well-trained eighteenth-century soldier could fire four shots a minute in an exercise under optimum conditions, but less in battle. If the action lasted 15 minutes, their rate of fire would have to be two shots a minute, despite the fact that they were under fire from the privateer.

[124] Holland later concluded a treaty with France, thus turning her shipping into a legitimate target for the British. In 1795, off St Helena, nine VOC ships were taken, ruining the Dutch company at a single stroke.

[125] Mallet could expect to be treated courteously as a prisoner of war.

[126] Commanders of East Indiamen did not view such duties as an honour. They were personally out of pocket, often seriously so.

[127] Sir John Brathwaite 1739–1803, son of the Governor in Chief of the African Company's factories on the south coast of Africa. Ensign in 53rd Foot, 1765; Colonel in 1779; taken prisoner at Seringapatam. After Pondicherry appointed Major General. Died London, August 1803.

[128] *History of the Madras Army* Vol. 2, L C W J Wilson, Madras 1822.

[129] PRO ADM/1/1910.

[130] There are some inaccuracies in the names: Henry Quinn Brownrigg was given as W H Brownrigg.

[131] The MS in the South African Library is signed by Dale but may have been copied by a clerk.

[132] PRO WO12/8130.

Chapter Sixteen

[133] The equally ancien-regime Port Bourbon was renamed Port South East.

[134] F10 No. 547 25/9/1793 Declaration de Sieur William

Dunn. National Archives of Mauritius.

135 A104/3, 1794: Nottes des Prisoneriers de Guerre qui sont à Bord de la Prison Flotante, National Archives of Mauritius. The names of Joseph Carr, William Bowman (Beaumont) and John Kindler are present; there were also unnamed English sailors in the hospital.

136 William Hotham, later Admiral Sir William Hotham recalling an incident in 1798, quoted by F D Ommanney in *The Shoals of Capricorn*, two years before Malartic's death. Commodore Losak was blockading Port Louis, and there was much friendly social intercourse between the two commanders, including dinners and trips to the opera.

137 According to Essex Institute Historical Collections 1864 Vol. 6, the *Henry* was a 180-ton ship, i.e. three masted and square rigged, launched in 1793 by Enos Briggs of Salem and measuring 84 feet in length, 22.6 feet in beam, and 11.3 feet in depth. Vol. 79 for 1943, in the article *East India Voyages of Salem Vessels* which drew on a report in the *Salem Gazette* 18 November 1794, states she was a French ship bought at Mauritius before the war.

138 Ralph D Paine: 'The Old Merchant Marine' (published 1921, now available on the Internet by Project Gutenberg).

139 *La Route des Iles* (information supplied by the Archives of Mauritius).

140 OIOC E/190/103. The lists are not with the letter and do not appear to be listed separately.

141 Dubuc led an adventuous life, assisting his countrymen in their war with England, until shot on the orders of Napoleon for getting too friendly with the British.

142 'Discipline and obedience to the law'.

143 'The people of France – liberty or death!'

144 The report which Dale wrote for Cornwallis ended with his arrival in Madras, as did the later account (based on it) which he loaned to George Buchan. Between 1804 and 1808 Archibald Duncan published *The Mariners Chronicle*, and included in Volume 2 was an account of the *Winterton* attributed to Dale and clearly based on his first report. It ends with the following paragraph: 'Of the fate of those that remained on board their own vessel when taken by Le Mutin and ordered to steer for the Mauritius, no intelligence has ever been received in this country, notwithstanding the most diligent search was set on foot to ascertain it by the direction of the H.E.I.C.'

Chapter Seventeen

145 Her presence at the base was noted by William Money in a letter to his son dated 7 February 1794.

146 Letters from the Crowninshield Papers, by kind permission of the Peabody Essex Museum, Salem.

147 Quoted by Northcote Parkinson in *Trade In the Eastern Seas*.

148 *Calcutta Gazette* 24/9/1794.

149 'Master Mariner' by James

Connolly 1943, now published on the Internet. It is based upon Delano's journal.

150 OIOC F/4/20.
151 *Les Gloires Maritimes de la France*, P Levot and A Doneaud, published by A Pigoreau, Successeur, Paris (no date).
152 PRO FO/5/6 – f147. The blank shows that Hamilton did not know the name of the 40-gun Frenchman.

Chapter Eighteen

153 PRO FO/5/6 Folio 151, 22/1/1794.
154 ibid Folio 158.
155 ibid Folio 161/162 19/2/1794.
156 ibid Folio 78, 9/6/1794.
157 ibid Folio 171 28/3/1794.
158 ibid 23rd Feb, Phineas Bond to Grenville.
159 Archives de France, Marine FF2 107 f126/ Marine BB4 44 f55-60.
160 PRO FO/5/6/f194.
161 OIOC E/1/231 MISCELLANIES 12/9/94.

Chapter Nineteen

162 PRO WO/12/9458.
163 *The Gentleman's Magazine*.
164 PRO WO/42/b446; also Burke's *Peerage*.
165 Hodson's Index, National Army Museum, states he was given a medal, implying distinguished conduct.
166 M Milit. 1794 22/4 & 25/5 94 – OIOC.
167 Hodson.
168 National Archives of Scotland GO45/14/884 Dalhousie Muniment, by kind permission of the Earl of Dalhousie.
169 *Monthly Magazine* September 1808.
170 NAS GO45/14/509 Dalhousie Muniment.
171 Duncan's *Mariner's Chronicle* published Dale's account of the wreck of the *Winterton* but instead of ending with his arrival at Madras went on to state that he and some of the seamen with him embarked for England on the *Scorpion*. Totally ignoring the American interlude, the penultimate paragraph ends: 'we were chased by a French Frigate and experienced foul winds and continual calms, by which our progress was so retarded that it was generally supposed the Scorpion had been taken by the enemy. At length, however, we arrived in safety on British ground, and so eager were the poor fellows to see their different relatives, that they got on shore at the Land's End, having first received protections from the Captain of the sloop'. This looks like an editor's clumsy conflation of events, so there could be enough truth within it to explain the dates on which the sailors collected their wages. They must have been part of Jolly's group on Anjouan since Dale's companions on *Le Mutin* were pressed at Madras and the others were still at Mauritius when the *Scorpion* sailed.
172 OIOC ref. B/120 p 1118, 4th March 1795.
173 Allen, *History of the Indian Navy*.
174 *Illustrations Of A Particular Providence*, George Buchan,

published in Edinburgh by William Oliphant.

175 Hardy, Register of Ships.

Chapter Twenty

176 She was actually chartered at 1200 tons; the chartered tonnage of a ship did not always match its actual capacity. Tonnage was a measure of cargo rather than of the ship; the very word comes from 'tun' (a barrel of wine). In modern shipping, 1 gross registered tonne equates to 100 cubic metres, confirming tonnage as a measure of cargo capacity.

177 Confirmed on 24 December 1799.

178 Letter written by Uvedale Price of Foxely Esq. in 1795, quoted in 'The Family History Of Thomas Jones The Artist Of Pencerrig' by R C B Oliver 1970 J D Lewis and Sons Ltd, Gomerian Press, Llandysul.

179 The portrait was in the possession of a descendent until stolen during a burglary. It was subsequently sold at auction with a date of c.1805. Other Dale items remain missing.

180 *The Gentleman's Magazine.*

181 Log of the *Streatham* OIOC L/MAR/B.

182 There are understandable discrepancies of time in the reports given by the captains of the *Europe* and *La Caroline* – standardised times, much less time zones, were still in the future. However, while Gelstone states that the engagement with the *Streatham* lasted from 7.30am until 8am, Lieutenant Feretier's account makes it over an hour. There are

other discrepancies, in that according to the French report both the *Europe* and the *Lord Keith* attempted to attack *La Caroline*, while Gelstone observes that his ship was too crippled to intervene.

183 *The Times.*

184 Letter from Admiral Bertie 29/8/1809, aboard HMS *Raisonnable*, St Paul's Roads.

185 James Thomas had earlier mortgaged his share in the ship so that Mortlock's son, Charles, could sail as Second Mate on the *Streatham* on her maiden voyage. Like so many families with fingers in the HEIC pie, the two were related by ties of friendship and marriage. (R H J Griffiths, The Banking Mortlocks', published on the Internet).

186 Bode was the maiden name of her grandmother who came from the Hague.

187 Dale's great-grandfather, William had had a sister, Suzanna, who married Daniel Andrews. Daniel's grandson, Joseph, a Major in the Royal Berkshire Militia, was created a Baronet in 1766, and on his death the title passed to his nephew, Joseph, born in the year before Dale, and a Lieutenant in the 1st Regiment of Footguards. Lieutenant Sir Joseph Andrews Bt owned Shaw Place, Speenhamland Berkshire, very close to Speen, and it is fair to suppose that he and Dale were on friendly terms.

188 PRO BT107/8. Certificate of Registry.

189 Annals of the Strand, E Beresford Chancellor 1912.

[190] Pierce Egan's 'Walks through Bath...' published in 1819 describes the locality around Newbury: 'SPEENHAMLAND, (55 m. 6 f.) On the right of which is Shaw-Place, the seat of Sir Joseph Andrews, Bart. Immediately adjoining *Speenhamland* is NEWBURY, (55 m. 7 f.) a corporate town...The buildings are old and irregular, and it contains no feature of any particular interest. Its inhabitants are estimated at 5000; but the houses do not exceed 1100. NEWBURY is considered about the half-way to BATH; and some of the coaches make a short stay here to dine; indeed the time allowed for this necessary refreshment is so *short,* that the traveller has scarcely swallowed a few mouthfuls, when he is interrupted by the coachman that *"all is ready,"* and he must either go without his belly-full, or stand a chance of choking himself by bolting the remainder of his food, if he means to make any thing like a dinner, in order to accommodate the coachman. This may be deemed one of the *"miseries of travelling,"* and it should almost seem that *coachy* has a secret understanding with *"mine host"* to turn these things to good account. SPEEN, (56 m. 6 f.) is surrounded both on the right and left with a variety of seats, belonging to the following ladies; Mrs. Wasey; Mrs. Craven; Miss Hulberts; and Mrs. S. Quintins; Donnington, or Chaucer's Grove, belonging to John Bebb, Esq. and Donnington Castle-House, Col. Stead. Also the residences of F. C. Parry, Esq. and the Rev. G. Wyld: but the most prominent and attractive to the mind of the traveller is Goldwall-Hall, the seat of George Canning, Esq. BENHAM-PARK, (57 m. f.) the seat of Anthony Bacon, Esq. and at the end of which is Hemstead-Lodge, belonging to the Earl of Craven. This nobleman elevated to the rank of his countess, Miss Brunton, belonging to Covent-Garden-Theatre, a lady of great personal beauty and attractions, and possessing considerable theatrical talents. About three miles on the right is Welford-Park, belonging to the Rev. John Robinson. HALFWAY-HOUSE, (59 m. 5 f.) within one mile and a half of this place, on the left, is Barton-Court, the seat of C. Dundas, Esq.'

Appendix II

[191] 'Le Tresor du Winterton', Dr Robert Sténuit, written after the expedition to Madagascar. (Author's translation)

[192] Hollow iron balls into which explosives were packed. A fuse was added, and just before the ball was fired from the mortar – a short-barrelled, large-bore tube – the fuse was lit, the whole operation being timed so that the ball exploded as or just after it hit the target.

[193] John Dale recorded this fact in his private journal: it never appeared in Buchan's book.

Sources

The starting point for the research was George Buchan's book *A Narrative of The Loss of the Winterton East Indiaman Wrecked on the Coast of Madagascar in 1792* **(Buchan 1820)**. This was supplemented by Buchan's untitled manuscript **(Buchan MS)**, clearly written shortly after the events they describe, John Dale's 1793 manuscript presented to Cornwallis **(Dale 1793)**, and Dale's private journal **(Dale *Journal*)**. Various accounts of the disaster, based on Dale's formal account appeared as individual publications or in maritime magazines in the early 1800s.

The records of the HEIC are preserved in the Oriental and India Office Collection, which has its own Reading Room at the British Library **(OIOC)**. These records contain a vast amount of information – much of it indexed – on ships, marine and military officers, civil servants, expatriate families in India and the Company's military and civil operations. Among the most important classes of records are the L/MAR series relating to ships, logbooks and marine officers, L/Mil dealing with the Company's military operations, and J/ which houses, among other documents, letters of application from aspiring civil servants. In addition to formal records there are microfilms and card indexes for births, marriages and deaths.

The events described in the book extend into areas of government, where the records are held at the Public Records Office, Kew **(PRO)**. These include the War Office (WO), the Admiralty (ADM), the Foreign Office (FO) and the Board of Trade (BT).

Papers relating to Captain Dundas are held at the National Library of Scotland's Department of Manuscripts **(NLS)**, and the Dalhousie Muniment is deposited in the National Archives of Scotland **(NAS)**.

An invaluable source of genealogical information is Hodson's Index, a large card index held at the National Army Museum. Some of Hodson's information was published (see below) but the card index has a far wider scope, and has been hand-annotated for many years when new information has been received. Its scope goes beyond military officers to cover marine officers, surgeons, etc. For security reasons, it is necessary to apply well in advance for a reader's ticket.

Other sources, where not stated in full in the Notes, can be found below.

Banbury, Philip, *Shipbuilders of The Thames and Medway*, David and Charles, 1971.

Barnard, John, *Building Britain's Wooden Walls*, Anthony Nelson, 1997.

Bellasis, Margaret, *Honourable Company*, Hollis and Carter, 1952.

Bevan, David, *Drums of Birkenhead*, Larson Publications, Aylesbury, 1972.

Bombay Courier.

Bradshaw, A R, *Anglo French Naval Terms*, Williams and Northgate, 1932.

Buchan, George, *A Narrative of The Loss of the Winterton East Indiaman Wrecked on the Coast of Madagascar in 1792*, Edinburgh, 1820.

Buchan, George, *Particular Illustrations of a Particular Providence*, Oliphant, Edinburgh, 1829.

Buchan, George, Untitled MS, MS South African Library, Cape Town, 1793.

Bulley, Anne, *Bombay Country Ships*, Curzon, Richmond, 2000.

Burke, John and Sir John Burke, *A Genealogical and Heraldic Dictionary of the Landed Gentry of Great Britain and Ireland*, 3 volumes, Colburn, London, 1846.

Burke, John, *A General and Heraldic Dictionary of the Peerage and Baronetage of the United Kingdom* (known as Burke's Peerage), Periodical Publications, London, 1826.

Calcutta Gazette.

Chatterton, E Keble, *The Old East Indiamen*, T Werner Laurie, 1914.

Cook, Dr Andrew S, 'Alexander Dalrymple and John Arnold: Chronometers and the Representation of Longitude on East India Company Charts', *Vistas in Astronomy*, Vol. 28, 1985.

Dale, John, 'A Narrative of the Loss of the Winterton', Tegg and Castlemain, not before 1802.

Dale, John, 'A Narrative of the Loss of the Winterton', C Withington for B Crosby, c. 1796.

Dale, John, *Journal*, private collection.

Dale, John, 'The Loss of the Winterton', MSB158 1793 (a copy of the narrative presented to the Marquis of Cornwallis at Madras), South African Library.

Dalyell, Sir J G, *Shipwrecks and Disasters at Sea*, 1812.

Dictionary of American Biography.

Dictionary of National Biography.

Duncan, Archibald, *Duncan's Mariner's Chronicle*, 1810.

Findlay, Alexander, *A Directory for Navigation of the Indian Ocean*, published for Robert Holmes, 1882+.

Fletcher, R A, *In the Days of Tall Ships*, Brentano's, London, 1928.

Gardiner R (ed.), *Fleet Battle and Blockade*, Caxton, 2001.

The Gentleman's Magazine

Hall, Richard, *Empires of the Monsoon*, HarperCollins, 1995.

Hardy, *A Register of Ships Employed in the Service of The Honourable East India Company*.

Harland, John, *Seamanship*, Conway Maritime Press, 1984.

Hickey, William & Peter Quennel (ed.), *Memoirs of William Hickey*, Purnell Book Services, 1975 by arrangement with Routledge and

Kegan Paul.

Hodson's Index (unpublished), National Army Museum.

Horsburgh, James, *Directory For Sailing to and From the East Indies*, 1809+

Kingsford, Charles Lethbridge, *The Story of the Royal Warwickshire Regiment*, D P & G (Doncaster) available from the Regimental Museum.

Kirby, Percival, *The True Story of the Grosvenor East Indiaman Wrecked on the Coast of Pondoland South Africa on 4th August 1782*, Oxford University Press, Cape Town, 1960.

A List of the Officers of the Army (annual publication listing army officers by regiment).

Lloyd's List.

Low, Charles Rathbone, *History of the Indian Navy*, London, 1877.

MacGregor, David R, *Merchant Sailing Ships 1775–1815*, Argus Books Ltd, 1980.

Madras Courier.

Mariners' Marvellous Magazine, London, 1809.

Mason, Philip, The Men Who Ruled India, Cape, 1985.

Miller, Nathan, *Broadsides*, John Wiley & Sons Inc., 2000.

Muntz, Captain Pierius, 'Account of what happened on board of the VOC Ship Ceylon on 15th July', (unpublished, hand-written report) 1.04.02 VOC 6836, Nationaal Archief Den Haag.

Northcote Parkinson, C, *Trade in the Eastern Seas*, Frank Cass and Co.

Ltd, 1937 (reprinted 1966).

O'Brien, Patrick, *The Mauritius Command*, HarperCollins, 1998.

Oliver, R C B, 'The Family History of Thomas Jones of Pencerrig', 1970.

Ommanney, F D, *The Shoals of Capricorn*, Longman's Green & Co., London, 1952.

Paine, Ralph D, *The Old Merchant Marine*, 1921 (now published on the internet, see below).

The Register of Ships (annual publication with details of merchant ships from 1760s to date), Lloyd's Register of Shipping.

'Remarkable Account of the Loss of the Ganges…also the Loss of the Winterton', London, 1808.

Schebesta, Paul, *Portugals Konquistamission in Sudost-Africa Missiongeschichte Sambesiens und des Monomotaparreiches*, Steyler Verlag St Augustin, Studia Instituti Missologici Societatis Verbi Divini XIV.

Society for Army Historical Research, *Journal 1974*.

Steel's Original and Correct List of the Royal Navy (and the Hon. East India Company's Shipping) (annual publication of ships and officers of the Royal Navy).

Sténuit, Dr Robert, 'Le Trésor du Winterton', private MS.

Sutton, Jean, *Lords of the East*, Conway Maritime Press, 1981.

Taylor, Alistair and Henrietta (Ed), *The House of Forbes*, Aberdeen 1937.

The Times.

Tuck, P (ed.), *The East India Company 1699–1858*, Routledge, 1998.

Wallis J P R (ed.), *Zambezi Journal of James Stewart*, Chatto and Windus, 1952.

Wilson, L C W J, *History of the Madras Army*, Madras, 1822.

Woodman, R, *The Victory of Seapower*, Caxton, 2001.

Websites

Aquatic Ape, African Eve, by Denis Montgomery:
www.sondela.co.uk/Aqua/aquaindex

The Banking Mortlocks, by R H J Griffiths: www.com.sg/~tonym/mortlock

The Blackheath Connection (undergoing major change).

Ilha da Mocambique: www.geocities.com/b_veronik/ilha/monuments

Indian Ocean Privateers, by Henri Maurel:
www.perso.wanadoo.fr/henri.maurel/corsair

Paine, Ralph D, The Old Merchant Marine:
www.digital.library.upenn.edu/webbing/gutbook/lookup?num=3099.

The Money Family, by Adrian Money:
www.members.lycos.co.uk/adrian_money/william

Glossary

back. Position of the sails so that the wind bears on the opposite surface from that which will propel the ship forward, to slow the ship, hold it relatively stationary or actually 'reverse' it.

able seaman. A knowledgeable and experienced seaman.

aft. To the rear of the vessel.

amidships. In the middle of the vessel.

astern. Behind.

beam. The width of the ship.

bilgewater. Water that collects and stagnates in the ship's bottom.

booms. A spar to which the lower part of a sail is attached.

bowsprit. A heavy spar, in effect a mast, angled forward over the bow.

brace. Rope used to hold the direction of the sail.

brails. Rigging lines used to reduce and control the area of sail catching the wind.

bring to. Heading the ship into the wind so that it almost stops – a technique for slowing down.

bulkhead. Internal partitions created by the ship's structure.

cable. Heavy rope.

cable. 240 yards.

capstan. The mechanism by which the anchor if raised.

chains. Chains attached to both sides of the ship abreast of each mast. They held the shrouds which gave lateral support to the masts.

close hauled. Rigged to sail directly into the wind.

club-hauling. A method of moving against the wind using two anchors. The first holds the boat in positing while the second is thrown out. Then the first is weighed while the boat is pulled up to the second, and repeated.

corvette. A flush-decked warship next in size to a frigate.

country trade. This was the trade round the coast of India or between the HEIC's other trading posts – as distinct from the trade between India and England.

cutter. In this context, one of the ship's boats.

driver. A fore-and-aft sail set on the mizzenmast.

flush deck. A deck without a break or step.

fore. Front of the ship.

forecastle. The forward part of the ship / a small raised deck.

foresail. The lowest sail on the foremast.

frigate. A class of Royal Navy ship.

gig. A ship's boat, usually for the captain.

Great Cabin. A large cabin at the rear of the main deck.

halyards. Rope to raise or lower sails.

hawser. A small cable.

hove to. Stationary above the anchor.

jib. A triangular sail from the top of the foremast to the jib-boom (an extension of the bowsprit which projected forward).

jolly boat. One of the four boats carried by a ship for the purpose of taking people to and from the shore and supplying the ship.

kedge anchor. The smallest anchor.

lanyards. Small ropes.

larboard. The left side of the ship (when looking forward from the stern).

lazarette. The after part of the ship, used for stores.

leeward. Same direction as the wind.

letter of marque. The formal commission that granted privateers the right to acct against the enemies of their country.

longboat. The largest of the ship's boats.

lying to. The position of the ship after it has been brought to.

midshipman. A very junior officer.

mizzen. Rear of the ship.

nabob. A corruption of the Indian word, nawab, and used to signify a man who has returned to England after making a fortune in India.

orlop deck. The lowest deck of a ship which has three or more decks.

Petty officers. Men with specific responsibilities, e.g. ship's surgeon, quartermasters, carpenter, boatswain.

Pool of London. The wide stretch of the River Thames below London Bridge.

quarterdeck. The deck forward of the poop. On naval ships of the period it looked down into the ship's waist. It was the preserve of the officers.

round house. A large cabin on the upper deck, beneath the poop.

schooner rigged. Rigged fore and aft as opposed to square rigged.

sextant. A navigational instrument to measure the altitude of celestial bodies.

sheets. Ropes attached to the bottom corners of sails.

sloop of war. By this period, a warship carrying less than 20 guns; the largest of them looked like miniature frigates.

snow. A two-masted square-rigged vessel almost identical to a brig.

spars. A general nautical term for wooden poles. Depending on its use, it could be a yard, a boom or even a mast.

stand on. Keep the same course.

standing rigging. The rigging which is set up permanently to support the masts and tops, as opposed to the running rigging which was used in sail handling.

sternway. Moving backwards.

topgallantmast. Each mast was in three sectionsl the topgallantmast was fitted to the topmast, which in turn was fitted to the lower mast.

Trade Winds. Winds that blow continually towards the Equator, e.g. the North East Trades will carry a ship from Europe south west towards the coast of South America.

transom. Timbers secured at right angles to the sternpost to form the back of the ship.

yard. A spar from which the sail hangs.

yawl. A ship's boat, very similar to the jolly boat.

Index

Introduction

Those concerned with the task of meeting all children's educational needs, special or otherwise, will be aware of the impediment of previous thought and action, within the short history of education, which has created a legacy of inappropriate attitudes. The major part of this legacy, which we have inherited from a predominantly category-based development of special educational needs, reveals that decision makers, at every level, are actively involved in passing **the problem** to someone else. The meeting of individual children's needs, no matter how special, within the structure of the **school for all**, with its concomitant view of **personal responsibility**, is a relatively new, and for many radical, idea: one which is actually discouraged by the legacy.

The legacy brings with it seemingly insurmountable barriers: segregated and diverse provision; imprecise legislation; poor communication; professional isolation; an attitude of unwillingness to be involved; and above all, a crippling inertia borne out of the view that resources are inadequate and that the problem is best dealt with by those who are better resourced and more qualified.

This book is about an alternative viewpoint. A viewpoint which proposes a new concept, that of the resourced school, where the resources are as much human as physical, and where human resources are thought of as **personnel educated in meeting the needs of all children**, personnel who have a common perspective, through an agreed policy, where personal responsibility leads to full participation in providing a curriculum for all.

Recognizing that such a goal will be hard to achieve, the authors offer a route from the present to the future, using **in-service activities** and **clear LEA policy direction** as the vehicle. Within these two aspects of change, planned phases of development are discussed, which incorporate the need for: a radical realignment of LEA resources; the adoption of an approach to integration which begins with the integration of the working practices of current personnel; the construction of a whole-school policy; and the realization of a continuum of in-service activities which spans the school, Local Education Authority and Institute of Higher Education.

The central concern of the book is teacher development. Nothing will be achieved, it is argued, if in-service activity fails to address the ultimate issue of personal responsibility. It is personal responsibility, through the growth of personal development, which will dictate the teacher's attitude towards children's needs and influence their response to the range of needs they are prepared to meet.

Amongst the many possible spheres of decision-making, two are selected for scrutiny, the Local Education Authority and the Institute of Higher Education. The authors believe that the future of provision for meeting special educational needs depends very much on the relationship which exists between these two bodies, and that in the wake of recent government sponsored initiatives which substantially alter the balance of power between the Local Educational Authority and the Institute of Higher Education, the time has come to re-examine the quality of this relationship, particularly as it affects the personal development of teachers.

In order to propose appropriate adjustments in the relationship between the Local Educational Authority and the Institute of Higher Education, it is necessary to examine at length the needs of the school, the teacher and the child. The last of these, in the form of a case study, occupies a large proportion of the earlier part of this book. Although case studies are a frequently used device, they rarely explore the full range of influences acting upon a child, and the authors therefore have thought it appropriate to extend this device, both to illustrate the central issues raised in this book and to introduce the reader, in as practical a way as possible, to the **legacy of inertia**.

Locked into a Legacy

Chapter 1

The Case Study

Introduction

The case study serves to illustrate the points made in chapter 2, 'How It Came About', and provides, in one composition, practical examples of the central issues raised in this book.

To successfully accomplish the latter, we have thought it necessary to concentrate on one case, presenting it in some detail. However, we would stress that whilst the study is based on actual case history, we have carefully bowdlerized and altered the material and not only as regards dates and events, since in some instances it has been necessary to re-write correspondence and eliminate confidential items. The integrity of the study, however, remains intact. For obvious reasons, the Authority remains anonymous.

We reviewed a number of cases from several Authorities, all equally interesting and demonstrative of the legacy, but finally we decided on the case of John because it so comprehensively illustrates the *feelings and attitudes* of all involved. It also allows for a full exploration of the roles of those professionals currently concerned with children with special educational needs. And whilst John's case can not be regarded as 'typical', particularly in view of the number of people involved, it is, in our experience, a 'true' reflection of what can and does happen, despite recent advances following the Education Act 1981.

Part One: Events Leading up to a Formal Assessment under the 1981 Act

John (born 22.11.1969) and his family live in a semi-detached house on a small Council estate in a rather remote area. John's father is a Grocery Manager at a large supermarket in a town 18 miles away. His mother is unemployed. John is identified in the third year of his 9–13 middle school as 'easily the least able child in the class', but his involvement with special education began in his First School, where in his final year he received individual help from a peripatetic 'remedial' teacher.

On his SE1 form (evidence submitted by a school on referral) he is quoted as 'unable to recognize print (letters) and relate sounds — it is impossible to decipher his spelling', and as having 'very limited retention powers'. His 'practical skills are very limited'. He is, however, 'happy at school and a regular attender'. The school is not optimistic about his future. In three sections of the SE1 the Headteacher responds:

Has he/she made progress in the last 12 months?
'seems to have made none'
If not, are there signs of deterioration?
'Little room for deterioration'.
Any special characteristics of child noticed?
'No — tends to worry about things he is not sure of, but tries not to show it'.

At this point the parents are quoted as

very concerned and anxious for John to make progress. They have even had private consultations with various experts in an effort to find the possible cause for John's lack of progress. They are so concerned that they are prepared to allow him to be placed in a residential school.

The Headteacher's concluding comments are:

John is a very pleasant boy who has severe learning problems (word blindness). Reading and word recognition are beyond his capabilities. He needs specialist help in a small group, which he is not likely to receive in a normal school. I feel that the only solution for John is to be placed in a residential school which has the staffing to deal with his particular problem.

This report is concluded in Autumn 1981. The initial referral to the School Psychological Service is dated Spring 1979 and was made by the Headteacher of the First School. The SE3 is completed by the Educational Psychologist in December 1981.

In his report the Educational Psychologist suggests that John has been discussed on several occasions, and that:

he has specific learning difficulties not responding to the limited, though willing and sympathetic help available at his school. His teachers and parents are increasingly concerned about him.

The Psychologist's impression of John is that:

he is an extremely pleasant, likeable boy who has always acknowledged his difficulties and been fairly philosophical about them, opting, if he can, for active, practical pursuits and avoiding difficult areas. In this way he has avoided much of the distress and frustration

he might have suffered, but I am afraid these are coming. At 12 he
remains at 6–7 year level as far as formal work is concerned.

It transpires that the Educational Psychologist has carried out two assessments
of John using the Wechsler Intelligence Scale for Children. In January 1979
a 'performance' IQ of 91 is recorded, with the following comment:

> No verbal IQ can be quoted since two sub scores, for Information
> and Similarities, were very poor and two, for Vocabulary and
> Comprehension, were average.

The scores obtained in October 1981 were similar.

Significantly, the Educational Psychologist states that 'this year John has
moved into the more secondary type organisation at the top end of the
Middle School and life has certainly become more complicated and difficult
for him.' He concludes:

> John is a home loving boy, very much involved with his family,
> and rather immature. At one time I would not have felt the academic
> advantages of specialised schooling would outweigh social and
> emotional disadvantages, but I now think John could cope quite
> adequately with residential placement and that he will cope less and
> less well in his present school.

In mid-November 1980, John was visited at school by a teacher from the
Services for the Hearing Impaired. This teacher was alerted by the Remedial
Service. John is found to have hearing well within the normal limits, and
no further action is proposed.

Following referral, John's case is taken up by the Local Education
Authority, and it is at this point that we monitor his progress.

In mid-February 1982, a clerk from the special education branch of the
Education Authority writes to the Remedial Service to ask if they can provide
extra help. At the same time the SE forms are passed to the Authority's
Adviser for Special Education with the note 'John attends a Middle School
but has now been recommended for residential placement'.

The Adviser replies:

> He is not ESN. It is suggested by Ed. Psych. that a school for
> specific learning difficulties is required. Re-route!

John's file is 're-routed' to the Principal Psychologist, who replies:

> I fail to see why we need to consider residential schooling when the
> residential component isn't necessary. Can we have a report from
> the Remedial Service. Can they give extra help? If necessary, can we
> appoint a tutor for a couple of terms working with/under the
> direction of the Remedial Service for an hour each day — preferably
> Centre based? To place him in a residential school solely on account

of reading problems seems to be extraordinarily profligate — not to say an indictment of the system.

The Main Education Office writes to the Local Officer:

> This boy has been recommended for residential placement in a school which could cater for his specific learning difficulties. In order that consideration may be given to John's educational requirements, I should be glad if you would arrange for him to be assessed by the Remedial Service, as soon as possible, and let me have a copy of their report.

In the meantime, the Education Welfare Officer is requested to visit the family. The EWO reports that both parents have doubts about John leaving home, but are now convinced that this is the best for him. The EWO describes John's father as 'outspoken but pleasant' and his mother as 'polite and anxious'. The EWO adds to the 'picture' of John by stating that:

> he couldn't care less about his appearance — needs reminding to clean his teeth, etc. Has a good sense of humour and whilst normally quite placid, can be quick tempered. He is an 'outdoor' boy who likes rugby, cricket, swimming, fishing, etc.

The EWO's recommendation is for residential education as soon as possible, despite a strong relationship between mother and son. At the beginning of June 1982, a reminder is sent to the Remedial Service.

On 28 June 1982, the Head of the Remedial Service files his report. This points out that John was referred to the Service in the Autumn of 1980 and that a preliminary assessment showed that he required a 'basic sight vocabulary', before learning phonics, and that there were a number of letter/sound confusions. A programme concentrating on building sight vocabulary with the introduction of initial letter sounds was prescribed in September 1980 and John received one hour's tuition per week. The report continues:

> John's reading was tested in October 1981 and assessed as RA 6.9, and in May this year, 1982, RA 7.6. Some progress had obviously been made but the report on John commented on his 'poor retention despite constant practice and repetition'.

A more detailed assessment is made by the Remedial Service. Using a battery of tests, this concludes that:

> reading ability is affected by continued difficulty with sight words and poorly developed word attack skills and these are probably due to inadequate visual memory . . . the severity of John's learning problems, without doubt, warrants very prolonged and structured teaching, preferably one-to-one on a daily basis, and this should provide a supportive framework for the rest of the teaching timetable. I stress that John's difficulties cannot be dealt with in isolation. They

require a fully integrated, programmed approach, and one which meets his individual and specific needs.

No comment is made as to whether this could be met by the Remedial Service. On receiving this report, the Adviser suggests:

a tutor for five hours per week based at the school, working for and under the guidance of the Remedial Service, if this is the most economical in terms of liaison with others who teach him.

This is endorsed by the Principal Psychologist. The Assistant Education Officer responsible for Special Education supports this request, but writes to the Adviser asking him:

1. What period of time should the additional help run for?
2. Does John need to be formally assessed?
3. This is an expensive precedent, can I have more detail?
4. Where do we go when the additional tuition stops?

But in the meantime he issues an order for the additional support to be given:

. . . exceptionally agreed that a tutor may be appointed for five hours per week for the Autumn Term 1982 only. The tutor must be appropriately qualified and experienced and should work under the guidance of the Remedial Service, possibly working at the Centre initially and then at John's school. An individual programme should be prepared in liaison with the Remedial Service and John's school. I must advise you that it will not be possible to continue this arrangement beyond the end of the Autumn Term 1982, and in the particular circumstances of this case, I should be grateful if you would arrange for a report to be provided at half-term.

At half-term the tutor submits her report, the most significant comments being:

John has become more relaxed and open, as over the past five weeks he has happily settled to the tutorial sessions . . . he is most aware of his problems in learning but still remains motivated . . . there is particularly good contact between the Head, Deputy Head, form teacher and myself . . . during each session some link-up work with John's classwork is covered, supported by his form teacher . . . John's parents visited the school at the end of September and were pleased with the extra help available.

Much of the tutor's assessment of John accords with that of the Remedial Service.

In late November the Headteacher writes to the Education Office saying that John is very happy with his tuition and gives the impression of being more confident in his approach to school work.

The Tutor's extensive report is sent to the Adviser for comment; he replies:

> The Tutor has written a good informative report and is clearly helping John a lot. Regretfully, we must stick to the original limitation of one term only, so she should clearly indicate to the form teacher what she is doing and how, so that the form teacher or others in the school can continue the 'remedial' work.

In the meantime the local office has written to the Assistant Education Officer to ascertain whether the additional help can continue after the Autumn Term. He quotes the Educational Psychologist as being entirely in accord with this proposal.

In December, the Assistant Education Officer writes to the local office, '. . . in the light of all the circumstances it will not be possible to agree to the continuation of school based tuition beyond the end of the Autumn Term', requesting that the Tutor liaise with the form teacher. At this point, the Educational Psychologist writes to both the local and main Education Office:

> John is clearly happier and more confident now than he was last year . . . he feels he is achieving success . . . he is certainly working hard and is not 'fed up' with reading and writing anymore! He actually managed to copy a simple sentence for me, largely 'joined-up' and without any reversals or combination letter. At thirteen this may not sound impressive, but it represents, in John's case, real and significant progress. I have heard nothing about any planned placement for John for many months and wonder whether the individual tuition was agreed as an <u>alternative</u>. In this case, it is absolutely essential that it continue if progress is to be maintained.

A clerk at the main office sends a memorandum to the Adviser informing him of the view of the Educational Psychologist. The reply is:

> No need for residential placement as he is progressing well and if the programme is transferred to the form teacher it should continue.

This information is imparted in an official memorandum to the local office.

No more is heard of John's case until March 1983, when for the first time John's parents write to the Chief Education Officer. This is a long letter; we quote the main parts only:

> I do hope you can help me and more especially my son.
>
> Since he first started school he has had problems. Most of his teachers as he's gone through school have said the same thing at one time or another, he's . . . lazy . . . he's backward . . . he can't be bothered.

I knew he was neither of these things but didn't know exactly what was wrong and although I voiced my opinion <u>no one listened</u>. Finally I and my husband had to spend our own money to have him assessed. He was found to have learning disabilities. Since then both the teachers, head master and Psychologist and us, his parents, have been trying to get something done for him for his future education and working life. Last term you sent a teacher to see him for an hour a day and the difference was quite amazing, we thought that at last you were doing something, then, just as things were going great guns you <u>stopped it</u>. Poor John is getting quite frustrated. He is doing his best but he can't keep up. He takes a lot of ridiculing from the boys at school and one <u>teacher</u> even made him stand up in front of the class to read and made him look a fool. <u>I will not have this</u>. I saw the head master and he sorted things out. <u>BUT PUT YOURSELF IN JOHN'S PLACE KNOWING HE CAN'T READ</u> and the thought becomes very frightening. The Psychologist and I talked about trying to get him into a residential school; while I'm loathe to do this for my own selfish reasons I realise that for John's sake I must take this step.

I've had John assessed, I've seen <u>all</u> the teachers, I've seen the heads of school, seen Drs and they all try, but you won't <u>listen</u>. I think it's time you started to listen and to take action especially as John is due to go to X Comprehensive in September and it's a sure fired bet they won't be able to do anything for him. Please find a place for him; give him a chance otherwise what else can I do to help him.

This passionate plea is met with the response:

Thank you for your letter, John's educational needs are being considered and I shall write to you again as soon as possible.

In the meantime, unknown to the parents, the local office writes to the main office requesting to know why the Authority thinks it no longer necessary to provide tuition, particularly as the Educational Psychologist supports continued help. The Adviser replies:

I can't justify awarding further tuition, there is only a limited amount of tuition and this has to be thinly spread. Please put to the Principal Psychologist for his opinion as to when this boy qualifies for extra help because of specific reading difficulties.

The Deputy Principal Psychologist's reply is:

If we cannot provide for John in school, in school backed up by Remedial Service help — in school backed up with tuition, then personally I think it is legitimate to proceed with consideration for residential school. Policy may dictate, but bricks need straw!

On reading this, the Adviser telephones the mother and as a result writes the following memorandum to the Assistant Officer:

> . . . she wishes to proceed with an application for a residential placement in a school for specific learning difficulties as suggested by the Educational Psychologist. This will presumably mean assessment, etc. and if successful considerable cost. It will be better if we try to fix him up locally with Remedial Service/Tuition help after all. Could we find out what would be the minimum time the Tutor could work to get maximum results? As the cost of a residential placement would be considerable, can we vire this cost to appoint someone to the Remedial Service who has expertise in specific learning difficulties? Such cases will become more numerous I'm sure.

On receiving this memorandum, the Assistant Education Officer writes to the local office asking that a case conference be convened with the Educational Psychologist, Head of the Remedial Service and a representative from the local office. They are charged with discussing John's needs and recommending a joint plan as how they should be met. The parents are not informed of this meeting. The local office return the memorandum saying that they will comply, albeit reluctantly, since everyone is agreed at local level that additional tuition is required.

On 5 April 1983, a member of the political ruling group of the Council receives a letter from John's mother and promptly writes to the Chief Education Officer:

> . . . I am enclosing a photostat letter of a plea for help from a parent in my area. The letter is well written and needs no explanation from me. I have seen the parents, and am of the opinion that a more genuine and deserving case would be very hard to find. The worry expressed by the parents, is having a profound effect on the whole family. I have sent a copy of my letter to the Chairman of the Education Committee. May I ask your support and help in this matter as soon as possible.

In her letter John's mother has written:

> I wrote a six page letter to the Education Office and received a one and a half lines letter back saying John's education was being looked into. The point is, how long are they going to take? John will be fourteen in November, he hasn't a great deal of time left. My worry for John is now getting so great because it's on my mind all the time, that I'm driving all the family mad because I'm getting more and more depressed about the whole thing.

On the 16th, the Chairman writes to the Member saying that he has made a request to the Chief Officer and has asked to be informed of developments. On the 19th, the Assistant Officer replies to the Member:

> . . . John's needs have been under discussion following his mother's letter to me of the 7th March. This reappraisal indicates that John's needs can be met by his attending an ordinary school with supplementary help from a tutor rather than by placing him in a residential special school.
>
> It is proposed therefore to appoint a tutor for the start of the coming Summer Term for 10 hours per week. I have written to John's mother advising her of this.

Subsequent half-term and end-of-term reports show that John is making good progress and is again confident and enjoying his work.

In mid-July the Headteacher of the Upper School writes to the local office seeking assurance that John's tuition will continue when he transfers. This request is supported by the local office and passed to the main Education Office. Without referring the case to the Adviser or Principal Educational Psychologist, the Assistant Education Officer replies that he cannot agree to additional daily tuition, since he considers that 'a school as large as the one John is transferring to should be able to cope'. The final report from the Tutor indicates that John will fail without additional support. At the last moment the Assistant Officer reverses his decision and agrees to support until half-term. The subsequent report again suggests improvements, but also stresses the need for continued support. At the same time, the Head of the Special Needs Department also compiles a report which indicates that John has settled well but concludes, 'It is imperative for his future development that the tuition continues, uninterrupted, for at least the rest of this school year, and may still be required into the fourth year'.

The Assistant Education Officer agrees to extend the tuition until the end of the term, but requests that the Educational Psychologist re-assess John's needs. At the same time he recommends a reduction from ten to five hours.

A memorandum is issued to the local office on 2 November 1983. This immediately prompts a letter from John's mother

> . . . After all the fighting I've done over the last years to get extra help for him I think it's sheer bloody mindedness of the so called Education Committee to put his educational needs aside so that someone else who will probably be a vandal can go to special school. John is fourteen on the 22nd of November which leaves him about two years left at school not a lot of time without the correct help but I don't suppose that bothers many people on the Education Committee . . . I am sorry about all the mistakes in this letter but I am angry and it shows . . .

This elicits the response:

> Thank you for your letter concerning your son, John. I am looking into the position concerning the extra tuition given to John as a matter of urgency and will write to you again as soon as possible.

John's mother also writes to the Local Officer, though shows her appreciation of his efforts by offering a more conciliatory tone.

In the meantime, the Headteacher has also written to the Local Office expressing 'dismay' at the reduction of tuition time, describing the frustration felt by all: parents, school, Educational Psychologist, John and his tutor.

The Local Office responds by asking the Main Office for urgent consideration to be given to John's case, enclosing copies of the letters sent by his mother and the Headteacher.

The immediate response of the Main Office is to restore the 10 hours tuition (by telephone), and to request an urgent review by the Educational Psychologist. The Assistant officer also writes to John's mother:

> I have now had an opportunity of reviewing your son, John's case and have informed the Local Office that the level of Tuition should be restored to 10 hours a week for the remainder of the Autumn Term . . . I have also asked the Educational Psychologist to review John's educational needs as quickly as possible so that I may have his views before I consider the question of the level of individual tuition which should be given to John for the Spring Term.

On 10 December, the Department of Education and Science ring the LEA offices, informing that John's mother has written to them regarding the reduction of school tuition hours. The Department is informed that the hours have been re-instated.

On 7 December the Education Office receives the following communication from the Educational Psychologist:

> . . . I am afriad that I shall not be able to carry out a review until February at the earliest, and I must admit I wonder what I could add to the information already provided by the teachers involved. . . .
> You have my SE3 of November 1982 recommending residential provision for John and my memo of December 1983 after he had had additional help in school for one term — the help was then discontinued. We had a case conference in March this year when John's mother made her 'representations' and the help was reinstated for the Summer Term and half of this term. It was then reduced.
>
> . . . I must admit that I can see no benefit in this see-sawing from help to no help or reduced help and back again. John <u>was</u> a remarkably pleasant, well-motivated boy considering his difficulties, but I am not surprised to hear from the Head of the Special Needs Department that he has again been confused, upset and discouraged

by recent events. His mother is an anxious lady and the strain of these crises and her efforts on his behalf must be stressful for the whole family. I gather that she has asked for residential placement at a school specialising in specific learning difficulties, and since it appears the only way that John is likely to receive the help he needs consistently, I must support her request. John's problems are such that they will not go away, neither this year nor next and I do feel strongly that his special needs must be acknowledged and provision made for the remainder of his school career. I realise that this means formal assessment under the 1981 Act and I would be pleased to make my contribution.

The Assistant Education Officer issues a directive for tuition to continue and a full assessment to be initiated. The Local Officer is asked to counsel John's mother. The DES is informed.

On 8 February, John's mother gives her consent for a formal assessment.

Aspects of the Legacy

It is quite common and necessary in such cases to try to resolve the difficulty without entering into formal procedures, even if the referral suggests that a full assessment is required. Clearly, in John's case, the reason for deferring the assessment is strongly linked to the understanding of those involved as to the purpose of the assessment. It is not viewed as a means of providing John with a viable response to his special educational needs, but as a **final act** and one which has major resource implications. This view of assessment is consistent with the omission of an appropriate communication network which endeavours to develop, over a period of time, a profile of the child's needs: a profile which can be contributed to, in a systematic way, by a widening circle of personnel, as and when required. In John's case, the personnel exist, but there is no structure for communication, nor is there a **positive** procedure whereby the involvement of new personnel can be seen as part of the development of a programme of positive response, rather than negative crisis intervention.

Much of the growing frustration experienced by John, his parents, his teachers, the Educational Psychologist and to some degree the Local Officer, might well have been alleviated by an early identification of need and the early involvement of the parents. Indeed, the five stages of assessment outlined by the Warnock Report (DES, 1978), would have been sufficient in this case to have provided an appropriate educational response.

The lack of a sound procedure for identification, assessment, recording and intervention, both at school and LEA level, is in part responsible for the Headteacher's inability to accept that the responsibility for educating John lies with him. In using the term 'word blindness' he distances John's difficulty, and uses the label to express an 'expectation' that John will be removed from the school, since it is clear to him that there must be other people, perhaps in a residential school, who have the expertise to deal with such problems. It is unlikely, therefore, that much will be attempted in the school.

This too is a common point of inertia. Having decided that the problem belongs to someone else, the school can but wait for the 'powers that be' to complete their task of removal. Unfortunately, as in so many cases, the time lapse between request and response is an inordinately long one, and equally long is the time lapse between response and decision. In the meantime, matters are not made easier for John and his parents by the expectations of failure expressed by the Educational Psychologist, and this despite the encouraging response to personal tutoring.

It could be argued that the Educational Psychologist's pessimism is founded in reality, in that he views the increasing formality, which characterises the secondary curriculum, as presenting insurmountable barriers to John. In this he is quite correct, but the formal nature of his assessment procedures, namely the use of standardised tests such as the Weschler Intelligence Scale, indicate that he has not assessed the curricular needs of John in the context of the current learning situation; nor has he suggested ways in which the school could modify its approach, albeit by ameliorating the effects of John's language difficulty on areas of the curriculum to which he has entitlement.

As the Principal Psychologist points out, the use of residential school, to **solve** this problem, does indeed seem 'extraordinarily profligate'. This is, however, in our experience not an unlikely suggestion. It illustrates the relationship between the LEA's inability to respond, at a local level, to an emerging category of need, and the subsequent drain on resources which occurs when the number of cases dealt with in this way exceeds, sometimes out of all proportion, the level of funding available for alternative, more effective, and often less-expensive, forms of intervention. As DES-backed research has shown, once the pattern of provision is developed, even if fortuitously, it is extremely difficult to find the appropriate level of funding to change direction. Hence, despite the apparent success of the tutor, the support cannot be continued because it falls within a severely restricted budget.

Poor communication is evidenced throughout this case. Too many people only have partial knowledge of what has gone before, and most of the information is fed 'up' to the Assistant Education Officer and not across to the school, Educational Psychologist and parents. Others act as go-betweens, thus interrupting the flow of communication between those making decisions and those most affected by the decisions. The Education Welfare Officer, the Educational Psychologist and the Local Officer all act as 'message carriers'. Even at the centre of decision making, the Main Education Office, there are too many people involved. Officers, advisers and clerks all contribute, often without receiving feedback, or without informing others outside the office of their actions. Indeed, some contributions appear to be made in a 'vacuum'. All of this proceeds without the consent or participation of the parents.

Poor communication, at the levels described, has profound implications for the quality of intervention as experienced by the child. Early help is not related to the curriculum on offer, and much that follows is 'crisis oriented' and subject to financial decisions which vacillate according to the pressure brought to bear on the decision-maker. There is no long-term strategy, agreed by all those involved. Quite the reverse, there is considerable uncertainty about the status of the support given, its duration, and even the amount of hours available at any one given period of time. The expectation that the school will take over the programme from the tutor within one term, exhibits a simplicity of thinking which has no regard for the origins of the problem nor the complexity of the school organization in which John finds himself.

Such inadequate levels of communication often lead to violent outbursts from parents. Underlining and the use of capital letters is common; it signifies a level of frustration which stems from a perception of the LEA as 'unresponsive', 'unfeeling' and 'uncaring'. If parents are ill-informed as to progress, they are quite likely to believe that little or no action is being taken. Our case study illustrates that this is a misperception, that in fact a great deal is happening, but that this is not communicated. Further, when such outbursts occur, the administration has no effective, humane, way of responding. The only response it can make, in the shadow of the gathering storm, is to initiate a formal assessment; this, with luck, may relieve those involved of further responsibility, since a decision in favour of a special school placement will transfer that responsibility to someone else. The only contribution the parents are asked to make is that they agree to this assessment.

Part Two: Events Following the Decision to Assess

On 15 February John's mother receives the following from the DES:

> . . . I understand that the Authority have, with your agreement, begun a full assessment of John's learning difficulties. I do hope that as a result of the assessment a satisfactory outcome will be achieved.

On 8 May 1984, John's mother rings the Main Education Office, informing them that she is very concerned about 'delays' in getting an assessment completed. As a result, the Local Office is asked to pursue the matter with some urgency and to telephone her to explain the position.

In his reply, the Local Officer writes:

> . . . A draft statement is attached. You will see from this that it is still felt that John requires residential education, a recommendation made a few years ago but not supported at the time . . .

John's statement read as follows:

Special educational needs
John is a boy of low average ability who it was felt should be placed in a school able to cope with his learning difficulties. He requires constant reassurance and help, and is currently placed in a small remedial class at X School. John lacks self-confidence and becomes easily disillusioned when unable to cope with situations or school work.

Special educational provision
John requires tuition in a small group where he can receive as much individual help and support as possible. This will not be available at the X School after the end of the Summer Term 1984 and alternative provision will therefore have to be made to cater for John's special educational needs.

As it is not possible to make adequate long term provision for John locally, it is felt that a place should be sought for him at a residential school catering for children with learning difficulties, i.e., the Authority's residential school for children with moderate learning difficulties.

The evidence which contributes to the statement is extensive and includes evidence from the Educational Welfare Officer. There is no written evidence, however, from the parents. The Educational Psychologist's evidence, in particular, is very full, but the recommendation is for a residential school 'specializing in children with severe specific learning difficulties' not 'moderate learning difficulties' as is now specified on the statement.

In June, John's mother finally receives a copy of the draft statement. The parents agree the statement and visit the Authority's school with John.

In July, the Educational Psychologist telephones the Main Office expressing surprise at the school chosen and equal surprise that the parents have accepted this. He makes it clear that he intends to speak to the Authority's adviser about this.

In the meantime, John and his parents attend the interview.

At about the same time, the Educational Psychologist writes to the Main Office:

. . . I have not seen a copy of the statement, but it appears from this letter that John's parents have agreed to the description of him as a child with moderate learning difficulties. I would not myself agree with it and did not use the term: if we had thought John an ESN(M) boy, we could have admitted him to our local special school years ago. Even allowing for increased flexibility in our use of provision I would not envisage him at X Special School and was hoping, when I recommended residential placement (not for any other reason than lack of suitable local provision) for something more specialised . . . . I have had no recent contact with John's parents. I did ring the headmaster of the proposed school and understand from him that the school is now taking some children of somewhat higher ability than in the past. If the family contacts anyone after they visit the school it may well be me (assuming it isn't their MP, Sir Keith Joseph or the DES as in the past) and I would be grateful for further information on how this decision was reached . . . ..

In reply, the Main Office state:

. . . I attach a copy of John's Statement of Special Educational Needs which was completed by the Local Office and approved by the Authority's adviser for Special Education.

On 25 July, the clerk at the Main Office writes a memorandum to the Assistant Officer which records a telephone conversation with John's mother:

. . . John's mother rang today re her interview. The Headmaster asked why John was recommended to his school when the boy had no problems at home.

She told him that there are no vacancies at local day schools and since she has pushed hard for appropriate provision for John, she agreed on his school. On seeing the school, John's mother has doubts that it is suitable for John and she is writing to the Authority expressing her doubts. She feels that John is dyslexic and there is an independent school within travelling distance of the home that has provision for this problem. Although the parents agreed John's statement, she did this without knowing or seeing the school proposed.

On the same day an urgent note is passed to the adviser for comment, and confirmation is received from the Authority's school that John is to be offered a place.

In reply to the Educational Psychologist's query, the Authority's adviser writes:

I read all the information most carefully before recommending X School. I appreciate that John has specific learning difficulties, but he has a great number of other problems as well. Much centres around the interpretation of 'moderate' learning difficulty. We are no longer referring to intellect but level of learning difficulty. In this respect John has moderate and specific learning difficulties which ought to be catered for by our own residential school for moderate learning difficulties as proposed. John is described in the 'evidence' as slow, low average ability, very poor in all basic skill areas, emotionally immature, has no friends, nervous and anxious. The advice also calls for a situation which will help him develop practical abilities and be given work oriented skills. All this seems to point to a school such as that proposed. We also have to bear in mind that John will soon be 15 and we are therefore looking for a placement that will continue at 16+. The school proposed has excellent provision of this nature. I believe the nature of John's emotional and social difficulties (i.e., no friends, anxious, etc.) does call for residential education. It is far too late to be looking for a Specialist School (i.e., dealing with dyslexia). I doubt one would take him in any case, his profile is too mixed and complex, and he is not average to above average ability as measured on intelligence tests.

A memorandum is received from the Educational Psychologist:

> John's mother contacted me on return from her visit to X School. She had appreciated the opportunity to visit the school . . . she felt however that most of the pupils at the school had more serious difficulties than John and that 'he stuck out like a sore thumb'. She was not certain that he would receive specific, appropriate help for his reading and writing difficulties or that he would be able to take part in a full range of practical and sporting activities. She understood, for instance, that he would not do cookery, something he is enthusiastic about. . . . John's parents now feel that the situation at John's present school has deteriorated and with it, John's attitude and motivation. She was suggesting that she might have to withdraw him from school and educate him at home. . . . I am now at a loss as to what to suggest.

Shortly following this, John's mother addresses the following to the Assistant Officer:

> . . . I thought when we heard that you had found him a place at X School that the answer had finally come and it was the end of years of writing and phoning and talking to people trying to make them realise that John needed proper help and specialised teaching in the right environment. How wrong can I be. I don't know who made the decision to recommend X School for John but whoever it was obviously didn't care where he went the attitude seemed to be that because I had been fighting and trying so long for something or somewhere for him that I would accept anything. WELL YOU ARE WRONG. John will not be going to that school nor will he be going back to the 'Comp'. They have done nothing at all with him this term. After he's been to school in the morning he's totally negative because they just can't be bothered. I feel that John has had to put up with third rate education because you can't find the answer. If I had the time and money, I would consider sueing the Education

Committee because John should have been having help a long time ago, you have thrown all his schooling away, however, there are other ways. I have decided that if you find nothing for John before the school year starts I'll teach him at home. Who can tell probably we'll make quite a good job of educating John and getting more from him. It's a sure thing we can do no worse than all of your efforts.

A version of the adviser's memorandum is sent, in the form of a letter, to John's parents.

Further attempts are made within the Main Office to resolve the problem of placement, but in the meantime the Educational Psychologist forwards the following memorandum:

> . . . I shall try and see John and his parents before the beginning of term and suggest to them that we need to visit his present school and discuss John's timetable and the help that can be offered to him should he remain there. I certainly do not think John's mother would be wise to attempt to educate him at home. . . . I am concerned about the suggestion that the term 'moderate learning difficulties' should not be taken to refer to a level of intellect. Since I and my colleagues agreed to use the term precisely to refer to a level of intellect and have been doing so for the past two years. I can only forsee further confusion and misunderstanding both between ourselves and between us and parents . . .

A memorandum circulating the Main Office in early September reveals that the Adviser has suggested three independent residential schools catering for children with specific learning difficulties with a note from the clerk which says:

> John's mother is not, however, keen on boarding and I doubt she will agree to the distance of these schools. She is seeking a day school for dyslexic pupils. John's ability for Z School (an independent school) is too low.

At the start of the school year, John does not return to his Upper School, but the Authority continue with the five hours per week support, transferring this to the home. Some consideration is given to enforcing the statement, particularly as it has the signature of the parents.

On 10 September, the Assistant Officer offers 10 hours per week support if John will return to school. This is transmitted to the Educational Psychologist, who in turn is unable to contact the family.

The Educational Psychologist eventually manages to catch both parents at home. He reports that the parents are adamant that John will not transfer to the proposed residential school nor return to his present school. John's mother is reported as having organised a timetable for John which includes the Home Tutor's help. The Educational Psychologist acknowledges that the Authority is now in a very difficult position regarding John's Statement of Special Educational Needs. He also reports that John's mother is only too happy for 'the School Board or whoever to come and see what John is doing!'

In September, the Authority's Adviser, responding to a memorandum from the Assistant Officer, writes:

> I have no further suggestions. Either we compromise on one of the three schools listed, or we enforce the statement, or we allow John's mother to 'educate' John at home — presumably until the enthusiasm runs thin. Appeals procedures at this point are likely to take up to his statutory leaving date.

Finally, in October, a case conference is called, which includes the Assistant Officer, Educational Psychologist, the Adviser and the Head of Special Needs from the Upper School. The parents are not invited. It is resolved that:

1. The Upper School has neither the experienced or qualified staff to provide sufficient support.
2. The school named on the Statement is unacceptable to the parents.
3. That an independent school outside the Authority would best meet John's needs, if one could be found that had vacancies.
4. The current arrangements at home, as reported by the Educational Psychologist, are thought to be 'enterprising' and quite successful. Such an arrangement should be the subject of an 'inspection' by the Authority's Adviser, and it is thought unlikely it would meet with approval.
5. It is agreed that the informal views of schools outside the Authority be sought, with a view to financing an additional year. This could then be put to parents.

In a carefully worded letter, John's parents are informed that the placement of John at the proposed school is now disregarded and that the Authority's Adviser will arrange for a visit to 'inspect' the current arrangements. The Assistant Officer also telephones John's mother to talk to her personally about the difficulty of finding a residential placement.

Following the home visit of the Adviser in December, a report is filed:

> I found John's parents most helpful. They are clearly concerned parents, quite capable of articulating their problems. We discussed John's difficulties and reviewed the present arrangements. . . . My overall impression of John is that he might well have benefitted from attendance at our Residential School for Pupils with Moderate Learning Difficulties, but that boarding education is not now an acceptable option. His needs are much as I have described them on file . . . John was present throughout the discussion and participated appropriately. I found him relaxed. He appears to be coping well

with the somewhat peculiar demands of being taught by his own parents. John's mother struck me as quite capable of teaching John. My only concern is that she has not been given the necessary advice as to appropriate methods and materials. . . . I would not doubt her claim that since John has been at home his handwriting, reading and general approach to learning have all improved. The evidence seems to substantiate this . . . I was able to hear John read, and it is my opinion that he is now at a stage where he will derive more from sustained periods of reading aloud than from any other form of instruction. Providing, of course, that the accompanying adult is sympathetic. This is what he is now experiencing. . . . However, the nature of John's specific learning difficulties is such that some 'structured' teaching is necessary, particularly for spelling, and this should be multi-sensory based. . . . In total, it would be difficult to conclude that John is getting the range and balance of curriculum suited to his age, aptitude and ability as described in the 1944 Education Act; but it is not difficult to conclude that his parents are educating him in a manner which is more appropriate to his needs than was the case at his previous secondary school. . . . It is this consideration which causes the difficulty. In addition, it is undoubtedly the case that John is well motivated, and this is largely due to the enhanced relationship he now enjoys with his parents. This motivation may not survive in some educational settings, i.e., a return to his secondary school or a transfer to residential school. . . .

Option one: John remains at home. Attendance at his local secondary school for practical subjects only. Continue 5 hours tuition. Transfer to appropriate 16+ day provision.

Option two: Remain at home. Negotiate specialist help from local Dyslexia Association Centre. This may involve travelling two or three times a week (I strongly favour this). Attendance at local secondary school for practical subjects. Transfer to 16+ provision. In both of the above options John's parents ought to have support from the Authority in terms of appropriate materials and advice. I would undertake to do this providing a minimal amount of money were forthcoming for materials.

Option three: Attendance at independent school suggested by John's mother. There appear to be no other options. John's parents deserve support. At this stage, attendance at residential school is not acceptable.

The Officer's file note reads:

I am not happy about providing the support requested by the Adviser to allow John to be educated at home until we have looked into all other possibilities. Please press the Educational Psychologist in the area of the independent school quoted by John's mother for a view on the school.

On 25 February 1985, the Assistant Officer writes to inform the independent school chosen by Mrs Right of John's position, requesting consideration for placement. This elicits the response:

> . . . I have to tell you that it would be difficult to consider this boy for a place at this school as things are at present. We operate an ordinary school with about 32 pupils most of whom have some degree of learning difficulty and taught in groups of about eight pupils. Our full time remedial teacher feels that John would need considerable one to one tuition to be effective and the time she has available for this, at the present time is fully taken up. . . .

On 25 April, the main office receives a letter from the DES:

> We have received a letter from John's mother regarding the education of her son, John, who has apparently received no tuition since July 1985. . . . John's mother is concerned that nothing seems to have been done about John's education by the Authority since before Christmas, when she was visited by one of the Authority's Advisers. . . . We have a copy of the draft statement. . . . I should be grateful to know what provision the Authority is considering for John's future education. . . .

The Adviser is asked to re-visit the family, but replies that he does not feel a visit would be useful unless there is movement on the points he has put forward in his previous report.

In May, John's mother again writes to the Main Office:

> I feel I have to write to you to let you know how I feel regarding my son and his education or lack of it . . . . I last spoke to you on 13.11.85 on the telephone we had a rather heated discussion where on you then asked for an adviser to come and see me which he did I can't remember his name off hand. He came in December. He talked to us and to John and agreed that something should be done as quick as possible and that we should hear something to our advantage soon in the new year. Well we are now into May with John having one year left of his education and still we have heard nothing. I'm not sure quite how to take this attitude of the Education Department. To say that they couldn't care less about John is an understatement. No one has been in touch at all. The last time we saw or heard from the Educational Psychologist was last September. I think that you now have had long enough to get things sorted out and I fully believe that you haven't tried and that the attitude now is that as he has so little time left school wise you might as well not bother. I agree with you, I shouldn't bother and may I add that I

think you, unfeeling, uncaring, unconcerned and totally inefficient because if nothing else you could have kept in touch, its quite obvious that you considered the situation unimportant.

In the following weeks the DES are assured that the statement ought not to have been upheld. The DES write to John's mother informing her of the answers given by the Authority, and that they are satisfied that the Authority has done all it could reasonably be expected to. The Assistant Officer tries to accommodate John in another secondary school but fails. No one seems to be able to suggest a viable solution. In September 1985, a meeting is held at John's local secondary school involving the Educational Psychologist, the Headteacher, and the Local Officer. Again the parents are not invited.

In early October John is re-admitted to his local Upper School, initially for mornings only; the five hours tuition continuing. This is agreed by the parents. At the request of the Assistant Officer, a school report is written in March 1986:

> . . . It was agreed at the meeting with John's parents that we try to give him a practical-based course and leave the Maths and English to the work he did with his private tutor. His progress has been somewhat slow due to his absences and the fact that he misses various afternoon lessons in the same subjects. However, he is a quiet, concerned boy who shows maturity in his oral answers. Unfortunately because of the nature of CSE exams covering course work and continuous assessment, we have been unable to offer John any exam entries. . . . In discussion with him, it would appear that he will leave school at Easter and is already writing off for jobs. I feel his social development has been enhanced by this short contact with his peers, even at this late stage in his school career, and he has always shown a cheerful acceptance of the problems which arise in a group situation.

The report is sent by the Assistant Officer to the Adviser, asking for his comment. The reply:

> In essence, we have failed this boy.

Culpability is indeed plural, but, as is so often the case, throughout the course of events related above there were changes in personnel in the form of the Assistant Officer, the Adviser, the Principal Psychologist and the Headteacher of the Upper School. No one informed the parents of these changes, either as they occurred or afterwards. In fact, it could be said, that no one informed them of anything very much at all.

Out of Control

The procedures for Formal Assessment, laid down by the Education Act 1981, offer the parent no guarantee that communication will be any less fractious than it might otherwise have been. Indeed, it could be said that some LEA officers view the period of Formal Assessment as a 'breathing space'. It is not uncommon for a year or more to go by before completion. In this respect John's mother's anger at what she perceives as a delay, is somewhat unjustified.

The final product, however, is very unsatisfactory. The assessment does no more than confirm an earlier position, and in the process ignores the good results achieved by the tutor. In recommending a residential school for children with moderate learning difficulties, the administrator, and apparently at this stage without reference to the Adviser, is making the Statement of Need fit the provision available.

The actual Statement of Need represents a poor summation of the range of difficulties exhibited by John, and clearly the choice of school is based on the primary handicap which best approximates to the LEA's own provision. No programme is prescribed, the provision being somewhat simplistically described as 'tuition in a small group' and 'alternative' — this, despite the wide range of evidence available. The parents are not encouraged to submit evidence and make an informal 'representation', only via the Educational Psychologist.

We can learn much from the argument which ensues between the Educational Psychologist and the Adviser. Clearly the Educational Psychologist has substituted the former category of Educationally Sub-Normal (Moderate) for a label, and is not using it in the way the 1981 legislation intended, that is, that the child **is** MLD, rather than, the child is **experiencing** learning difficulties of a moderate kind. The Adviser appears to be attempting to change the nature of the provision, so that it accords more with the 'spirit' of the '81 Act, emphasizing meeting individual need rather than category; but this has not been transmitted either to the Educational Psychologist or the residential school involved.

No one explains this difference to the parents, and they, in good faith, sign a legal document which they believe reflects their views. In the event, it does not.

The situation is not helped by the lack of communication between the Education Office and the residential school. The Headteacher demonstrates a considerable degree of insensitivity in questioning the parents as to the reasons for John's referral, expressing surprise that John is not experiencing difficulty at home. It is not surprising, therefore, that the parents reject this school.

The independent sector must also take some responsibility for the difficulties which follow the assessment. Clearly someone has convinced John's parents that John is 'dyslexic', and they are anxious that John should attend a school, albeit outside of the LEA control, which deals with 'dyslexia'. On this matter, the LEA is forced to consider this option, and indeed approaches a number of independent schools. The problem that the LEA faces at this point is very common. Once the Formal Assessment is complete, it is possible to consider alternatives for John which are considerably more expensive than those suggested prior to assessment. That they are more expensive, however, does not guarantee that they are more appropriate. The most appropriate provision may well be less expensive but unavailable. This problem is due solely to the rigidity of budget headings, which are often weighted towards the 'assessed' 2 per cent of children thought to have more complex needs. In reality, this reflects an out-moded philosophy, one which responds to special educational needs as they become more severe, and not the philosophy and practice more appropriate to the spirit of the '81 Act, which deals with early intervention and prevention.

In such cases, if parents wish to exercise their limited power, often out of frustration or as a gesture to the LEA, they only have two courses of action open to them. The first is to pay for private education, which in any case may well be as inappropriate as that which is currently on offer, or they can educate their child themselves. John's mother's decision to do the latter is a clear sign that she has reached the point of desperation. This is heightened by the fact that both the Educational Psychologist and the Adviser, in addition to those involved at the local level, have 'opted out' of the case because their advice has seemingly been ignored.

Unsupported, the parents are eventually worn down, and in their letter of May 1985, demonstrate that they have finally abandoned what little hope they might have had of achieving appropriate special educational provision for John. John returns to his local mainstream school, but is allowed to keep his five hours per week tuition. John is no further forward, his present position reflects exactly that which pertained when his case was first brought to the Authority's notice; and this despite the intervention of Council Members and the DES.

One cannot help but wonder what might have been the position had the response from the LEA included early identification, assessment and intervention which was 'coordinated', 'communicated', 'flexible', and 'participatory'.

Nicki Cornwall (1987), in her investigations of the statementing procedure under the 1981 Education Act, has written:

> . . . I did not discover malignant aspects, simply human beings struggling and enduring badly-devised and poorly-connected systems. It is, above all, a picture of individuals caught in machinery they had not devised and over which they had little control. . . .

This would indeed appear to be the case.

Chapter 2

How It Came About

Introduction

John's case is not typical, yet parents, LEA officers, advisers, Educational Psychologists, Education Welfare Officers, and others will recognize many of the intractible problems it presents. Indeed, it would be no exaggeration to suggest that the elements of John's case are enacted somewhere in the education system almost daily. In this chapter we attempt to say why this should be so, and in order to do this, we have felt it necessary to give some account of the historical development of provision, thought and attitudes in meeting special educational needs.

Since 1945 special education has developed rapidly. The perspective established since that time reflects roots firmly established in educational and medical traditions, and accompanying expectations. Our present working experiences and future opportunities are therefore very dependent upon a legacy of separateness. It is from these traditions, and the knowledge of its creation as a system, that our views are informed. If we are aware of how things have been accomplished in the past, and how they operate at present, we possess at least one standard against which the present service can be measured and evaluated. We can also observe if changes have meant progress, what has interfered with progression, whether it has been maintained and whether there is any likelihood of change continuing.

In addition, the focusing of attention upon such areas as special educational needs, also places in the spotlight the underlying trend of integration. Practitioners may need to ask why, when for the length of time the education system has existed within this country there has been a segregated sub-sector of education, does legislation now give a direction which is contrary to this notion. Additionally, practitioners may also wish to examine the effects that such a lengthy period of segregated provision may inevitably incur in planning changes of the magnitude envisaged in the process of integration.

The 1944 Education Act: A Signpost to Change

The signpost to change may well have been the 1944 Education Act which overhauled the existing national system of education. It implemented many of the recommendations of the Bryce Commission (1895) and drew heavily upon the Spens (1938) and Hadow Reports (1926). The inspiration for the changes in special education was to be found in the recommendations of the Wood Committee (1929) and the reports of the committees of inquiry on the 'partially sighted' and 'partially deaf' (Board of Education, 1934, 1938). All three committees had stressed the importance of bringing the special schools within the general education framework. All had deplored the tendency to look upon the 'handicapped' as a class apart and all had felt the stigma attached to special schools could be lessened.

The Education Act 1944 gave expression to this outlook or change in outlook but also helped to intensify the change. It was best exemplified by the fact that provision of special educational treatment was merely made part of the general duty laid upon Local Education Authorities to ensure that children were educated in accordance with their 'ages, aptitudes and abilities'. Earlier legislation had dealt separately with the education of the 'handicapped'.

Tomlinson (1982) notes that the 1944 Education Act's tripartite system of secondary schooling by 'age, aptitude and ability' meant that

> selection by ability sanctioned selected by disability. Thus the duty was laid upon local education authorities to arrange provision for pupils suffering from 'any disability of body or mind'. This requirement was vague and general enough to incorporate all children who might conceivably upset normal education.

The section of the 1944 Education Act which called upon Education Authorities to provide primary and secondary schools also required them to have regard 'to the need for securing that provision is made for pupils who suffer from any disability of mind or body by providing, either in special schools or otherwise, special educational treatment' (Ministry of Education, 1944).

It is worthy of note that reference was made to special education being given 'in special schools or otherwise'. The Education Act 1944 also instructed LEAs to

> provide for the education of pupils in whose case the disability is serious in special schools appropriate for that category but where that is impracticable, or where the disability is not serious, the arrangements may provide for the giving of such education in any school maintained or assisted by the LEA (Ministry of Education, 1944, c. 31, s. 33).

The reference to 'any school' meant that not only could special education be given in schools other than special schools, but it need not necessarily be given in a special class. This was also confirmed by the Ministry's Pamphlet No. 3 (Ministry of Education, 1956).

The intention may well have been praiseworthy. The Ministry went further, saying it served –

> to emphasise that physical or mental handicap existed in all degrees, from the very slight to the serious, and that special educational treatment was not a matter of segregating the seriously handicapped from their fellows but of providing in each case the special help or modifications in regime or education suited to the needs of the individual child (Ministry of Education, 1956, Pamphlet No. 3, p. 1).

Pritchard (1963) states that unfortunately the wording of the Education Act, 1944, allowed LEAs to evade their responsibilities in terms of handicapped pupils and placement in the mainstream of education. The evasion was not so much in the level of provision of special schools, but in the lack of facilities in the ordinary schools. As LEAs ignored this alternative perspective, then special education became inextricably associated with *special schools*.

A Medical Model

The notions of disability of mind or body found in the Education Act 1944, where appropriate placement was seen as a special school environment, also implied a relatively simple concept of causation, analogous to the disease model of causation in medicine. Not surprisingly, the assessment of these 'disabilities' was made the responsibility of medical officers. No doubt this was because none of the other relevant professions was, at that time, sufficiently developed to take on the task. Special educational provision was organized according to categories of handicap and allocation to these was through a type of classification process — the handicapped pupil form reports on children.

The handicapped pupils forms, introduced under the Handicapped Pupils and Health Service Regulations (Ministry of Education, 1945) defined eleven categories of handicap, later to be modified to ten discrete categories, with, as discrete implies, a separate existence in separate provision.

Those children who were not considered capable of education — the 'ineducable' — were passed to the Health Authorities and were categorized as being severely subnormal. The less severely handicapped were therefore processed through the handicapped pupils procedure. The policy ideas recognized that some parents may not readily accept the arrangements suggested for their children and may need coercing into accepting that their children would be excluded from 'normal' education. A certificate could be issued, signed by a doctor, which would compel unwilling parents. Therefore, this HP1 Form was used to secure compulsory attendance at a special school.

This inevitably made a nonsense of the idea of providing special education in ordinary schools, for to threaten one child with compulsory attendance, whilst allowing another to remain in ordinary school was a manifest contradiction. Only medical officers were given statutory powers in the assessment procedure under the Education Act 1944. More and more, special educational treatment came to be associated with provision in separate schools.

A curious feature of this legislation was the power given to medical officers to make decisions affecting the placement of children in educational terms. The medical model of assessment employed collected a series of symptoms exhibited by the child, and from this aetiology a diagnosis was arrived at, and a treatment plan suggested, reliant upon placement in a special school treating pupils with a primary handicap.

Whilst the less seriously 'handicapped' could well have been educated in mainstream provision, this may well have conflicted with other educational interests, particularly where children were geared to a system of 'credentialling'.

Growth and Separation

Special education's expansion began from this time, and the professionals involved within it grew at a corresponding rate. As momentum gathered it was not surprising that provision for special education failed to develop in ordinary schools to any large extent.

Training for staff involved in the work followed the pattern of the establishment of special schools dealing with separate and discrete categories. For instance, as pupils were assessed as being handicapped in terms of physical handicap, so they were treated in a school for physically handicapped youngsters, and taught by teachers trained in that category. There was little overlap and the special schools were not only isolated from other special schools because of their discrete nature, but particularly isolated from their local mainstream schools, for contact was not required in day-to-day terms. Children attending special schools were likely to remain within them for most, if not all, their school career. Teachers, similarly, tended to remain outside the mainstream of training provision, and transfer from one sector to another proved very difficult in career terms. Very little understanding of the workings of special schools was therefore known to mainstream schools, and vice versa. This separateness, and isolation, is a further element of the perspective.

A great interest in mental testing, particularly following the work of Burt (1921), had meant that mental testing had become a part of the procedures in 'processing' children destined for special education, and psychological as well as medical and educational interests were served by the expansion of special education. The increasing emergence of a psychological orientation amongst professionals, particularly dealing with the categories of educationally subnormal (moderate) and maladjusted children, did not alter the underlying perception of 'an illness' and a personal disorder (Ford *et al.*, 1982). Thus psychological theories and practices followed this model in individual assessments, observations were made, symptoms noted and a diagnosis made. A treatment plan could then follow which could lead to 'a cure' or more likely an adjustment to a less than normal adult life.

When the Ministry of Education published their Pamphlet No. 5 in 1946 (Ministry of Education, 1946) they sought to more clearly define the categories of handicap. The pamphlet envisioned a special education system reaching as many as one-sixth of British youngsters. Yet special education developed very differently, as a distinct service reaching a tiny fraction, fewer than 2 per cent of British schoolchildren. The structure of the policies at this time goes a long way in helping to explain this outcome, for the child was assessed as handicapped and a category of handicap assigned to him/her. A further factor was that special provision was made the norm and linkages to the ordinary system of education the exception. Thus a small and separate service grew and expanded to its present considerable proportions.

Because this growing clientele was identified in essentially medically orientated ways, the medical profession had figured large in policy changes in special education. Behaviours were attributed to individual organic deficiencies, deficits, whether the behaviour in question was within the category of maladjustment or that of deafness, blindness, physical incapacity, etc. The belief in innate intelligence and the use of suitable tests and measures to allegedly gauge intelligence, meant a job market was created for Educational Psychologists as professionals who would be uniquely able to identify and sort certain kinds of special children. It also helped to foster the development of distinct institutions often well away from mainstream schools and centres, in philosophy and practice as well as physical location. The special institutions had their own resource requirements and staffing patterns, and were given generous allowances in comparison with schools in the 'ordinary' system. So, just as the pupil numbers in special education grew, there was an accompanying growth in the teachers, resources, and the specialist professionals allocated to them.

The expansion continued and Tomlinson (1982) suggests

> . . . what was happening was that teachers in ordinary schools were taking full advantage of the deliberately vague and complex definition of an educationally subnormal child and were using the category for the purpose of removing children who were troublesome in both learning and behavioural terms.

Most significantly, the Education Act 1970, which transferred the responsibility of pupils, previously considered ineducable, from Health Authorities to Education departments, saw the emergence of pressure groups seeking more appropriate provision for youngsters now categorized as educationally subnormal (severe). Pressure groups and allied voluntary bodies were now able to contribute to the shaping of special education. Very often these groups remained locked into the legacy of separateness and segregation, and were linked to the discrete categories.

The LEAs, in responding to the Education Act 1970, were assisted by the general expansion of local government, including social services and education, for a considerable bureaucracy concerned with special education was emerging and beginning to dominate what had been a medical interest. Many of the bureaucratic structures were separate in their organization from other facets of the LEA organization, and designed to support the separate categories of handicap. Thus, clerks and officers would have particular discrete categories under their purview and case files would be dealt with on the basis of handicap category.

Resisting Integration

The Education Act 1970 suggested the erosion of the boundaries of the discrete categories and the possibility of overlap between categories, and the difficulties of apportioning priority of handicap in placing a child with more than one major handicap added fuel to such a position.

The inclusion of mentally handicapped children within the category 'educationally subnormal' acknowledged that mental handicap can be viewed as a continuum. This idea of a continuum of defect had developed alongside ideas of very discrete categories — which was yet another contradiction.

Such concerns over the overlaps of categories and the unease about their separateness were to be answered by the setting up of the Warnock Committee. Accompanying changes in the assessment procedures (DES Circular 2/75) recognized that the causation of handicaps was complex and that their manifestation did not necessarily occur within the boundaries defined by the statutory categories. It was also seen that the main focus of intervention was through education and that decisions about provision should be based on developmental and educational principles rather than medical expertise.

As Welton *et al.* (1982) point out, this new SE forms procedure was issued in the context of this developmental idea:

> the multiple causation of special needs was recognized in a recommendation that assessment should have an educational and psychological, as well as medical component.

The wish for more involvement with mainstream schools, and a departure from the legacies of attempting to classify handicaps more and more precisely, and catering separately for those discrete handicaps, was embodied in the

Education Act 1976, as it had been in the 1970 Chronically Sick and Disabled Persons Act.

The Education Act of 1981 similarly sought an improved involvement with mainstream provision but through its impreciseness, and its susceptibility to individual LEA interpretation this involvement may be difficult to achieve. It abolished the ten categories of handicap, replacing them with the term 'special educational needs', and adjusted its system of classifying pupils by gauging the interests, capabilities and individual needs of children in the light of evidence from various professionals. Parents, as suggested by the Warnock Report, were to be involved in all stages of assessment on a partnership basis.

Many practitioners responded in a less than enthusiastic way to the Education Act 1981, suggesting that because of lack of financial resources little change was likely to be achieved. There was, too, the view that pupils with special educational needs were competing for scarce resources, this was not just financial support but often human support and understanding. As a group, such pupils and their families are seldom in a position to plead their cause with much success and are not always treated seriously when they do. Ignorance, prejudice, and stigmatization have much involvement in the preservation of the legacy.

'Special educational needs' is regarded by Barton and Tomlinson (1981) as tautological rhetoric which attempts to present whatever passes for 'special' education as a good thing for the child. Despite the benevolence behind this rhetoric, special education is an exclusion from mainstream education. The concept 'special need' is often used in a mystifying manner, directing attention away from the needs that are actually being served by the expansion of special education.

Categorizing or assessing children into special education disguises the reality that they are not wanted in the ordinary schools. Barton and Tomlinson (1981) see the unproblematic acceptance of the concept of special need being assisted by the assumption that there is a foolproof assessment process which will correctly examine children and define their needs:

> Special needs has become the rationalisation by which people who have the power to define and shape the special education system and who have vested interests in the assessment of and provision for more and more children as 'special' maintain their powers. The rhetoric of 'needs' is humanitarian, the practice is control and vested interests.

An International Problem

Interestingly, this passage of development is mirrored in other countries. Almost universally, governments have followed a policy of separateness in the way they have produced reports directed towards scrutinizing one section or aspect of the education service at any one time. The result has meant that various sections compete for slices of the resources cake, and the whole picture, as a total set of ingredients and range of possible mixtures and quantities, has been avoided by successive national regimes.

The expansion of the special education system in other countries has also reflected the medical dominance of special education, although not always using the social welfare model which Kirp (1983) believes has characterized British special education. He sees this as being based upon benevolence and paternalism and best suited to periods of social prosperity, where professionals and particularly administrators work on behalf of an ever-expanding clientele toward an agreed upon common good.

Scandinavia has been a focus for many international educationists to examine approaches to pupils with special educational needs. The Warnock Committee for example spent a deal of time gathering evidence from these countries concerning integration initiatives, and the Open University courses in special education, devised in the late 1970s, similarly used events in Scandinavian countries to signal future direction. In Sweden, as well as Norway and Denmark, there has been a continuing impetus and commitment to the integration of pupils previously placed in special environments. This has resulted in a diminution of the special schools and a gradual re-distribution of 'specialist' resources to the mainstream environments. In Denmark, developments have moved quickly, and mainstreaming has become the norm with 'schools for all' a reality.

Italian legislation brought 'handicapped' children into mainstream classes in a manner akin to the 'designated' approach adopted by many LEAs in this country. This provided places within classes alongside peers but limited the number of handicapped pupils and, importantly, also placed a restriction on the total class size to accommodate the 'special' children. The USA, through its Public Law 94/142, also sought to educate 'handicapped' pupils in the least restrictive environment possible, and safeguarded such pupils through a pattern of individualized education programmes. The latter also harnessed the involvement of parents in planning appropriately for pupils and interestingly, incorporated *pupil* involvement as a vital aspect in the production of such plans.

Policy-making and the Professionals

Central direction, as a result of committees of enquiry, has been the pattern of change for most of these countries. The resource allocations have been markedly different but the direction and intentions clear. Perhaps impreciseness of legislation and the complexities of attempting to dismantle what in effect has taken over a hundred years to erect, make breaking out of the legacy in Britain all the more difficult. Central government, through the DES, in its recommendations for policy change, has viewed progress in special education as synonymous with continuing the expansion of a distinct enterprise. These policies have been geared to providing for children who have differed from the 'norm'. Whilst not directly allocating resources, it did approve building requests and during periods of expansion favoured special school construction. During the period between 1950–1977, for instance, the number of such schools increased from 685 to 1882 (DES, 1978).

The distinct categories, and the Circulars affecting them, fit the social welfare model and its administrative ease and pragmatic approaches. Circulars and reports concerning aspects of special education issued since the 1950s have reinforced the professional character of the service. Some have set standards of good practice, others have identified particular categories of handicap. Others have catalogued and implicitly made legitimate new developments in special education, such as behavioural units (HMSO, 1978).

Centrally-promoted change was clearly exemplified in Circular 2/75 (DES, 1975). The new assessment forms gave effective control to the psychologist who co-ordinated the appraisals of a number of professionals. It codified what was regarded as sensible practice and backed up the professional claim to competence even as it altered the balance of the authority among professionals within the special education system. For the legacy of special education is also about power and decision-making as well as personal responsibility, and the personnel able to make decisions and the effects that such decisions have upon others.

The professionals involved, in particular, have done much to affect policy change. They have regarded themselves as specialists, which may well bolster their claim to expertise which in turn distinguishes 'special' from ordinary. The separateness of special education has meant that policy-makers have arisen from a small self-interest group with a shared commitment to basic assumptions — notably of their own expertise in shaping policy.

This 'professionalism' refers not only to the skills and knowledge that professionals bring to their work but also to the power they wield over their clients. Many have enjoyed considerable discretion in the way they interpret and implement policy. Special education has been seen as a humanitarian, caring process, undertaken solely in the interests of children, and has therefore precluded any questioning of the powers vested in professionals and practitioners to affect the lives of those they assess and teach.

The outcomes of policy may not always be as beneficial to the recipient as claimed by the practitioner. If the results do not quite fit the intentions of the policy makers, this becomes not only a challenge to the content and suitability of the policy, but also to the efficacy of the decision-makers, practitioners and policy initiators.

The assumptions of the professional knowing best, the dominance of the various models in policy-making, and the importance of bureaucratic ease are less easily accepted by those associated with special education in the 1980s. Unlike many other 'systems' within this country, special education has not been affected by pressure groups and interest groups. The nature of special education has meant that existing interest groups have tended to be hampered by their separateness, in terms of interest or category of handicap.

However, those involved in special education in the 1980s now find themselves under intense scrutiny. As economic growth has slowed and special education is competing for resources, a re-examination of how resources are distributed is in turn increasing or reducing professional discretion. Such attention has also affected the power relationships within the policy-making system, and suggests circumstances under which the unquestioned dominance of professional values in social welfare policy may be addressed very differently in the future.

In the future, policy changes may affect how individuals view pupils with special educational needs, such that special education no longer remains, as Lane (1981) describes:

> for long special education has been a cul de sac, well set off from the mainstream of educational inquiry, sociological study and political concern.

Chapter 3

Teacher Development

Introduction

We turn now to the effects of the legacy on teacher development, to the implications of the inertia and lack of personal responsibility, witnessed in the case study, and placed in historical context in the last section, for the relationship between the Local Education Authority and the Institute of Higher Education. In particular, we wish to highlight the need for a joint approach to policy construction and a renewed vigour in establishing a working partnership.

The Institute of Higher Education and the Local Education Authority: The Need for Partnership

As the concept of meeting special educational need moves gradually away from focusing on deficits within the child, and issues are raised concerning appropriate curriculum, whole-school policies, teacher competencies and attitudinal change, so the problem of meeting special educational needs will centre more on the development needs of teachers. Further, the fundamental re-structuring of provision within the Local Education Authority, which this re-orientation of emphasis suggests, will require that teacher development be a prominent feature within LEA policy. As a consequence, well-considered in-service activities will need to be constructed which reflect both the professional needs of the individual teacher and the policy decisions of the LEA.

It has to be said that to date the match of INSET to LEA needs has, for many LEAs, not been good, and as the principles of the Education Act 1981, rather than the letter, are implemented, so the gap may widen.

As far as the LEAs are concerned, the impreciseness of the Act led them off to a bad start. There was little in the Act to suggest how it should be implemented, and the only guidelines available were those concerned with the formal assessment of children and the production of statements of special educational need. Thus, much valuable time was lost in developing administrative structures and issuing interim statements. For many authorities this also came at a time of financial stringency, and in the context of an Act which specified that its operation must be 'within existing resources', this placed an intolerable administrative burden on those officers, including the School Psychological Service and Advisory Services, involved in its implementation.

Institutes of Higher Education, on the other hand, were less concerned with the administrative implementation of the Act and were therefore able to put their energies into examining the fundamental philosophical and educational aspects of change embodied in the Act. Whilst LEA personnel were endeavouring to cope with the vast increase in paper work, therefore, the more forward thinking Institutes of Higher Education were concentrating on the form new responses could take and developing models of provision more appropriate to the spirit of the Act.

Between these two positions, however, exists the vexed question of *how* provision should change, and it is perhaps indicative of the present relationship between the LEA and IHE that the LEA did not enlist the help of IHEs in resolving problems which arose from the imprecise wording of the Act, particularly in the area of assessment. Similarly, it is also indicative of the relationship that IHEs did not participate in devising viable pathways for change in order to put into operation models which they had developed.

In this light, the recently established Grant-Related In-Service Initiative could be viewed as recognition on the part of the government of the need for a closer working relationship between the LEA and IHE. Indeed, much good collaborative work was begun in anticipation of its implementation, and since its inception this partnership has continued to develop.

The meeting of special educational needs, however, whether through policy implementation or INSET activities, presents its own particular difficulties, and these difficulties we have described as a legacy. It will take no small effort on the part of the LEAs and the providing institutions to break with the past, and any serious attempt at implementing the recommendations of the Warnock Report and the Education Act 1981 will involve the LEA in a fundamental review of policy and provision. Such policies which may emerge must take account of the need for a re-appraisal of teacher development through in-service activities. The evidence to date would suggest some recognition of this priority but that LEAs and providing institutions have a considerable way to go before meeting the needs described in this book. Thus, the previous position whereby LEAs decided on policy without reference to the ability of the providing institutions to respond in terms of appropriate courses is no longer desirable. Conversely, the providing institutions can no longer expect to develop courses in isolation of LEA policies.

Just as there needs to be a corporate responsibility for special educational needs which extends to all teachers within a school, so the development of special educational needs provision, if it is to be seen in terms of teacher education, requires a corporate response from the LEA and providing institutions. Where the development of a seconded teacher, for example, becomes the responsibility of the providing institution, in isolation from the responsibility which the LEA has for articulating that development within the school, the change implicit in the new concept of special educational needs can not take place.

Where an LEA continues to consider the development of teachers in the field of special educational needs as someone else's problem and the providing institutions likewise consider the development of provision to meet special educational needs as someone else's problem, then the legacy we describe will continue to present insurmountable barriers to change.

Towards Partnership

> . . . it seems clear to us that a successful implementation of the 1981 Act is very much dependent on the development by an LEA of a clear and coherent policy, arrived at in a way which enables it to command the support of those — parents, teachers and voluntary organizations — who are most affected by it. (DES, 1987)

We would suggest that this falls short of what is required. If the development of provision, in the wake of the Education Act 1981, is to be based upon the professional response of teachers, then, in addition to the parties stated above, a meaningful policy will be one which has been contributed to by those directly involved in the professional development of teachers.

We would add that such a policy should also be arrived at in such a way that it enables the IHE to participate effectively in its implementation. We believe that it is unreasonable to ask IHEs to provide courses which deal with fundamental change in provision within the LEA if the personnel within the IHEs have not contributed to the process of reviewing existing provision. Often it is only through the process of review that the complex nature of certain aspects of provision, and their inter-relationship, can be appreciated. This understanding is part of the essential knowledge of the LEA's intentions and present structure, which leads to more realistic In-Service activities.

It would seem to us that either the LEA and IHE manufacture situations whereby each can participate in each other's activities, or a specific appointment is made which promotes participation. In the authors' case this takes the form of a joint appointment which is further described in chapter 6. We give below (figure 1), as an example, that part of an LEA review which follows from an examination of the existing provision and the development of an overall plan. It can be appreciated from this example that without prior cooperation and participation it will be extremely difficult for the IHE to understand, and therefore meet, the In-Service needs which this review generates.

PRIORITY AREA	IDENTIFIED NEEDS
Parents and Governors	Responsibilities / Partnership / Rights / Support
Pre-school	Parental involvement / Problem of assessment of very young children / Professional development of pre-school teachers (attached to nurseries, playgroups, child centres, etc.) / Development of multi-disciplinary teamwork / Planning programmes / Development of pre-school coordinator's role
Integration of personnel	Special school 'Outreach' role and the role of the special school headteacher / Curriculum continuity across special and mainstream / Creation of common working experiences for corporate responsibility / Facilitating clusters / Inter-personal skills / Encourage integration of various levels of intervention.
Primary support teams	Development of school coordinators / Development of primary INSET programme tutors / Facilitate new roles following 'four level' intervention model / Recording and evaluating change / Headteacher awareness / Class teacher development in classroom organization and use of support teacher.
Special schools	Management structure / Development of 'Areas of Experience' (Science, Humanities, CDT, etc.) / Moderate and severe school development in line with projected policy — continuum of curriculum provision / Constructing appropriate individual programmes / Integration (or re-integration) of pupils — constructing integration plans / Development of support, resource and INSET role.
Secondary schools	Senior management response / Coordinator / Head of special needs department / Subject teacher designated to coordinating group / Class teachers and curriculum modification / Implementation of secondary curriculum development policy.
14–19	School–college links / Development of 14–19 curriculum continuum / College coordinator / Access (physical and curricular) / Course development / Awareness courses.
Residential education	Care staff / 24-hour curriculum (integration of living and learning) / Referral criteria / Integration with mainstream.
Officers, advisers, inspectors, SPS, INSET Coordinators	Writing statements / Development of policy statements / Structure and organization / Making priorities / Development needs / Personal needs / Dissemination / Devolving responsibility.

Figure 1: Priority areas and identified needs

MODE	USE
Modular Diploma	In-school development / Encourage change agent role / Develop LEA policy / Theory to practice (personal reflection and development) / Policy-practice research / Appraise teaching force and guide personnel to appropriate posts.
One-term Release	*Free-standing*: Development of coordinator role in ordinary school / In-school development / Develop LEA policy / Develop relationship with Area Adviser for post-course support. *Offered as an Integrated module of Diploma.*
Schools Psychological Service	Based at SPS INSET Centre *Free-standing*: As for One-Term Course but biased toward practical skills / Open to class teachers (special and ordinary) who may or may not be a coordinator / Main vehicle for Support Service. *Offered as an Integrated module of Diploma.*
Teacher Fellowship	Exploring new developments / Evaluation of LEA projects / Evaluation of policy / Research / Relating practice to policy.
Medium Term (½-day–20 day)	Packages that underpin policy (Instrumental Enrichment, Primary Special Needs Programme, TVEI-related, etc.) / Cascade model / Consortia work / Cluster work / Main vehicle for senior and middle management development.
In-school	Release and in-school support of SEN Coordinator / Follow-up work to advisory visits and inspections / School initiated / Encourage staff development policy / Encourage home-made INSET packages.
1 day per week for one term	Based at SPS INSET Centre 'Specific Needs Courses' (Behavioural Difficulties, Speech and Language Difficulties, etc.). *Offered as an Integrated module of Diploma.*

The essential conclusions of the review on which the INSET activities are based, are the commitment of the LEA to a policy of greater integration into the mainstream of pupils and young people with special educational needs. This is to be achieved through a progression of three aspects of integration. Firstly, the integration of the personnel involved with pupils with special educational needs by the amalgamation of hitherto discrete services and the fostering of cooperative methods of working. Secondly, the integration of what are currently considered different and discrete forms of curriculum (often articulated in terms of the *category* of school or pupil), by developing a continuum of special needs provision not based upon placement but on a progressive modification of the curriculum and adaptation of the

3–4 day residentials	Based at LEA Colleges / Consultation about, and development of: guidelines for meeting special educational needs in primary and secondary schools; LEA initiatives and policy / Encourage personal relationships within specific groups (Heads of Moderate Learning Difficulty Schools, Support Teams, Secondary Coordinators, the whole staff of one school, etc.) / Intensive delivery of other LEA packages (Derbyshire Language, Makaton signing, etc.).
1 day course	Small groups, mainly area based / Dissemination of feedback / Up-dating / preparation or follow-up of residential courses or medium term INSET / Consultation / Preparation for organizational change / Develop curriculum development bids.
Full year Secondment	Training of those working with specific groups of children requiring particular expertise (Specific learning difficulties, Severe and complex difficulties, Emotional and behavioural difficulties, Hearing impairment, etc.) / Courses dealing with a defined curriculum area (for individual applications and LEA-sponsored 'specialists').
Masters Degree	Training Educational Psychologists / Development of Modular Diploma / LEA-sponsored research / Personal academic and professional development.
Area INSET Centre	Development of Area initiatives / Dissemination of LEA initiatives / Follow-up work to residential courses / Development of local special needs groups / Respond to local requests.
Out-county short and part-time courses	Day, week, weekend, evening, vacation / Association and Society run courses / Main thrust of support: minority interests and expertise outside scope of LEA INSET / Contact with other Authorities / National initiatives.

Figure 2: INSET modes: projected use

environment. Thirdly, the integration of the learner into the mainstream of education by the 'clustering' of schools — thus emphasizing corporate responsibility and resource sharing, thereby developing the necessary attributes of autonomy and self advocacy.

The left hand column in figure 1 represents an order of priority, but in order to achieve the objectives outlined above, all areas need some degree of simultaneous development. Many of these needs are expressed as new professional roles which arise through the introduction of new approaches.

Such an identification of needs does not in itself provide an adequate framework for the development of INSET activities, since it does not easily translate into the pattern of organization, and institutional constraints, which necessarily characterize the deployment of resources within the IHEs. However, by an examination of alternative modes of INSET delivery, which may include some existing activities, the IHEs could respond to the LEAs' needs more appropriately. A more flexible approach could create a variety of units or modules of INSET activity which when incorporated into an overall range of responses, including those of the LEA, can be suitably accredited and allow for personal, professional and LEA development. This would involve IHEs in adapting their traditional courses, thus providing for the requisite roles and concomitant skills.

Figure 2 demonstrates how a partnership between the LEA and the IHE can respond to identified needs by translating those needs into practical units of delivery. Whilst many of the units are free-standing, they can be combined to offer a pathway of professional development which may include an Advanced Diploma or Master's Degree.

Content and Delivery

Having established a framework for devising INSET activities, it is necessary to consider the ways and means by which cooperation can be achieved in the important areas of content and delivery. As far as content is concerned, LEA involvement is often restricted to the presence of the adviser on the course review or validation committee — where the role of the adviser is a consultative one — following the construction of the course by the course tutors.

Just as we have suggested that it is unreasonable to ask those in IHEs to provide courses which deal with fundamental change in provision within the LEA if the personnel within the IHEs have not contributed to the process of reviewing existing provision, so we would contend that it is reasonable to allow personnel within the LEA to participate in all stages of In-Service activity design, and for the same reasons, i.e., that it is only through the process of planning a variety of INSET activities, within the constraints of an institution, that the complex nature of certain types of delivery and their inter-dependency can be appreciated.

Further, it is important that the participating teachers perceive these activities as not only belonging to themselves and the IHE, but as part also of an overall strategy for developing special educational needs provision within the LEA. To this end, the level of cooperation should be such that it facilitates rapid response to emerging needs or imposed conditions. In the case of the latter, a good illustration is the emphasis on severe learning difficulties and sensory impairment contained in the government guidelines for the GRIST allocation 1988/1989 (DES, 1987). An example of the former might be the need to develop a pathway through a Diploma which addresses, say, the difficult issue of specific learning difficulty.

An important consideration in the development of course content through partnership is the considerable role INSET activities play in the appraisal and deployment of the teaching force, and in particular identifying hitherto hidden potential, in the reorganization of provision following review.

As far as delivery is concerned, there are a number of ways in which the LEA can participate. The most obvious and more traditional is the involvement of LEA officers, particularly Educational Psychologists and Advisers, in lectures and seminars. More recently, however, this has widened, with the same officers participating in negotiated developments, often school-focused, involving the teacher, the tutor, and the school. Others within the LEA's employ may also contribute. A greater degree of integration between the LEA and IHE will be achieved if, for example, change agents identified through the partnership are offered the opportunity to participate. In the authors' experience the practice of seconding senior staff to an IHE for the duration of one term to make a direct contribution to INSET activities, benefits professionally the contributor, the participating teacher, the LEA, and the IHE. Other forms of participation and collaboration include carefully planned teacher fellowships, with negotiated areas of research or evaluation essential to the development of provision, the secondment of tutors to the LEA Advisory Service, and the direct involvement of tutors in LEA initiatives.

Conclusion

In this part of the book we have described, and illustrated by way of a case study, what we call the legacy. We have suggested that this legacy has seriously reduced the potential to develop provision to meet special educational needs. In Part II, by widening the concept of integration, we offer an alternative to 'accepting the legacy'. Central to this is the development of a partnership which accepts a greater degree of closeness among participating professionals, and provides for a greater understanding of each other's roles through shared responsibility. In particular we will concentrate upon the partnership between personnel in the LEA and the IHE, because we believe that they have a common concern which is fundamental to meeting children's special educational needs. This concern is the professional development of teachers, which neither can be permitted to view as *someone else's problem*.

Unlocking the Legacy

Chapter 4

Accepting the Alternative

Teacher Competence and Educability

Traditionally, educability referred to a child's level of response to the education on offer. Thus, if a child did not respond within the mainstream classroom he/she was regarded as having special educational needs. In the respect that the child was ineducable within that setting, he/she was considered to be *someone else's problem*. Levels of educability, therefore, were defined as a progressive series of alternative settings. Hence the categories of handicap and types of provision reflecting those handicaps. Whilst we accept that a small percentage of children do have severe and complex needs, the argument in favour of an approach which emphasizes adaptation of the setting, for all children, through the development of the skills, competencies and attitudes of the teacher, cannot easily be dismissed. Indeed, the professional development of teachers concerned with such children is no less important, in that they share the common need for the support which shared responsibility affords.

In defining educability in terms of teacher competence we are drawing attention to a level of confidence which reduces the likelihood of pupils with special educational needs being excluded from the mainstream classroom. The two most important features to consider here are the support which the teacher enjoys through the shared responsibility of a whole school approach, and the *feeling* of confidence which comes with a better understanding of children's needs and how these needs can best be met. These two aspects of educability are inter-related to a point where it is difficult to sustain one without the other. Indeed we contend that successful In-Service activities, whether LEA or IHE based, are the result of carefully planned experiences which simultaneously address both the need of the teacher and the context in which that teacher operates.

This relationship is in itself a form of integration, since it concerns the integration (or re-integration) of the teacher into the whole school. One of the problems for In-Service activities in the past has been the isolation of teachers. This isolation was manifest both within a school and across groups of schools. Teachers were not always professionally involved with colleagues in a range of provision, nor were they sufficiently part of their own school's organization and subsequent response to children's needs. Shared responsibility, therefore, means both a *whole school* approach and an *inter-school* approach. This point was highlighted in chapter 3 in the example of an LEA and IHE partnership of INSET activities, where the concept of 'clustering' formed one of the basic principles for planning.

It is not surprising, therefore, that evaluation of In-Service activities in recent years has been based upon the success of the teacher as a change agent within the school setting. Concern has centred around the apparent inability of many teachers after a period of secondment away from the school, often for a whole year, to return and initiate change. At the very least it was anticipated that they would exhibit noticeable change in their own classroom practice, but this was frequently unfulfilled.

The above has clear implications for the organization of INSET activities and the nature of the relationship between the child, the teacher, the school, the LEA and the IHE. In recent years the move has been towards school-focused activities, but the necessary structure to integrate this with centre-based activities has not always been evident. The close partnership we are advocating facilitates the development of a rationale for integrating aspects of school-based and centre-based activities. We contend that a measure of success would be the level of involvement achieved by both the partners in both forms of activity. In chapter 7 we discuss the development and practice of school focused INSET activities, where they are viewed as an integral component of the concept of a *resourced* school.

To exemplify this notion of close partnership and reflect the nature and quality of the relationship between the school, the LEA, and the IHE, we describe two contrasting situations. One is a cautionary tale which highlights the problems that arise when preparation on the part of the LEA, IHE or school is inadequate. The second describes a successful outcome based upon sound preliminary investigation and subsequent negotiation. The pre-requisites for a successful outcome are identified.

Example 1: A Cautionary Tale

A medium-sized comprehensive school, in a shipping port which houses a large number of families associated with the Armed Forces, has established a link with a special school for children with emotional and behavioural difficulties. There are arrangements to accept these special school pupils on a part-time basis, and the staff group are thought to provide a caring environment for pupils with special educational needs. A science subject specialist applies, and is accepted, for attendance on a full-time special needs course leading to a Diploma. On returning to the school, he attempts to enlist the support of the senior management team to introduce a new structure for meeting special educational needs. The response is encouraging but no practical support is offered. Rather than commit resources to this development, the headteacher seeks to explore the issue further by inviting the LEA adviser to the school. The adviser arranges to meet the headteacher. However, the adviser is not aware that the science teacher has attended the course, and arrives with an impression of the school gained through her second-hand knowledge of the links with the special school. In response to the headteacher's questions, the adviser explains current thinking and outlines a possible course of action based on the designation of a senior member of staff as special needs coordinator. The headteacher fails to mention the science teacher, assuming that the adviser is already aware of his involvement. The headteacher, who is newly promoted, is seeking a role for the deputy headteacher, who has been at the school for some time and who, unbeknown to the adviser, has not yet established an effective relationship with the rest of the staff. The need for a coordinator, and the deputy head's needs, coincide in the headteacher's view, and he suggests that the deputy head attend a course of training. The adviser responds positively to this suggestion, and after discussion with the deputy headteacher, agrees to secure a place on a one term course for designated teachers.

Whilst the deputy headteacher is away from the school, a probationary teacher is appointed to act as a special needs teacher, and as a replacement for the now retired Head of Remedial Department. This recruitment enables the headteacher to allocate the available scale points to another area of the curriculum.

On completing the course, the deputy headteacher reports on his school-focused work to a meeting of the headteacher, the science teacher, the IHE tutor, the adviser, and the probationary special needs teacher. There is considerable conflict. The various factions are disparate in their views, and it is apparent that little communication has taken place prior to the meeting. It also becomes apparent to the IHE tutor and LEA adviser that the organizational structure and responsibility for special educational needs rests, inverted pyramid fashion, on the shoulders of the distraught probationary teacher. The science teacher, thwarted in his endeavours to initiate support teaching, tries to help the probationary teacher but is unwilling to cooperate with the deputy headteacher. The latter has failed to develop a realistic action plan, and is unable to give the meeting direction. The IHE tutor and LEA adviser become increasingly aware of the lack of serious involvement or commitment of the headteacher, and in the process become uncomfortably aware of their own shortcomings. The real situation within the school begins to emerge, and post-meeting discussion with the probationary teacher and science teacher reveals intense difficulties.

The communication gap and information mis-match, prevalent through-out, result in the probationary teacher leaving the school with feelings of resentment, the science teacher seeking re-deployment, and the deputy headteacher failing to complete the school-focused project. The LEA adviser is reconciled to the view that there will be no development of provision to meet special educational needs in this school for some considerable time.

Example 2: A Successful Outcome

A teacher from a secondary school, who is a Physical Education specialist, wishes to pursue a new career within teaching. He is unsure in what direction, or which INSET activities might offer appropriate advancement. He therefore seeks a career interview with the headteacher. The headteacher describes the current situation in the school as one which requires a change in direction, and explores various possibilities with the teacher as to the acceptable future roles which he may perform. A specific area for development is that of the existing Remedial Department. The school is experiencing falling rolls, and the present head of the Remedial Department has applied for, and been granted, early retirement. The teacher is asked if he is prepared to take on the responsibility of organizing this department to meet the needs of the school. The teacher expresses some concerns; these centre upon feelings of inadequacy. The headteacher suggests enlisting the support and guidance of the LEA adviser.

A meeting takes place involving the headteacher, the adviser, and the designated teacher. The adviser signifies the need to review and analyse existing arrangements for special educational needs within the school, and suggests that the teacher should consider undertaking a suitable series of INSET activities to complement the review process. During the process of review, certain needs will be identified and a plan of action developed.

The school is situated in a densely populated area surrounded by heavy industry. The premises are Victorian and in a state of disrepair. There are plans for re-locating the school into new premises but these have been temporarily shelved. There is little available space and only limited possibility of re-arranging the accommodation. Many of the staff have worked at the school for a long time, and to date, have been accustomed to remedial pupils being withdrawn from the occasional lesson. However, the staff is united in its resolve to make the best of the resources available and generally works well together. Despite the degree of unemployment in the area, and the general level of social deprivation, the parents are supportive of the school and the headteacher has developed a strong pattern of liaison and communication.

The designated teacher is offered a one-term secondment to attend INSET activities at a local IHE. The intention is to negotiate a school-focused project which the headteacher will utilize to bring about change. However, the designated teacher attends these activities not only to fulfil a commitment to a school-focused project, but also to heighten awareness, broaden vision and to be involved in shared working experiences. In particular, through an examination of whole-school approaches, the teacher gains confidence and group support through interaction with like-minded designated teachers, who are also developing projects within their schools. As a group, they are able to sustain one another, build a degree of competence, and establish through their workshop activities a common view and understanding of what constitutes special educational needs. Thus the teacher's own education is enhanced, supporting the proposed direction of the school's development. This improved level of confidence is a vital ingredient, in that he will engender similar feelings of confidence in colleagues, and through interaction and participatory activities, provide a rationale for their involvement with pupils identified as having special educational needs.

The nature of the school-focused project and accompanying school-based activities, help to firmly establish alternative ways of working which are consistent with a new perception of special educational needs which places emphasis on in-class support, departmental identification of need and a policy of entitlement and access for all pupils to all areas of the curriculum. It also emphasizes a requirement to develop relationships across departments, such that adequate support and resources are appropriately deployed. Only through this improved network of communication will the inter-departmental and cross-curricular approaches be secured. This will entail an integration of all personnel, which is in itself a major objective of the school-focused project.

The designated teacher formulates a plan of action which includes identifying staff who are willing to undertake an element of support teaching within their own department. These teachers then form themselves into a group which takes on the function of a steering committee, developing a number of aspects of special educational needs provision which can be presented to the whole staff for discussion, modification and implementation. This is guided and supported by the Senior Management Team, Heads of Departments and the LEA Adviser, with continued support from the IHE.

Both examples highlight the fact that successful involvement of all the partners is often contingent upon the school perceiving a need for action. Sometimes this comes about because the school is actively seeking a change of direction, sometimes because of the appointment of a new headteacher, sometimes because of external pressures, sometimes because the levels of learning/behavioural difficulties reach a degree which can no longer be ignored or tolerated, sometimes because of a change of personnel, or a combination of these. However, as the first example alone demonstrates, whatever the catalyst, success will not be achieved if the necessary pre-requisites are not established.

These pre-requisites would be identified by the adviser in his dealings with the school over a protracted period of time. This assessment is a difficult and complex exercise, since it requires a more intimate knowledge of the organization of the school than is normally readily available. In order to prevent the kind of situation outlined in example one, the adviser will need to work collaboratively with the school to establish the point at which the designated teacher can act as an effective change agent. In some instances it may be necessary to furnish the school with a school-based awareness course for all staff; to debate over a period of time possible scenarios with the designated teacher; to convince the senior management team of the need for change; to encourage other members of staff, through LEA subject advisers, to think about the implications of identifying and meeting the needs of ALL the pupils in subject classes; and to develop stronger links with available support agencies.

Only when this groundwork is complete can the pre-requisites be assessed. The following are not in order of importance, but cover what we believe to be pertinent:

A prevailing attitude within the staff group which is accepting of change, and a willingness to respond to new initiatives.

Accord amongst the members of the senior management team in establishing special educational needs as a priority development.

A designated teacher willing to undertake the responsibility for initiating the development, and to partake in INSET activities.

A structure within the school which allows for discussion, and encourages active participation and contribution.

An organizational pattern which promotes optimum communication.

A resource policy within the school which facilitates rather than hinders priority developments.

In the second example needs are no longer expressed as someone else's problem. The pupil is now regarded, by most staff, because of the support available, as educable within the classroom setting; but more important, the class teacher has acquired feelings of competence through the confident articulation of the agreed policy by the designated teacher.

We wish now to turn to a detailed exploration of the appropriate skills, competencies and attitudes which are pertinent to a new perception of meeting special educational needs.

Skills, Competencies and Attitudes

It is very difficult to identify the skills, competencies and attitudes which should be available to professionals involved in teaching pupils with special educational needs, and yet without doing so it is impossible to alter perceptions regarding special educational needs and how they are to be met.

Traditionally, special education has been characterized by teachers eager to discover a different and more successful method of overcoming difficulties, thus improving the quality of life for pupils with whom they were involved. Hence, many of the approaches used in special environments have tended to be experimental, where pioneering work has been passed on by those with gathering reputations, through colleagues working cooperatively and through the medium of journals where practitioners can 'talk' to one another. Much of the advancement in the work has been through this route, and conferences of professional organizations have waited with eager anticipation to hear word of new developments in their chosen field. Voluntary organizations, created to fill the gaps left by statutory bodies, have similarly contributed to change and development, providing much needed funding to allow, via experiment and projects, hypotheses to be tested, monitored and reported upon. Through the wider dissemination of the voluntary body network, the initial trialling has often been refined, adopted and adapted.

The segregated nature of special education, and particularly the discrete handicaps, often prescribed separate routes for staff training, where the separateness and difference was emphasized rather than diminished, giving rise to separate approaches, methods and content. The very nature of this separateness, in terms of special and mainstream, discrete handicap and discrete handicap, and differing approaches to 'treatment' within one category of handicap, made the identification of particular skills and competencies difficult.

The emphasis on training rather than 'education' is not new. It has its beginnings at the turn of the century when teachers involved with deaf children were provided with university courses at specific centres of expertise such as Manchester. Courses specializing in other aspects of special education work quickly followed, some dealing with discrete categories, others employing a slightly more generic approach. Such courses grew around their handicap, so that courses in educational subnormality vied for funding with those of maladjustment, remedial work, the visually handicapped, etc.

In many ways it could be argued that the pattern of In-Service activity has paralleled that of the caring services and the changes they experienced in the 1970s. Social Services Departments mushroomed during the early 1970s and with their re-organization and increased staffing came a new direction in policy requiring an underpinning programme of INSET. The move to restructure the social and caring services was centred upon adopting a generic approach. In this approach it was anticipated that every social worker would be able to deal with every case presented to him/her. The difficulties and complexities of situations encountered in an individual case, where, for instance, the 'client' was elderly and infirm, would be taken into account alongside the intricacies and complications of a further case involving, perhaps, a young person in need of care and protection. The 'expertise', it could be argued, has been lost through this generic approach, and the setting up of specialist teams in Social Service Departments in very recent times, and the subsequent change in the pattern of training, does in some part reflect recognition of this.

More importantly, however, the expansion of the service made the decision-making process more complex and those promoted to the many senior posts thus created often were those with the 'expertise', whose vital INSET role was lost and subsumed in their new administrative duties and responsibilities. As time elapsed, the decision-making regarding INSET provision was left to those well removed from the new training needs.

To return to the sphere of special educational needs, the situation whilst mirroring many of these issues, is somewhat different. The specialization route and the generic approach are present, but the underlying need has been one of attitudinal change and a series of INSET approaches which reflects the requirements of schools, both special and mainstream.

The qualities required by those teaching in schools catering for 'special' children, and those in mainstream schools, were at one time thought to be very different. Qualities in teaching the blind, for example, would differ from those associated with teaching the maladjusted. The need for a critical examination of the education and certification of teachers of 'exceptional' children was recognized within the Canadian education system in the early 1970s following the publication of Dr David Kendall's report (Kendall and Ballance, 1969). A series of committees for exceptional children looked into teacher education and professional standards relating to exceptional children and raised certain issues pertinent to this discussion. Particularly, in recognizing that many children have special needs because they are exceptional, yet have a number of characteristics in common with each other and with other non-exceptional children, there should be common elements in the education of teachers of exceptional children, and common elements relating to exceptionality in the education of all teachers. They recommended a series of stages of skill-gathering for the teacher, where a communication model provided a framework for viewing exceptional children. It acknowledged that the current classification systems used in the education of exceptional children did not cater for the growing number of cases regarded as sub-categories, or where children were considered multiply-handicapped.

They also envisaged an alternative to traditional teacher education programmes consisting of a number of courses which included short inputs of teaching experience. This alternative was to be a concept of teacher competencies

> . . . based upon the premise that the first consideration in determining how professionals are to be developed should be the tasks that are to be performed, the knowledge needed, and the skills required in different situations. . . . They constructed a hierarchy of competencies as an '. . . outgrowth of an understanding of children's needs which the teacher must be prepared to meet . . .' (Hardie *et al.*, 1971).

Below is what was described as an example of teacher competencies:

A. To Develop Sensitivity to the Needs of Children, as Individuals and in Groups,

TEACHERS SHOULD DEMONSTRATE OR DISPLAY:

1. understanding of physical human growth and development as it applies to the education of children
2. understanding of human emotional development
3. understanding of human intellectual development
4. ability to relate and communicate with children with various kinds of physical, intellectual, and behavioural development
5. warmth and kindness in relationships with children
6. ability to make children feel valued and accepted as individuals
7. sensitivity to individual behaviour
8. ability to identify sources of various kinds of behaviour
9. ability to deal effectively with various kinds of behaviour
10. professional interest in areas in the lives of children, outside of the school, which are relevant to their education
11. active interest in understanding the communities in which children live
12. ability to make learning in school relevant to the lives of children
13. ability to assist children through counselling
14. ability to assist parents and families through counselling
15. ability to recognize the teacher's limitations in counselling
16. knowledge of the various agencies, services, clinics and professional specialists in the community to whom referral may be made and knowledge of procedures for referral of children
17. ability to prepare a comprehensive, written report on a child for whom the teacher has some responsibility
18. ability to interpret into positive action, a written report on a child supplied by another professional worker

The authors suggest that a much more comprehensive list of competencies could be developed — detailed and analytical sets of competencies.

What this would signify is that such competencies would be competencies appropriate for all teachers and the teacher of 'exceptional' or 'special' pupils would view them as essential to their repertoire. The difficulty comes not in recognizing such competencies but in their measurement.

In industry, personnel are often expected to have 'know how' about their chosen area of professional interest, and yet this is often measured against their practical experience as well as theoretical grounding. In education we similarly recruit, select and promote those teachers thought to be outstanding practitioners or potential future leaders within the education system. The criteria for such selection, however, is often based upon experience and further qualification through courses or INSET activity.

Whether such courses have traditionally provided teachers with the necessary competencies is doubtful, and most courses would never claim to do so.

The appropriate school environment for staff development is all important if colleagues are expected to make wide ranging changes and take on more onerous responsibilities. Where changes in direction require considerable shifts in thinking, as well as practice, and where a different repertoire of skills is called for, management teams in schools must be aware of how colleagues can perceive having both choice and control over their future development, otherwise a passive response at best, and feelings of 'anti-task' at worst, will result. Ideally, individual change in direction and orientation should accompany and support the changes in the institution as a whole, and consistently support individuals to ensure success.

This 'whole-school' approach is consistent with other aspects of meeting special educational needs (chapter 7) and in encouraging such an approach, each school would need to look at its existing practice, but particularly, it has implications for the close examination of prevailing attitudes within the school. An additional, rather than a different, set of competencies begins to emerge if such an approach is to be adopted, and the following describes some of these:

1. The devising of a review process to view such areas as identification and assessment.
2. A knowledge of organizational patterns so that a whole-school response can be judged within the context of the whole school organization.
3. A knowledge and experience of group work, from the point of view of management and change, and to promote group responses within the classroom.
4. Knowledge and experience of task setting where a balance can be made between individual, group, and whole-class approaches.
5. Experience of working alongside colleagues in cooperative settings, joint planning and shared working experiences.
6. Developing awareness and attitudes in others appropriate to meeting individual needs.
7. Experience of and disseminating skills regarding supporting colleagues. Supportive roles of both leader and follower experienced. Experience of organizing support strategies.
8. Experience of colleagues being able to evaluate each other's approaches, so that techniques can be improved.
9. A knowledge and experience of differentiation within the curriculum so that individual pupils can demonstrate what they know, understand and are able to do. This would also include the setting of appropriate tasks for individuals and ensuring that success and achievement are pre-requisites and where they are acknowledged and built upon.

Further competencies concerning classroom practice for individual teachers are described in more detail in chapter 7.

As suggested above, the implication is that management teams in schools need to attain a positive climate for staff development. It must also be recognized that available resources may lie beyond the school. For mainstream schools this may employ the services and 'expertise' of the local special school or unit personnel, or draw upon the cluster of schools in the locality, the division or the area.

We suggest that an appropriate atmosphere for the development of teacher competencies, skills, and attitudes is one which encourages teachers to maintain interest and seek out further information, or undertake more formal INSET activity. There will, therefore, be expectations placed upon staff which will go beyond practitioners talking to one another, and where account will be taken of devising consistent, uniform programmes for meeting the needs of ALL children. Concentrating solely upon skills, with an orientation directed towards practice, will exclude vital time for reflection, research and a period where a number of models can be considered in a critical light.

Consequently, the new INSET funding patterns have given rise to a number of anxieties, particularly regarding coherence, and recent changes in INSET delivery have prompted queries concerning the balance of needs between the school and the individual teacher. It is therefore important that we examine more closely the obligations of all those involved.

Obligations: IHE, LEA, School and Teacher

Successful participation is contingent upon each participant accepting a degree of responsibility for his/her own level of involvement. The education of children with special educational needs is both a corporate and individual responsibility. The type of relationship between the teacher, school, LEA and IHE we are advocating is only possible, therefore, if each recognizes the obligation it owes to the other three, in addition, as it were, to its obligation to children. This relationship of obligations can be expressed in diagrammatic form thus:

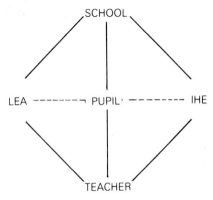

A clear understanding of obligations is an essential starting point for all INSET activities concerned with meeting special educational needs, and before proceeding further we would wish to clarify what we understand these obligations to be. They are not solely based on the demands of the Education Act 1981, but on our perceptions of the kind of relationship required between the parties, which is most likely to succeed in persuading the teacher to accept responsibility for educating all pupils.

Institute of Higher Education

Until the advent of the Grant Related In-Service Training scheme, only a small number of institutions acted in a pro-active fashion. Most were content to consider teachers as potential Full-Time Equivalents, and accordingly 'court' teachers to courses, often not out of any feeling of responsibility, but self-preservation. Occasionally a Department engaged in market research with schools and Local Authorities, but for the most part, needs were assumed. Responsibility was taken for course construction and delivery, but not for match of INSET activity to LEA, school or individual teacher need. Although some lecturers attempted to involve themselves with particular schools and groups of teachers, their time allocations were not conducive to this type of development, and often their best attempts were frustrated by unsympathetic colleagues or management structures. In larger institutions, such as Polytechnics, advancement was viewed, and still is for many, in terms of committee involvement or the production of academic papers. The lecturer who committed time to developing close relationships with LEA advisers or school staff groups went unrewarded when advancement committees met or resources were re-distributed. For many, a commitment to the personal development of teachers or the corporate development of a staff group effectively cut them off from professional advancement within the institution.

The advent of the Grant Related In-Service Training initiative has to some degree altered this, but not significantly. Many institutions are still unable to offer a viable way of involving their lecturers with schools and LEAs, though the threat of devolving INSET funds to schools and clusters of schools has resulted in a more concerted effort.

The obligation of the institution is therefore two-fold. Lecturers need to appraise their role in the light of the development of a special educational needs response, nation-wide, which focuses on LEA and whole-school policy; and those responsible for decision-making need to reconsider their approach to staff development, particularly as regards the criteria for deployment and advancement.

A good starting point, as far as the Institute of Higher Education is concerned, is the principle of integration as advocated by the Education Act 1981. The move away from the medical model, and the fundamental change in thinking which has taken place in recent years, demands a level of response which goes well beyond that which is implied by a change in course content. It is inappropriate to lecture teachers on the need for a whole-school approach and the need for an individual commitment to teaching all children within the classroom, if the content is not demonstrated in the mode of delivery and in the form of follow-up. The lecturer and administration have an obligation to ensure that the teacher is supported in his/her efforts to translate theory into practice, and to demonstrate the fundamental tenets of what they are advocating in their own approach to identifying and meeting the teachers' personal and professional needs.

As far as our model is concerned, it can be demonstrated that the strongest link exists between the teacher and the IHE, and that stronger links must now be forged between the IHE and the LEA and school. In order that lecturers can meet the challenge which this presents, principal decision-makers within the IHE must address their obligation to support the lecturer in his/her efforts.

Local Education Authority

Whilst Institutes of Higher Education have to some degree had their obligations highlighted by market forces, the Local Education Authorities have had theirs forced upon them by legislation. The introduction of GRIST, although welcomed by many Authorities for the increased flexibility it provides, has caused all LEAs to undergo a fundamental re-structuring of INSET activities. Before GRIST, many LEAs did not have the appropriate machinery to allocate resources according to prioritized needs. The system of pooled secondments, divorced as it was from LEA INSET activities, ensured discontinuity between what the LEA was endeavouring to achieve, via policy, and what the IHE provided in course construction. Indeed, many LEAs did not have a framework for reviewing INSET needs, and consequently had no overall structure for deciding on priorities and this resulted in an inequitable distribution of resources.

The development of machinery, therefore, for reviewing In-Service needs within an LEA, which for many LEAs is a new phenomenon, brings with it clear obligations to consider the needs, and value, of both school and IHE involvement, in addition to that of the teacher.

It is an unfortunate fact that some LEAs have not yet found the appropriate balance between the three sets of obligations depicted in our model. In the fervour for devolution of finance and decision-making to schools and clusters of schools, there has been a tendency to undervalue, and subsequently erode, the essential contribution of the IHE. In part the blame for this erosion must rest with the IHEs, particularly where innovative Departments have been frustrated in their development by unnecessarily cumbersome validation procedures. The concentration, too, on academic qualifications, to the detriment of observable change within schools, has also persuaded some LEAs to re-direct funds towards an Authority structure, which often includes expensive new posts related to coordination and staff development advisory work within schools, which in turn precludes spending on IHE-related activities. The danger which this poses for the IHE is all too evident, but the danger which it also poses for the LEA and teacher, may not be so easily recognized.

It is important that individual teachers and LEA personnel, including advisers and officers, have access to an 'independent' source of knowledge and expertise. The research and development base fostered by the IHE is founded on a national, and objective, perspective. Such a perspective operates as a crucial 'touchstone' for the LEA. The drift into isolation and unchallenged precepts is altogether too possible under the current arrangements. A determined effort is required by the LEA, in the form of its officers and advisers, to maintain a degree of objectivity and outside involvement. Advisers and officers need to be challenged, at least as regularly as their teachers, as to the soundness of their assumptions and policies. There is, therefore, a very real, if somewhat old-fashioned, role for the IHE to play in the realignment of attitudes, values and practices, through scrutiny and vigilance which leads to proper criticism and challenge.

The LEA, therefore, has an obligation to the IHE to maintain and extend its role in monitoring, evaluating and questioning developments, in the light of national and international trends, and in the light of its own accumulated objective knowledge and experience. The LEA also has an obligation to the teacher, to ensure a balance between its own needs, in terms of policy development and whole-school approaches, and the personal development needs of the teacher, which at times will require the kind of intellectual stimulus most readily available in the IHE.

The School

Earlier in this chapter we described two important features of educability: the support which the teacher enjoys through the shared responsibility experienced through the whole school approach, and the feeling of confidence which the teacher enjoys through obtaining a better understanding of children's needs and how these needs can best be met. We also pointed out that these two aspects of educability are inextricably inter-linked, and that the most successful INSET activities address simultaneously both the need of the teacher and the context in which he/she operates.

The obligation of the school to the teacher is a relatively straightforward one. It is that the school, through its senior management, and in particular its headteacher, facilitate the teachers development *in situ*. This lays a clear obligation on the school to produce and operate a dynamic and unambiguous staff development policy. Part of this policy will include the ways and means by which INSET activities inside and outside the school can be coordinated. This will involve appropriate arrangements to enable the teacher to carry out school-focused and school-based activities, so that the maximum effects and advantages of these forms of INSET, discussed in chapter 7, can be realized.

In meeting its obligation to the individual teacher, the school will also, to some degree, be meeting its obligations to both the LEA and IHE. In our Cautionary Tale we drew attention to the waste of effort and resources, both on the part of the LEA and the IHE, which can take place if schools are ill-prepared to participate in whole-school, school-based, INSET activities. This obligation, of course, cannot be met by the management team alone. No amount of facilitation by the headteacher and senior staff will be productive if the teachers themselves are intransigent in their beliefs as to what constitutes In-Service, and as to what is an appropriate level of cooperation to afford colleagues involved in school-based activity.

The Teacher

In the context of the 'shared working experience' advocated by the authors as the essential vehicle for change and development at all levels, it becomes clear that the teachers' obligation to fellow teachers is paramount. Throughout this book, we consistently argue that the personal development of teachers is the most important factor in developing provision to meet special educational needs. This personal development will not take place unless teachers, as individuals, participate in the development activities of their colleagues. The inability of some teachers to 'share' experiences in this way, is, we believe, the biggest stumbling block to progress. Providing the Local Education Authority, the Institute of Higher Education and the School Senior Management are meeting their obligations as described above, the teacher will, by entertaining *both* his/her personal development and the development of colleagues, meet the obligations placed on him/her by the school, LEA and IHE. More importantly, all four parties will have gone some considerable way to fulfilling their corporate obligation to meet the educational needs of ALL pupils.

A Possible Way Forward

It follows from the above that the main consequence of not accepting the legacy is increased responsibility at all levels. A greater degree of ownership is required in the planning of a coherent approach to meet special educational needs, and this will be achieved through shared INSET activities. If the resourced school has as its main characteristic teachers who are confident in their dealings with individual needs, then it is possible that ultimately the necessity for INSET activities to address the development of support systems will decrease, whether such support systems take the form of external services, or internal mechanisms as in the case of the present role of many special needs co-ordinators. Such developments as we are currently engaged in may well be viewed as an *interim phase*: one part of a longer term plan which is directed towards establishing resourced schools, as described in chapter 7. The fundamental difference between this approach to planning INSET activities and our current practice, is that both the process and the product of both planning and delivery is dynamic. We appreciate that this point may not be readily accepted by those who are currently the focus of INSET activities, since the roles which they are presently developing will be transitory ones: but this all the more emphasizes the need for INSET activities to be concerned essentially with process rather than product.

A significant element in the equation is the realignment of resources which the LEA will necessarily undertake as part of its re-organization of provision. The devolution of resources from more specialized forms of provision, including support services, to facilitate the development of resourced schools, will require a plan which not only specifies possible interim phases, but which also details the type of INSET activities which will bring this about. It is difficult to see how such a re-organization or realignment of resources can take place outside the type of framework for partnership we are advocating. We are particularly concerned that support should be viewed as an interim phase in the development, because it would seem to us that many LEAs perceive this response as a final target. Such a perception raises important questions. If LEAs continue to build on support models, they may well become institutionalized to the point where teachers and schools continue to view themselves as being without the necessary skills, and therefore the confidence, to respond to individual needs. This lack of confidence, and allied lack of competence, is incompatible with the view of teacher development thus far proposed. Our analysis of LEA policy documents which are reviewed in chapter 6 would seem to reinforce this view.

The relationship between the required realignment of resources, INSET activities and the view of educability described above, is best expressed in the form of an equation:

$$\frac{\text{LEA realignment of resource} \times \text{INSET}}{\text{Planned interim phases of development}} = \frac{\text{greater educability in the}}{\text{mainstream environment}}$$

As the formula indicates, the first step is the realignment of LEA resources. Without an appreciation of what this is likely to entail, it will be difficult to plan appropriate INSET activities. The formula emphasizes the inter-dependent nature of these two aspects of development. Once the resource components have been identified and quantified, the INSET activities can be constructed to coincide with the needs specified in the phases of development.

In order to identify and quantify the available resources, the LEA would need to undertake a review. In essence, the proposed reorganization which follows such a review is the LEA's policy for development. If, as we have advocated, personnel within the IHEs are to be involved in the production of policy, then they must also be involved in the review of provision. Indeed, it might be argued that a review, if it is to be prescriptive, must in part contain evaluation, and it could be further argued that evaluation is precisely one of those areas of expertise which is to be found within an IHE rather than the LEA.

If we examine now, by way of example, one LEA's response to support, we see that existing support services were dismantled and a new structure erected. The new structure incorporated schools' discretionary remedial teachers, peripatetic remedial teachers and some additional posts to act as co-ordinators within three areas of the Authority. Additionally, a signal was given to mainstream schools to appoint special needs co-ordinators who would liaise with the new advisory and support service. The personnel of the latter would perform new roles at four levels: help with individual pupils; discussions with class teachers; providing additional materials; and monitoring individual children. The INSET activities consisted of weekly team meetings to discuss difficulties and devise new approaches.

The three areas were allowed to develop separately, and as a consequence the roles of the advisory and support service differed considerably from area to area, becoming institutionalized within each area. The expectations of schools were also different, with many resenting the loss of their traditional 'extra' remedial teacher. This loss was perceived as a replacement of a valued service by an inferior service. At the same time a change was also signalled to the day and residential special schools, which because of falling rolls, could be replaced by learning support departments in local primary and secondary schools. The intention was to redeploy the existing staff of the special schools into the learning support departments, and to provide access to relevant training for these new roles through existing special needs courses at IHEs. The latter were not involved in the development nor in the processes which proposed such radical change.

Clearly the scope for partnership was considerable, and the omission of this part of the formula assumes a reallocation of resources without the ability to plan the development through phases which are supported by appropriate INSET activities. In the event this LEA may have unwittingly created a support system, albeit within the mainstream setting, which does not constitute an interim phase, and may indeed prevent further development towards the resourced school with its constituent educated personnel. Such a development, whilst in many ways laudable, we view as ultimately inappropriate to achieving the goal of greater educability within the mainstream environment.

Chapter 5

The Support Model as an Interim Phase

Introduction

In this chapter we highlight the consequences for INSET activities of an LEA adopting a dynamic approach to the development of special educational needs provision.

The starting point is a policy which contains a clear statement of philosophy or perspective, a perspective which we have argued should include the concept of the resourced mainstream school. In order to move towards a position where the resourced mainstream school with its concomitant educated personnel is the norm, it will be necessary for the LEA to pass through *interim phases*. It is suggested that these phases need to be encouraged in such a way as to prevent their institutionalization, and that the most important interim phase is that of support. It is further suggested that without a clear policy and the appropriate match of INSET activity, the support model will obstruct development of personal responsibility which is central to meeting the needs of ALL children.

Policy and Perspective

In order to gain a better insight into how various authorities have approached the development of a policy to meet special educational needs we examined a sample of twelve documents obtained from the Education Management Information Exchange. The authorities were chosen to represent a cross-section of characteristics relating to size and location. Having scanned the documents, we identified a series of headings and then carefully analysed the documents to measure the LEA's response to these headings. These were as follows:

1. An overall statement of policy which gives clear direction and informs the subsequent review of provision (the perspective).

2. A description of present provision.
3. A review of provision which has an element of evaluation.
4. An analysis of the information obtained in the review phase.
5. Specific recommendations.
6. The degree to which the review is category-biased.
7. The degree to which the review or recommendations is biased towards a 'service-delivery' model.
8. The degree to which ordinary and special schools are reviewed separately.
9. The degree to which pilot projects informed recommendations.
10. Proposals for changing management structures.
11. The inclusion of an action plan.
12. The level of involvement, both in terms of the review and subsequent consultation procedures.
13. The inclusion of an underpinning programme of In-Service activities.

A positive feature of all the documents was the manner in which an historical account aided a clearer understanding of how present provision had evolved. In many, national and international examples were used to give insight into recent trends and developments, which in turn highlighted current shortfalls in needs and requirements. Where this was apparent, it helped the reader to form a clearer picture of how developments could be shaped, and how policy may be determined. The logical progression provided by these historical accounts meant that a formulation of strategies was more readily achieved. However, where this was not the case, the reader could well be confused by a wealth of unconnected material relating to the Warnock Report and the Education Act 1981. This tended to highlight the LEA's responsibility but provided no clear direction as to how this responsibility might be discharged.

The documents fell into two groups. The majority were characterized by a review leading to recommendations, which espoused a service-delivery approach and made recommendations regarding In-Service activities and management structures. The minority included these elements but also a clear statement of 'general' direction, wide consultation and participation, and an action plan.

It appeared from our examination of the documents that there was a wide discrepancy between LEAs as to the level of resourcing allocated to the review. We noted a high correlation between extensive resourcing of the review and the quality of the outcome in terms of participation, evaluation, consultation and forward planning.

In general, all the LEAs had employed some form of review procedure. This varied from a description of the various discrete provisions, their staff, rolls and physical setting, to a complex survey and analysis of relationships between the provisions leading to a critical evaluation. Importantly, less than half the documents provided this detailed analysis. Most, however, went on to list recommendations. This appeared to be an unwise undertaking if devoid of analysis, and furthermore, seemed to make the task of decision making for Elected Members more difficult. In many of the documents the list of recommendations cited was so extensive, in two examples numbering more than 130, that the process of prioritizing change, and indeed the ability to produce an overall statement of direction, became impractical.

Given that most of the LEAs used the review process to recommend change without analysis, it is not surprising that few documents contained plans for pilot schemes or experimental initiatives. There was a failure to test out models in order to support and give practical direction to proposed changes.

Perhaps one of the most important features of our document analysis was the discovery that all LEAs had embarked upon a review which led them to consider each category of handicap in turn. Whilst in some instances this was contained within more global descriptions of learning difficulty, all the documents made reference to discrete forms of provision for aspects of physical and sensory disability and emotional and behavioural difficulties. It would seem to us that without prior and extensive consideration of philosophy, or as we have discussed it in chapter 9, *perspective*, there is a very real danger of allowing the review of present categories to shape future development.

Such a category-based review of provision will hinder the development of the LEA's response to meeting special educational needs. Many of the documents emphasized deficits within the child and concentrated heavily upon identification and assessment procedures of a service-delivery kind, where responsibility for meeting the child's individual needs reflected a process of gradual devolution of responsibility away from the class teacher. All the LEAs viewed the support model as a permanent feature of future provision. None had thought through their developments sufficiently to arrive at a point where phases of development might be considered. Only one document embraced fully the concept of personal responsibility. There was a considerable discrepancy between the opening statements concerning the historical account of developments in the field of special educational need, with associated concerns for whole school approaches, and the final recommendations which relied heavily on providing support mechanisms to ordinary schools. The institutionalization of support, as discussed in this chapter, would seem therefore, at least for these LEAs, an inevitability.

The references to In-Service activities, whilst evidenced in the majority of the documents, ranged from a cursory consideration of the need for such activities without specifying for whom and at what stage of involvement, to a detailed set of proposals for named personnel, possible content and method of delivery. As a consequence of viewing the support model as a final goal, In-Service activities were adjusted to complement the requisite skills of the personnel likely to be involved. As a result, some of the LEAs concentrated heavily upon suggestions for testing and assessment and even linked such techniques to the traditional categories of handicap. Thus, whilst paying lip-service to the principles of integration, the In-Service activities were closely aligned to existing segregated provision.

More positively, we would wish to draw from the minority of documents those aspects of policy construction which appear to us essential to communicating a clear definition of purpose to all those involved in policy implementation. In the three most coherent documents, the LEAs had succeeded in under-pinning their policy statements with a consultation process; an analytical review; an In-Service plan; a management structure; and most significantly, clearly communicated intentions. In consequence they had arrived at a coherent perspective and constructed a plan of action. The plan of action so derived embodied the perspective, transmitting a clear message of continuity and integrity of purpose, thus alleviating the problem of communication and allowing for the possibility of planned phases of development, which would enable the LEA to reconsider its policy on support, exchanging it for the more desirable goal of the resourced school and the acceptance of personal responsibility.

Adopting a Dynamic Approach

If the process of development, following a review, is indeed dynamic, the perspective will relate more readily to all schools. As a consequence, and largely following a development of commitment and initiative within the schools, there will be 'interim phases' which are unpremeditated by the LEA but which nevertheless provide creative routes to the goal. Likewise, those working within existing support services may develop practices which demonstrate an acceptable alternative pathway. In order to be responsive to possible alternative 'interim phases', INSET activities need to be harnessed to support such initiatives. This is not to suggest that creative initiatives should lead to arrangements which are *ad hoc* or *laissez-faire*. Providing the statement of perspective is clear and the final goal understood, those charged with policy-making can carefully monitor developments and encourage the initiative, or redirect it, in accordance with the overall goal. INSET activities would play a crucial role in this process.

However, because of accountability and the need to justify change, it will be necessary, particularly in large authorities, for the LEA to plan a series of possible 'interim phases'. Such phases will mostly be concerned with the restructuring of resources, and as previously suggested, this is likely to follow a pattern for the integration of personnel. The nature of decision-making within the LEA (chapter 10) will make the necessary flexibility difficult to achieve, but without it the dynamic process of incorporating initiative into planning cannot be accomplished. Further, such changes as may ensue cannot be imposed, for as some LEAs may have discovered, many of those required to change their methods of working have chosen instead to perpetuate existing practice. This has been especially true of remedial advisory services, which overnight have been required to adopt support methods using existing personnel.

Even if an LEA adopts a quite different model, perhaps dismantling existing support mechanisms and thus placing immediate obligation and responsibility upon mainstream schools, it cannot be assumed that this will be achieved without the assistance of some form of dynamic process which encourages initiative. Evolution through 'interim phases', based upon the acceptance of local initiative which is supported by INSET activities is essential.

'Interim phases' can be represented in a diagrammatic form which is more easily communicated to those involved in the dynamic process of change. Below we offer one series of 'interim phases', which provide a pathway for moving from a known position of discrete services toward the suggested position of the resourced school. Apart from the initial act of re-organization required to unify the discrete services, the phases are enabling rather than prescriptive, in that they facilitate initiatives, albeit within a particular direction. It is quite possible that the nature of the phase could change and/or some phases be omitted/replaced. The important point is that there is a perceived direction with a known goal, and that there is a framework through which INSET activities can be developed.

Having established a series of 'interim phases' the LEA and IHE must be prepared not only to respond to creative initiatives, but also be flexible in the organization of its INSET activities — to accommodate different rates of progress or different types of initiative, in different locations of the authority. Clearly this cannot be achieved if 'courses', rather than INSET activities, are in themselves prescriptive and institutionalized in content.

Phase 1

Within this phase, our representative authority will be involved in the integration of personnel. This will entail amalgamating those currently employed as peripatetic remedial teachers with teachers working in special classes attached to mainstream schools. The support teams thus created would be made larger by the inclusion of remedial teachers allocated to mainstream schools by way of discretionary points. As we have explained elsewhere, the interim nature of this phase lies in the transitory quality of this type of support in establishing confidence and competence amongst mainstream teachers. If this is the case, then the INSET activities embarked upon in this phase must contain a large element which addresses the following two needs: the role of the support teacher as change agent, and the personal needs of the support teacher brought about by sustained adaptation of role as a response to changes taking place in the mainstream, as the concept of the resourced school is realized.

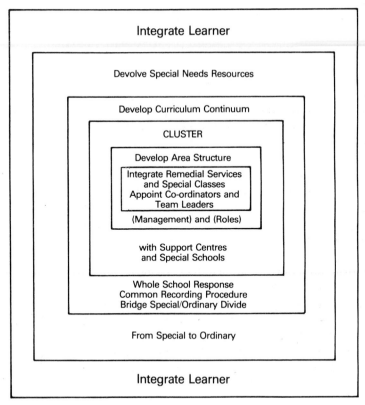

Figure 3: Patterns of change

Phase 2

Having integrated the personnel, a management structure is required, which to some degree defines roles and establishes relationships. The LEA will need to address issues which arise from placing the integrated personnel into a new context. For example, the roles of the advisory services and the school psychological service may have to be reviewed alongside those of headteachers and special needs co-ordinators in schools. This suggests that INSET activities will be required which include a wider group of people, wider than might at first be suggested by the management functions of, say, support service co-ordinators or team leaders, or the new inter-personal professional skills of team members. Such re-organizations rarely confine the repercussions of role change to those directly involved. This will be an interim phase because the prime function of the devised management structure is to facilitate change, and the management structure itself is included in that change.

Phase 3

In order to meet special educational needs, a clustering approach is to be adopted so that scarce resources can be shared across a group of schools — these resources include materials, educated personnel, specialist facilities, etc. The clustering will also involve the local special school and the facilities and personnel they may make available. The interim nature of this phase is that it establishes the bridge whereby resources can be devolved from specialist institutions to resourced schools. As far as INSET is concerned, it will be necessary to organize activities which not only address the needs of individual schools but relationships between schools, in particular the relationship between the special school and the mainstream.

Phase 4

To sustain the movement of resources from specialist institution to mainstream it will be necessary to devise a continuum of curriculum activities which responds to all children's curricular needs. For our representative authority, this will be achieved through the development of a curriculum which is increasingly and progressively modified. The nearer the cluster moves towards differentiation of the curriculum for ALL children, the more likely it is that the resource implications of the final goal, i.e., the resourced school, will be understood. The interim nature of this phase, therefore, is to some degree dependent upon the willingness of the LEA and the participants, once needs are established, to devolve and increase resources.

Phase 5

THE GOAL — the resourced school

The Support Model

The Warnock Report and subsequent Education Act of 1981 made many of the terms used prior to their inception either no longer pertinent or difficult to interpret within the new framework. Thus, such phrases as 'backward', 'retarded' and 'remedial', which had previously been every-day terms within education, became no longer fashionable or relevant. Similarly, the roles of professionals involved with 'backward', 'retarded' or 'remedial' pupils have also come under scrutiny, and traditional approaches of remediation to individual pupil deficits have been translated into a service offering support to schools, teachers and pupils, in addition to the individual pupils within a specific category of difficulty or 'handicap'.

Many of the Remedial Advisory Centres or Reading Centres were set up in LEAs as a result of the influences of Burt (1937) and Schonell (1942) and as a response to the various interpretations of the meaning of 'backward', 'retarded' and 'remedial'. However, the subsequent myriad of interpretations made coherence difficult, and responses to perceived needs, in terms of remedial education, were viewed differently by LEAs (Laskier, 1985).

The Remedial and Reading Centres which were established concentrated upon improving literacy skills, usually withdrawing children from their classroom situation and teaching them either individually or in a small group at a local centre. This role has persisted until recent times and teachers involved within it were often part-time, peripatetic teachers who specialized in the teaching of reading, gaining expertise through specialized courses which concentrated upon 'diagnostic' testing of individual children, and individual planning aimed at alleviating 'problems' within the child's repertoire of skills. It also involved the making of reading materials, and building up a bank of appropriate materials for youngsters regarded as needing remedial help.

Personnel recruited to such posts varied in background and experience, including those returning to teaching after a gap in their service, those wishing to work only part-time, those unable to secure a full-time post, those unhappy in dealing with larger groups of children, as well as those committed to helping children with difficulties, who were self-selecting in their chosen career path. In consequence, the status of such teachers varied considerably. Many teachers regarded them as a means of transferring responsibility from themselves, as classteachers, to the remedial teacher, encouraging the attitude that children recognized as not coping with the curriculum would be *someone else's problem*. Others, through a lack of understanding of the remedial teachers' commitment and skills, regarded such teachers as having an easy option in terms of teaching demand. Their status, in general, was often difficult to determine, and many who were involved in schools on a peripatetic basis, were often relegated to using store cupboards, corridors, or the medical room (Thomas, 1986) in order to undertake their duties.

The approaches adopted by remedial teachers tended to be characterized by a lack of continuity between what occurred in the classroom and what occurred in the withdrawal group or remedial centre. The experiences which were missed by the pupil as a result of withdrawal from their peers for 'remediation' often outweighed the possible benefits of the remedial programme. The pupils' own views of their performances as a result of the labelling process of 'remedial', resulted in feelings of inferiority and failure, which had further repercussions in terms of expectancy by both themselves and those involved in the learning process.

A further feature of this model of provision involved LEAs in making financial cuts to educational services. Often personnel involved in remedial provision were one of the first areas to feel the effects of stringency. To counteract this diminution of numbers and to spread thin resources as widely as possible, many remedial services became less involved with the teaching of individual children in the services they offered, adopting instead support to, and involvement with, teachers who in turn could be supportive to pupils. The use of voluntary assistants has also been a factor in many schools, where students, older pupils and adult helpers are involved. Alongside the financial effects, where part-time staff were likely targets for making savings, professionals were involved in questioning the efficacy and appropriateness of traditional remedial teaching. The Warnock Report and Education Act 1981 prompted changes which saw the traditional remedial services beginning to evolve as supportive agencies, consistent with the notion of a continuum of provision. Whilst recognizing the desirability of a change in direction, LEAs lacked a clear, central direction as to the most efficient and effective way of responding to the development of such a service delivery model. Hence, changes in the service were introduced as part of an experimental exercise, and pilot projects were instituted to measure viability. If successful, these were adopted as an appropriate support service. The imprecise nature of the legislation, and the extent and variation in interpreting that legislation, has led many LEAs to adopt different strategies. However, most LEAs appear to have adopted similar strategies in terms of support to schools (Gipps *et al.*, 1987).

Many LEAs, realizing the implications of the Education Act and an emphasis upon identification and assessment, expanded their advisory and support services particularly with personnel drawn from the field of educational psychology. As the new support services have evolved, those working within them have already changed from traditional remedial teachers, albeit retaining many facets associated with their former role. Consequently, schools, teachers and pupils have experienced a changing service, likewise personnel involved in the services have experienced change. However, where a change in role does take place, it is often most difficult to convince those affected by that new role that a change has occurred. To be a remedial teacher involved in teaching individual pupils one day, and to become a support teacher to class teachers the next, is a difficult adjustment from all points of view. In some LEAs it involved not only new roles, but new personnel, where induction, familiarization, and INSET activity were essential for staff — whether changing their role, or being new recruits to a burgeoning service.

The pattern of support which Gipps *et al.* (1987) outline in six LEAs has characteristics present in very many LEA support structures, where they have evolved from existing remedial provision and have expanded in response to the Warnock Report and the Education Act 1981. Other LEAs have abandoned the term 'remedial', and have a range of services which may have an integrated support for hearing-impaired, visually-impaired, behaviour difficulties, or additional services to meet requirements. The level of autonomy apportioned the support services would seem to vary, and line management for some occurs through the school psychological service, a Head of Support, or through divisional, area or central education offices.

Similarly, the range of involvement may be organized on the basis of a cluster of schools, a reactive role to requests by individual schools, or a targeted group of schools decided by a steering group of local Headteachers and support personnel. The width of focus also seems to vary markedly, where in some cases it is very specific and narrow in range and in others the role is extremely broad with participants very quickly experiencing 'burn out'.

Where the LEA has a written set of guidelines or a policy statement regarding the support services, this has overcome difficulties of overlap of support by different agencies and educational personnel. It assists in identifying roles more precisely, outlining particular responsibilities and placing the support service network within a wider educational framework. It also contributes monitoring features in order that the effectiveness of the service delivery model can be assessed and communication between elements of the support service enabled.

The resulting implications which the support structure suggests are far reaching, especially in terms of teacher development. An LEA needs to clarify its intentions and direction in a manner which is readily communicated to teachers in schools and to the evolving support services. This entails teachers being involved in the formulation of policy, ensuring their contribution and creativity, and subsequent commitment to its implementation. As the new roles entail new skills, further recruitment and future appointments need to reflect the changing role.

This change in role may include: working alongside colleagues; curriculum modification; adapting the environment; classroom organization and management; a knowledge of differing learning styles; an INSET role; assisting in making school policy changes; involving parents; advising professional colleagues; planning programmes; as well as the more traditional roles of withdrawal and small group work. More importantly, for many support teachers it may involve the acquisition of additional skills, knowledge and attitudinal change. Particularly, it will require an understanding of the management and organizational structure of the schools supported and the level of involvement specific schools require. This will aid the school in making the most of the support on offer. For some schools a clear indication of the type of support required must be matched with what the support service personnel are able realistically to deliver. This may entail the school making choices from a menu of possibilities and may also involve some form of contract, where targets are set, time spans are indicated and where monitoring and evaluation are integral features. This has further INSET implications in: organizing and allocating resources both human and physical; time management; identifying individual functions; the process of negotiating and possibly re-negotiating with schools; and methods of evaluation.

These advisory functions and consultancy roles also involve inter-personal skills where people can feel valued, and where personal contributions are fostered and encouraged. The range of role functions would suggest a need for flexible responses allied to tactful approaches. They also indicate the need for INSET activity focusing upon management skills.

Expectations of teachers to be involved in INSET without prior experience are unrealistic and may not take account of appropriate and necessary prior teacher development. Similarly, support linked to INSET initiatives such as the Coventry SNAP programme appeared most effective where there was continuing support and development by those involved in the initial INSET pathway, and where the 'trainers' were themselves adequately 'trained'. However, the needs of all LEAs are undergoing change and responding to those needs will continue to present difficulties. This presents particular difficulties for INSET providers, for as the needs of teacher development alter, no appropriate 'catch-all' INSET activity will adequately address the needs of individual support teachers. Alternatively, teacher development can address the issues outlined above, by responding to newly identified INSET needs in a dynamic way, such that it can involve individual teachers, school staff groups, clusters of schools, LEA officers and advisers, and IHE personnel.

The Problem of Institutionalizing the Interim Phase of Support

In the first part of this chapter we described the emerging models of support as being necessarily interim in nature. This follows from our view that the ultimate aim of meeting special educational needs is the transfer of responsibility to the classroom teacher. It is pertinent, therefore, at this point, to consider why so many LEAs have opted for the support model, and why there is so little evidence of intention to use support as a means to an end, i.e., the classroom teacher taking full responsibility for the education of all the children in his/her class.

The first observation to make is that those making decisions about policy, assuming that they are making those decisions in a non-participatory manner, have not themselves always accepted personal responsibility. The case study in chapter 1 clearly illustrates this. There is a constant movement to and fro as the responsibility for making decisions, or making a commitment to action, is passed from one professional to another. The advent of a support service in such a situation will undoubtedly encourage the attitudes that underpin this level of inaction. If the school cannot deal with the child, and the alternative options are too expensive, or educationally undesirable, then administrators, and associated professionals within the Advisory and School Psychological Services, will only be too grateful to pass the responsibility to the support teacher. Apart from the intolerable burden this will lay upon support teachers, such an abdication of responsibility will inevitably lead to an institutionalization of support work, with little or no development toward the resourced school. In a sense, the advent of special schools mirrors this scenario. So too has the introduction of statements of special educational need. We saw in the case study how the assessment became the final act, and its process the excuse for inaction.

If support teachers are viewed as the answer to awkward parents, or worse, awkward schools, then there is no possibility of development. The inertia we have described in chapter 1 will continue. Only when an LEA addresses the fundamental question *'whose responsibility is it?'*, and in the process replaces the answer *'someone else's'* with a deep consideration of the issues raised by *educability* and *teacher development*, will the notion of support as an interim phase be considered.

In considering the passage of LEA provision from its present, predominantly segregated, separate and varied forms, towards the stated goal of the resourced school, it is necessary to identify the constraints likely to be encountered on the way. In many respects, this book is about those constraints and about the strategies which will be required if the goal of the resourced school is to be realized. There is, however, one particular constraint which we believe has yet to be fully appreciated. Because this constraint has the potential to undo much of the good work currently in evidence, both in the LEA and IHE, it deserves closer attention. We have chosen to describe this constraint as the 'institutionalization of support'.

The term 'planned interim phases' was deliberately chosen so as to contrast with the idea of development. As with curriculum development, the development of provision to meet special educational needs can be taken to mean *change giving rise to enrichment*. This represents a process of growth; improvement through evolution. Planning, in contrast, may be understood as *the production of a scheme for accomplishing a purpose*. Development implies a certain open-endedness as to outcomes, with outcomes dependent upon complex relationships operating between teaching methods, beliefs, attitudes, management systems, interactions between personnel, facilities, buildings, etc. In the case of planning, the outcome is clearly stated, i.e., the resourced school, and the complex relationships manipulated accordingly.

This manipulation can itself give rise to distrust and lack of enthusiasm for participation, and in our opinion, the only way to avoid the product of manipulation, which we agree is necessary to some degree in planning, is to involve all the participants, fully, and from the start. This means stating the goal clearly and involving those who are to be part of the interim strategy in the production of the plan.

Each phase must be successfully accomplished and established before the next can begin. The process of establishing the phase is called 'institutionalization'. In order to achieve a sound basis for further change it is essential that each phase is firmly established, or institutionalized. If those participating are not involved in the original plan, it quite often transpires that institutionalization can only be brought about if those participating actually believe that what they are involved in *is* the end product. Clearly such an approach to planned change raises ethical and professional issues regarding manipulation and the covert nature of its method. We believe, quite apart from ethical issues, that in the long term such manipulation is counter-productive; even though, in the short term, it may achieve the interim position more quickly and smoothly.

The problem therefore arises that in order to be effective in the support phase, the practice, which includes the development of a working relationship between support teacher and classroom teacher — which in itself will be hard to establish and require considerable effort on both parts — must become so ingrained as to be almost 'second nature'. When this occurs, institutionalization will have occurred, but further development, through to the next phase, will be extremely difficult, since, as with all institutionalized practice, it will be difficult to change. This is a well-recognized phenomenon to those involved in curriculum development. If a new innovation does not reach a state of institutionalization it will fade away. Conversely, if it does become institutionalized, it may be difficult to develop further, or indeed change if subsequently viewed as inappropriate. This is the Catch 22 of education.

From the outset, then, support must be viewed as interim, and if, as many LEAs would want, those taking part are not to be manipulated, or hood-winked into working towards a temporary goal, steps must be taken to ensure that those participating understand the need to firmly establish support, but equally understand the need to move into personal responsibility.

To achieve this it will be necessary, from the start, for the LEA to make plain its goal and its plan for achieving it. For most authorities, this will require something more than the current 'review' or 'policy' statements we have encountered. As Liz Allan (1987) points out, in the report of the Centre for Studies on Integration in Education, *Duty to Review*, of the 46 per cent of LEAs that had completed a review of provision as required by the 1981 Education Act, by February 1987, the quality of the reviewing was such that direct comparisons were almost impossible. One LEA's 'review' was another LEA's 'policy statement'. Some LEAs had reviewed their provision by category, others had taken a 'snapshot' of the whole service. Very few had embarked on a wide-ranging consultative exercise across the whole authority. In some instances, the review was represented by a briefing report to the education committee as part of a continuous process of looking at provision.

Following this, and our own analysis of LEA policy statements and subsequent follow-up of support strategies, it would seem unlikely that many LEAs will consider support teaching as an interim phase. As a result, where support teaching has been introduced, or is to be introduced, it is most likely that it will be institutionalized and remain institutionalized, and therefore present a major obstacle to further development.

From the point of view of introducing support teaching with the intention of devolving the responsibility to the classroom teacher, the accumulated evidence, regarding the way in which LEAs have conducted their reviews, is equally disquieting. Participation is essential, both in the construction of a coherent policy and in its implementation, as indeed is advocated by the House of Commons Committee of Enquiry into the workings of the 1981 Act, if the support phase is to develop into a form of provision which does not encourage the view that special educational needs are *someone else's problem*.

If participation is the key to moving from the phase of support to the phase of personal responsibility, as envisaged in the resourced school, then the institutionalization of support, which we agree is necessary to developing the skills and competencies of classroom teachers, must be characterized by certain participatory demands. Hughes, as long ago as 1957, suggested that these demands could be thought of as feelings — feelings of personal worth, identification, satisfaction, real responsibility in decision making, and interaction.

Of particular concern to a support service is identification. Partial identification is one of the least desirable attitudes in any educational organization. Such attitudes are common enough in schools, where teachers identify with a department rather than the whole school, and it is important that the support teacher identifies fully with the school or schools he/she is supporting. This must be achieved in such a way as to lead to integration with other personnel within the school, so deriving satisfaction from the development of both the whole school response and the development of individual members of staff.

Dissatisfaction, or frustration, as a negative feeling, not only leads to poor participation, it also creates barriers to the integration of personnel which is essential if the support is to evolve, or devolve, into personal responsibility. To achieve this, the interim phase of support must avoid feelings of 'ownership' on the part of the support teacher. Ownership is characterized by the degree to which an individual teacher views their part of the organization as personal property and is possessive about the privileges and rights of his/her position. It is not difficult to see how such 'ownership' might occur in the 'interim phase'. Just as 'remedial' teachers can be possessive and protective about *their* children, so support teachers may be protective about *their* role or service; and in a way which is not conducive to 'letting go' when the school or class teacher reaches the point of accepting responsibility, and perhaps only requires 'another pair of hands' rather than 'expert advice'.

Such attitudes, even if teachers are not aware of them, are constantly given overt expression and this has a deteriorating effect on human relationships. Good human relationships are, after all, at the heart of innovation which seeks to integrate personnel in a manner that establishes a common perspective through shared working experiences.

Role-clarification for the support teacher is paramount here. Such clarification is perhaps made even more difficult by the knowledge that the support is interim, and that the role must necessarily, in time, change. Feelings of satisfaction play an important part in this process. As Shipman (1975) points out:

> But role performance must not only be learnt, it must be felt to be right, efficient and rewarding, for individual satisfaction and group solidarity.

Feelings of worth, one of Hughes' participatory demands, is only likely to be achieved if the role, and its proposed evolution, feels right, efficient and rewarding.

Much of this will depend upon good communication systems and for this reason we have explored this issue elsewhere. The inadequacy of present communication systems is one of the major themes and conclusions of the case study. Sufficient to say here that the development of good human relationships depends on good communication, and that good communication depends largely upon how authority is used, or managers manage or mismanage. The connection between communication, authority and human relationships is emphasized in the two participatory demands of interaction and real responsibility in decision making. How authority is used, both in terms of the decisions made by the Senior Management Team of the supported school and the decisions made by the leadership of the support team, will very much influence what actually happens in the classroom between supporter and supported. Communication, therefore, between the management of the support team and the management of the school is vital. Between the two, the support teacher must feel that he/she is interacting with both parties and that responsibility in decision making is a reality, both in terms of what is agreed, by and for, the supported school, and in the development of the LEA plan at large.

The feelings of participation outlined above, affected as they are by communication, authority and human relationships, are more likely to be achieved if the vehicle for the development of support, and indeed its eventual devolution into personal responsibility, is dynamic In-Service activity — In-Service activity which reflects the movement from one phase to another. Participation, as we have described it, and INSET as a vehicle for change, are, we believe, the two necessary ingredients which will help prevent the permanent institutionalization of the interim phase of support, and it is to INSET as a vehicle for change that we now turn.

INSET as Both Vehicle and Process

Having outlined a pattern of development for the realignment of provision to meet special educational needs which is dynamic, we contend that such a realignment without sufficient partnership between the LEA and IHE will not be adequately fostered. Indeed, throughout this chapter we have drawn attention to the need to consider INSET activities as the vehicle through which phases of development are realized. If INSET is dynamic it will mirror the journey undertaken by the LEA; but more than this, as we would expect the LEA interim phases to accommodate local initiative, so we would expect INSET activities, which are truly dynamic, to contribute their own pathways towards the commonly understood goal. In this sense, dynamic INSET activities are more than a vehicle, they are an integral part of the process by which initiative is generated.

Neither the LEA nor the IHE should underestimate the strain that will be placed on their partnership, if in fact they undertake the dynamic process we are suggesting. Our observations indicate that at the present moment most LEA/IHE partnerships do not contain the necessary symbiotic characteristics to withstand even a relatively small degree of misunderstanding. Over recent years, through numerous re-organizations of Higher Education, notably following the James Report and more recently the introduction of GRIST, a mistrust has developed; differing goals of LEA and IHE, and the aura of severe financial constraint for both, have further contributed to this. Consequently, serious attention should be given to the following.

The LEA must realize that its plans can be diverted or channelled in different directions. For, if the IHE is to mirror the journey undertaken by the LEA, and adopt a dynamic process, it will inevitably adapt, divert, or extend and develop the LEA plans. Similarly, if the IHE is to be successful in fulfilling this sensitive aspect of the partnership, it must understand fully the constraints and the potential of the present provision. For through this understanding the IHE will often provide the catalyst which provokes the change that fundamentally affects parts of that provision.

Participants within IHE INSET activities will represent one part of the overall provision. Given the commitment of the participant to contribute initiative, and the IHE's ability to foster and encourage such initiative, participants can be the providers of new or alternative pathways. However, a lack of an appreciation of the repercussions for the total provision of an adjustment in one part of that provision, no matter how obviously self-contained, will result in *ad hoc* and piecemeal development, which may obstruct progress towards the commonly understood goal.

Therefore, whilst in the short term localized developments may contribute to the relationship between LEA and IHE, in the longer term it may produce issues which strain the partnership and diminish the relationship. We would argue that to some considerable degree this can be avoided through the mediating role of the 'joint appointment' or similar facility. The partnership must therefore be built on solid foundations, where constraints and potential, both within the structure of the LEA and the IHE, are clearly recognized and understood. To this end, the IHE and the LEA must acknowledge that neither can be the prime mover in change and development. The relative merits of each must be codified, so that each other's strengths and weaknesses can be accepted — for example, the IHE's superior access to a wider range of current thinking, and therefore their ability to act as a catalyst and clearing house for ideas; and the role of the LEA as enabler through the appropriate political/structural decision-making machinery.

This would seem to strengthen the argument for both a plan of interim phases, however loose and open to modification, and the full involvement of the IHE in its inception. Indeed, this may give practical direction to the perspective and policy already jointly agreed. Such an exercise, whether or not each phase is adhered to, clearly indicates the nature of the INSET activities required. Whilst there may be alternative pathways to that described in our example of interim phases, it is likely, as our example illustrates, that the common denominator is 'change' — how it is initiated, developed, maintained, adapted to, coped with and measured; change in a wide variety of aspects — provision, roles, attitudes, working practices, the processes of INSET, how INSET is organized and entered into, decision making, and the understanding of whose problem this is.

As far as INSET activities are concerned, the most important change will be the manner in which participants are involved. Whilst it may be necessary to change INSET content because of the different requirements of participants in terms of new skills and competencies to be acquired, their preparation for articulating these skills and competencies in a way which reflects the underlying flexibility required of a post which has in-built into it rolling role change, will require a fundamental re-appraisal of the way in which those skills and competencies are developed. It is certainly no new idea that INSET activities should take participants through a process of change which is indicative of the points to be made, but this rarely takes place. This was most graphically illustrated to the authors in their dealings with course development in the Netherlands, where the principles of curriculum development were in fact not taught. Course members experienced curriculum development by negotiating the content and methodology of their whole course within the first few months of that course. Principles for curriculum development were deduced by action and reflection.

The intrinsic nature of change mitigates against its characteristics being taught through the traditional mode of delivery. Further, it demands that INSET activities themselves should be open to renewal and, by implication, defended from institutionalization. This is no small matter, since as with all teaching and learning activities, the organizational constraints and pressures of time lead to sterility.

If a dynamic approach is adopted, this will be avoided.

Chapter 6

The Problem of Communication

Introduction

In this chapter we examine ways in which the partnership of the Local Education Authority and Institute of Higher Education can best service the notion of *dynamic* INSET. The central issue is one of communication, and in exploring new structures designed to enhance communication, we highlight the positive and unique contribution of the *joint appointment*.

Towards Better Communication

Traditionally, teachers applied for courses at IHEs and applied for secondment from the LEA. In the least-developed form of communication, secondment was granted on the basis of the LEA recognizing the right of the teacher to secondment, subject to such criteria as length of service; availability of funding; appropriateness of the course to the teacher's position and subject taught; and whether the LEA, through its advisory service, valued the course or particular IHE. At this level of communication, special educational needs were often viewed by the LEA as a subject, and LEA advisers played no other part than selecting candidates from those already offered a place on a course. The emphasis was on the course providing a qualification which could be recognized by both LEA and teacher as a step on the ladder to promotion. Little thought was given to the professional development of the teacher, either in terms of the needs of the current teaching environment or its place in the overall development of provision within the authority. It was commonly expected that teachers would not return to their own school, or if they did, would actively be seeking positions elsewhere, thus minimizing their impact on development within that school. Clearly, such a view of INSET does not demand the same kind of involvement as is the case with the concept of teacher development proposed in this book. As promotion prospects decreased and redeployment became an accepted method of dealing with falling rolls, so the need for advisers (who were also involved in the deployment of staff) to be involved with course development became more apparent. However, for many authorities, involvement in terms of attendance at a course committee prescribed the limit of their participation. Even where communication has developed beyond this point it is still restricted to the arena of the adviser and course director. It is interesting to note that this limited form of communication has to some degree been formalized in recent times with the advent of the INSET co-ordinator in IHEs, whose role it is to negotiate with their counterpart in the LEA structure, the INSET adviser/inspector. From our point of view, such a development will, in the longer term, be unproductive, since our view of teacher development, by necessity, demands a much wider sphere of involvement. The communication which this kind of negotiation implies does not facilitate the development of working relationships which encourages integration of personnel — which we believe to be essential to the construction and implementation of commonly understood goals.

Communication, to be effective, must encompass all those in the IHE and LEA who are part of the decision-making and enactment process. Such a view has two consequences. Firstly, it is necessary to identify the participants. Secondly, the participants need to engineer an appropriate *shared perspective*. We choose the word 'engineer' because we believe that a shared perspective results from shared experiences.

To take the first, it may appear self evident that in order to gain participation one needs to identify the participants. However, in the case of the LEA and IHE this is not so obvious. Many authors refer to LEAs and IHEs in a manner which would seem to indicate that such bodies have a single will and are able to respond accordingly. To a certain extent this is true, in that political decisions are made within the Council Chamber or Board Room, but, for most practical purposes, it is more useful to envisage both the LEA and the IHE as complex human organizations, where decisions and actions, at all levels, contribute to what makes the LEA or IHE what it is (chapter 10). If we view the LEA and the IHE in this way, then it is possible to regard partnership as the integration of personnel within these complex human organizations, and at many levels.

Indeed, it is only through this interpretation that the concept of a shared perspective, through shared experiences, can have practical meaning. Having identified the participants, it is possible to engineer shared working experiences. These can then be divided into two types. Firstly, there are those experiences that relate to the administrative roles of the participants, and careful thought needs to be given to selecting the most appropriate arenas for contributing to, and understanding, each other's viewpoint. Of the many meetings that take place at various levels of administration within the LEA and IHE, there are those where a permanent representation is desirable, and those where selective inputs need to be planned in advance. Referring back to our example of partnership in chapter 3, we identify the following forums for participation in an authority which has six administrative areas:

Permanent Representation

i) *Special Needs Advisory Team*
All the advisory staff concerned with special educational needs, including Inspectors, Advisers, and the Joint Appointment.

ii) *Wider Special Needs Advisory Team*
The Special Needs Advisory Team, the senior members of the Schools Psychological Service, and the staff representing the hearing impaired and visually impaired services.

iii) *Area Management Special Needs Teams*
The Area Education Officer, the Area INSET Co-ordinator, the Area Senior Educational Psychologist, the Area Adviser for Special Educational Needs, IHE Lecturer.

iv) *Special Needs INSET Team*
The Principal Lecturer, Senior Lecturer and Joint Appointment.

v) *Interviewing/selection for appointments to the IHE*
Principal, Vice-Principal, Heads of Departments, Principal Lecturers, Governing Body representative and LEA Inspector.

vi) *Course Steering Committee*
Head of Department, Special Needs INSET Team, Teacher representative, Educational Psychologist, LEA Inspector.

vii) *Examinations Board*
Vice Principal, Dean of Studies, Head of Department, Special Needs INSET Team, University representatives, external examiners, LEA Inspector.

Selective Inputs

i) *Full Inspectors meeting*
Chief Inspector, Senior Inspectors, General Inspectors, Specialist Inspectors, and Chief Educational Psychologist.

ii) *Area Inspector/Adviser meetings*
Area Education Officer, Area INSET Co-ordinator, Inspectors, and Advisory teachers.

iii) *Adviser/Officer meetings*
Assistant Education Officer for Special Educational Needs, Special Needs Section Leaders (finance, welfare, case work, etc.) and Chief Educational Psychologist.

iv) *Area INSET*
Area INSET Co-ordinator, Staff Development Co-ordinators, Area Inspectors, Area Advisory Teachers, and IHE personnel.

v) *IHE Education Department*
Head of Department, Lecturers, and Joint Appointment(s).

vi) *IHE INSET*
Vice-Principal, IHE INSET Co-ordinator, Lecturers, and Joint Appointment(s).

vii) *Special Educational Needs Resource Centre*
Special Needs INSET Team, Professional Assistant, Clerical Assistant, LEA Special Educational Needs Advisory Team, and MSC.

Even though we have only selected those forums that are most pertinent to a shared perspective within the field of special educational needs, it can be appreciated that this alone represents a considerable commitment of time and energy. There are, of course, other forums for special educational needs, as well as other aspects of education which have some bearing on decisions made for special educational needs provision. What this illustrates is the complexity of the two organizations and the importance of establishing priorities as far as relevant, efficient, and effective communication is concerned. Faced with the enormity of the task, and given a finite level of staffing, and assuming a reasonable allocation of working time to meetings in relation to other roles which have to be performed, this authority has found it more efficient to establish a Joint Appointment. If such an appointment does not exist, then the organization required for this kind of interaction is considerable, and indeed may not be achieved.

The second type of *shared working experience* comes about through participation in local or authority-wide initiatives/projects. An example of such an initiative is given below. It concerns the production of guidelines for the development of special educational needs provision in secondary schools. The focus of the initiative is the curriculum and the title of the document produced *Curriculum Modification In The Secondary School*. Since the document was intended to be a statement of policy on the part of the authority, it was essential that INSET providers from the IHE were involved at all stages of development and implementation. The Inspector for Special Educational Needs and the Joint Appointment planned a series of INSET activities for a three day period, which involved thirty senior staff from secondary schools. This took place in a residential setting. The activities were open-ended and endeavoured to explore the difficulties experienced by both pupils and teachers. At the end of the three-day period a document was produced which could act as guidelines for responding to special educational needs in the secondary school. The participants had set out a series of priorities; developed a taxonomy of difficulties relating to policy, pupils and teachers; suggested a series of steps for addressing identified problems;

developed a plan for changing the nature of special needs/remedial departments; and suggested alternative 3–5 year plans. The LEA undertook to continue this initiative by producing school-focused INSET packages to address each of the problems raised. The LEA and IHE personnel then collaborated in the writing of the final document, which was considered in turn by the Special Needs Advisory Team, the Wider Advisory Team, the Chief Education Officer, and eventually presented to the Education Committee through The Curriculum Group of Members for adoption as policy.

It will be appreciated from the above that shared experiences of this kind are dependent for their success upon the shared perspective achieved in the process of participating in selected meetings, as outlined in our first form of shared working experience. Indeed, in this example, it is difficult to see how continuity from inception to implementation could have been achieved if personnel from the IHE were not present at the various meetings at which the document was presented.

The next stage of the initiative involved the IHE in follow-up work, supporting participants engaged in school-focused projects which adapted and built on the guidelines, implementing suitable plans for further development. Those involved in the IHE activities were teachers nominated as special needs co-ordinators, who were recognized by the LEA as having sufficient status and credibility within their school to implement such a project. The activities were carried out either within the one-term Special Needs in the Ordinary School course, or the modular Diploma in Curriculum Studies (special educational needs). Without the initial involvement in planning and delivery, adequate support by IHE personnel would not have been possible, and the potential of the document would have remained unrealized.

The problems encountered in the pursuit of effective communication will be greater where more than one authority is attempting to relate to an IHE, or conversely, more than one IHE exists within the vicinity of the LEA. There are a number of ways in which this problem can be addressed. All depend, however, upon an initial realization, and therefore determination to achieve, the kind of partnership we have outlined.

a. A consortium of IHEs which agrees to rationalize INSET activities by the allocation of specialisms. This would lead, eventually, to one IHE within the consortium offering a wide range of activities concerned with special educational needs in consort with all the LEAs within the vicinity. In consequence, other IHEs would offer other curricular areas, e.g., multi-cultural education, health education. This approach would not only secure focused communication but would also allow for a greater concentration of effort on the part of the elected IHE to provide the width and depth of INSET required. However, it does raise the difficulty of ensuring appropriate initial training in special educational needs for all prospective teachers, the implication being that the special needs facility within one IHE would serve the IHEs in that consortium, possibly to the point of movement of staff or shared appointments.

b.   A consortium where each contributing IHE offers a specialist route, such as is required for teaching children with severe learning difficulties, sensory impairment, emotional/behavioural difficulties, etc., avoiding overlap with the other consortium members.

c.   A consortium policy, agreed with all the participating LEAs, to pair-off individual LEAs with IHEs. This would be unlikely to succeed, however, if the LEAs perceived an imbalance in resources, whether physical or human.

d.   The creation of joint appointments between individual IHEs and LEAs.

e.   The creation of corporate joint appointments between one LEA and a number of IHEs, or one IHE and a number of LEAs.

Whatever the approach, the fundamental aim is better communication, because, as we have outlined in this section, effective communication is critical to establishing the kind of partnership which enables both IHE and LEA to contribute to, and act upon, a clearly defined policy for the development of special educational needs provision within the authority.

We turn now to the approach we are specifically advocating — the joint appointment.

The Joint Appointment

Joint ventures and collaborative undertakings are always difficult to engineer in the initial stages, but experience would seem to indicate that once underway they usually prove extremely beneficial to all those involved. The nature of the collaborative undertaking we describe here is that which involves an Institute of Higher Education and a Local Education Authority. For a number of years this IHE, an independent College, has sought to work closely with its neighbouring LEAs and in particular has strengthened ties with, and consequently its understanding of the working practices of, one LEA with which it is most significantly involved.

The IHE has been in operation for more than two decades, and its role has changed markedly during that period. At the outset it was involved almost exclusively in teacher training, concentrating upon the training of potential primary teachers and upon a spread of subject areas likely to attract students with a range of skills. The College is linked strongly to the local University, which validates its courses, and while not having an education department, the University departments have many research interests closely related to education issues, and where colleagues can undertake cooperative ventures.

As courses were refined, and demands locally and nationally mirrored current trends, the College was able to readily adapt to innovations and respond creatively to these demands. A deal of diversification resulted, and the range of activities offered became no longer confined to teacher education but much more of a response to a wider set of needs. Departments were steadily increased and new building undertaken to promote special strengths.

An aspect of this diversification was the increase in INSET activity in many areas of the curriculum as the College was able to respond positively to the demands of the neighbouring LEAs. One important feature of this was the creation of a number of joint appointments between the College and one of the LEAs. Such areas included Language and Reading Development, Religious Education/Studies, Mathematics, Primary Science, Foreign Languages, Multi-Cultural Education, Pre-Vocational Education, Business Education, and Special Educational Needs. The joint appointments were used to cement relationships between the role partners and gave the post-holders opportunities to follow through initiatives and to be involved in INSET activities in two different forums — the LEA and the IHE. A further aspect of the role was to set up jointly-funded Resource Centres within the IHE which could be used by teachers, students, academics, researchers, parents, and the public at large. In many cases these Resource Centres would be guided by the joint appointment who ensured that they were kept up to date and that they reflected the work of the LEA and the IHE. People would be appointed to such posts from various backgrounds, but always, recent and relevant school experience was taken into account. They would be appointed by representatives of the IHE, the LEA and the University to the IHE, but seconded for 49 per cent of their time to the LEA.

Inevitably roles vary considerably between the various joint appointments, where some are involved only in INSET activities, which are College-based, and others act as Tutor/Advisers to all the schools within the LEA. Others are also involved in initial teacher training, and contribute to the various diversified courses in the BA and BSc programmes, and their teacher advisory role is therefore perhaps limited to the specific group of schools with which they relate.

The joint appointment described here is one which encompasses both the role of Adviser to the LEA and the role of INSET provider contributing to a wide range of courses. There are inevitably many practical difficulties in working in two separate, if closely linked, jobs and it was agreed by those concerned at the outset that the appointee's week would be divided clearly between the two areas of work, that of the IHE, and that of the LEA. Consequently, Mondays, Tuesdays, and Wednesday mornings are given over to the IHE, and Wednesday afternoons, Thursdays and Fridays are available to the LEA.

At the IHE, the joint appointment has been involved mainly in INSET activities: a modular Diploma in Curriculum Studies (Special Educational Needs), and 1/86 Certificate courses in Special Educational Needs in the Ordinary School. There are also contributions to the Year III BA/BSc, Year IV BEd courses which are an option in the students' final year, and occasional contributions are made to the PGCE courses and other courses which the College undertakes, such as Pre-Vocational, Care courses, etc.

There are closer links established between the LEA and IHE as a consequence of the joining of the two separate functions, and there are definite advantages to the dual role. Within the modular Diploma course, one integral feature is the school-focused project and much of the work within this can be supported directly through the dual role, replicated, adopted or adapted by other students from other schools, or be built upon by future INSET students. Perceived INSET needs within the LEA can be related to the course and specific schools can be identified where a particular set of skills, appropriate techniques, or series of support measures can be geared using the course as a vehicle to achieve this.

The joint appointee is part of the LEA team of Inspectors/Advisers who have general responsibilities and specific briefs either on an Area basis or across the LEA. This team is headed by a General Inspector, and also comprises a Specialist Inspector, an Area Adviser, and the joint appointment. Each has responsibility for one of the six Areas of the LEA. The General Inspector and Specialist Inspector each has oversight of two Areas, the Area Adviser and the joint appointment each having the oversight of one Area. This oversight involves relating to a large number of types of educational provision which includes selective secondary schools, non-selective secondary schools, Infant Schools, Junior Schools, Primary Schools, Day Special Schools, Residential Special Schools, Special Units, Pre-School Centres, and Colleges of Further Education.

As an Area Adviser, the joint appointment could be asked for advice on a very wide range of issues from both the County Education Officer and the Area Officer, as well as the General Inspector. They would also represent the General Inspector for Special Educational Needs and the County Education Officer within an Area of the LEA. They would be responsible for the overall development of services for Special Needs in all schools, and for monitoring and guiding developments of whole school policies in order to meet the requirements of the Education Act 1981.

The role has other facets:

a management role as part of the Advisory Team of four

a management role as part of a Wider Advisory Team together with the Chief Educational Psychologist, six Senior Psychologists, the Head of the Hearing Impaired Service, and the Advisory Teacher for the Visually Impaired

a management role as part of an Area based organization

the dissemination of information relating to developments within the County

to visit schools, advise, and assess response to special educational needs

to encourage developments, advise on funding, etc.

respond to schools' enquiries and assess needs in relation to Area and County developments

advise individual schools, teachers

liaise with INSET co-ordinators and assist with INSET activities

identify INSET needs and with others plan to meet those needs

attend case conferences and meetings regarding individual pupils when appropriate

advise on placement

encourage and enable efficient teaching methods and organization in all schools in relation to special educational needs

to keep informed regarding current practice, events, and literature pertaining to special educational needs

be available to parents to discuss, advise, and comment upon their queries and requests

assist in the co-ordination of multi-disciplinary services when necessary, especially in relation to pupils in special schools

to have a watching brief concerning residential special schools

to have a watching brief concerning the use of micro-technology with pupils with special educational needs

to liaise with all services pertaining to children with special educational needs

to have a special interest in INSET activities and their development

There have been a number of initiatives which have been to the fore in the LEA which have required particular support. These have been linked to the review body looking at special education for whom various papers have been written, and where they have been linked to specific INSET activities. These include support to primary schools, curriculum modification in the secondary school, designated schools for integrating the physically disabled, support services, special needs departments in mainstream schools, pre-school provision, etc.

Particular INSET links via the College, other than with the SENIOS courses and the modular Diploma, have been through TRIST funding, which has provided short courses in Information Technology and Special Educational Needs, a course for those involved in residential provision looking at aspects of caring for young people, in-school developments in secondary schools, and INSET activities and staff developments in the FE Colleges. It also provided a Management Issues in Special Educational Needs course for senior staff in special schools.

The Information Technology course, in particular, demonstrated a very great need. Many schools were at an early stage in developing the use of micro-computers and were unaware of contact points, sources of help, funding, and basic equipment. This course will now run a number of times in a modified form and link in with developments taking place in nearby Institutions, mainstream schools, special schools and units.

The College has also developed a programme of research in special educational needs alongside the LEA through the system of teacher fellowships. This has already provided an opportunity for monitoring and evaluating some of the initiatives referred to above.

A further development has been to enlist the help of local Headteachers and teachers with specific knowledge or skills to be involved with Initial Teacher Training students. Fortuitously, this has more recently developed into a full-time secondment where a local Special School Head has been seconded full-time to the College, for a term, contributing to a variety of INSET activities geared to special educational needs. This has many advantages — relating existing practice to elements of the activities undertaken by the IHE and the LEA.

The recent incorporation of an LEA one-term course for 'remedial' teachers within the modular Diploma structure, has also meant LEA involvement at a high level. The Advisory team contribute to the Diploma and SENIOS courses. In addition, the College special educational needs team and educational psychologists combine to devise appropriate INSET activities. Thus students are provided with the opportunity to be engaged in a wide spectrum of experience and involvement with schools and special educational needs provision. This also applies to an array of personnel from other support agencies involved with special educational needs who can relate their own practice to students interests and requirements.

This contributes considerably to closer ties between Initial Teacher Training, the Induction of new teachers in schools and INSET activity. The joint appointment allows a wider LEA perspective to be introduced into the IHE, and teacher needs, relating to special educational needs, can be viewed through an LEA perspective, supporting teachers from IHE into schools, through the Induction process and through INSET activities. Continuity of support is ensured. In particular, by knowing what is happening in schools regarding special educational needs, and knowing the problems which are currently affecting professionals, it allows the lecturer/adviser to bring an element of reality to students. It also promotes the identification of perceived INSET needs and Induction needs.

Where students can brain storm, be creative and set up models, it provides opportunities for schools to use these models, actually applying them to real situations within the school, unit, or classroom. This cooperative link between schools and the IHE has mutual benefits and focuses upon adopting and adapting models in a practical and useful way. In addition, the use of child case studies, which are current and real, help students to appreciate the dilemmas currently facing colleagues in school, and how the various role partners involved in a particular case may combine to provide appropriately for a child's educational needs. By inviting a 'problems and solutions' approach to present strategies to identify and assess needs and to provide for those needs appropriately, students can gain a deeper understanding of the limitations of particular packages and the need for 'holistic' approaches.

Case studies containing real issues which the LEA Advisers are currently facing, help students to devise responses which will meet real requirements. Working to budgets and to time limitations also heightens awareness and gives students the chance to experience deadlines. Strategies such as timed decision-making can then be used within a wider context of a series of problem-solving exercises, but where the problems to be examined are real and where the solutions may actually be put into practice. If the problems have appropriate solutions, and provide real outcomes, they can also become a blue-print for future action in a variety of settings.

If tasks expose students to situations with a real-life orientation, it encourages them to be involved in corporate decision-making, negotiation, and consensus, such that they will be better prepared for similar involvement within their own school. They can also become consultants to schools, in that they can be presented with planning problems, where time for reflection is limited but where creative activity is vital. Because the student group is varied in experience, and of different status, the need for collaboration and cooperation soon becomes significant and the process of DOING, REVIEWING, and APPLYING can begin.

Curriculum issues from a specific school, which may require a group design or a series of individual contributions, can be trialled, so that suggestions can be offered and possible ways forward identified. This can be exemplified in a cross-curricular way whereby students design a music input, or take part in constructing a play to reflect a school's reading or language work, or design packages to meet specific requirements laid down by the school and where teachers from the school guide the group.

Awareness of developing whole-school approaches, and how students may have a role to play within that, can also be assisted by the joint role. Students can discuss with teachers involved in curriculum modification and adaptation the difficulties with which they are presented, and how problems are tackled in schools and decisions taken. Often, students need to understand the workings of a special needs department within a school, the role of the special needs co-ordinator, the establishment of a special needs steering group and how subject departments can be adequately represented and a whole school approach undertaken.

Further, the joint appointment can outline the LEA's current strategies, such as support to schools, and prepare students for involvement in such initiatives. With Initial Teacher Training students, exposing them to such initiatives can be linked to placement in schools for periods of observation and involvement, so that practitioners can demonstrate how current strategies are employed to meet special educational needs. Similarly, the shadowing of a teacher, to gain some understanding of that teacher's role in participating with youngsters with special educational needs, can also bring considerable insight to a participant and via the joint appointment, suitable mentors can be identified who can exemplify good practice.

A particularly interesting possibility is that of the 'teaching hospital'. Close involvement with the LEA and schools allows some residential school settings to act as a teaching environment, where practice and theory can be linked. Constructing this type of teaching hospital environment, linked to a residential special school means that adequate support and guidance are available. This is an idea which began some years ago in Community Homes with Education premises, whereby induction of staff into work involving seriously disturbed youngsters could be organized to experience the combination of the living and learning environments. This affords students the opportunity to spend a few days in residence, where they can be involved beyond the school day, and where they can be carefully guided, with approaches thoroughly discussed prior to and following a particular input.

Whilst listing many of the advantages, a cautionary note should also be included. The joint appointment must always be wary of presenting only one model of support, organizational structure or specific technique, as exemplified by the LEA in which that person works. This may be avoided if the IHE is involved with other LEAs.

Inevitably the joint appointment means that total involvement in College life or LEA structure is not possible, and one has therefore to rely heavily upon colleagues in order to keep up-to-date and informed. The structure of the working week, split as it is between two significantly different, albeit closely linked roles, implies that meetings relating to one role may well occur during time set aside for the other, and the ability to be present at all crucial meetings is impossible. This reliance on colleagues may well present considerable difficulties for those involved.

To conclude, as the nature of INSET activity changes, the need to understand organizational structures becomes more important, and the ability to involve others in individualized approaches to learning takes on significance, so the need for close collaboration between LEA and IHE will increase. The pattern of INSET delivery, and a teacher's involvement with it throughout their career, will need the combined support of both IHE and LEA, and the joint appointment may have a great deal to offer this development.

Chapter 7

In-Service Activities and the Resourced School

Introduction

In recent times, the move towards devolving responsibility from the specialist teacher to the classroom teacher has required individual schools to develop a broader-based strategy for meeting special educational needs. In this chapter we examine the practical requirements of planning and implementing a whole-school policy, the consequences for school-focused INSET, and the development of the *resourced school* as the logical successor to the interim phase of *support*.

The Movement towards Whole-School Policies

In seeking to develop a whole-school policy, the school is recognizing that an approach is required which promotes a corporate sense of responsibility towards the development of necessary attitudes, patterns of organization, and curriculum modification. These are fundamental aspects of change which require a high degree of consensus, and we would contend that the formulation of such a policy for meeting special educational needs will, by necessity, be one which is contributed to by all, agreed by all and implemented by all. A whole-school policy which develops and sustains special educational needs as part of its *raison d'être*, will incorporate special educational needs into the total philosophy of the school. Colin McCall (1987) writes:

> The 'whole school approach' is a term used to convey the idea of a united school . . . whereby every effort is made to secure the best for all children as individuals.
>
> The approach means that every effort is made to promote a school 'climate' which recognises the right of pupils with special educational needs — those already in the school and those who might be on roll for part of their learning programme — not to stand out as different from the rest of their peers.

The whole school approach means that:

a. Low-value terms for describing some pupils are not used by the teaching staff, and their use by others is actively discouraged.

b. The school has accepted to review its existing arrangements, seek improvements and implement identified changes with all possible speed.

c. There is acceptance of the point of view that the task is one of shared responsibilities to meet the needs of all pupils. The special needs that some children display are addressed primarily as a TEACHING PROBLEM which the school is in a position to significantly address.

d. The whole school commits itself to a written policy statement on how it intends to implement the approach.

These four critical points: the abolition of low-value labels, the determination to review all aspects of school life which may impinge on appropriate provision, the recognition of the problem as a *teaching* problem, and the commitment to write clear policy statements, dominate the newly evolving concept of special educational need, even at LEA level. There are, however, five further points we should wish to make regarding the development of policy. In part they represent the logical assumptions on which the foregoing are based, and in part they provide the direction for practical interpretation. In some ways they are relatively simple assertions but their impact on a school, if accepted, will be considerable.

The first is that all pupils are *entitled* to experience all elements of the curriculum. This point has been highlighted in recent times by HMI and DES documents dealing with a variety of curriculum areas. In particular it has been recognized that pupils in special schools follow a narrow range of curriculum subjects, with vital areas of experience, such as can be provided by the sciences, humanities and craft, design and technology, conspicuously missing. These omissions have been made all the more poignant by the introduction in recent times of increased opportunities for problem-solving approaches in these subjects and the acceptance that such strategies are crucial to many children exhibiting learning and behavioural difficulties.

The case for *entitlement* applies equally to the ordinary school, indeed our second point emanates from this assumption. This is, that the traditional model of segregating the so-called low ability pupil, either within the primary setting or, as is not uncommon, the first two years of the secondary school (in order to concentrate on basics) impoverishes curricular experiences by depriving the pupil of depth and breadth.

Sufficient depth within a subject or area of experience is not so much a matter of pupil ability, or inability, as the ability or inability of the teacher to understand the skills, facts, concepts and attitudes necessary to be acquired, and the best way of acquiring them. The *specialist* remedial/special needs teacher may understand a great deal about how children learn, but this is arguably useless knowledge if that which is to be learned is not sufficiently understood by the teacher. Our third point, therefore, is that wherever possible, and particularly in the secondary school, the subject should be taught by those teachers trained in the disciplines of that subject. Clearly this raises many issues regarding the appropriate deployment of teachers who have traditionally extracted children from lessons, or worse, have taken remedial/streamed sink groups; particularly where such people have been found to be effective in forming relationships with difficult pupils, and indeed, in their own way have provided a degree of stability within the school for both pupils and teachers. But, this potential problem can only be addressed if, as part of the whole-school policy, there is a policy for school-focused INSET.

Our fourth point draws on the previous three. It is that pupils should not be judged to be incapable of learning concepts, skills, attitudes and facts, related to such areas as science, humanities, modern languages, etc., solely on the basis of literacy skills and general levels of intelligence. That *access* to vital areas of experience is barred to some children on the basis of the teacher's inability to adapt his/her materials to the conceptual level of the pupil, or because appropriate alternative strategies cannot be found to reading and writing as methods of learning and recording, was illustrated in the case study in chapter 1.

Finally, our fifth point is that in order to gain *access* to all elements of the curriculum, fundamental changes are required in such practical areas as classroom organization, material presentation and pupil assessment. If the school policy does not address itself to these kinds of practicalities, no amount of appropriate attitude or climate is going to produce a learning environment in which individual differences in pace and style are respected.

As the Fish Report concluded, the higher the percentage of special educational needs identified, the more it becomes an issue of what the school is offering ALL children. The relative nature of special educational needs, as outlined in chapter 1, would seem to demand a whole-school approach which addresses the current failing of the school. For many this will be a painful process.

The Implications for School Management

A whole-school policy which incorporates special educational needs into the total educational philosophy of the school will require a change in teacher attitudes which can only be achieved through the energy and commitment of the Senior Management Team. At both primary and secondary phases it will be necessary for the Senior Management Team to appoint in the interim phase a senior member of staff to act as the Special Needs Co-ordinator, someone who has responsibility for the implementation, monitoring and evaluation of the school policy. It may also be necessary for the Senior

Management Team to ensure that every department within the school increases its awareness and expertise, through greater liaison with those teachers involved in supporting pupils with special educational needs. Such coordination should lead to:

(i) a positive commitment by the school to a programme of INSET for meeting special educational needs, i.e. perhaps of the sort described in this chapter;

(ii) an evaluation of the present position which leads to a positive commitment to the development of relationships between the pupil, teacher, parent and outside agencies, and to some form of appraisal of direct benefit to the classroom teacher;

(iii) increased communication at all levels;

(iv) the creation of pupil assessments which are:
(a) pupil-specific
(b) criteria-related and
(c) developmental and formative;

(v) pupil records which provide for access and dissemination of information pertinent to pupil difficulties, and ensure accurate recording and updating, involving both parents and pupils.

More specifically, there will be a need to examine the special educational needs particular to the school: the problems that any re-organization will raise, and the practical consequences of change either for the class teacher or members of the special educational needs department or other support agents such as the 'discretionary allocation' for remedial teaching in the primary school. Discussion of a whole-school policy, therefore, is likely to lead to a plan of development which may extend over several years. As a first step, the Senior Management Team may need to review and evaluate the present position, and the following is offered as an *aide mémoire* to identifying the school's special educational needs.

The Senior Management Team may find it helpful to divide the difficulties experienced in their school into the three areas of policy-based difficulties, teacher-based difficulties, and pupil-based difficulties. We offer the following as pertinent questions for review. Which of these statements applies to your school?

Policy Based

There is no policy for special educational needs.

The predominant mode of instruction is class based with few individual or group approaches.

The school is creating a negative learning environment for some pupils by not addressing itself to the issues of classroom management, inappropriate teaching styles, pace, and the needs of groups and individuals.

Traditional remedial programmes, where they do exist, are ill-defined and unstructured.

There is an overall lack of variety in teaching method.

The curriculum is dominated by staff strengths rather than the creation of essential experiences for pupils.

The school does not provide a welcoming and sympathetic environment for pupils, parents, teachers and visitors.

The interaction between school, parents, and other agencies is less than positive.

The timetable is not sufficiently flexible to accommodate the changes necessary to enact a new policy of provision for pupils with special educational needs.

The present approach to pupils with special educational needs is fragmented, with each department, including the special needs department, working in isolation.

The disciplinary framework is inconsistent.

There is little or no modification of existing curricular materials.

The present courses leading to public examinations are inappropriate for pupils with special educational needs and there is no alternative curriculum available for the 14–18 range.

There is no system of profiling which can record their achievements outside the examination system.

There is no register of pupils with special educational needs, defining their requirements and safeguarding provision.

The school does not provide its teachers with a clear statement of aims and objectives for pupils with special educational needs.

Teacher Based

Teachers are failing to appreciate the relationship which exists between learning difficulties and behavioural problems.

The school is experiencing behavioural difficulties which primarily stem from a lack of achievement. The lack of achievement is linked to the low expectations of teachers.

The school is not honestly addressing itself to the problems of isolation experienced by teachers in the department of special educational needs.

The special needs department does not have equal standing with other major departments and may therefore lack the necessary influence and credibility for a change in role.

Teachers are not receiving sufficient support and training enabling them to deal with the variety of problems encountered.

There are inadequate resources within the school to support teachers in their efforts to provide appropriately for pupils with special educational needs.

Pupil Based

The school does not recognize that pupils with learning difficulties do not communicate with teachers or others about those aspects of their learning in which they know they are failing, likewise, the school does not recognize that parents may not be able to satisfactorily communicate their concerns.

The language of the classroom, both spoken and written, is inappropriate in level and content.

The school is alienating pupils with special educational needs by maintaining a system of segregated provision.

Work within the classroom is not adapted either in content or approach. It does not achieve the learning goals set by the teacher.

There is no system of support for pupils experiencing periods of intense difficulty, whether physical, emotional, educational or social.

The pupil with special educational needs has no way of evaluating his own achievements.

You may wish to add items pertinent to your school which are not mentioned in the above.

This type of review is essential both for the construction of short, medium and long term goals, and for the appropriate development of INSET activities. The questions have clear implications for the acquisition of skills, competencies, and attitudes at several levels. Most schools will want to begin by offering a series of sessions aimed at raising awareness. If a whole-school policy is to develop, it will be necessary to arrange In-Service activities which meet the needs of various groups of teachers according to their level of involvement. The Coordinator and Senior Management Team will need a broader and deeper appreciation of the issues commensurate with their function of allocating and balancing resources, and their supportive role. The special needs personnel may require In-Service activities which focus on role change. All members of staff will need In-Service activities which take them beyond attitudinal and organizational change to actual skills associated with changes in teaching style, classroom management, recording techniques, and any other activity which reflects the change from separate curriculum provision to a modified and integrated curriculum which meets the needs of all pupils.

School-focused In-Service Activities

From the above, it will be appreciated that we regard the *resourced school* as not only requiring appropriate levels of personnel and materials, but also appropriately *educated* personnel who can articulate the agreed whole-school policy, and influence school-focused activities. In our opinions, if such personnel are to be successful it will be necessary for them to concentrate on the development of activities which foster interpersonal skills. As with the development of the relationship between the IHE and the LEA, we consider this most likely to be achieved if such activities are formulated to provide common working experiences. Such experiences ought, eventually, to lead to a shared perspective on what constitutes an individual need, and how this is to be met.

To this end, the critical arrangements which we argue characterize the *resourced school* will form the subject of these activities. The development of such working relationships can not be brought about within a vacuum, but must be linked to activities of common interest, and where individual's skills can be expanded, enhanced or more finely tuned. They may relate to specific roles that participants will play or to a particular context within the school, and they may be geared to a developmental process which can provide personal satisfaction, as well as institutional change.

As the stages of a whole school policy materialize, are refined and delineated, they must be accompanied by INSET activities which aid the achievement of those stages. A whole-school policy, by its nature, needs planning over a period of time. The traditional approaches to INSET activities, which are not school related, are unsuited to this development. Clearly, if INSET activities are not allowed to develop in an *ad hoc* fashion by teachers attending one-off courses, priorities for the development of critical arrangements need early consideration. However, following the principle of establishing a shared perspective, the initial activities will be geared to group/team building, and at this stage the content of the activity is subsidiary to the process involved. To be consistent with the principle of a shared perspective, it is necessary that the group itself generate a taxonomy of need, from which a sequence of responses can be elicited to form the stages of the whole-school policy.

To this end, it is important for IHE providers to recognize the nature of the process. In locating, recruiting, and selecting an appropriate designated teacher, particular skills in the sphere of inter-personnel relationships must be considered alongside potential as a catalyst to further INSET activity. The selection of the school-focused project is of equal importance, in that it will assist in identifying the needs of the school, enhance the opportunities for working together, and provide the necessary impetus to raise staff consciousness to the need for change. Consequently, the personnel of the IHE need to recognize that the institution is not simply dealing with another student on another course, but that it is taking on the support and development of a whole school, and all that entails in establishing a relationship with the senior management and teaching force of that school. This, if seriously undertaken by the IHE, represents a radical departure from present practice, and will require additional human resources. At present, this is not necessarily taken into account by those responsible for devising formulae for full time student equivalents, or indeed by the LEA in the way it funds INSET activities based upon full time equivalent secondments, although in recent times there is evidence that both IHEs and LEAs are adopting a more flexible approach.

In this respect, there is a particular case to be made for IHE Departments dealing with special educational needs INSET activities, since their involvement is, by necessity, whole-school oriented. If this is to be realized to greater effect, it is essential that the IHE and LEA share in the production and communication of a comprehensive profile of INSET for individual schools. Although this presents obvious difficulties of a political nature, of the sort normally associated with record-keeping, it could provide information on other activities within the school integral to establishing continuity and coherence, thus avoiding competing demands, duplication of endeavour, and conflicting priorities.

Returning to the designated teacher, all of this would signify that as far as the institution-based element of INSET activities is concerned, change is not the immediate goal. More important at this stage is the support which the designated teacher requires from the tutor and other course members in establishing his/her role as a change agent. This has fundamental implications for the further development of relations between IHE and LEA, since the bulk of the school-based work, which is a logical extension of the school-focused activity, will be the responsibility of the LEA. Therefore, the early stages of forward planning must be, in every sense, cooperative. It must assist in denoting the priorities for the design of a series of school-based INSET activities which will follow the initial 'planned shared experience', which is the subject of the designated teacher's school-focused project.

At this point, we think a note of caution is required, particularly regarding those LEAs that are moving quickly towards school-based INSET activities which are unsupported by the kind of IHE activities described. The 'power' which an LEA now has, under the GRIST initiative, to organize and develop its INSET activities according to its own perceptions of need, could well tempt the LEA to place far more emphasis on the school-based element than it is capable of supporting. An LEA which chooses to devolve the majority of its INSET resources to individual schools must address the following difficulties:

1   The structure of the school day, irrespective of directed or non-directed time, is such that depth, continuity, and coherence requires the undivided attention of at least one person. This person requires appropriate knowledge and a range of experiences, and these can only be provided

by a period of intensive exploration away from the day-to-day mêlée of the school.

2   No school can be expected to develop sophisticated structures for dealing with special educational needs if it only has recourse to its own pool of experience and expertise. Whilst the concept of consultation as a role for the IHE lecturer and LEA adviser is to be encouraged, it is not possible to resource a large number of schools across all the phases of education in this way.

3   Although we support the principle of staff development through shared activities within the school, based on cooperative exploration, the best of leaders, i.e., co-ordinators, are not able to harness and articulate such activities to advantage if they themselves are not first exposed to opportunities which enable them to assimilate knowledge and accumulate experiences which provide them with a firm basis on which to make informed decisions.

4   Similarly, if the total experience of the staff group is limited in time, diversity and range, as would be the case for example in a school where there was little staff movement (with perhaps a large percentage of staff having served for 15 years or more in the same school), a substantial input is required to give at least one member of staff the necessary breadth and depth of vision.

5   Without such inputs, it would indeed be possible for the staff of a school to conclude that further development, or possible change of approach and/or direction, was not necessary. It is an essential element of the IHE input that the designated teacher is exposed to the skills of instituting a critical review of the school, and that he/she is supported and guided in using such an instrument within the school.

6   The IHE input also enables the chosen teacher to review accounts of similar developments, thus obviating the need to re-invent the wheel. As with all developments, a judgement has to be made as to the comparative benefits of a staff resolving its own problems, against the time taken to achieve this. Clearly, we support the notion of process, since developments arrived at in this fashion are likely to be *owned* and therefore acted upon. However, without appropriate input, the time taken to secure a special educational needs response may be such that the immediate and medium term needs of the school are unnecessarily deferred.

7   In the absence of models which can both clarify and improve understanding, further development is likely to be severely restricted. It is a central feature of Higher Education that theoretical models are constructed and practical models collated.

8   Finally, care needs to be taken not to see INSET activities solely in terms of training. There has been a tendency, with the introduction of school-based activities, to drop the word 'Education' from the phrase 'In-Service Education and Training'. The development of the resourced school requires educated personnel, with the word 'educated' used in the widest

possible sense. In addition, there may well be a tendency for schools, because of the pressures placed upon them, to avoid the philosophical analysis which such an exercise requires, and which can be successfully furnished through the involvement of members of staff with the IHE.

It is not, therefore, a simple matter of compromise between the two extremes of IHE-based and school-based resourcing. A positive structure is required which integrates the various modes of INSET activities, and which by so doing diminishes the difficulties raised in 1–8 above.

We would suggest that a structure is required which clearly relates the IHE resource to school-focused, school-based, and cluster-based activities. Each of these critical modes of INSET activity requires careful examination, since the relationship established between them will necessitate detailed monitoring, if, indeed, as we suggest, resources are to be appropriately balanced across them.

This further underlines the dynamic nature of the relationship which exists between the modes, whereby one mode may expand and take on greater significance as another mode recedes. Typically, we would expect that the LEA and the IHE would initially come together to resource the school-focused element, which we conceive as mainly IHE-based.

The resourcing at this level is intensive, often requiring a full-time one-term secondment, which prepares the designated teacher for the role of change agent and sets the scene for the shared activity which is to take place within the school. In the second phase, the school-based activity evolves, relating critical arrangements of the whole-school approach to knowledge and experiences gained in the school-focused, IHE-located, phase.

The nature of the relationship between these two phases is such that continued support will be required from the IHE, but that the transfer of support to the LEA, through its cluster group arrangements or Teacher Centre/ Staff Development initiatives, will lead to greater advisory involvement. Once the initiative is underway, the responsibility for supporting the initiative gradually devolves towards the LEA, with the logical conclusion that in the final phase the school is responsible for developing the initiative through its curriculum policy. However, involvement of the IHE may continue through the further development of the teacher by attendance at INSET activities which lead to higher qualifications. This should result in stronger links with school-based activity and provide professional development of a personal kind, within the overall development of the school.

As IHE involvement diminishes within a particular establishment, further medium-term support can be offered through cluster-based work. The local INSET centre will at this stage require resources to organize and facilitate INSET within the cluster. We have suggested cluster-based INSET activities as a separate mode, because it seems to us that there are important advantages for both the designated teacher and the individual school, as well as clear advantages for the LEA in the development and dissemination of policy.

Providing clusters involve all forms and phases of education, a great deal can be achieved, in terms of integration of personnel and integration of the curriculum, by the introduction into a cluster of a school-based project. Such a project would have initially been the concern of the IHE and LEA as school-focused activity. For the school and the teacher, the cluster offers the opportunity of a wider exchange of experiences which may help the school to test the validity of its initiatives in a wider forum.

The professional development of teachers within the cluster will be further enhanced by such an input. In resource terms, the LEA takes prime responsibility, through its local INSET organization, to offer a structure of shared facilities, mutual support and facilitates the link with other important initiatives and/or curriculum areas. However, although much decreased, the IHE involvement at this distant level can still be evidenced, since other schools within the cluster may also benefit from a school-focused input which they will wish to share with the cluster. There is a sense, therefore, in which it can be said that the cluster-based activity, centred on the local INSET organization, is the constant factor to which the more fluid relationship between school-focused and school-based INSET relates.

From IHE to Cluster: Case Examples

Example 1

A newly appointed secondary school Headteacher contacts the LEA's adviser for special educational needs to urgently gain support in changing the school's approach to meeting children's needs. The Headteacher has recognized that a number of his staff, whilst eager to adopt a new approach, lack the requisite skills and 'education' to fulfil this requirement. From the staff group he has elicited a commitment to change and a desire to establish a broader-based response.

The adviser discusses proposals for a whole-school response whereby all children would be entitled to access to the whole curriculum. An integral feature would be a post of Co-ordinator who would be part of the Senior Management Team. A senior teacher with considerable experience and credibility within the staff group is suggested by the Headteacher as an appropriate candidate. The adviser describes an IHE INSET pattern which will enhance skills, allow time and space for research, and most importantly, involve the school in a review of critical arrangements. Further discussions take place involving the designated teacher, Headteacher, adviser and senior lecturer from the IHE. As the designated teacher embarks on the INSET package, the school-focused project is more clearly defined. With the particular support of the IHE, the project develops, and after one term's work is delivered to the school as the first stage in the production of a whole-school policy.

The project chosen is one which will highlight prevailing attitudes to pupils with special educational needs, and establish a range of teaching styles appropriate to such pupils. As a result of this project, a discussion document is produced for the whole school with a view to staff agreement as to successful implementation. Additionally, the LEA is able to offer facilities and release time for the school to build on these initial developments.

With heightened awareness and the experience of working in collaboration with colleagues from all phases of education during the one-term IHE-centred activity, the designated teacher sets out to foster closer links with neighbouring primary, secondary and special schools. This cluster responds positively to his/her request for a meeting. They explore the areas of common concern and identify their INSET needs. The designated teacher takes the opportunity to present the needs of the cluster to a follow-up school-focused project meeting attended by the LEA adviser, the Headteacher and senior lecturer from the IHE.

Fortuitously, within this cluster there are two other designated teachers who are involved with IHE one-term activities, and they are also able to positively influence colleagues and provide support both to the general group within the cluster and to each other. As well as drawing on their own experience as educated personnel, they are now able to call on others that they have identified during their IHE experience and offer appropriate pathways of INSET activity to the local LEA INSET Coordinator, thus establishing the link between the main LEA resource and the LEA/IHE endeavour.

Example 2

Two teachers — one in a secondary school and one in a school for children with severe learning difficulties — are both attending a one-term INSET activity. This INSET activity is one element in a series of activities culminating in the award of an Advanced Diploma. The teacher in the secondary school is concerned in his school-focused project with the integration and support of pupils previously placed in remedial classes. As with the first example, the new Headteacher has called in the LEA adviser to discuss proposals for re-organizing classroom groups. The LEA adviser had proposed a steering group comprising members from each of the major subject departments. The teacher is a member of this group, and it is suggested that they experience a series of activities which will enhance their skills and knowledge and better prepare them to co-ordinate the group.

In the meantime, the teacher in the school for children with severe learning difficulties is charged with designing a more appropriate curriculum for pupils 14–19. He draws on national and international perspectives and develops a network of contacts to better provide for this group. This network includes local secondary schools, one of which happens to be the school which is forming the steering group and whose teacher is also embarking upon the IHE one-term INSET activity. As a result of this shared working experience, a closer professional link is fostered, and as a consequence, a plan emerges to locate the group of 14–19 year olds from the school for children with severe learning difficulties at the secondary school. The IHE involvement can now be devolved to the LEA, via the adviser who has specific responsibility for pupils with severe learning difficulty. This presents little problem, since the development is consistent with LEA policy on integration.

The relationship between the two school-focused projects encourages follow up school-based activity, not only in each of these schools, but also between them. The school-based INSET activity organized by the steering group will have the advantage of the change in perspective which comes about by the introduction of pupils with severe learning difficulties into the school, and the assimilation of the pupils with severe learning difficulty is likely to be aided by the work of the steering group in examining alternative groupings and support for pupils with special educational needs. The commonality between the two settings leads to a better understanding as to how the teachers in the two groups work; this in turn leads locational integration towards functional integration, the resourced school and educated personnel.

Example 3

A senior member of staff in a primary school chooses to examine an awareness-raising strategy concerning special educational needs within a cluster of eight local primary schools. This has two strands. One strand looks at existing attitudes and perceptions relating to a proposed support structure for staff and pupils. The second sets out to develop a series of INSET activities to heighten perceptions and exemplify skills. The designated teacher, having completed a questionnaire and structured interviews, analyses various teachers' responses in order to inform the participants of their present level of understanding and involvement. As a result, a programme of meetings is negotiated whereby involved personnel, from various facets of support agencies, explain their roles and inform the cluster members as to how they will be involved with staff and pupils.

This has advantages for the cluster, as there are now established points of contact and reference who can be enlisted in a consultative and supportive context. The result suggests that there is a corporate responsibility which is not confined to individual teachers, individual schools, or individual agencies. Instead, through the integration of these personnel, and an informed group that recognizes the advantages and necessity of shared working experiences, the level of teacher competence and confidence is raised and closer liaison fostered. As a further development, this wider group, which includes the various supportive agencies and therapists, can identify new areas of INSET activity which will enhance their joint contributions. It also identifies new school-focused interests which act as a catalyst for better provision.

Example 4

A school attempts to map out a rolling development, such that a number of staff will take specific foci and together interlink them to form medium- and long-term proposals for INSET activity. The school is a residential facility offering specialized help to pupils with specific learning difficulties. A designated teacher examines aspects of mathematics teaching as a starting point to reviewing the curriculum. This brings about a series of staff discussions which explore teaching strategies, classroom practice, material resources, recording, etc. In turn, these discussions identify other aspects of the curriculum which require investigation.

A particular emphasis is placed on the relationship between the learning and living environments, and this raises the need for a second designated teacher to devise an INSET package which will provide an interdisciplinary approach to integrating these two aspects of the child's experience.

A third member of staff is able to extend the initiative and looks at how the institution can avoid possible isolation through closer involvement with the local community. This includes identifying interested and interesting groups of individuals, other professionals and support agencies, services, employers and other educational settings.

The rolling programme of development produces school-based INSET activity, shared working experiences with a wide group of contributors, and involvement of all staff. It also identifies new areas of interest, and by necessity, school-focused projects.

The three school-focused projects, associated with this one institution, have resulted in very close contact between the school and the IHE, providing a forum for the IHE to act as a resource for the school, and enabling a heightened interaction between LEA and IHE. They have also promoted a high level of school-based activity with the potential for further, independent, INSET activity.

Example 5

A designated teacher from each of two schools — a secondary school, and a nearby all-age special school for children with moderate learning difficulties — examines the feasibility of aligning the curricula of their respective schools to provide a common programme accessible to both groups. Their projects also endeavour to encourage a common perspective between the two groups of staff. The first teacher, from the secondary school, is able to investigate an alternative curriculum for the 14+ age group. The second teacher is to explore areas of the special school curriculum accessible to pupils in the secondary school. Together the teachers will identify the common areas and heighten interaction between the schools and their curricula. Various aspects of development are presented. The opportunity to create modules of common interest, packages which reflect a mainstream and special, focus, and the possibility for pupils from either school to attend courses offered in either setting, increase the level of integration for personnel, curriculum and the learner.

An additional advantage of the IHE setting at this stage is the link established with teachers involved in associated INSET activities, particularly where the focus of attention is upon pre-vocational pathways which have similar cross-curricular dimensions. Thus, a teacher attending pre-vocational INSET activities is able to relate closely to the objectives of these two school-focused projects.

In all these examples we have tried to demonstrate how a school-focused initiative can develop into school-based INSET activity and eventually lead to cluster-based developments. The IHE initially supports and directs the projects, the LEA resources it and thereby encourages transfer of responsibility to the school and local INSET centre. In turn, as involvement widens, a cluster may accept 'ownership', thus achieving a greater impact for the time and resources offered by the IHE and the school.

We have also used these examples to demonstrate a range of possibilities for providing shared working experiences which encourage greater integration of personnel across and between institutions, support services and the community. We have identified the prerequisite features for a form of INSET which is self-generating and self-supporting. The key components are: a designated teacher; an IHE supported school-focused project; an LEA resourced school-based INSET development; mutual support and development within a cluster; planned transfer of responsibility from IHE/school to LEA/school/Local INSET Centre; and a re-introduction of the IHE to support newly identified needs through further school-focused projects.

Personal Development

As well as developing the school's response to meet special educational needs, and positively adjusting the pace of change for that school, the designated teacher's personal and professional development must also be considered. There is a danger in the format we have suggested of concentrating solely upon the needs of the pupil and the institution, disregarding the personal educational needs of the staff involved.

If our main concern is with a school-focused project, as may be the case for example with the one-term course, we will not appropriately address the personal needs of the teacher. These teachers in particular require some recognition of their achievements, and through their contribution, both within the IHE activities and those which are school-based, they can acquire feelings of worth, enhance their confidence, and gain skills important to career progression. However, there is also a need to take account of other areas associated with personal development. These encompass the need for a new impetus and intellectual challenge sufficient to allow for different experiences, opportunities to reflect on these experiences, and explore avenues for application. We should also endeavour to provide opportunities which refresh the individual by presenting new horizons — through the exploration of issues, not necessarily related to their current teaching concerns, with teachers and others — and engagement with personnel whose interests lie outside the teacher's present responsibilities or experience.

To ensure the teacher's continued development and future career progression, the school-focused project is best incorporated into a one-term secondment which forms an optional module of a wider qualification, possibly an Advanced Diploma or In-Service Degree. Further progression may be available through a Teacher Fellowship or Higher Degree. If this one-term activity allows exemption from the initial stages of more advanced courses, other pathways such as those associated with pre-vocation, multi-cultural, or specific curriculum areas, could be pursued.

This kind of personal development also offers the opportunity for the 'educated personnel' to contribute to the development of other teachers by their planned inclusion in the INSET activities of the IHE and LEA. This effectively ensures a growth and development of INSET activities which goes beyond the parameters of the traditional course.

Such a view of personal development also encourages appropriate ways of monitoring the professional progress of the teacher, thus enabling the LEA to better match the attributes of its personnel with the particular requirements of posts as they become available. This would suggest that the closest of links between IHE and LEA is required to consider the best possible deployment of educated personnel to resourced schools.

The Resourced School

Throughout this book we have referred to the ultimate goal of special educational needs provision as the *resourced school*. In the following chapter this is linked, through the process of integration, with the concept of *The School for All*; the two terms, however, are not synonymous. The main focus of the resourced school is the interplay between suitably educated personnel and appropriate material resources. Whilst we would wish, therefore, to support the idea of the School for All, more so as our view of special educational needs demands an individual approach to meeting the needs of all pupils, and this suggests a comprehensive structure, we would not place the emphasis on the range of intake, but on the abilities of the teachers and others to articulate knowledge, expertise and equipment to maximum effect.

It might, of course, be argued that a more diverse intake necessitates, indeed stimulates a more diverse response, but experience would suggest that this is not always the case. Neither is it the case that the best equipped school, in material, physical and human terms, always offers the best education possible to all its pupils. By placing the emphasis on the teacher, on his/her professional development, we are signifying the overriding principle that meeting children's educational needs is first and foremost about the quality of relationship between teacher and taught; and that this relationship, whilst subject to factors of personality, will be greatly enhanced, in educational terms, if the teacher is well informed; indeed, well educated to the wide variety of approaches available to identifying and meeting pupils' individual educational needs.

As the movement towards whole-school policies and school-based INSET activities signifies, this has as much to do with the relationship between teachers and others as it does between teacher and taught. At the level of the whole-school policy, it is essential that most, if not all, the teachers, whether in a senior position or not, work to one aim. A central aspect of teacher education, therefore, must be the fostering of the ability to work with and alongside colleagues. Since we are proposing that the integration of children with special educational needs will best be achieved if the development of provision is based on a prior phase of integrating personnel, we would place evidence of such integration high on the list of criteria for identifying a resourced school.

By making the integration of personnel the main focus of attention, it is possible to examine more precisely those material resources which are critical to establishing a viable whole school approach, and which also, therefore, describe the *resourced school*.

In this sense, the word 'resource' takes its meaning from the stage of segregation which now exists as a result of the historical development of special education, which was, prior to the Education Act 1981, based on a philosophy of within-child difficulties. The appropriate level of material and human resource required, therefore, is that level which enables the integration of all children, and this can be directly related to the maximum efficiency which can be obtained by staff working in a variety of integrated ways.

In concrete terms, we are concerned with certain critical arrangements which vary considerably from school to school. These arrangements include: teacher–pupil ratio; classroom management; careful distribution and use of materials; appropriate forms of assessment and recording; flexible arrangements for combining and exchanging groups of pupils with teachers and others; effective introduction and use of resource people other than teachers; and flexible cooperative/team teaching arrangements in staff deployment. All these arrangements can, if well organized, enhance the chances of integration by meeting individual pupil needs, but all require effective interpersonal behaviour, and this requires sufficient staff development activities to ensure integration of personnel.

Critical Arrangements

The critical arrangements, mentioned above, should not be viewed as a list, since there are clear connections between the various but discrete elements.

In total, they form a logical sequence, beginning with the Teacher–Pupil Ratio (TPR).

To date, the TPR has been crucial in the efficacy of meeting individual need. Teachers have often argued that given smaller class sizes they would be able to cope with, and cater for, the individual style and pace of every child. However, experience would suggest that the optimum class size is not easily ascertained, and that the teacher's attitude and techniques in classroom management are of equal importance. The relationship between these factors is such that where the TPR is high, for example in a primary school where classes are in their thirties, developments in attitude and classroom techniques are very slow to evolve. Indeed, where classroom numbers remain high, there is every chance that development will not take place.

However, the reduction of TPR is not a sufficient method *per se* of achieving more appropriate attitudes and classroom techniques, since it is also essential for the teacher to make fundamental changes in practice. Where teachers have become accustomed to dealing with large groups of pupils by addressing them as a class, they will not change unless adequate INSET activity is available for them to adopt different strategies.

In this context, TPR might represent Technology, Personnel and Resources, rather than Teacher–Pupil Ratio. The technology available to the teacher would include the flexibility to use materials, support, and other personnel to create groupings and individual approaches more likely to meet pupil needs. The personnel element reflects attitudinal change required before, during and following such a re-arrangement, with resources holding the balance between what is desirable and what is possible.

The above would suggest that all schools require coherent policies for the important areas of staff development, and resource acquisition and deployment. If this is achieved, and more flexible grouping arrangements are advanced, it is possible to develop curriculum-based individual assessment which leads to the promotion of recording, which in turn establishes appropriate individually oriented teaching plans.

Only then can teachers justifiably consider and quantify the amount of support they need. This may be met initially within the school by new teaching arrangements which bring teachers together in cooperative or team-teaching situations. Such arrangements would also facilitate the introduction of other support personnel, including parents. This might in itself give rise to a review of the physical resources required, leading to an up-dating of the policy for resource acquisition and deployment.

Given the confines and focus of this book, it would be difficult to cover in detail those critical arrangements which relate to classroom management techniques, nor is it appropriate that we should do so. However, we feel it important, for the sake of clarity, to suggest a number of areas worthy of closer consideration. In our experience, if these aspects of management are not introduced into the classroom, then learning and/or behavioural difficulties may well arise. Alternatively, evidence of their presence may establish the degree to which a school can be said to be a 'resourced school'. We have grouped these under three headings, pupils, classroom and teachers.

PUPILS

An awareness of how to:

differentiate effectively between individual learning patterns

help pupils of differing abilities to demonstrate what they *can* do, and what they understand

make sure assignments are at an appropriate level

provide a range of assignments commensurate with interests and capabilities

allow pupils to experience different levels of pupil/pupil and pupil/teacher interaction

organize a daily routine which satisfies the need for breadth and balance

provide extension activities for extending and broadening concepts, skills and attitudes

provide attainable targets within specified time periods which give positive feedback and reinforcement

provide pupils with ways of demonstrating their learning which do not demand impoverished skills such as writing or reading

use individualized learning techniques such as precision teaching and task analysis

the need to make explicit the rules of the classroom with visual reminders.

CLASSROOM

An awareness of how to:

make the classroom environment one which is achievement oriented, and where success is acknowledged

organize the furniture in a way conducive to quick and efficient changes of grouping

take account of friendship groupings

take account of group dynamics

organize learning centres appropriate to the pupils' learning needs use display material to foster further learning

alternate the roles of the adults available in the classroom to maximize on the number of teaching/learning situations required by pupil needs

recognize the need for a degree of negotiation in what is to be learned, how it is to be learned and when.

TEACHERS

An awareness of how to:

make sure that the various experiences within the classroom are seen by the pupil and the teacher as worthwhile

make sure that all contributions are recognized

vary the presentation and methods of teaching

accommodate individual interests, capabilities, and rates of work output

present material in a novel way

provide adequate concrete examples and utilize alternative sense modes

vary the speed and form of instruction

use language at different levels for purposes of understanding and reinforcement

place different emphases on practical, oral and visual sequences within the lesson

use techniques such as 'proximity control', which ensure a more controlled pattern of behaviour.

Finally, as a product of all three, pupil, classroom and teacher —

the need for careful devolution of responsibility for learning from teacher to child.

Chapter 8

Rethinking Integration

Introduction

In its third report (May 1987) *Special Educational Needs: Implementation of the Education Act 1981*, the House of Commons Education, Science and Arts Committee concluded: that in order to support the principle of integration, it is not necessary to support the principle of insisting that all children be educated in primary and secondary schools rather than special schools. At first sight this may appear to contradict both the letter and the spirit of the Education Act 1981, but on further reading it becomes evident that this position is entirely consistent with the first of the two major conclusions of the report, that the present levels for resourcing education are inadequate, and that this position is in itself consistent with the conditions laid down by the Act for the integration of children with special educational needs in ordinary schools. The committee evidence points both to the lack of specific resources to implement the Act and to the general shortage of resources in schools, which if less acute, would minimize the numbers of pupils requiring special education. There is, in addition, some recognition within the report that perceptions have changed, and that whilst some LEAs continue to define integration as *placement*, the majority regard it as *a process in which children with special educational needs mix with their peers in a regular and planned way.* The report therefore accepts that the term also embraces collaborative ventures between special schools and ordinary schools.

In view of our comments in the previous chapters, this represents a disappointingly shallow description of integration. Whilst there is some recognition that the concept of special educational need has changed, in so much as the committee points to a direct relationship between levels of resources and numbers of children deemed to have special educational needs, it says nothing about the effect of this change on the actual processes of integration. Indeed, because of this omission, the report adds little to our understanding of what must surely be the main focus of attention in meeting special educational needs post-Education Act 1981. The committee, however, is largely reporting evidence collated in England and Wales, and the complex nature of integration to which it alludes might best be attributed to the low level of commitment, both in terms of policy and finance, of central and local government. The logic of accepting integration as an educational issue rather than a philosophy or ideology, is that it inevitably leads towards a position of establishing *resourced* schools. Given the current financial climate, we are undoubtedly in danger of accepting a hotch-potch of compromises based on political and financial expediency. If finance is to be the guiding factor, then we need to be truthful, and it behoves us to be explicit, for example, about our reasons for initiating collaborative ventures between special schools and ordinary schools.

In this chapter, therefore, we explore the implications of accepting a concept of integration which closely relates to the *resourced school*, and in particular, focus on the need for an integrated INSET programme to support the LEA's efforts in integrating discrete aspects of provision, which we have argued are a dominant feature of the legacy.

The Illogicality of Segregation

Ironically, it is not the legislation pertaining to integration which has had most effect on our attitudes towards segregation, but another aspect of the Education Act 1981, that dealing with de-categorization. As far as integration is concerned, the Act is very weak. It requires LEAs to make provision in ordinary schools, but only if this is compatible with the child's educational needs, the efficient education of the other children with whom he or she is educated and the efficient use of resources. As many commentators have pointed out, unless there is a sufficient infusion of new money at an early stage, it is unlikely that provision within the ordinary school will satisfy both the first and third criteria simultaneously. The Act, however, did, as from April 1983, remove the ten categories of handicap, and whilst many LEAs may have found the specific legislation referring to integration useful in maintaining the status quo, they may have also found the logical and practical consequences of de-categorization quite problematic. It is this part of the legislation, whether intended or not, that provides the argument for integration at the level of the *school for all*.

In removing the ten categories of handicap, the Act also removed the administrative concept of primary handicap. As discussed in chapter 1 in the case study, the notion of primary handicap has long been used by decision-makers within the LEA to reduce the difficulty associated, and rightly associated (chapter 10), with making decisions about placement. By replacing primary handicap with individual need, the Act has shifted the focus of attention. What is now required is an examination of a variety of contributory factors, all of which require careful and balanced consideration before placement is determined. Balanced judgements, however, involving a variety of factors, are more difficult. It is no longer possible to rely on cut-off criteria, arrived at via assessment techniques primarily designed to signify a level of deficiency within a defined handicap. Assessments are required which are more closely related to the actual learning requirements of the child.

This gives rise to the notion of a continuum of learning, behavioural and physical/sensory difficulties which is more closely allied to the educational context currently experienced by the child; and it is precisely at this point that the wider concept of special educational needs acquires meaning. If we reject cut-off points and accept the notion of a continuum, it becomes necessary to acknowledge a much larger group of children with special educational needs, in particular, those children whose pattern of contributory problems suggests a significant learning difficulty, but who, under previous assessments, would not have been deemed to have a significant problem in any one area of primary handicap. Once we accept this level of complexity in meeting individual need, it becomes clear that the previous practice of investigating causation, sometimes referred to as the 'medical model' (chapter 2), was inappropriate, and that what is actually required is an approach which is *educational* in character; one which primarily considers the needs of the learning and teaching environment. Clearly, if all contributory factors are to be taken into account, this will include the curriculum. The nearest that previous legislation came to this was the creation of the category of Educationally Sub-Normal, where the legislation, at least, allowed for reasons other than limited ability, though in practice IQ was often the deciding factor. Since all children, irrespective of their particular pattern of contributory factors, have access to the curriculum as a common educational goal, the curriculum itself must constitute a central cause for concern.

It follows from the above that the concept of special educational need must to some degree be relative, and that this relativity is born out of an interactive model of special education, whereby two children presenting the same degree of internal and social factors may be judged differently; one as having special educational needs, and one as not, according to the appropriateness of the curriculum or the degree of access afforded. The teaching of children with special educational needs, therefore, has less to do with labels such as 'dull', 'remedial', 'slow', etc., and more to do with appropriate content, methods and materials. Inadequacies in teaching are nowhere more apparent than when dealing with pupils with special educational needs; inadequacies, as described in the previous chapter, associated with classroom management and the inability of the teacher to analyse skills and concepts, or present material at an appropriate level or in a motivating fashion.

As the case for meeting individual need increases, so the case for segregation, whether physical or curricular, diminishes, and new concepts appear relating the needs of the pupil to the education on offer. These concepts carry the notion that all children are entitled to experience all elements of the curriculum; that too many pupils have been distanced from the curriculum of their peers; and that access to the curriculum means more than physical adaptations for the physically handicapped. Curriculum modification becomes a major consideration, with integration viewed more as a continuum which is curriculum-based rather than provision-based, provision, that is, in the physical sense. The question to be asked is, how much should the pupil's curriculum be modified? Not, where should the pupil go? The concept of integration, therefore, should be firmly linked with its antithesis, segregation, and in the light of the above argument, the onus of justification should be placed on those concerned to maintain a segregated form of education. The authors are doubtful that this can be achieved, other than in terms of the realistic arguments of financial constraint, and the reason for this is the demonstrable connection between integration and the notion of individual educational need. Any LEA or Government wishing to promote maximum educational opportunity for all must address this issue.

Integrating Existing Provision

If in the future individual educational need is to be met through the development of the curriculum and not by reference to category of handicap, so that curriculum modification forms the main continuum of provision for meeting special educational needs, most LEAs will, by necessity, have to embark upon a radical reorganization of schools and services. The degree of reorganization in terms of integrating personnel and services, and indeed integrating special schools, will depend upon the commitment of the LEA to the principle of resourced schools and whether or not the LEA views the process as evolutionary, through carefully thought-out interim phases, or revolutionary through the closure of special schools and services with a corresponding resourcing of ordinary schools.

Whilst we have advocated an evolutionary approach based on a parallel evolution within in-service training, we do recognize that this strategy may present a considerable problem for the LEA that has a wide variety of provision, since, somewhat paradoxically, the more types of provision, the greater the difficulty in meeting individual need. The larger the LEA, the more acute the problem, and the greater the variety and number of provision, the greater the task of integrating services and personnel. The existence of a large number of schools for pupils with moderate learning difficulties, the divorced nature of the remedial/support services and 'specialist' units, and the distinctly separate administration of some services such as those for the hearing impaired, will present a considerable challenge.

Further, the present system of distributing resources according to category leads to a form of provision which is dominated by 'late intervention', since time is required for some categories to emerge, at least with sufficient evidence to confidently form the subject of a statement. This is clearly illustrated in the case study. Not only is the category of specific learning difficulty (dyslexia) 'diagnosed' late for John, but there is further delay caused by doubt as to which 'category' he should be placed in — an inevitable consequence of category-related provision. In this way the argument for prevention is weakened, since the argument can only be won in the political arena by demonstration of proof. Whilst provision remains category-based, only severe and more easily identified cases will accrue resources.

The task, therefore, is two-fold: to integrate forms of provision by a deliberate and bold act of de-categorization assisted by assessments of need which are curriculum-based and truly individual; and to further this by integrating the working practices of those currently involved in discrete provision. Encouraging people to work together, however, is no easy task. Garry Thomas (1986) describes both the difficulties and the advantages of professionals working together in one classroom but performing different roles. He draws our attention to the 'alien' nature of this work to teachers, and to the preparation required to bring about maximum efficiency. Paramount is role clarification and In-Service activities which highlight inter-personal skills. Once we move out of the classroom, however, to the more complex levels of integrating personnel across existing support services and special schools, the inter-personal skills and role clarification identified by Thomas need to be greatly supplemented by changes in attitudes and beliefs. A clear policy is therefore required, and the LEA that does not communicate to its support services and special schools what its response to the Education Act 1981 is to be, will not achieve integration of personnel, but simply encourage both archaic practices and the development of harmful rifts between those who cling to a 'category' related service and those who wish to contribute to a more flexible view of individual needs.

As already intimated, integration of personnel can not take place outside a radical reorganization of LEA resources. Such a reorganization will involve a detailed analysis of the provision, how personnel are presently deployed, how work is organized, what criteria are used for prioritizing children's needs, and what the current thinking is amongst personnel concerning the Education Act 1981. As indicated in chapter 5, *Policy and Perspective*, such an analysis does not figure highly in LEA reviews.

Planning for Integration

To date the move towards integration has been somewhat piecemeal. Although all of the LEA policy statements analysed in chapter 5 contained a strong commitment to integration in principle, few described the path by which it is to be achieved. Where large-scale integration has been achieved, it has been on the basis of primary handicap using the system of a 'designated' school, serving a wide catchment area, usually confining itself to the less problematic cases of physical or intellectual disability, although in recent years some LEAs have expanded this system to provide education for children deemed to have disabilities not originally incorporated into the ten categories of handicap and for which there was little LEA provision, such as Autism, Dyslexia, and Speech and Language Disorders. Since many of these children were previously either not diagnosed, or were educated at independent schools, this development can be recognized as a form of integration, at least in the sense that the child is integrated into the LEA, and as such can remain at home, even if he/she has to travel a considerable distance to school. Designated schools, however, do not in themselves guarantee integration.

The Warnock Report's three levels of functional, social and locational integration can be observed at and across a variety of institutions: within the ordinary classroom; the ordinary school; the special school classroom; the special school; the unit (whether attached or unattached to an ordinary school); the support services; and across the special/ordinary divide. The permutations are almost limitless. At one extreme, it is possible to observe the almost total segregation of children with multiple and complex difficulties within schools for children with severe learning difficulties; at the other, total functional, social, as well as locational, integration for children with quite severe physical disabilities.

Whilst the designated school may be viewed by some as integration, it is clear to us that it does not fulfil the aspirations of the *resourced school*. Some LEAs will have already faced opposition from parents who wish their child to be educated at the neighbourhood school. In the context of the Education Act 1981, and despite caveats regarding the 'efficient use of resources', this would seem both a reasonable and desirable request. The arguments against the designated school are largely concerned with inappropriate travel and the development of friendship groups. If we widen the definition of locational integration to incorporate *the neighbourhood* (as against the narrower definition of 'near to normal peer group' as expressed in the Warnock Report), then it could be argued that functional and social integration are gained at the expense of locational. In addition, there has been a tendency to regard these three forms of integration as progressively more desirable, with functional integration the main aim and locational integration only marginally better than segregation. In reality, integration *per se* demands all three, and the designated school, therefore, can only be regarded as a 'compromise' or a 'stage' in the development of an LEA's response to the Education Act 1981.

Whilst it is true that an argument can be made for designated schools on the basis of a more efficient use of resources, particularly where this pertains to Non-Teaching Assistants and the development of a body of 'expertise', this argument is no more than that used to retain, or indeed establish, special schools. In reality, neither the literature nor experience indicates that there is a coherent body of knowledge or expertise available within a designated school. It is not uncommon for the majority of the staff in such schools to feel ill-informed or inadequate, often quite unnecessarily. In-Service training is a commonly identified need in such schools, though on closer examination it is often difficult to suggest what activities are required.

It is often suggested that the argument for integration is at heart an ideological one, and this would certainly be true of attempts in recent years (Sayer, 1987; Booth and Statham, 1982; Booth and Potts, 1983a, 1983b; Booth and Coulby, 1987; Booth and Swann, 1987; Booth, Potts and Swann, 1987) and in particular these involved with the Open University, to establish a rationale for the *school for all*. Indeed, it would be possible to argue that this type of thinking also forms the basis of the influential Fish Report (1985) *Equal Opportunity for All?* From the point of view of the resourced school, however, the argument lies not so much in ideology, though this is not dismissed, as in the justification for segregation on financial grounds. Integration is an educational argument. Segregation, we have argued, initially came about because of the inability of the education system to cope with what it now defines as 'differentiation' and the quasi-medical stance it took on disability. However, despite consistent government proclamations to the contrary, education has developed, and it is now possible to view every child as not only educable but educable within the mainstream of provision. We have consistently argued this point through the concept of the educated teacher, because it seems to us that the Education Act 1981 was quite correct and timely in re-focusing our view of special educational needs — away from the quasi-medical — towards the educational. Educationally speaking, in the wake of the Act, there is no defence for segregation other than that of finance, and therefore, public and political will. Designated schools and units, viewed in this light, are either half-way houses or institutionalized forms of categorization. By the same token, the ultimate position of the LEA wishing to fulfil the principle of integration, is that of establishing *every* school as a resourced school, where the resources are sufficient to embrace *any* child with special educational needs whose parents live within its catchment area and who wish him/her to attend the neighbourhood school.

Such an undertaking would indeed be enormous, and given the reality that resources will not appear overnight, but will be fought for pound by pound, it would seem prudent that the LEA have some form of plan, whereby both existing resources and 'new' money, as and when available, can be used to greatest effect. Such a plan might well involve a series of integrations, whereby services such as those related to remedial services, hearing impaired, visually impaired, behavioural difficulties, etc., are brought together to form one support service. This new service might then concentrate on integrating with special schools and ordinary schools, with a view to providing an initial link between the special and ordinary school sector, whilst developing classroom practice through in-class support. A third stage might then be the devolvement of these services into the main teaching force, beginning the process of establishing resourced schools. Such an integration of services, and therefore personnel, will require a variety of In-Service activities carefully planned to develop in tandem. Here too the stricture of finance will play its part. In-Service activities, however financed, are not cheap. In addition to the massive undertaking which is required to develop those teachers within current services, there is an even greater undertaking required for those in ordinary schools. Timing in such matters is essential. Concentrating on one group, to the detriment of the other, will only produce a mis-match of expectations in both. Such a disharmony may well mitigate against the intention of the plan. Unfortunately, and somewhat ironically, this may be the eventual result of the current GRIST arrangements. What originally promised immense flexibility, is now immensely restricting. Not because of any inherent fault in the structure of the scheme, but because of the ill-advised interference of the government in delineating the areas within special educational needs which the grant should cover. Hence, whilst the spotlight has been focused on a much needed initiative to train co-ordinators in ordinary schools, LEAs have little encouragement or latitude to develop, and therefore change, special schools. This can either be viewed as a genuine attempt to meet the needs of the wider group of children identified by the Act, or as a cynical attempt to discourage developments within, and therefore bring about the demise of, special schools. The latter, though a little extreme, gains some credibility from the disquieting lack of direction from the government, DES, or HMI regarding the future of special schools; the prime example being schools for children with moderate learning difficulties which make up the majority of special school provision. Such an approach to special schools can only result in determination on the part of those involved with such schools, parents, governors as well as teachers, to maintain the status quo.

Devolution requires the participation of all those involved in the continuum. In-service activities must address all groups simultaneously. Special schools ready to devolve resources, through the medium of an interim phase of outreach work, will make little headway if the ordinary schools they wish to support have scarcely heard of the 1981 Act, let alone developed a comprehensive whole-school policy. Likewise, the most sophisticated whole-school approach will be under-utilized if the supporting services and adjacent special schools continue to deprive them of the necessary resources to see them established. Since we are advocating a plan of development which views integration as a continuum of curriculum-based opportunities which may have to be arrived at through a series of evolutionary measures, it is only logical that we should also advocate that all parties be involved in each phase of that development, and that the common denominator be teacher development.

Integrating INSET

It should be clear from the above, that if integration is to be more than a statement of principle, a concerted effort is required to provide in-service activities which span a wide range of interim and final roles across a variety of institutions and services. This in turn will generate a wide variety of activities operating across an equally wide spectrum of modes: Neither the LEA nor the IHE can satisfy this demand, though both may contribute a unique element.

Unfortunately, it is more often the case than not that LEA and IHE in-service activities are planned and delivered in isolation. This isolation takes several forms. Courses are frequently self-contained, offering little continuity with other courses, either within the LEA or IHE. Courses or activities offered within the LEA or IHE are isolated from the development policy of the LEA. LEA- and IHE-initiated courses are sometimes at best unrelated and at worst contradictory in direction, occasionally to the point of overt criticism or hostility as to content and approach. Courses are isolated in the sense of accreditation, in that many do not lead to, nor contribute to, a recognized qualification.

We have elsewhere pointed out the difficulties such issues raise for the academic autonomy of the IHE, and it is well understood that what we propose in terms of joint planning, delivery and accreditation, requires careful consideration if the integrity of both the IHE and LEA is to be upheld. Clearly the IHE cannot submit itself to one view of special educational needs and its development, but something of a compromise must be reached if partnership is to be achieved. In chapter 6 we have suggested, in some detail, how the IHE and LEA can achieve a *common perspective*. The rest of this chapter, therefore, is devoted to the issues of continuity and accreditation, and how these may be encouraged by a greater degree of integration between IHE- and LEA-financed in-service activities.

One of the chief products of partnership between the LEA and IHE is evaluation through justification. Courses and activities cannot be integrated, with the purpose of achieving continuity, unless they can be communicated. This requires both parties to reflect on their activities, their rationale and effectiveness. A further gain is the clarification of objectives, since each element of in-service, whether predominantly LEA- or IHE-inspired, will have to fit an agreed overall pattern.

In chapter 9 we argue that this overall pattern is best achieved through a continuum of activities, rather than any pre-set notion of levels of training which relate to the roles teachers and others are thought to perform. This approach does, of course, colour our view as to the nature of the integration of INSET activities, since our main focus is the professional development of the individual rather than pre-conceived skills required at set levels of involvement. Whilst we acknowledge that in the interim phases (or indeed in the longer term if LEAs opt for a form of provision somewhere between segregation and integration as we have described it) there will be a need for a greater concentration on the particular knowledge and expertise required within a narrowly defined set of roles such as Support Teacher, School Co-ordinator, Special School Teacher, etc., we would suggest that, as is the case with the school curriculum, certain attitudes, skills, knowledge, and concepts pervade all aspects of special educational needs provision, and that the acquisition of these is likely to be developmental, with the speed of refinement dependent upon personal, as well as experiential, factors. Since the main resource of the resourced school is likely to be the educated teacher, it would make more sense to develop every teacher's sensitivity to individual need rather than select limited skills for defined roles. The first task required of continuity, therefore, is the examination of what constitutes a good teacher within a resourced school, 'good' being related to the teacher's ability to participate fully in a whole-school approach which is aimed at meeting all pupils' educational needs.

Such an examination is indeed a major task, but only when such an exercise is complete can the various contributions made by the LEA and IHE be identified. It may then be possible to establish the relationship between, say, the LEA blanket cover course such as the Coventry Special Needs Action Programme, the DES GRIST-funded SENIOS course for co-ordinators in ordinary schools, and the IHE Diploma. The whole variety of INSET modes, ranging from evening sessions in Teachers Centres, Day and evening sessions within schools, residential settings, twenty-day courses, etc., can then be thought about in terms of what they can offer to the development of these identified characteristics by virtue of their unique setting, duration and format.

Continuity may also be enhanced by the development of accreditation. There are perhaps more difficulties here for the IHE than the LEA. LEA INSET, although in more recent times subject to the scrutiny of the GRIST evaluation, is for the most part answerable only to itself, and is largely regulated by the demands and comments of its own teaching force. The IHE, on the other hand, if it is not a University, must satisfy the demands of a validating institution such as the Council for National Academic Awards or affiliated University, the External Examiner and the DES. In this context, a relationship with an LEA or a number of LEAs can be, and predominantly was so before the GRIST arrangements, viewed as an optional extra. Fortunately the GRIST arrangement has not only made some form of partnership indispensable, it has also freed some IHEs from unnecessary and over-burdensome mechanisms of change. It was not until very recent times, for example, that Polytechnics were allowed by the CNAA to make the kind of quick and easy adjustments, to both the mode and content of their courses, demanded by those LEAs determined to institute change following the Education Act 1981. Although both the DES and the validating bodies have, if somewhat sluggishly, responded to the IHE's needs, the situation is still such that accreditation of a Local Authority's course into a formal qualification, such as a Diploma, is extremely difficult. Indeed, at the time of writing, it is still a complex, and therefore unusual matter, for two IHEs to offer inter-institutional accreditation, particularly if one is validated by a University and the other by the CNAA. This in turn makes it very difficult for an LEA to deal with more than one IHE, and restricts the development of the wider range of expertise which could be achieved if IHEs were able to contribute specific elements to a formal qualification, perhaps, on a modular basis. Clearly this must change.

As LEAs devote more energy to In-Service activities, through the mechanisms of GRIST, so they will want, on behalf of their teachers, their efforts to be recognized as worthy of inclusion in formal professional qualifications. To date, only one or two LEAs have succeeded in achieving accreditation of a course at the level of a full module. Most LEA courses gain credit as an element of a foundation course only, and this does not seem to satisfy the criterion of equal partnership. Clearly there is a great deal of scope for further development.

In conclusion, in accepting a view of integration which is closely related to the development of the resourced school, we strongly advocate, in addition to the integration of existing provision and working practices, the integration of IHE and LEA In-Service activities. We turn now to an examination of the continuity which this implies.

Chapter 9

A Continuum Approach to In-Service Activities

The Traditional Model — a 'Taught' Course

The traditional model of INSET reflected the separate categories of handicap and allowed seconded teachers access to specific pathways such as a Diploma in Maladjustment, a Diploma in Educational Sub-normality, a Diploma in Handicapped Children, a Diploma in Residential Education, etc. Such courses were comprised of taught elements which gave the history of handicapping conditions, how they would be identified, and diagnostic techniques which would provide the teacher with a treatment plan and suggest possible strategies for dealing with the problem. For instance, the various medical problems and associated sensory difficulties, linked to a main category of handicap, would be considered, so that an aetiology, or collection of presenting symptoms exhibited by the child, could be collated. From the resultant diagnosis, a treatment plan would be devised to treat the collection of symptoms, and the likelihood of success expressed in terms of a prognosis.

The seconded teacher would be instructed in the skills and techniques associated with a particular handicap. For example, in the case of Behaviour and Emotional Difficulties, taught elements might include the origins of behavioural difficulties, the history of pioneer work illustrating the development of psychodynamic approaches, the use of rating scales such as the Bristol Social Adjustment Guide and the Rutter Scale, psychiatric and psychological theory, behaviourist methods, delinquency and criminology, and psychiatric conditions. The taught elements would be given different emphases according to the predilections, research interests, or strengths of the course team. Thus, some would be viewed as essential, some optional, and others peripheral. Because the course was primarily based on a transfer of knowledge and skills, there was little scope for the joint participation of those involved in the teaching and learning, and as a result little opportunity for transfer of learning to serve the 'development' needs of the service, or a wider, more integrated perception of special educational needs response to be encouraged. Logically, if the teacher was involved with children displaying a range of interrelated 'problems', such as those associated with behaviour *and* learning, it would be necessary for that teacher to undergo a further year's taught course in Learning Difficulties.

Such an arrangement also had repercussions for career development. A teacher seeking promotion in a special school, having completed a Diploma in Maladjustment, say, was destined to remain in a school of this category, mainly because this very specialized Diploma did not carry credibility with those appointing in other institutions, both special and mainstream. As a consequence, this form of INSET maintained the 'mythology' surrounding distinct categories of handicap and actively ensured the continuation of segregated provision. The numbers of teachers able to participate in the taught courses therefore were limited to those who were perceived by the LEA as having potential for senior posts in particular categories of special schools.

Because of the regional distribution of courses to IHE departments, specified by the DES, many teachers either travelled a considerable distance to their chosen course, or they accepted the philosophy and direction of their nearest institution, or indeed chose to forego opportunities for further training. In accepting the philosophy and direction of their nearest institution, they were also accepting distinct features which sometimes conflicted with other institutions.

Depending upon the philosophy of the course undertaken, a school could find itself in a position whereby different senior staff held, if not opposing, uncomplementary views. For example, in the field of Educational Sub-normality, it was possible for a Head of Department to have studied for a Diploma which was heavily oriented towards learning theory, leading to a consideration of learning programmes and curriculum organization, whilst members of his/her department may have studied in a different IHE, where a heavier emphasis was placed on a sociological model of causation. A conflict did arise in some schools, and this often interrupted the flow of development.

The Concept of Levels

The taught course, as described above, became one feature of a wider pattern of INSET for special educational needs. It tended to be a course offered to special school personnel only, but with changing perceptions, following the Warnock Report and the implementation of the 1981 Act, it was recognized by LEAs that INSET activities would be required by teachers in the mainstream of education.

The very specialized Diploma courses were not accepted as an appropriate route, since they neither provided for sufficient teachers to participate nor offered the required content. The development took place over at least four identifiable phases. In the first phase, the existing Diplomas were added to by awareness-raising courses for mainstream teachers, mainly those in primary schools. Many LEAs adopted a cascade model such as the Special Needs Action Programme developed by the Coventry LEA, although a few LEAs, such as Oxfordshire, offered a broader approach for all primary school teachers. In the second phase, three levels were identified: a short awareness course for mainstream teachers, a specialist one-year Diploma, and the additional one-year Diploma for both mainstream and special school teachers, offering a broad, generic, programme. The third phase incorporated the further level of a one-term Special Educational Needs in the Ordinary School (SENIOS) course, aimed primarily at those teachers in the mainstream 'designated' to develop a special educational needs response within their school. Finally, the fourth phase included a modular structure to the 'generic' Diploma, which paved the way for an integration of the one-term course, an awareness-raising course, into the overall structure of the Diploma.

The LEA tended to view these levels of INSET as being commensurate with the teacher's level of involvement with children with special educational needs. Thus, a classroom teacher in a mainstream school was unlikely to be accepted for a Diploma course. With the introduction of the one-term SENIOS course, teachers in mainstream schools could be identified as co-ordinators of special educational needs, and therefore as requiring a greater degree of training than those teachers attending awareness courses, although not as great as those involved in special schools.

The Warnock Report had also pointed to the importance of a special educational needs input into initial teacher training, and consequently, IHEs responded to such recommendations either through option courses, core courses, or attempts at permeation throughout all courses. Nevertheless, despite developments in both initial training and INSET, there was little evidence of continuity or co-ordination between the two. Further, schools were unable to offer substantial elements of special educational needs in their induction programmes. This suggests that a closer relationship between the IHE and LEA was required, so that a coherent and continuous programme of teacher development could take place, incorporating all three aspects, initial training, induction and INSET. The direction this could take was exemplified in the IT-INSET project, organized by the School of Education at Leicester University at the turn of the decade. The project encouraged lecturers, students and teachers to participate in a joint learning experience. We take up this vital theme later in this chapter.

The Introduction of Role-Related INSET

The levels of INSET, outlined above, were established at a time which coincided with a major shift of emphasis in the development of provision for meeting special educational needs. This emphasis suggested a different response from both the ordinary school and the special school. The ordinary school would need to take greater responsibility for ALL pupils and allow for differentiation of learning needs, and in so doing enlist the support of specialist services; either in the form of a re-organized remedial service, or outreach worker from a special school. These descriptions of the available services signify the early patterns of support which were to be improved and developed through appropriate INSET. This INSET became more desirable as the role functions of those involved widened, particularly as it became evident that support was to be directed towards the teacher and the whole school, rather than the individual child.

As the response required of the ordinary school became more clear, so the role of the designated teacher became that of a co-ordinator charged with the responsibility of leading a whole-school approach to meeting special educational needs. The nature of the support required by the school also changed, requiring of the support teacher more sophisticated consultation, inter-personal, curriculum development and systems analysis skills.

It also became clear that the hitherto undeveloped role of the outreach worker based at the special school needed to be reconsidered in the light of developments taking place between the co-ordinator and support teacher. The notion of the special school as a centre of excellence, an INSET agency, and a physical and professional resource, required a level of response more sophisticated than that suggested by outreach alone. This was particularly the case when the idea of a continuum of curriculum modification, or realignment of the curriculum to reflect mainstream provision, was mooted.

It seemed that the new levels of INSET offered a useful time allocation for these various emerging roles, and hence the concept of *Role Related INSET* was introduced. Whilst this would seem a pragmatic solution to the problem of matching restricted resources to a widening circle of INSET need, the case for discrete, and somewhat arbitrary, allocations of time to a pre-conceived hierarchy of role functions, has not yet been adequately argued. Indeed, it is a central argument of this book that the responsibility for meeting children's special educational needs rests with all teachers. This can only be achieved if all teachers are presented with opportunities pertinent to the concept of the educated teacher proposed in this book. This does not preclude management roles, nor does it preclude interim roles as required by the interim phase of support. However, in working towards the resourced school, equal consideration should be given to the development of all those involved in its realization.

If developments in INSET for special educational needs have failed to provide educated personnel on the scale required, an alternative approach will need to be developed which identifies those arrangements which are integral to the act of sharing responsibility.

Initial Teacher Training, Induction and INSET

At present there are few links between these three phases of teacher development. Whilst the LEA has increased its involvement with the IHE in the area of INSET, there has, to date, been little cooperation, other than in the placement of students in LEA schools, in the initial training of teachers. Neither has there been involvement by the IHE in the induction process. Clearly, if continuity is to be achieved, a way has to be found to involve both parties in all three phases.

As regards Initial Teacher Training, the indications point to some form of nationally agreed framework which stipulates the range of issues and alternatives for meeting special educational needs which should, as a minimum, acquaint the student with current practices across the country and prepare them for working in a range of Authorities. In addition, guidelines need to be issued to staff in IHEs as to the mechanisms for permeation. If special educational needs are to be addressed within departments, by department staff, it is essential that there is agreement as to the scope of this involvement.

The House of Commons Committee (1987) suggests that there is a need for a National Advisory Body, and indeed many professional bodies have been of the same opinion for some years. Such a body, if instituted, might well construct the framework and guidelines required.

There are also implications for the next phase of the teacher's development, namely induction. At present the probationary teacher is inducted into the school by whomever is responsible for staff development. In some schools this may be the Headteacher, in others the deputy head or senior teacher may have this as a specific responsibility. They are also inducted into the Authority by a variety of arrangements, which range from local teacher centre involvement to authority-wide probationary teacher days. All those involved in the induction process must, therefore, have knowledge of what has gone before in Initial Teacher Training, and be prepared to negotiate with the probationary teacher a programme of development. Since special educational needs permeate the whole of the curriculum and relate strongly to the organization of the school, they should be included in the induction programme. This is particularly important if the school has a policy for addressing special educational needs, and if the Authority has a policy for the development of provision.

As the process of induction is undertaken, it sets in motion the longer term development of the teacher and leads to identifying strengths and weaknesses, untapped competencies, and opportunities which are presented to enhance performance. The teacher will be involved in a review of his/her performance at an early stage. This review will indicate further INSET requirements which are clearly related to what is available within the school, the cluster or the Authority at large. It may also indicate the need for the teacher to be involved in shared working experiences, with colleagues recognized for their particular strengths and skills, or to impart their own strengths in the process of participation. This would recognize that the probationary teacher also has a part to play as a change agent. Indeed, such a role may well be actively encouraged by the LEA if such strengths are brought to the attention of those outside the school.

It is important that the content and format of the induction programme be grounded in an understanding, and expectation of, what is available to the teacher in the form of INSET activities within the Authority beyond the probationary period. If this is the case, continuity will be upheld, both with LEA and IHE INSET activities, since the LEA and IHE will have jointly planned these activities on the basis of a shared policy perspective.

This goes beyond the needs of the probationary teacher, because all staff will require a profile of development from which a school's needs can be identified and responded to by the LEA/IHE programme. The profile will suggest how staff development will proceed at the level of the individual school, across a group of schools or across the Authority. This can usefully form a wider profile for a cluster of schools or an Area within the LEA and most importantly give the LEA/IHE a clear indication of the responses it needs to make in key areas of INSET activity.

The responses could be subject-based or cross-curricular, and whilst taking account of special educational needs, would re-orientate emphasis to common needs in other areas of INSET. Providers for staff development could be drawn from the school, but also from the cluster, the Area, the LEA and the IHE. All these contributors would gain in confidence, and reflect leadership qualities, which in turn would provide the school and its partners with a clear direction for future development. This would have the effect of encouraging teachers to take initiative and to engage in offering colleagues the opportunity to contribute in a worthwhile manner. Inevitably, new skills will be imparted, especially enhancing the effective communication within the school and providing a continuous process of review and response. It will also allow teachers some control over their own development and sustain flexibility and choice in their chosen pathways.

Opportunities will be presented by the IHE for cross-fertilization of developments, as they bring together personnel from different schools, Areas, and LEAs. As a continuing process, the teachers attending the IHE INSET activities will be able to feed in alternative practices and models for meeting special educational needs in their schools, leading to further review and possible adaptation or adoption of viable alternatives. This will help to maintain the good intentions, enthusiasm, and positive attitudes brought by the probationary teacher to the school and LEA, and allow the LEA/IHE to decide which priorities need to be addressed.

All the participants can then be seen to be contributors to policy formulation, articulation and communication. As teachers enter into professional development within the service, they can be recognized as contributors, and valued members, who can be seen to enhance their personal worth and avoid stagnation through their individual intellectual development.

The possibilities of adopting the role of catalyst and development agent will depend upon the degree of accuracy achieved in assessing the teacher's strengths and weaknesses, and the proper realization of their current aspirations. The potential for development will therefore not be restricted to a few individuals within the Authority, who have been identified fortuitously, but be available to ALL.

Essentially, a pattern of continuing research and development would need to support this process through a programme of accreditation, which includes modular diplomas, higher degrees, teacher fellowships, and the secondment of teachers to teach on IHE/LEA INSET activities. This can not be achieved over a short period of time, and as with the goal of the *resourced school* and *educated personnel*, various interim phases will need to be identified.

Permeation

One way of ensuring a continuum, whilst at the same time integrating In-Service activities, is to operate the principle of permeation. As a practical example, we cite the case of a secondary school of approximately 600 pupils in an urban area. The newly-appointed Deputy Headteacher realizes that there is an urgent need to address the quality of provision for the 'least able' pupils. The school does not have sufficient staff to create a department for special educational needs, and over the years, has evolved a system whereby the fourth set in each subject contains the least able pupils with a more favourable teacher–pupil ratio. The Deputy Headteacher realizes that a policy of radical change would not be supported by the Headteacher but that the Headteacher is sympathetic to an appraisal of pupil needs. The Deputy Headteacher forms an alliance with the Head of the English department and between them they discuss tactics. The favoured strategy is that of calling together a voluntary working party. The working party has the brief of considering the extent and variety of skills required by the least able pupils, to enable them to be more successful in benefiting from these smaller classroom groups.

The working group decide to organize an INSET activity which will replace the staff meeting. The activity consists of the staff group dividing into small working units to identify these skills. In plenary session, it is discovered that the skills so identified are similar in each group, and that they cross subject boundaries. The working group, on analysing the results, decides to set aside one of the five directed INSET days to further explore the implications of this finding. Both the Deputy Headteacher and Head of English arrange to discuss the content of the day with an adviser. In the interim, they attend a seminar arranged within a local cluster of schools, where the topic is the direction of LEA policy regarding special educational needs in secondary education.

Following these two experiences, the Deputy Headteacher and Head of English realize that what they have in fact achieved in their school-based In-service to date is the identification of 'access' skills appropriate to all pupils. They resolve that the In-service day should focus on the permeation of these skills across the whole curriculum at all levels of ability. They also realize that their discovery has important consequences for the way in which groups of pupils are organized within the school, and that the development of access skills, in the areas of comprehension, reading, writing, oracy, etc., will focus on teacher development in the form of lesson construction, classroom arrangements, attitudes toward cross-curricular activity, etc. As a result, the working group begins to look more closely at the contribution which can be made by the LEA advisory services in other subject areas, but maintain the cross-curricular skills approach.

The working group decides to use the INSET day to raise awareness amongst the staff of the LEA's policy of meeting special educational needs by meeting the needs of all children. In addition, and on the advice of the adviser, they construct workshops around the level of understanding of the staff, noted from previous activity. The workshops, therefore, are targetted at prioritizing the skill needs already identified, examining these further for levels of competency and constructing observation schedules. They intend to take the INSET activity into the classroom via the observation schedule, and in identifying the highest priority, create a shared working experience.

Further, the working group realizes that some teachers may already have strengths in these areas, which are as yet unidentified, and that two probationary teachers in particular, because of their recent course input, have strategies available to them which it will be useful to disseminate to a wider group of staff. Thus, the school is able to use existing, and perhaps previously unused competencies from within its own staff strengths and can now look beyond the school's boundaries for further support and guidance. Within the school setting, therefore, there is a clear link between initial training, induction and In-service activities.

In this context, permeation can be thought of as operating in a number of ways. Initially, the permeation is discovered to be cross-curricular. That this had not occurred to the staff before must be a matter of concern, not only to those presently involved in constructing INSET activities, including the advisory services, but also those involved in initial training. However, we would contend that such a position is more common than current thinking or literature indicates, and that this has important implications for the approach made to permeation of special education issues at all levels, initial teacher training, induction and post-qualification in-service activity. Quite often permeation is viewed within the course team as one person's responsibility, where the task is to monitor inputs in terms of content and delivery so that the special educational needs aspect is given sufficient focus. Permeation is less likely to be viewed as the responsibility of all lecturers and In-service agents through the consideration of common skills, concepts and attitudes which give access to all areas of learning. If the responsibility is transferred to all participants within the school and/or Institute of Higher Education, this personal responsibility for the analysis of what occurs within the classroom or seminar room will quickly identify access skills common to all situations of learning, thus permeating the notion that pupils are entitled to access to all aspects of the curriculum, and that the quality of the skills, concepts and attitudes displayed by a pupil both demonstrates the level of acquisition and the degree to which this capability is enabled by the teacher.

A second level of permeation, operating in the above example, is that of strengths identified within the teaching group. By identifying those teachers, including those newly qualified, who have the ability to articulate skills demonstrated by the pupil, it is possible to consider ways of transmitting those skills to other members of staff. The logical extension of the activities identified by the Deputy Headteacher and Head of the English Department is that of facilitating shared working experiences which take these identified members of staff into other classrooms or arrange for members of staff to work cooperatively with them. A practical example might be mutual observation using an agreed checklist of identified pupil skills, with the purpose of discussing together ways and means of modifying lesson content or delivery to maximize and develop the skills thus observed.

A third level of permeation might be achieved by the introduction into the school-based In-Service activity an element of LEA policy through the advice and involvement of the advisory service. It is important that the discovery concerning access skills, made by the staff themselves, be reinforced and explored by an outside perspective. At some point, this permeation of ideas will be expanded further by the introduction of specific members of staff to INSET activities organized by the Institute of Higher Education. This offers a fourth level of permeation, that of ideas and concepts regarding the meeting of special educational needs across institutions and other professional groups.

What this example demonstrates is that permeation, of the sort described above, does lead to the formulation of a whole-school approach. It demonstrates that a whole-school approach is a vehicle, a legitimate means to an end, and not an end in itself. It is possible for a school to by-pass the interim phase of support, and by concentrating on personal responsibility, through activities which are of concern to all, achieve a whole-school approach, even without intention.

Conclusion

In this second part of the book we have drawn attention to the notion of educability as teacher competence, and have suggested ways in which the teacher, the school, the LEA and IHE can promote teacher development. The nature of INSET activities and the requirements of the resourced school, alongside a realignment of LEA resources and a redefinition of integration, has led us to the conclusion that a carefully devised continuum of activities is required, one which reflects the needs of teachers, schools and LEA policy — a continuum which operates throughout the teachers career, from initial training to INSET, whilst at the same time offering a multiplicity of activities at school, cluster and IHE level.

Part III

Decision Time

An Overview

Conclusion

We began this book with a consideration of the legacy of thought and action which adversely affects all those contributing to the development of special educational needs provision. We have described the sum of that legacy as inertia. This inertia, we have argued, is maintained at its present high level by the unwillingness of the participants to accept responsibility at a personal level. We have explored the legacy, and concluded that the inability of the individual to accept responsibility is founded upon a view of special educational need which has not fully assimilated the implications of meeting the individual needs of all children. Amongst the issues raised, one stands out as critical to the unlocking of the legacy — the personal development of the professionals involved: administrators, advisers, teachers, lecturers, and agents of allied services. We have, however, concentrated on the teacher, since it is the teacher who is at the centre of the development of the *resourced school* and the notion of *educability*, with its allied notion of integration, which we view as the final goal; the resourced school, in terms of the educability of all pupils, being the key which will unlock the inertia. The personal development of others we have viewed as instrumental to achieving this goal, and to this end we have pursued the question of the IHE and LEA evolving a common perspective on policy direction and INSET provision.

The structure of INSET, and in particular, the proposed model of continuity, which we have emphasized should reflect a measure of supported devolution from IHE to school, with the attendant issues surrounding the whole-school approach, the role of co-ordinator, and the dynamic process, should, we have argued, lead to a transformation of policy into practice. This, we contend, is best achieved through a series of planned interim phases. In offering this view of development, we have rejected the development of support services as a permanent feature of the resourced school, and thereby re-emphasized our view that the development of INSET activities must be personal and school oriented, and not, as is currently the case, level and/or role dominated.

In this final section, we are concerned to make the point that none of this can be achieved without deliberate action on the part of the LEA and

IHE, through the vehicle of policy making and implementation. Without a bold and imaginative consideration of what policy is, how it comes into being, how it is contributed to, and how it is enacted, special educational needs will always be *someone else's problem*.

We consider it crucial, therefore, that we conclude this book with a closer examination of the mechanisms of policy-making and decision-making, both in the IHE and the LEA.

Chapter 10

Decision-making Mechanisms

Introduction

Throughout this book we have referred to the Local Education Authority and the Institute of Higher Education but as yet we have offered no definition of these terms. Whilst it is common practice to refer to these two authorities in this way, it is, we believe, quite wrong to make criticism without first identifying what is actually meant by these terms, and that more consideration should be given to addressing the elements of decision-making and responsibility within the two structures.

This need was particularly emphasised when one of the authors of this book attended a seminar to discuss the implications of recent research into support teaching. The author of the research concluded the day by offering a catalogue of 'negligence' on the part of LEAs, and listing a number of actions the LEA should take. When asked what she thought an LEA was, the author of the research offered no answer, and indeed appeared to consider the question somewhat mischievous. In the heated debate which followed, it became clear that the author of the research had no working knowledge of LEAs and had very little idea as to their complexity. This lack of understanding is of course two-way. Much of the defensiveness, as exhibited in recent publications against the GRIST initiative, by 'academics', stems from a genuine fear that those taking decisions within the LEAs do not understand the role of the Institute of Higher Education in INSET. It is important, therefore, that some attempt be made to explain the complex structures of both institutions, and this is probably best done by reference to decision-making processes.

The authors of this book are fortunate in that they both have dual experience of working within an Institute of Higher Education and a Local Education Authority, and the following observations are drawn from that experience.

The Local Education Authority

At one extreme the LEA can be considered as the sum of all those who work within it: elected members, teachers, administrators, advisors, etc. At the other, it can be regarded as a service within a democratic system which has customers, rate-payers and service consumers, and therefore has its corporate identity in the administration of local politics. Between these two extremes there is a hierarchy of decision-making, stretching from school policy to LEA policy, which includes a wide range of employees, all of whom contribute, but not equally. The inequality of contribution is, to some degree, inevitable, but it is this which leads the teacher to consider that he/she is but an employee of the LEA, can make criticism of the LEA, and by implication is not part of the LEA. A parent, on the other hand, might not agree with this perception, particularly if he/she is dissatisfied with the quality of performance exhibited by that teacher.

The more involved an individual is with decision-making which affects relatively large parts of the service, the more it is likely he/she will consider themselves to be part of the LEA. An adviser, for example, will identify with the Authority, because his/her advice affects the overall policy and decisions made. He/she is unlikely, however, to feel as much identity as an Assistant Education Officer, since the adviser lacks the executive power of the Officer. Likewise, the Officer, in the face of a strong political group, is likely to identify less with the Authority if his/her decisions are heavily constrained by Member involvement. Whilst, therefore, Members are the only group within the LEA to have the actual power to ratify policy, the process by which that policy reaches the Council Chamber ensures the involvement of others; and the degree to which it does determines what the LEA is.

The decision-making machinery may vary from LEA to LEA, but certain fundamental structures remain the same. Within the Council Chamber, education will only be one of a number of services provided by the Council, albeit the largest. General policy will be dictated by the 'ruling' group and the strength of this policy will largely depend upon the current majority. The day-to-day work of the Education Committee is largely dealt with in smaller committees responsible for such aspects of the service as schools, curriculum, and finance and general purposes. The sub-committees, themselves, will have working parties, which may or may not have wider representation, and it is in this context that special educational needs will be debated. Some authorities will have established working parties which report to sub-committees, others will debate issues and policy statements brought by officers direct to sub-committee. It is possible, therefore, for three levels of decision-making to be involved, even within the immediate orbit of the Council Chamber.

The second sphere of influence is that of the Chief Education Officer. Whilst all committee documents will pass through his/her hands before 'Member involvement', much of the decision-making, particularly in terms of what issues are to be addressed and how they are to be presented, will have already taken place at the level of the Assistant Education Officer. Most

LEAs will have an officer who has responsibility for special educational needs. In larger LEAs, important documentation, such as policy statements, may need to pass through at least three levels of officer before reaching the Elected Members. In the largest LEAs, where there are Divisional or Area Education Officers, this may increase to as many as five.

The third level of influence is that of the Professional Adviser. Within some LEAs this will include the Principal Educational Psychologist, but in general will be confined to a general or specialist adviser. Within larger LEAs, there may be a specialist adviser working to a general adviser. Most LEAs will, in addition, have advisory teachers for special educational needs.

At this level there will be copious working groups, mostly minuted as 'meetings'. These will variously represent the opinions of advisers and Educational Psychologists; advisers and Officers; advisers, Officers and Educational Psychologists; advisers and advisory teachers etc., depending upon the structure of Officers, advisers, advisory teachers, and Educational Psychologists within the LEA. At this level alone, a major proposal may require discussion by as many as four to eight groups of people, and usually in a pre-determined order.

Depending upon what is debated, and the decision-making structure within the LEA, teacher representatives and representatives from other services may be involved at any level from adviser to elected member. Below this sphere of decision-making, however, most debate is 'consultative'. This will include governing bodies, staff meetings, teacher associations, etc.

It will be appreciated from the above that no decision is made easily or lightly. When all four spheres of decision-making and consultation are taken into account, it is likely that a new proposal will have been debated, and some aspect of decision-making taken place, in at least ten to twelve forums, the exact number being somewhat dependent upon the origin of the initiative.

The question of the origin of a proposal is an important one because it highlights the complexity of the decision-making process. Change may be enforced from without, via the Government and the DES, or it may originate from within, and at any one of the four levels so described. It is this which makes the statement prefaced by 'the Local Education Authority ought', so naive and misguided. Responsibility and accountability are not easily identified.

The quest for a coherent policy, therefore, is not an easy one. The initiative for change may arise from any layer of authority, and the length of time it takes to come to fruition, will, to some degree, depend upon its point of origin. Clearly, a pronouncement from the Chairman of the Council will meet with a more rapid response than if the same idea is propagated by the adviser. The lower down the chain, the more people there are to convince, and the more groups will debate and find fault. Most initiatives do not come from the Chairman, they have to be nurtured, shaped and brought to fruition through a long series of 'political' arenas. Initiatives within an LEA are not for the faint-hearted, they require staying power and considerable patience. At the end of the day, however, success will be a matter of personal responsibility.

The Institute of Higher Education

Institutes of Higher Education differ in their organizational structure, but a common underlying pattern exists. One way of describing this is to follow the route of an advanced diploma, from its construction to its adoption as an In-Service qualification, and the decision-making machinery involved.

This process would typically begin with a small group of colleagues working as a team in the area of special educational needs. This group, who may well represent different departments, would construct a course proposal for discussion with an *ad hoc* steering group consisting of teachers, advisers, academic staff and students. Following this informal consultation, the outline would then be submitted to a departmental meeting. From this meeting the proposal would progress to a sub-committee or working group of the faculty, and if approved in principle be tabled at the faculty as a whole. If supported by the faculty, it would progress to the committee responsible for course submissions before going on to the academic board for final approval. Depending upon the implications for resources, in some institutions it may be considered by the governing body. Between these various stages there would be involvement and consultation with both the proposed external examiner, more so if the decision is concerned with re-validation or major change to an existing course, and the external validating body. If the institute is a university, the latter may be an internal body. In the case of a polytechnic this will be the National Council for Academic Awards, and for an independent college it may well be an associated university department. Having completed this cycle of proposal, modification and consultation, the final approval rests with the validating body. However, at each and every stage, modifications of considerable proportions may be suggested, with consequent delay. At each stage of modification it may be necessary to return to previous groups/committees to re-enter the cycle of decision-making machinery of the IHE; progress is very much dependent upon appropriate timing in order that proposals can pass as smoothly as possible through committee 'cycles'. A delay at any point may have significant repercussions.

Although this may appear a cumbersome procedure, as with the passage of proposals within the LEA, no decision regarding the worth and relevance of a course, or In-Service activity, is made lightly. Indeed, it could be argued that such checks and balances are an integral part of ensuring quality.

As various government initiatives have placed pressure upon LEAs, and in turn IHEs, to respond more quickly to priorities in INSET activity, this somewhat drawn out process of decision-making has rendered the Institute of Higher Education incapable of responding within the time limits required.

In addition, the move towards customer-orientated INSET activity has signalled the demise of traditional INSET courses, which, some LEAs claim, have failed to meet changing circumstances. The INSET activities for special educational needs, for example, as a priority area within the GRIST initiative, have resulted in LEAs, possibly unrealistically, expecting IHEs to shape their activities to meet LEA requirements. A lack of understanding as to the decision-making processes within the IHE has perhaps contributed to a misperception of the IHE's response.

Working Together

Given the complexity of the two decision-making processes outlined above, it follows that progress will be impeded unless some consideration is given to the amelioration of the constraints which these processes inevitably raise. Realistically, despite attempts by the IHEs to circumvent bureaucracy, there is very little that can be done to rationalize these processes. Indeed, we have argued that such processes are necessary if individual responsibility is to be exercised at all levels of authority, and that such processes ensure participation and consultation. If we accept this position, then it would seem to us that the most useful way forward is to ensure that as many personnel as possible within the LEA decision-making process become *au fait* with the decision-making processes operating within the IHE, and vice versa; and that shared working experiences be 'manufactured' in order that common ground can be established. Given the nature of what is to be achieved in the development of provision to meet special educational needs, it would seem to us that this common ground is best established in the area of policy. In contributing to the development and implementation of policy, the IHE and LEA will enter into a venture which will inevitably lead to In-Service activities which properly address the development needs of the LEA. In our opinion, this will be more so if the policy itself is grounded in the notion of personal responsibility, with consequent focusing on the teacher's personal development. We, therefore, now turn our attention to the question of policy, its formulation and implementation.

Chapter 11

Policy

Introduction

A classroom teacher's view of policy may well be closely linked to their view of the curriculum, namely that it is 'received' and therefore acted upon. It is unlikely that teachers will be willing to participate in the process of policy-making if their experience of other critical decision-making processes, such as those involved in curriculum development, has been a passive one. What this suggests, therefore, is that the development of a special educational needs response within a school, is contingent upon both a degree of development within the curriculum which is conducive to the education of all children in one setting, and, in consequence, a degree of involvement in decision-making which makes participation in the development of LEA policy an expectation rather than an imposition.

An examination of what policy is, and how it is disseminated, must reflect this position, and to this end, we have chosen to include in the policy-making process aspects of preparation, consultation and organization which, together with the actual written document, ensure that the policy is a dynamic one, initiating and fostering change. As a means of articulating our ideas, we have chosen to use the word 'policy' as a mnemonic, expressing those ideas under the headings of:

P perspective
O organized change
L leadership
I initiatives
C communication
Y yourself

Perspective

A perspective will be based upon an amalgam of current thinking and examples of practice, culled from national and international trends. This perspective will give direction to future strategies and will outline a review process which will enable the LEA to move forward from its present position. It would include a process of consultation, whereby ideas can be set out and possible structures exemplified. During this period of consultation, the underpinning philosophy will be established, aspects of which will, by its nature, not be open to negotiation, but which will invite adaptation and refinement. This should also encourage creativity, vision, and imagination, and will draw upon a range of experience within the Authority. A suitable example is the perspective of the resourced school and educated personnel, as described in this book, whereby such a perspective would have some non-negotiable elements relating to the philosophy of integration, shared working experiences, and personal acceptance of responsibility for educating all children currently within the school. The negotiable elements would include the practicalities of adopting such a philosophy, alternate pathways, the stages essential to achieving the goal, and the time scale involved.

The perspective, as well as providing direction, would give much-needed leadership to disparate viewpoints, many of which will be isolated, entrenched, and may indeed actually fetter possibilities for taking initiative and responsibility. The perspective could be presented by the IHE, the LEA advisers, or ideally, through a joint process. It would begin the policy-making exercise and invite further development. To date, many of the LEA advisers and IHE personnel have entered the domain of special educational needs from specialized, segregated, environments, and consequently have been unable to present an alternative perspective. In our examination of the available statements of LEA policy, we noted that these were heavily constrained by a perspective which stemmed from a review of existing provision. To generate a different perspective we are suggesting that consideration be given to philosophy and direction before a review is undertaken, otherwise, the sheer size and complexity of traditional forms of provision will impose a method of review which considers each category of handicap in turn. Each attempt at review may suggest its own, segregated, form of advancement, which finally mitigates against a coherent and cohesive strategy for meeting individual need.

This isolated and segregationist approach has tended to lead professionals into consolidating their own position, determined as they are, through concerns of self-interest and self-preservation, to maintain as much of the status quo as is possible, given the prevailing climate of opinion. Without a clearly stated philosophy and effective structures for participation and consultation, such vested interests will flourish, reinforcing the state of inertia earlier described.

This in turn raises the very important question of the origin of the perspective. If the LEA relies entirely upon its advisory service to generate policy statements, albeit in conjunction with officers and teachers, it may not in the long term be effecting the best possible change at its disposal. A heavy responsibility is placed on Members to both make appropriate appointments and be aware of current thinking. It also requires them to take more than a passing interest in the formulation of strategies for developing special educational needs provision, and this means formulating a perspective. Likewise, the personnel in the IHE have a responsibility to involve themselves in the formulation of such a perspective, and if necessary, speak out against entrenched positions. Clearly, to prevent discord, it would be better if the machinery for establishing a perspective, possibly in the form of a document for debate, did, at the outset, include all interested parties.

If the LEA adviser or IHE personnel are to make a substantial contribution to the generation of a perspective, they must be exposed to alternative viewpoints, and be supported by a substantial programme of research and development. This in turn should generate meetings across LEAs and IHEs, and ideally would encompass colleagues in other countries.

A clear perspective is the corner-stone of development; without it there is no direction. The following illustrates one LEA's attempt at establishing a perspective. The document is the culmination of a long series of participatory activities, which also involved a local IHE. It does not at this point represent policy, but a stage in policy development.

TOWARDS A COHERENT POLICY FOR MEETING SPECIAL EDUCATIONAL NEEDS: A CONSULTATION DOCUMENT

POLICY DIRECTION

1.1 The following is based upon three years of consultation and discussion with representative groups involved in special educational needs across the Authority. In particular, residential conferences have been held to debate the direction of the service, in the light of the 1981 Act, with Headteachers, senior staff and teachers-in-charge of support services; this has included representation from ordinary primary and secondary schools. A wider consultation is now required, encompassing parents, voluntary bodies, the social services, health services, and teacher organizations as well as schools and colleges.

1.2 The development of policy for meeting special educational needs provision should be based on four major assumptions:

1.2.1 The *integration* of all children with special educational needs is a prime target, and that this can best be achieved through the process of integrating the working patterns of those currently involved in separate provision, both with each other and with the mainstream. In its third report (May 1987) *Special Educational Needs: Implementation of the Education Act 1981*, the House of Commons Education, Science and Arts Committee concluded that in order to support the principle of integration, it is not necessary to support the principle of insisting that all children be educated in primary and secondary schools rather than special schools. Integration is a process in which children with special educational needs mix with their peers in a regular and planned way. The report accepts that the term also embraces collaborative ventures between special schools and ordinary schools.

1.2.2 *'Parents as partners'* becomes a reality within the Authority by the introduction of clear guidelines for the involvement of parents at *every stage* of assessment, intervention and review, and the active encouragement of parents to participate, wherever feasible, in the education of their child.

1.2.3 The changing concept of special educational need, brought about by the Education Act 1981, suggests that fundamental changes be made to the service, but such changes are unlikely to be successful without a strong In-service Education and Training policy acting as the vehicle for change. An INSET policy is required which addresses the professional development of teachers in the areas of attitudes, skills and competencies.

1.2.4 Wherever possible, resources be re-distributed to early identification and intervention. Pre-school provision for children with special educational needs will therefore be a priority; so will the establishment of preventative measures in ordinary schools.

1.3 There is a very wide diversity of provision in the Authority, most of this is based on special schools and units developed prior to the Education Act 1981. This provision is a tribute to the Authority's vigorous commitment to meeting special educational needs as it was under the ten categories of handicap; and in its extensiveness, offers considerable potential for the future. The 1981 Act has replaced the ten categories with a broader view of special educational needs which is more consistent with meeting the needs of individual pupils. It is now recognized that in its present form the organization of provision does not easily allow for this, and therefore, to some degree, militates against further development.

1.4 The meeting of individual need, without recourse to category of handicap, can be fostered in the future by the introduction of support to the ordinary school, support both for the child and his/her teacher. This support can be developed over a period of years, and achieved by the gradual devolution of resources away from specialist provision towards integrated provision. However, in seeking to meet individual need, whilst at the same time honouring the commitment of the Authority to the principle of integration, we cannot suddenly move children into ordinary school unsupported and unprepared. We cannot change the provision overnight, nor can we in the short term provide the mainstream teacher with the necessary skills and confidence to meet every child's individual needs. A degree of separated provision, therefore, albeit integrated into a cluster of ordinary schools, is envisaged for the foreseeable future.

1.5 As part of the process of change, the notion of 'special educational needs' will be subsumed in the broader approach of meeting the educational needs of all children.

1.6 If pupil needs are to be considered on an individual basis, a broad spectrum of integration and educational possibilities will be required, from support in the ordinary classroom to separate provision. The 1981 Act will require the Authority to continue to issue *statements of need*, but as support to the mainstream of education develops, it is possible that this might reduce significantly from the 2 per cent currently involved in this procedure. The provision for meeting special educational needs should reflect the Warnock Committee's suggestion that 20 per cent of all children, at some time, will require some form of additional support. A continuum of provision will avoid the necessity to differentiate sharply between those with statements and those without.

1.7 One way of achieving this, is to find ways for the teachers in each of these separate provisions to work together to support ordinary schools, to devolve resources to ordinary schools, and thereby change current staff into supportive agents. In the process, the barriers will be broken down between the special and ordinary schools.

1.8 An approach is required which fosters a closer relationship with other agencies, particularly those related to the Area Health Authorities and Social Services; an approach which devolves the responsibility for encouraging such links to the special school(s) within a cluster, a cluster being a small group of ordinary and special schools seeking to share a common view and responsibility for pupils with special educational needs in their locality.

1.9 An Authority-wide strategy is required, but the needs of each locality within the administrative Areas should be recognized. Each Area will therefore need to develop its own Area Support and Development Plan, possibly with regard to the INSET clusters already devised.

IMPLICATIONS FOR SPECIAL SCHOOLS

2.1 It is proposed that each child be provided with an integration plan, this plan to specify the development stages for involvement with mainstream education.

2.2 The special school to develop as a *centre of excellence* as regards assessment, intervention and support of children with more complex and multiple needs, and as such, to serve a local cluster of ordinary schools for development, support and advice. To maintain this excellence, the special school may need to retain an element which functions specifically as a school. As a first step, they should be required to embark on a thorough review of the curriculum, and thereby develop common ground with mainstream provision.

2.3 In order to allow for the development of an appropriate curriculum in special schools, some consideration will need to be given to the difficulties and desirability of all-age schools.

2.4 The relationship between 14–19 education in special schools and other possibilities offered by Further Education Colleges and ordinary schools, requires further examination, with a view to providing the best possible opportunities for all pupils with special educational needs in the 14–19 group.

2.5 It follows from earlier discussion that in adopting an approach to meeting special educational needs which reflects the 1981 Act, the Authority will be developing a continuum of provision which no longer reflects discrete categories of handicap, and it will therefore be necessary to encourage the growth of the special school as a support and resource centre. In order to achieve this, it may be necessary to review the way in which special schools are staffed, making it possible for teachers within the special school to operate a support role which is effective in reducing the numbers of children entering their school, thereby releasing further staff for support in ordinary schools. This method of devolving resources from specialist provision to mainstream education requires further investigation.

IMPLICATIONS FOR MAINSTREAM SCHOOLS

3.1 The development is two-way; the special segregated provision needs to be changed to accommodate a supportive role, but at the same time, a response is expected from the ordinary school. This should be based on guidelines to be issued to every primary and secondary school. These guidelines should be produced by working parties of primary and secondary school senior staff, encouraging the formulation of a whole school policy, and should be issued by the end of the academic year.

3.2 It is expected that The Senior Management Team of each school will designate a senior member of staff to act as the Co-ordinator. Following the guidelines, the school will produce a written policy which reflects the above considerations, and which involves all members of staff.

Organized Change

There comes a point in the development of provision when decisions have to be made as regards wholesale re-organization of facilities and personnel.

In our own perspective, for example, it would be necessary to physically re-organize, on the basis of our belief that the integration of children with special educational needs is best achieved through the integration of the working practices of those currently involved in discrete services. The devolution of resources away from segregated provision to integrated provision, i.e., from the special school to the resourced school, could not be left to chance.

Clearly, the timing of organized change is critical. We would consider it inappropriate for an LEA to embark upon a programme of restructuring its services, without first devising, disseminating and developing, a shared perspective indicating the direction of change, as in the example above.

The relationship between the IHE and the LEA as regards the provision of INSET activities which both prepare for, and support, a re-organization, is fundamental. We would consider that organized change of the sort, say, that devolves the LEA personnel from a school for children with moderate learning difficulties into mainstream support, would require a considerable amount of joint planning to establish acceptable pathways of personal development for those teachers undertaking this change. Organized change must, therefore, include organized INSET activity.

A first requirement of change is leadership, and quite a large element of the INSET activities must be about coping with change and assuming the role of change agent. INSET activities, at this stage, therefore, must essentially facilitate those wishing to adopt leadership roles.

Leadership

As far as the development of policy is concerned, leadership is also the vehicle for effective participation, and whilst the management of organized change requires a form of leadership conducive to implementing structural changes, and therefore a greater degree of managerial skills *per se*, what is actually required throughout, if the organized change is to be seen as part of a wider strategy, are qualities which encourage, enthuse, support, guide, build confidence and self esteem, share a sense of purpose, and above all foster good channels of communication. Leadership, in this sense, requires a wider view of INSET activity than that described above. It is essentially concerned with enhancing personal qualities with a view to encouraging spontaneous initiatives.

Referring back to our example of a documented perspective, it is clear that leadership is required at several levels of responsibility and stages of implementation. Initially, those formulating the perspective would describe the needs of the LEA and match these to the existing provision, as reviewed.

The leadership characteristics would be exemplified in the way current legislation, recent national and international trends, and different LEA responses to both of these, are interpreted. Leadership at this level requires both an imaginative stance and a willingness to diverge from national trends if these are perceived to be inappropriate or insufficient to meet the needs of the LEA. There are, however, dangers in this process. Checks and balances must be an integral feature. In order to monitor any proposed change in direction, it will be necessary for the leadership to receive a critical analysis and an appraisal of the proposed changes, so that the perspective may be further informed.

As we have already pointed out, an element of the IHE's obligation to the LEA is to judge the merit of any initiative through a process of trials, surveys, and interpretation, leading to a forthright assessment of its viability and the implications for implementation. IHE personnel would also be able to test out and pilot particular aspects, and through its programme of INSET activity, involve teachers at every stage.

The next stage of leadership would be that of initiative taken by interested teachers who wish to explore aspects of the emerging perspective. From this they would adapt and modify the practical interpretation, and in so doing, give feedback to the initial perspective for further development. This procedure, therefore, further informs and shapes the perspective, prior to its adoption as policy. Such refinement acts as a supplementary check on the efficacy of the perspective and provides a real and practical model for others to emulate. A new level of leadership therefore emerges, where personnel practised in new modes of working confidently articulate the issues and give support and direction to others, including those leaders who have initiated the debate.

Following this, a further level of leadership can be identified. As previously stated, there must at some stage in the development of the LEA response be organized change, where personnel are appointed to be responsible for the implementation of the policy, and where clear direction can be indicated. Development of the policy would be one aspect of leadership at this level, and evaluation of its effectiveness another. Once the policy is in operation, a fundamental feature of leadership will be the ability to communicate aspects of change, as they happen, to all those involved and affected.

Effective leadership promotes, sustains, evaluates and communicates initiatives, in a way which allows the perspective to evolve into policy, and leads the LEA through organized change to its desired goal.

Initiatives

Initiatives are the bed-rock of development. Within the perspective, initiatives would be encouraged in order to test out models and provide feedback. But initiatives of a different kind can also be fostered. These would be of a spontaneous nature and would help to clarify issues, difficulties and management implications affecting future proposals. For many teachers, such initiative-taking will be linked to their changing role *vis-à-vis* their perception as to how the perspective will develop and be practically implemented. Initiatives of this type are not to be confused with those planned by the LEA, often in the form of pilot projects which have a formal recognition and therefore operate within the constraints laid down by the Authority. Spontaneous initiatives, in the context of an LEA that is receptive to a dynamic form of policy development will be encouraged and facilitated in the expectation that new avenues of development will emerge which will enrich the current perspective. In our opinion, a policy for meeting special educational needs will be impoverished if it does not encompass this form of dynamic activity.

In the context of the Policy Consultation Document outlined above, we describe below a range of spontaneous initiatives which might contribute to the translation of perspective into policy.

1.2.1 Collaborative ventures between special schools and ordinary schools

A school for pupils with severe learning difficulties initiates with a local secondary school a programme of locational integration. A teacher, through negotiation, acquires a room within the secondary school, and establishes a work base for pupils aged 14+. The intention of the initiative being thus far successfully realized, a further, unplanned, phase evolves, whereby some pupils with severe learning difficulties attend mainstream practical lessons. This involvement increases to a point where both teachers and pupils, from both schools, exchange classes, thus providing a model of integration which operates at the functional and social level, as well as the locational level first intended.

1.2.2 Parents as partners

The staff of a special school for pupils with emotional and behavioural difficulties decide to invite parents to contribute to the review procedure by involving them in the construction of a detailed individual programme. Most of the parents respond enthusiastically and some request opportunities for involvement within the school setting. The staff group decide to accede to these requests, and the interests of some of the parents are employed in broadening activities within the curriculum. This brings about a better understanding of the pupils' needs, both for the parents and the teachers. In addition, it heightens the pupil's awareness of his or her response to the programme on offer. As a result relationships improve all round.

1.2.3 INSET activities as a vehicle for change

A support teacher attached to a cluster of primary schools responds to the request of a group of teachers to talk about reading difficulties. An evening meeting is set up in one of the schools where the support teacher decides to widen the topic to include aspects of paired reading. Following a declared interest by a number of teachers, the support teacher arranges for a demonstration to be given, which involves a parent and pupil. The teachers, under the guidance of the support teacher, embark upon a plan to involve parents in paired reading. The unforeseen aspect of this initiative is that the parents become further involved in the classroom, working alongside both the teacher and the support teacher. This development requires the support teacher to re-consider her role as In-Service agent, since the follow-up support is focused on changing parent/teacher perceptions rather than giving direct advice about children's reading difficulties.

1.8 Fostering a closer relationship with other agencies

A Headteacher of an infant school is concerned to meet the needs of pre-school children within her school's catchment area. She is approached by the local play-group leader who asks for access to a room and possible teacher help with a group of disadvantaged children. The Headteacher, whilst offering support, needs further resources to accomplish what is required. She decides to contact as many professionals as possible to act as a pressure group. A meeting is held within the school attended by representatives from various social agencies. Each visitor briefly describes their role and some common understanding is achieved. The meeting decides to hold further sessions to explore the issues regarding better links and improved communications. The LEA representative is able to locate resources to establish a nursery unit and the various agencies represented agree to a joint-funding arrangement which ensures the continuing support and cooperation of those involved.

Communication

Throughout this book we have made reference to the central issue of communication. In chapter 6 we explored the problem of communication between LEA and IHE, in chapter 5 the need for participation and consequent demands on communication between the management of the school and the support services, and in chapter 7 the major role of communication in the development of a whole-school policy. Further, in chapter 4 we focused on the need for good communication in developing school-based INSET, and at the other end of the continuum of INSET activities, we have argued, in chapter 9, the need for communication in the construction of a continuum of INSET activities. However, no matter how good the communication at these levels, little progress will be made in meeting individual need, through the process of personal responsibility, if communication is found to be poor *across* these levels. What is most striking about the case study is that it clearly demonstrates the link between communication, personal responsibility and the meeting of individual need. Communication must therefore be addressed at the macro level of co-ordinating and integrating the work of the teacher, school, associated agencies, support teacher, LEA officers and advisers and INSET-providing institutions. The best way to achieve this, we believe, is to construct communication systems around the needs of the child. Figure 4 attempts to illustrate this.

By examining an individual child's needs in some detail, through the case study, we have highlighted the fact that whilst an LEA can establish a communication system, this system often fails to address the individual needs of the child. As with any organizational structure within an institution, the areas of responsibility and the concomitant duties of personnel, whilst clearly defined, have boundaries which are less easily delineated. Where one person's responsibility begins and ends, therefore, means that there are fuzzy areas of overlap, where the taking of responsibility can be avoided or abdicated. The very large 'role set' of those attempting to meet an individual child's needs makes the number of overlaps considerable, and there are all too many opportunities for fuzzy areas to exist, with accompanying undetermined responsibility.

The process of communication is itself the starting point for identifying where the child is, in terms of his/her development, and if the communication between teacher and pupil is of a satisfactory nature, the quality of the identification process will be raised. If the communication is inadequate, the child's needs may well be overlooked, information will not be gleaned from other sources, and continuous assessment will not to be instituted. If the communication is appropriate, the teacher will take responsibility for instituting a planning process which meets the child's needs; selecting priorities; setting targets; sequencing the programme; identifying resources; timing the interventions and their frequency; and collating those items of information essential to meeting the child's needs. Similarly, in an effort to maintain momentum, the teacher will seek support from others within and without the school, so that motivation will be sustained. The relationships will continue, and a consistent approach be encouraged. To monitor progress, further communication will be required so that essential modifications, adjustments and involvement can be transmitted to others associated with meeting the child's needs.

The teacher's position within the school will be such that he/she will seek assistance and support in order to widen the responsibility and contribute to a whole-school approach to meeting the needs of all children. Personal responsibility moves towards collective responsibility, but in the process the personal responsibility accepted by the teacher is not abdicated.

Figure 4: Communication and the needs of the child

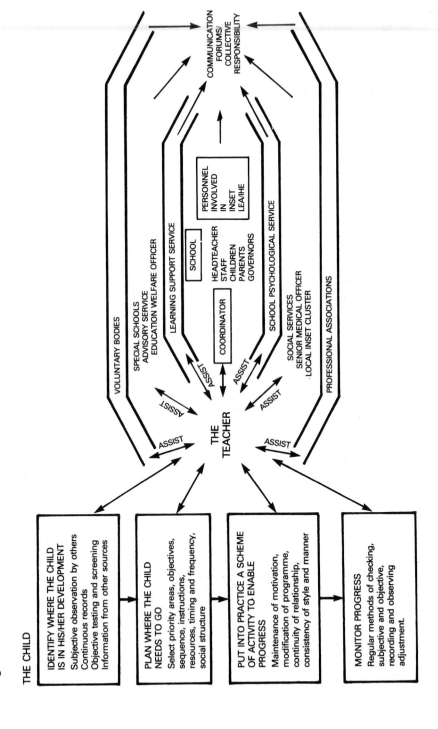

Beyond this, assistance will be sought from the support service external to the school, which will include the various social, health and educational agencies indicated in the diagram. In order to avoid the fuzzy areas of overlap, responsibility for meeting the child's individual needs would seem to require forums where collective responsibility is accepted, so that less effective forms of communication, such as those associated with the collation of isolated, and often conflicting, written reports, can be avoided. All too frequently, as exemplified in the case study, the passing of case files and partial information through memoranda leads to unacceptable delay in initiating practical responses. It also leads to a confusion as to where individual responsibility lies, with the main burden of responsibility resting solely with the parents.

A good example of such a forum can be found in the Dagenham and Barking LEA, for example, where corporate responsibility is assumed in a caucus which establishes needs, with the same caucus writing the legal statement. Rather than one person writing the statement from collated written evidence, the various contributors, including the parents, discuss the needs of the child, and arrive at a consensus to specify the needs and provision.

As far as the development of policy is concerned, the process of communication is cyclical. Good communication systems inform the perspective and the perspective generates good communication systems. The vital thread which holds them together and sustains continuity and coherence across all the elements of communication thus far mentioned, is a policy which has at its heart the notion of meeting special educational needs through teacher development. As previously stated, the vehicle to achieve this is dynamic In-service activity. It is self evident, therefore, that the most appropriate form of communication to bring cohesion to the perspective, organized change, leadership qualities and initiatives outlined above, is In-service activity which is planned to encompass all these elements.

We conclude this section by posing the following questions which all parties will need to address if communication is to be enhanced.

1. Is the teacher aware of the LEA structure and the mechanics of accessing support from available agencies?
2. What is the quality of relationship between teacher, school, parents, local community and others?
3. Are teachers and other professionals allowed sufficient time and opportunities to communicate effectively?
4. How influential are those responsible for communicating essential information?
5. Who decides who is to be involved in identifying, assessing and meeting the child's needs? Having taken the decision, how are teachers' untapped competencies and skills utilized?
6. Are all the participants given adequate opportunities to contribute?
7. Is the quality of information being passed sufficient to make the best decision possible?

8. Is there an element of sharing responsibility, resources, and expertise across traditional boundaries?
9. Are *all* the relevant parties consulted and involved?
10. Are teachers actively encouraged, both by the communication system and the decision-making machinery, to take personal responsibility?
11. Did the above considerations inform the development of LEA policy?
12. Did the above considerations inform the development of INSET activities?

Yourself

Whoever you are, parent, teacher, administrator, manager, co-ordinator, adviser, Educational Psychologist, support teacher, lecturer, or representative of an outside agency, your contribution is not given in isolation. Your action or inaction can, and does, have a profound effect on the quality of education experienced by the individual child. Personal responsibility, therefore, must first and foremost address itself to the quality of human relationships between all those involved with children.

Secondly, personal responsibility must be taken for the quality of communication as and where it affects the individual. Whilst good communication systems can be set up by those in authority, the effectiveness of those systems is entirely dependent upon individual contributions and commitment. That this is a critical aspect of meeting special educational needs is borne out by the case study, where communication is severely restricted by the poor quality and efficiency of the communication structure set up by the LEA and the actions of inefficient communicators at a personal level.

Thirdly, personal responsibility is demonstrated when the individual actively seeks to improve their performance by endeavouring to enhance skills, competencies and attitudes by entering into a process of personal and professional development.

Chapter 12

A Vehicle for Change

In figure 5, *A Vehicle for Change*, we have attempted to summarize all of the aspects pertinent to meeting special educational needs discussed in this book, and in so doing, place them in a relationship which illustrates the central importance of the interdependence between *dynamic In-service activities* and *clear policy direction*. On the journey from the legacy to the resourced school, these two fundamental aspects of the *vehicle for change* form the point of focus for decision-making within the two frameworks of the local education authority and the institute of higher education, and provide the rationale for partnership in decision making and implementation at all levels.

The legacy, embodied in the case study, has shown that decision-making processes, both within the Local Education Authority and the Institute of Higher Education, have failed to address the central issues of the diverse nature of provision and associated segregation and isolation; the lack of involvement coupled with poor communication; and the excessive bureaucratic procedures which inappropriately act upon imprecise legislation, lacking, as it does, any clear policy direction. This has accumulated, and culminated in inertia which has led to the tendency for all groups of decision-makers to regard the meeting of a child's individual needs as *someone else's problem*.

The unlocking of the legacy, we have argued, lies in the attainment of the resourced school. This goal requires a form of decision-making which leads to the establishment of full participation and effective communication; the creation of a common perspective which fosters personal responsibility; the acceptance of the concept of a school for all, with its concomitant, the entitlement curriculum; and where the notion of educated personnel is a guiding principle.

The vehicle for change, embodied in clear policy direction and dynamic In-service activity, as the focus for decision-making, will necessarily address the progression of initiative, leadership, and personal development through the medium of shared working experiences; a review of provision, leading to a radical realignment of resources, which employs organized change through a series of planned interim phases; and the integration of personnel through the reorganization of provision and the encouragement of whole-

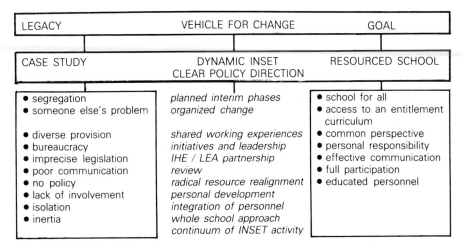

LEGACY	VEHICLE FOR CHANGE	GOAL

CASE STUDY	DYNAMIC INSET CLEAR POLICY DIRECTION	RESOURCED SCHOOL
• segregation • someone else's problem • diverse provision • bureaucracy • imprecise legislation • poor communication • no policy • lack of involvement • isolation • inertia	*planned interim phases* *organized change* *shared working experiences* *initiatives and leadership* *IHE / LEA partnership* *review* *radical resource realignment* *personal development* *integration of personnel* *whole school approach* *continuum of INSET activity*	• school for all • access to an entitlement curriculum • common perspective • personal responsibility • effective communication • full participation • educated personnel

Figure 5: A vehicle for change

school approaches, the whole to be under-pinned by a continuum of In-Service activity which emanates from the closest possible partnership between the Local Education Authority and Institute of Higher Education.

If these are the concerns of those responsible for making decisions within the Local Education Authority and Institute of Higher Education, then personal responsibility will be achieved and special educational needs will be met through the personal development of teachers.

References

Advisory Committee on the Supply and Education of Teachers (ACSET) (1982) *Advice: The Initial Teacher Training System*, London: ACSET.

—— (1984) *Advice: Teacher Training and Special Educational Needs*, London: ACSET.

—— (1984) *Advice: The In-Service Education and Training of Schoolteachers*, London: ACSET.

Ainscow, M. and Muncey, J. (1981) *Special Needs Action Programme — Small Steps*, Coventry, Coventry LEA.

Ainscow, M. and Tweddle, D. (1979) *Preventing Classroom Failure: An Objectives Approach*, Chichester: John Wiley.

Allan, L. (1987) *Duty to Review*, London: Centre for Studies on Integration in Education.

Barton, L. and Tomlinson, S. (Eds) (1981) *Special Education: Policy, Practices and Social Issues*, London: Harper and Row.

Bell, P. and Best, R. (1986) *Supportive Education*, Oxford: Basil Blackwell.

Bines, H. (1986) *Redefining Remedial Education*, London: Croom Helm.

Board of Education (1926) *Report of the Consultative Committee of the Board of Education on the Education of the Adolescent (Hadow Report)*.

—— (1929) *Report of the Mental Deficiency Committee of the Board of Education and Board of Control (Wood Committee)*, London: HMSO.

—— (1934) *Committee of Inquiry into the Problems Relating to Partially-Sighted Children*, London: HMSO.

—— (1938) *Committee of Inquiry into the Problems Relating to Children with Defective Hearing*, London: HMSO.

—— (1938) *Report of the Consultative Committee of the Board of Education on Secondary Education with Special Reference to Grammar Schools and Technical High Schools (Spens Report)*, London: HMSO.

Booth, T. and Coulby, D. (1987) *Producing and Reducing Disaffection*, Milton Keynes: Open University Press.

Booth, T. and Potts, P. (Eds) (1983a) *Integrating Special Education*, Oxford: Basil Blackwell.

Booth, T. and Potts, P. (1983b) *Creating Integration Policy*, Oxford: Basil Blackwell.

Booth, T., Potts, P. and Swann, W. (Eds) (1987) *Preventing Difficulties in Learning — Curricula for All*, Oxford: Basil Blackwell.

Booth, T. and Statham, J. (1982) *The Nature of Special Education*, London: Croom Helm.

Booth, T. and Swann, W. (1987) *Including Pupils with Disabilities*, Milton Keynes: Open University Press.

Bryce Commission (1895) Report of the Royal Commission on Secondary Education.

Burt, C. (1921) *Mental and Scholastic Tests*, London: Staples Press.

Burt, C. (1937) *The Backward Child*, London: London University Press.

Cornwall, N. (1987) *Statementing and the 1981 Education Act*, Department of Social Policy: Cranfield Institute of Technology.

Department of Education and Science (1970) *Education Act*, London: HMSO.

—— (1972) *Teacher Education and Training (James Report)*, London: HMSO.

—— (1975) *The Discovery of Children Requiring Special Education and an Assessment of Their Needs*, Circular 2/75, London: HMSO.

—— (1978) *Special Educational Needs. Report of the Committee of Enquiry into the Education of Handicapped Children and Young People (Warnock Report)*, London: HMSO.

—— (1981) *Education Act*, London: HMSO.

—— (1986) *Report on the Implementation of the 1981 Education Act*, London: HMSO.

—— (1987) *Third Report of the Education, Science and Arts Committee: Special Educational Needs: Implementation of the Education Act 1981. Vol. 1: HC 201–1*, London: HMSO.

Dessent, A. (1987) *Making the Ordinary School Special*, Lewes: Falmer Press.

Fish, J. (1985) *Special Education: The Way Ahead*, Milton Keynes: Open University Press.

Ford, J. (1969) *Social Class and the Comprehensive School*, London: Routledge & Kegan Paul.

Ford, J., Mongon, D., and Whelan, M. (1982) *Special Education and Social Control*, London: Routledge & Kegan Paul.

Galloway, D. (1985) *Schools, Pupils and Special Educational Needs*, London: Croom Helm.

Gipps, C., Gross, H. and Goldstein, H. (1987) *Warnock's 18 per cent: Children with Special Needs in the Primary School*, Lewes: Falmer Press.

Gross, H. and Gipps, C. (1987) *Supporting Warnock's 18 per cent: Six Case Studies*, Lewes: Falmer Press.

Gulliford, R. (1986) 'The training of teachers in special education', *European Journal of Special Needs Education*, 1, 2, pp. 103–112.

Hanko, G. (1985) *Special Needs in Ordinary Classrooms: An Approach to Teacher Support and Pupil Care in Primary and Secondary Schools*, Oxford: Basil Blackwell.

Hardie, M.I. (1972) 'Standards for educators of exceptional children in Canada', in Hermelin, R. (Ed.) *Teaching the Handicapped Child — Report of The International Conference (EASE)*, London: The College of Special Education.

Hardie, M.I. *et al.* (1971) *Standards for Teachers of Exceptional Children in Canada*, Toronto: The Canadian Committee, The Council for Exceptional Children.

Hegarty, S. (1987) *Meeting Special Educational Needs in Ordinary Schools: An Overview*, London: Cassell.

Hegarty, S. and Pocklington, K. with Lucas, D. (1982) *Integration in Action. Case Studies in the Integration of Pupils with Special Needs*, Windsor: NFER-Nelson.

Hodgson, A., Clunie-Ross, L. and Hegarty, S. (1984) *Learning Together: Teaching Pupils with Special Educational Needs in the Ordinary Schools*, Windsor: NFER-Nelson.

Hughes, J.M. (1957) *Human Relations in Educational Organizations*, New York: Harper and Brothers.

Inner London Education Authority (1984) *Improving Secondary Schools (Hargreaves Report)*, London: ILEA.

—— (1985) *Education Opportunities for All? The Report of the Committee Reviewing Provision to Meet Special Educational Needs (Fish Report)*, London: ILEA.

—— (1985) *Improving Primary Schools (Thomas Report)*, London: ILEA.

Kendall, D.C. and Ballance, C.E. (1969) *Report on Legislation and Services for Exceptional Children in Canada*, Toronto: The Canadian Committee, The Council for Exceptional Children.

Kirp, D.L. (1983) 'Professionalisation as a policy choice: British special education in comparative perspective', in Chambers, J.G. and Hartman, W.T. (Eds) *Special Education Policies — Their History, Implementation and Finance*, New York: Temple University Press.

Lane, D. (1981) 'Foreword' in Barton, L. and Tomlinson, S. (Eds) *Special Education: Policy, Practices and Social Issues*, London: Harper & Row.

Laskier, M. (1985) 'The changing role of the remedial teacher', in Smith, C. (Ed.) *New Directions in Remedial Education*, Lewes: Falmer Press.

Leach, D. and Raybould, T. (1977) *Learning and Behaviour Difficulties in Schools*. London: Open Books.

McCall, C. (1983) *Classroom Grouping for Special Needs*, Stratford-upon-Avon: National Council for Special Education.

McCall, C. (1987) *Helping Children with Special Educational Needs — The Whole School Approach (Module One)*. Unpublished.

Ministry of Education (1944) *Education Act*, London: HMSO.

—— (1945) *Handicapped Pupils and School Health Service Regulations*, Statutory rules and orders no. 1076, London: HMSO.

—— (1946) *Special Educational Treatment*, Pamphlet No. 5, London: HMSO.

—— (1956) *Education of the Handicapped Pupil 1945–1955*, Pamphlet No. 3, London: HMSO.

Moses, D. and Hegarty, S. (Eds) (1987) *Developing Expertise: INSET for Special Needs*, Windsor: NFER-Nelson.

Moses, D., Hegarty, S. and Jowett, S. (1987) *Local Authority Support Services*, Windsor: NFER-Nelson.

Pritchard, D.G. (1963) *Education of the Handicapped 1760–1960*, London: Routledge & Kegan Paul.

Robson, C. (1984) 'A modular in-service advanced qualification for teachers', *British Journal of In-Service Education*, (11) 1, pp. 32–36.

Robson, C., Sebba, J., Mittler, P. and Davies, L. (1987) *In-Service Training and Special Educational Needs: Running Short School-focused Courses*, Manchester: Manchester University Press.

Rogers, R. (1985) *Caught in the Act*, London: CSIE/Spastics Society.

Sayer, J. (1987) *Secondary Schools for All? — Strategies for Special Needs*, London: Cassell.

Sayer, J. and Jones, N. (Eds) (1985) *Teacher Training and Special Educational Needs*, London: Croom Helm.

Schonell, F. (1942) *Backwardness in the Basic Subjects*, London: Oliver and Boyd.

Sewell, G. (1982) *Reshaping Remedial Education*, London: Croom Helm.

Sewell, G. (1986) *Coping with Special Needs: A Guide for New Teachers*, London: Croom Helm.

Shipman, M.D. (1975) *The Sociology of the School*, London: Longman.

Smith, C. (Ed.) (1985) *New Directions in Remedial Education*, Lewes: Falmer Press.

Thomas, G. (1986) 'Integrating personnel in order to integrate children', in *Support for Learning*, Vol. 1, No. 1.

Tomlinson, S. (1982) *A Sociology of Special Education*, London: Routledge & Kegan Paul.

Welton, J., Wedell, K. and Vorhaus, G. (1982) *Meeting Special Educational Needs*, Bedford Way Papers No. 12, Tadworth: Heinemann Educational Books and Institute of Education, London University.

Wolfendale, S. (1987) *Primary Schools and Special Needs: Policy, Planning and Provision*, London: Cassell.

Index